CHILE PEPPERS

Dave DeWitt

CHILE PEPPERS

A Global History

University of New Mexico Press, Albuquerque

LIBRARY OF CONGRESS CATALOGING-IN-PUBLICATION DATA

Names | DeWitt, Dave, author.

Title | Chile peppers: a global history / Dave DeWitt.

Description | Albuquerque: University of New Mexico Press, 2020.
  Includes bibliographical references and index.

Identifiers | LCCN 2020008831 (print)
  LCCN 2020008832 (e-book)
  ISBN 9780826361806 (paperback)
  ISBN 9780826361813 (e-book)

Subjects | LCSH: Hot peppers—History.
  Cooking (Hot peppers)

Classification | LCC SB307.P4 D487 2020 (print)
  LCC SB307.P4 (e-book)
  DDC 633.8/4—dc23

LC record available at https://lccn.loc.gov/2020008831

LC e-book record available at https://lccn.loc.gov/2020008832

Cover illustration | The peperoncini of Italy.
  Photograph by Harald Zoschke. Used with permission.

Design | Mindy Basinger Hill

Composed in | 10/15 pt Adobe Caslone Pro

THIS BOOK IS FOR NANCY GERLACH, MY COAUTHOR OF 10 BOOKS, AND FOR THE MEMORY OF HER LATE HUSBAND AND MY GOOD FRIEND, JEFFREY GERLACH.

CONTENTS

Hundreds of people from all over the world have helped with this
project over many years. In addition to the individuals mentioned in
the text of this book, the following people were particularly helpful:
Mary Jane Barnes, Marlin Bensinger, Paul Bosland, Pat and Dominique
Chapman, Marco Del Freo, Nancy and Jeff Gerlach, Antonio Heras,
Patrick Holian, Sharon Hudgins, Stephen Hull, Gianluca Luisi, Lois
Manno, José Marmolejo, Scott Mendel, Robert Spiegel, Richard
Sterling, Mary Jane Wilan, and Harald and Renate Zoschke.

ACKNOWLEDGMENTS

I have been writing this book for 44 years, and I'm not done yet, despite the fact that you're holding it in your hands. That's because my research on the subjects of chile peppers and fiery foods never ends. Just like the archaeological discoveries at Cerén that are documented in chapter 1, some new disclosure about chile peppers will crop up, and, by the sheer force of my interest, I'll compulsively write about it. This is my writing niche; it's what I do and why I'm called the Pope of Peppers.

Over those 44 years, I've written, sometimes with coauthors, 42 published books on chile peppers and fiery foods, and hundreds of articles published in magazines and on blogs and websites. I've chosen some of my best writing from past projects for this book and also added new material that's previously unpublished in print form. So this book is partly a culinary history and partly a memoir about my trips around the world to research chile usage in many different cuisines.

Although this book is not designed to be a cookbook, I have selected several representative recipes for each chapter so readers can create the flavors they are reading about in their own kitchens. If readers want more recipes, I have thousands posted on FieryFoodsCentral.com, and there's always my book, *1,001 Best Hot & Spicy Recipes*.

Please remember that I am writing about the past, not the present, and that things have changed over the decades. Some of the people mentioned in this book are no longer with us, unfortunately, but fond memories of them linger. Some of the countries my wife and I explored are edgy to the point of being dangerous in certain circumstances, so be careful in all the countries mentioned in this book, and especially when visiting Mexico, Jamaica, and South Africa. Travelers are safer if they stay in designated tourist areas and should always try to find locals as guides, even if they have to be hired. That's the way Mary Jane and I have traveled over all these years and we've never had any problems at all.

We were warned about pickpockets in Rome, *narcotraficantes* in Mexico, Asian gangs in Cabramatta, Australia, thieves in Belize, and muggers in every large city, but by following a few basic rules, none of the bad guys bothered us. Hang with the locals; don't try to buy any illegal drugs; don't get drunk; don't be loud or call attention to yourself; but do use credit cards; and avoid showing a lot of cash. We had a street-smart guide named Tony in Jamaica who drove us all over the island, and I told him to take us only to restaurants where there were no white faces. "No problem, mon," he said, and he was right—there were none because he was with us. One of our black guides in South Africa was shocked when we invited him to have lunch with us; in Barbados, the same thing was a common occurrence. So be adaptable and go with the flow. If offered a choice between an American breakfast and a local one, choose the latter. Smile a lot wherever you travel, and don't be the stereotyped "ugly American."

THE FIVE DOMESTICATED *CAPSICUM* SPECIES

Because the species names of the *Capsicum* genus are mentioned so often in this book, I'm placing the definitions here for quick and easy reference.

Serrano chiles in the author's garden. Photograph by Dave DeWitt.

annuum   The name means annual, which of course is inaccurate as chiles are perennials in climates where there are no freezes. The is the most-grown species in the world in both gardening and agriculture, and its varieties are commonly known all over the world. The bells, jalapeños, cayennes, anchos, serranos, New Mexicans, paprikas, and ornamentals are all of the *annuum* species.

Ají amarillo in the author's garden. Photograph by Dave DeWitt.

baccatum   The species name means berry-like, and it is native to South America, where the varieties are commonly called "ají." There are at least two wild forms (varieties *baccatum* and *microcarpum*) and many domesticated forms. The domesticated ajís have a great diversity of pod shape and size, ranging from short, pointed pods borne erect to long, pendant pods resembling the New Mexican varieties. They are cultivated in most South American countries.

Bolivian red habanero in the author's garden. Photograph by Dave DeWitt

chinense   This species was misnamed *Capsicum chinense* in 1776 by Nikolaus von Jacquin, a Dutch physician who collected plants in the Caribbean for Emperor Francis I from 1754 to 1759. Jacquin, who first described the species as "chinense" in his work *Hortus botanicus vindobonensis*, wrote, mysteriously, "I have taken the plant's name from its homeland." He was dead wrong, of course—all capsicums are New World plants. Many people, including myself, believe that the species name should be changed to *Capsicum cheiro*, which would mean "perfumed pepper," because *cheiro* is Portuguese for aroma or smell. All *chinense* have a unique aroma similar to apricots. Habaneros and all the superhots, including the 'Carolina Reaper,' the hottest *Capsicum* in the world, belong to this South American and Caribbean species.

frutescens   Tabascos are the most commonly known peppers in the *frutescens* species and the name means shrub-like. There is very little pod diversity, and the Brazilian malagueta variety looks the same as a Tabasco. Tabascos are grown in Central and South America to make the famous sauce of the same name.

Malagueta pepper in the author's garden. Photograph by Dave DeWitt

pubescens   This is the most obscure *Capsicum* species and it, too, has little or no pod diversity. It is the only species with black seeds, and its name means hairy, an allusion to its fuzzy leaves. The pods resemble small apples, hence the common name *manzano* in Mexico. In South America they are commonly called rocotos. This species has no wild form, and it is grown in the Andes and also in Oaxaca, Mexico. There are two forms, red and yellow (canarios), and the pods are quite hot, 30,000–50,000 Scoville Heat Units (SHU).

Rocoto chile. Photograph by Dave DeWitt

For more than 10,000 years, humans have been fascinated by a seemingly innocuous plant with bright-colored fruits that bite back when bitten. Although the chile pepper has risen in our estimation from lowly weed to celebrity spice, the secrets of its domestication, its discovery by Europeans, and its subsequent spread around the world are still being uncovered. Often mistakenly thought to be of African or Indian origin, chile peppers are absolutely American; along with corn, squash, potatoes, and beans, they are among the earliest and most important plants domesticated by mankind in the New World.

THE TOLERATED WEED

According to botanist Barbara Pickersgill, the genus *Capsicum*, to which all chiles belong, originated in the remote geologic past in an area bordered by the mountains of southern Brazil to the east, by Bolivia to the west, and by Paraguay and northern Argentina to the south. Not only does this location have the greatest concentration of wild species of chiles in the world, but here, and only here, grow representatives of all the major domesticated species within the genus. Another chile botanist, W. Hardy Eshbaugh, believes that the location for the origin of chile peppers was further east, in central Bolivia along the Rio Grande.

Scientists are not certain about the exact time frame or the method for the spread of both wild and domesticated species from the southern Brazil-Bolivia area, but they suspect that birds were primarily responsible. The wild chiles (like their undomesticated cousin of today, the *chiltepín*) had erect, red fruits that were quite pungent and were very attractive to various species of birds that ate the whole pods.

The seeds of those pods passed through their digestive tracts intact and were deposited on the ground encased in a perfect fertilizer. In this manner, chiles spread all over South and Central America long before the first Asian tribes moved east and settled the New World.

When humans arrived in the Americas between 15,000 and 25,000 years ago, about 25 species of the genus *Capsicum* existed in South America. Five of these species were later domesticated; however, some of the other wild species were and

Garden terraces, Machu Picchu, Peru. Potatoes and early forms of chile peppers were grown on the terraces. Photograph by Mark Blumenthal (2005). Wikimedia. GNU Free Documentation License.

African grey parrot munching on a pepper pod. Photograph by Chel Beeson. Work for hire.

still are occasionally utilized. Two of the five domesticated species of chiles, *C. baccatum* and *C. pubescens*, never migrated beyond South America. *Baccatum*, known as "ají," merely extended its range from southern Brazil west to the Pacific Ocean and became a domesticated chile of choice in Bolivia, Ecuador, Peru, and Chile. Likewise, *C. pubescens* left Brazil to be domesticated in the Andes, where it is known as *rocoto*. Its range today is primarily in the higher elevations of Bolivia, Peru, and Ecuador, although it was introduced during historical times into mountainous areas of Costa Rica, Honduras, Guatemala, and Mexico.

Three other *Capsicum* species that were later domesticated are *annuum*, *chinense*, and *frutescens*. These closely related species shared a mutual ancestral gene pool and are known to botanists as the *annuum-chinense-frutescens* complex. They seem to have sprung up in the wilds of Colombia and later migrated individually to Central America and Amazonia. These three species were all in place when humans arrived on the scene, and, apparently, each type was domesticated independently—*annuum* in Mexico, *chinense* in Amazonia (and possibly Peru), and *frutescens* in southern Central America. These three species have become the most commercially important chiles, and the story of their domestication and further spread is revealed in the archaeological record.

The earliest evidence of chile peppers in the human diet is from Mexico, where archaeologist R. S. MacNeish discovered chile seeds dating from about 7500 BC during his excavations at Tamaulipas and Tehuacán. This find and an intact pod from Peru's Guitarrero Cave dated 6500 BC seem to indicate that chiles were under cultivation approximately ten 10,000 years ago.

However, that date is extremely early for crop domestication and some experts suggest that these specimens are chiles that were harvested in the wild rather than cultivated by man. The common bean (*Phaseolus vulgaris*) was also found in the same excavation levels, and scientists cannot be certain if they were wild or domesticated varieties. Experts are certain, however, that chile peppers were domesticated by at least 3300 BC.

Ethnobotanists—scientists who study the relationship of plants to mankind—have theorized that during the domestication process, chiles were first accepted as "tolerated weeds." They were not cultivated but rather collected in the wild when the fruits were ripe. The wild forms had erect fruits that were deciduous, meaning that they separated easily from the calyx and fell to the ground. During the domestication process, whether consciously or unconsciously, early Indian farmers selected seeds from plants with larger, nondeciduous, and pendant fruits.

The reasons for these selection criteria are a greater yield from each plant and protection of the pods from chile-hungry birds. The larger the pod, the greater will be its tendency to become pendant rather than to remain erect. Thus the pods became hidden amid the leaves and did not protrude above them as beacons for birds. The selection of varieties with the tendency to be nondeciduous ensured that the pods remained on the plant until fully ripe and thus were resistant to dropping off as a result of wind or physical contact. The domesticated chiles gradually lost their natural means of seed dispersal by birds and became dependent upon human intervention for their continued existence. Because chiles cross-pollinate, hundreds of varieties of the five domesticated chiles developed over thousands of years. The color, size, and shape of the pods of these domesticated forms varied enormously. Ripe fruits could be red, orange, brown, yellow, or white. Their shapes could be round, conic, elongate, oblate, or bell-like, and their size could vary from the tiny fruits of chiltepíns or Tabascos to the large pods of the anchos and New Mexican varieties. However, no matter what the size or shape of the pods, they were readily adopted into the customs and cuisines of all the major civilizations of the New World.

PRE-COLUMBIAN CHILE CUSTOMS AND KITCHENS

Chiles were the major spice of the New World and played a role similar to that of black pepper in the Old World; ancient New World cultures from Mexico to South America combined the pungent pods with every conceivable meat and vegetable. Our knowledge of the pre-Columbian culinary uses of chile peppers is derived from many sources: archaeological finds, Indian artifacts and illustrations of the period, Spanish and Portuguese explorers of the sixteenth and seventeenth centuries, botanical observations, and studies of the cooking methods of the modern descendants of the Incas, Mayas, and Aztecs.

This examination of the culinary uses of chiles begins in one of the major regions where they were first cultivated, the Andes. It was there that the great Inca civilization came to depend upon the chiles as their principal spice and a major crop. At the heart of the Incan Empire was farming, which determined nearly every aspect of society: the calendar, religion, law, and even war. The Incas were farmer-soldiers, likely to be called out of their elaborately terraced and irrigated fields at any time to defend the empire or extend its boundaries. But farming took precedence over

fighting, and some later uprisings against the Spanish failed because the Inca soldiers left the battlefront to return to their fields. It has been estimated that more kinds of foods and medicinal plants were systematically cultivated in the Andes than anywhere else in the world at any time. The result of the Incan agricultural expertise included 240 varieties of potatoes, nearly as many kinds of beans, 20 types of maize, plus sweet potatoes, peanuts, pineapples, quinoa, chocolate, avocados, papayas, tomatoes, and—of course—several varieties of the beloved chile pepper.

The Incan historian Garcilaso de la Vega, known as El Inca, wrote in detail about chile peppers and their place in Incan culture. In his *Royal Commentaries of the Incas* (1609), he noted that chiles were the favorite fruit of the Indians, who ate them with everything they cooked, "whether stewed, boiled, or roasted." He traced the nomenclature of the plant: the pods were called "Uchu" by the Incas, "Pimiento de las Indias" by the Spaniards, and "Ají" by the people of the West Indies, a name that became quite common in the Andes in later times.

The Incas worshiped the chile pepper as one of the four brothers of their creation myth. "Agar-Uchu," or "Brother Chile Pepper," was believed to be the brother of the first Incan king. Garcilaso de la Vega observed that the chile pods were perceived to symbolize the teachings of the early Incan brothers. Chile peppers were thus regarded as holy plants, and the Incas' most rigorous fasts were those prohibiting all chiles.

According to El Inca, the Incas raised three types of chiles. The first was called *rocot uchu*, "thick pepper," which described the long, thick pods that matured to yellow, red, and purple. The most likely identification of these chiles would be the ají type, *Capsicum baccatum*. El Inca forgot the name of the next type but wrote that it was used exclusively by the royal household. The third chile he described was *chinchi uchu*, which "resembles exactly a cherry with its stalk." This type, with its name and cherry-like pods both still intact, has survived to this day in Peru and Bolivia; it is the rocoto, a variety of *Capsicum pubescens* and the only *Capsicum* with black seeds. El Inca noted that the chinchi uchu was "incomparably stronger than the rest and only small quantities of it are found."

El Inca also collected some chile anecdotes. Chiles were reputedly good for the sight, were avoided by poisonous creatures, and had been offered as one of the gifts to appease Pizarro and his invading soldiers. As a final culinary note, El Inca unconsciously predicted the spread of chile around the world when he noted, "All the Spaniards who come to Spain from the Indies are accustomed to it and prefer it to all Oriental spices." Thus the invaders were conquered by the fiery foods of the Incas!

Most Incan dishes were vegetarian because fish and meat were luxuries—at least for the commoners. The Incan royalty, however, did consume fish caught in the rich coastal waters and Lake Titicaca, and also ate deer, wild llama, guanaco, and viscacha, a large rodent. But the royalty would not consume dogs, domesticated ducks, and *cui* (guinea pigs)—meat sources beloved by the peasants when they could obtain them.

The Incas' morning meal was extremely simple: leftovers from the previous evening and a cup of chicha, a mildly intoxicating beverage made from fermented corn. Around noon, an Inca family would gather for the midday meal, which was prepared by boiling or baking because cooking fats and frying were uncommon. Corn was often boiled with chile peppers, potatoes, and herbs to make a stew called *mote*. Another midday meal of the Incas was *locro*, a stew made from sun-dried llama meat, dehydrated potatoes, and chiles.

The evening meal was eaten at about five o'clock in the afternoon and was usually a soup or stew similar to the midday feast. Potatoes were ubiquitous.

But food was not the only use for the beloved chiles. According to historian L. E. Valcárcel, chile peppers were so highly valued in Inca society that they were probably used as currency. Since there were no coins or bills in those days, certain preferred products like chiles became part of a rudimentary monetary system. He noted that until the mid-twentieth century, shoppers in the plaza of Cuzco could buy goods with *rantii*, a handful of chiles.

Vessel in the form of chile peppers, Peru, south coast, Nazca culture. First century BC– AD sixth century, earthenware and pigment, in the De Young Museum, San Francisco. Photographer unknown. Wikimedia. Public domain

Tello Obelisk,
Chavín culture,
Peru. Carved gran-
ite. Photograph
by DC Columbia.
iStock.

The Incas decorated bowls, dishes, and other vessels with chile pepper designs, as shown in the accompanying photograph of a unique Nazca stirrup vessel with chile pepper legs from the southern coast of Peru. The exact date of this vessel is not known.

Chiles also were the subject of embroidery designs. One example of textile art of the early Nazca period is a yarn-embroidered cotton cloth showing the figures of 23 farmers carrying their crops. One of the farmer figures is wearing chile pods around his neck and carrying a plant bearing pods.

About AD 900, a sculptor of the Chavín culture in Peru carved elaborate designs into a sharp-pointed granite shaft measuring eight feet high and a foot wide that has become known as the Tello Obelisk. The principal figure on this obelisk is a mythical creature, the black caiman. The sharp point of the stone corresponds to a real caiman's narrow snout, and the end of the stone is carved with the feet and claws of the reptile, which are holding the leaves and pods of a chile plant. As yet, no scholar has deciphered the meaning of a magical caiman grasping chile peppers in its claws, but the image is suggestive of the magical powers that the people of the Andes Indians believed were inherent in the powerful pods.

As chile peppers spread north through Central America and Mexico, they gained the reputation of being not only a spicy condiment but also a powerful medicine. The pre-Columbian tribes of Panama used chiles in combination with cacao and tobacco (and probably other plants) to enter into hallucinatory trances. According to scientist Mary Helms, these Indians used chiles to "travel" to the heavens or to the underworld to negotiate with the good and evil spirits on behalf of mankind. Today, the Cuna Indians of Panama burn chiles so the irritating smoke will drive away evil spirits during a girl's puberty ceremony. They also trail a string of chiles behind their canoes to discourage sharks from attacking. (I should caution modern sportsmen that the efficacy of chiles as a shark repellent has never been verified.)

In southern Mexico and the Yucatán Peninsula, chile peppers have been part of the human diet since about 7500 BC and thus their usage predates the two great Central American civilizations, the Maya and the Aztec. From their original usage as a spice collected in the wild, chiles gained importance after their domestication, and they were a significant food when the Olmec culture was developing, around 1000 BC.

About 500 BC, the Monte Albán culture, in the Valley of Oaxaca, began exporting a new type of pottery vessel to nearby regions. These vessels resembled the hand-held *molcajete* mortars of today and were called Suchilquitongo bowls. While the metate was used for heavy-duty grinding, the Suchilquitongo bowl was used to mash relatively soft foods. Like a food processor today, the new bowl made it possible to mash foods together to make a sauce. Because the molcajetes are used to crush chile pods and make salsas today, the Suchilquitongo bowls are probably the first evidence we have for the creation of crushed chile and chile sauces. Scientists speculate that the Suchilquitongo bowls were specifically developed for the purpose of sauce making, and both the tool and the product were then exported.

THE LEGACY OF THE MAYAS

A carved glyph found in the ceremonial center of Monte Albán is further evidence of the early importance of chile peppers. It features a chile plant with three pendant pods on one end and the head of a man on the other. Some experts believe that the glyph is one of a number of "tablets of conquest" that marked the sites conquered by the Monte Albán culture.

By the time the Mayas reached the peak of their civilization in southern Mexico and the Yucatán Peninsula, around AD 500, they had a highly developed system of agriculture. Maize was their most important crop, followed closely by beans, squash, chile peppers, and cacao. Perhaps as many as 30 different varieties of chiles were cultivated. They were sometimes planted in plots by themselves but more often in fields already containing tomatoes and sweet potatoes. The Mayas also cultivated cotton, papayas, vanilla beans, maniocs, and agave. They kept domesticated turkeys, ducks, and dogs, and their main game animals were deer, birds, and wild boars. Armadillos and manatees were considered delicacies.

For breakfast the Mayas ate a gruel of ground maize spiced with chile peppers, which is usually called *atole* but is sometimes known as *pozol*. A modern equivalent would be cornmeal or masa mixed with water and ground red chiles to the consistency of a milk shake. For the main, or evening meal, stews of vegetables and meats heavily spiced with chiles were served. Various *pipiáns*, still served today, are early forms of the mole sauces to come and use two common Mexican chiles, ancho and

pasilla. Of course, the Mayas would have served turkey rather than chicken (which was introduced by the Spanish), but either fowl is acceptable.

Using the same technology that proved the use of chocolate at Chaco Canyon, New Mexico, researchers have analyzed the contents of the residue of pots from ancient Mexico and discovered traces of chiles without chocolate. This indicates that either chile sauces were being made or they were used to spice up other beverages, about a thousand years earlier than the Cerén archaeological site in El Salvador.

Terry Powis, associate professor of anthropology, and colleagues at Kennesaw State University in Georgia have chemically analyzed the residue in 13 pottery vessels, including spouted jars, pots, and vases—dating from 1,700 to 2,400 years ago—that were found at an archaeological site in the state of Chiapas, which was at that time inhabited by the Mixe-Zoquean people.

"The best and most direct evidence for chile pepper use in Mesoamerica prior to our study is from Cerén," says Powis.

So our work pushes back this date from circa AD 540 to circa 400 BC. To be honest, our study is the only one of its kind to show direct evidence of chile pepper use. In all of the other examples listed in the paper there is only indirect evidence—of chiles and pots found together. We actually linked the two together for the first time, and that is an important development. Therefore, we actually have the earliest known consumption of the peppers.

Powis adds, "During the mass spec analysis we were completely surprised by the fact that no cacao was present in any of the pots tested. In fact chile was present." The exact species of chile present was not identified, but Powis hopes to accomplish that in the future. The most logical species is *Capsicum annuum*, which was domesticated in Mexico.

Because of the absence of cacao and the fact that the artifacts were found in places associated with high-status individuals and rituals, the team speculated that chile peppers were possibly used to produce a spicy beverage or alternatively a chile sauce that was stored in the spouted jars and subsequently poured as a dining condiment, possibly during ritual feasts.

Powis wonders, "Was the chile ground up to produce a paste or a salsa and subsequently used as a seasoning in foods that were offered to the Zoquean gods or chiefs? Or, were the peppers left whole in the pots? We assume that the presence of chile is in the form of a sauce or paste, and not whole given that no seeds or other macrofossils were identified in the interiors of the vessels."

If the residue is not from a chile paste, was it a spicy beverage other than hot chocolate? "Why would there be evidence of chile peppers in a spouted jar?" Powis asks in his article. "It is commonly assumed that spouted jars were used for pouring a liquid into another container. Perhaps the peppers were not made into a sauce but a spicy beverage or alternatively a chile sauce that was stored in the spouted jars and subsequently poured as a dining condiment."

And if the chiles were used in a beverage other than hot chocolate, what might it have been? Further analysis will be required, but two possibilities come to mind: chicha, the ancient corn beer, or pulque, the precursor to mescal, which is made from fermented agave sap. If the Mayas and other cultures loved their hot chocolate spiced up with chiles, why not these other favorite beverages?

The Mayan civilization had declined considerably by the time the Spanish arrived in Mexico, so there are no Spanish observations about the height of Mayan culture. All that exist today are Mayan hieroglyphics, which are slowly being transliterated, artifacts from Cerén, and ethnological observations of the present Maya Indians, whose food habits have changed little in 20 centuries.

According to the *Ethnology* volume of the *Handbook of Middle American Indians*, chiles are highly visible today in areas with a Mayan heritage. Today in the Yucatán Peninsula, descendants of the Mayas still grow chiles, tomatoes, and onions in boxes or hollowed-out tree trunks that are raised up on four posts for protection against pigs and hens. These container gardens are usually in the yard of the house, near the kitchen.

Despite the passage of centuries, the most basic Mayan foods have changed little. Still common are tortillas with bean paste, chiles, and a little squash. Meat, usually chicken or pork, is only consumed about once a week. The Tzeltal Indians of central Chiapas plant chiles in plots about 50 feet on a side, alternating cotton every other year. Interestingly enough, the seeds are planted by women, but only after the men have punched holes in the ground with a planting stick—a ritual with obvious symbolism. The only difference between this method and that used by the Mayas is that the planting sticks today have metal tips.

Among the descendants of the Mayas, chile is regarded as a powerful agent to ward off spells. For the Tzotzil Indians of the Chiapas highlands, chile assists in both life and death. The hot pods are rubbed on the lips of newborn infants and are burned during the funeral ceremonies of *viejos* (old ones) to defeat evil spirits that might be around. The Huastec tribe of San Carlos Potosi and Veracruz treat victims of the "evil eye" with chile peppers. An egg is dipped in ground chile then rubbed on the victim's body to return the pain to the malefactor. The Cicatec Indians of the southern Mexican highlands prepare tepache, a drink of fermented sugarcane juice, with cacao and chile, for use in various rituals. Such a concoction vividly recalls a similar combination of chiles and chocolate consumed by the Aztecs.

In 1529, a Spanish Franciscan friar living in Nueva España (present-day Mexico) noted that the Aztecs ate hot red or yellow chile peppers in their hot chocolate and in nearly every dish they prepared! Fascinated by the Aztecs' constant use of a previously unknown spice, Bernardino de Sahagún documented this fiery cuisine in his classic study, *Historia general de las cosas de la Nueva España*, now known as the *Florentine Codex*. His work proves that of all the pre-Columbian New World civilizations, it was the Aztecs who loved chile peppers the most.

The marketplaces of ancient Mexico overflowed with chile peppers of all sizes and shapes, including, according to de Sahagún, "hot green chiles, smoked chiles, water chiles, tree chiles, beetle chiles, and sharp-pointed red chiles." In addition to some 20 varieties of "chillis," as the pungent pods were called in the Nahuatl language, vendors sold strings of red chiles (modern *ristras*), precooked chiles, and "fish chiles"—which were the earliest known forms of ceviche, a method of

Tlatelolco Marketplace as depicted at the Field Museum of Natural History, Chicago. The largest Aztec market was located in Tenochtitlan's neighboring town, Tlatelolco. There is a bowl of chile peppers at the bottom center of this image. Photograph by Joe Ravi. Wikimedia. Creative Commons Attribution-ShareAlike 3.0 Unported License.

preserving fish without cooking. This technique places the fish in a marinade of an acidic fruit juice and chile peppers.

Other seafood dishes were common as well in ancient Mexico. "They would eat another kind of stew, with frogs and green chile," de Sahagún recorded, "and a stew of those fish called axolotl with yellow chile. They also used to eat a lobster stew which is very delicious."

Apparently the Aztecs utilized every possible source of protein. The friar noted such exotic variations as maguey worms with a sauce of small chiles, newt with yellow chiles, and tadpoles with *chiltecpitl*. De Sahagún classified chiles according to their pungency, as evidenced by the following chart:

ENGLISH	NAHUATL	SPANISH
Sharp	Cococ	Picante
Very Sharp	Cocopatic	Muy picantes
Very, Very Sharp	Cocopetzpatic	Muy, muy picantes
Brilliantly Sharp	Cocopetztic	Brillantemente picantes
Extremely Sharp	Cocopetzquauitl	Extremadamente picantes
Sharpest	Cocopalatic	Picantísimo

Father de Sahagún, one of the first behavioral scientists, also noted that chiles were revered as much as sex by the ancient Aztecs. While fasting to appease their rather bloodthirsty gods, the priests required two abstentions by the faithful: sexual relations and chile peppers.

Chocolate and chiles were commonly combined in a drink called *chicahuatl*, which was usually reserved for the priests and the wealthy. De Sahagún also discovered the earliest examples of dishes that have since become classics of Mexican cuisine: tamales and moles. The early versions of tamales often used banana leaves as a wrapper to steam combinations of masa dough, chicken, and the chiles of choice. De Sahagún wrote that there were two types of *chilemollis*: one with red chile and tomatoes, and the other with yellow chile and tomatoes. These chilemollis eventually became the savory mole sauces for which Mexican cuisine is justly famous (see chapter 3).

Aztec cookery was the basis for the Mexican food of today, and, in fact, many Aztec dishes have lasted through the centuries virtually unchanged. Since oil and fat were not generally used in cooking, the foods were usually roasted, boiled, or cooked in sauces. Like the Mayas, the Aztecs usually began the day with a cup of atole spiced with chile peppers.

Aztecs living close to either coast were fond of drinking *chilote*, a liquor made with pulque (fermented agave pulp), ancho chiles, and herbs. Since pork was not available until the Spanish arrived, the Aztecs would have used peccary (a medium-sized, pig-like hoofed mammal of the family Tayassuidae) meat. The main meal was served at midday and usually consisted of tortillas with beans and a salsa made with chiles and tomatoes. The salsas were usually made by grinding the ingredients between two hand-held stones, the molcajetes. Even today, the same technique is used in Indian villages throughout Central America. A remarkable variety of tamales was also served for the midday meal. They were stuffed with fruits such as plums, pineapple, or guava; with game meat such as deer or turkey; or with seafood such as snails or frogs.

It was this highly sophisticated chile cuisine that the Spanish encountered during their conquest of the New World. And it all started with the Mayas.

FLASHBACK. OUT OF THE ASH:
THE PREHISTORIC CHILE CUISINE OF CERÉN

On an August evening in AD 595, the Loma Caldera in what is now El Salvador erupted, sending clouds of volcanic ash into the Mayan agricultural village of Cerén, burying it 20 feet deep and turning it into the New World equivalent of Pompeii. Miraculously, all the villagers escaped, but what they left behind gives us a good idea of the life they led, the food they ate, and the chile peppers they grew.

In 1976, while leveling ground for the erection of grain silos, a Salvadoran bulldozer operator noticed that he had plowed into an ancient building. He immediately notified the national museum, but a museum archaeologist thought that the building was of recent vintage and allowed the bulldozing to continue. Several buildings were destroyed. Two years later, Dr. Payson Sheets, an anthropologist from the University of Colorado, led a team of students on an archaeological survey of the Zapotitán Valley. He was taken to the site by local residents and quickly began a test excavation, and radiocarbon dating of artifacts proved that they were very ancient. He received permission from the government to do a complete excavation of Cerén. The site was saved.

top Artist's rendering of the outdoor kitchen at Cerén.

bottom The remains of the original structure at Joya de Cerén, buried by volcano eruption around AD 600 (El Salvador). Photograph by Mario Roberto Duran Ortiz. Wikimedia. Creative Commons Attribution-ShareAlike 3.0 Unported License.

Dr. Sheets and his students returned for five field sessions at Cerén, most recently in 1996. Their discoveries are detailed on their web site http://ceren.colorado.edu. Dr. Sheets describes one of their most interesting discoveries: "We had no idea that people in the region lived so well 14 centuries ago."

The ash preserved the crops in the field, leaving impressions of the plants. The plants then rotted away, leaving perfect cavities, or molds. Using techniques that were developed at Pompeii, the archaeologists poured liquid plaster into the cavities. By removing the ash, the ancient fields were revealed and could be studied. Interestingly, the Native Americans of Cerén used row-and-furrow techniques similar to those still utilized today; corn was grown in elevated rows, and beans and squash were grown in the furrows in between. In a courtyard of a building, "we even found a series of four mature chile plants with stem diameters over 5 centimeters (2 inches)," writes Dr. Sheets. "They must have been many years old." Chile peppers are rarely found in archaeological sites in Mesoamerica, so imagine the surprise of the researchers when they discovered painted ceramic storage vessels that contained large quantities of chile seeds. "One vessel had cacao seeds in the bottom, and chiles above, separated by a layer of cotton gauze," Dr. Sheets reveals. "It is possible that they would have been prepared into a kind of *mole* sauce." Also found were corn kernels, beans, squash seeds, cotton seeds, and evidence of manioc plants and small agave plants, which were used for their fiber to make rope rather than being fermented for an alcoholic beverage, pulque, as was done in Mexico.

I e-mailed Dr. Sheets, hoping to discover the shape and size of the chiles and thus deduce the variety being grown. But no whole pods were found, just the seeds and some pod fragments. The size of the chile stem indicated that the plant had been grown as a perennial, but all chile plants are perennial in tropical climates and can grow to a considerable size.

Dr. Sheets wrote me back about an article by Dr. David Lentz, the botanist who had studied the plant remains, and I tracked it down in the journal *Latin American Antiquity*, which I found in the Zimmerman Library at the University of New Mexico. Dr. Lentz writes about the seeds and the pod fragments: "It appears that many of these fell from the rafters of buildings where they would have been hung for drying or storage." He adds that the chile seeds from the site were the first in Central America found outside Mexico, and he speculates that those seeds in vessels were probably being saved for future planting.

IDENTIFYING THE CERÉN CHILE

But what kind of chile was grown in Cerén? There was an intriguing clue in the article: a photograph of a chile seed compared with a bar indicating the length of 1 millimeter. The seed was 3.5 millimeters wide. Since the size of the seed is directly related to the size of the pod (generally speaking, the larger the pod, the larger the seed), perhaps it was possible to guess the size of the pod by comparing that ancient seed to seeds I had stored in my greenhouse.

Scientists, including researcher Linda Perry, writing in the journal *Science* (February 16, 2007), have proven that chile peppers were domesticated in South America at least by 6,000 years ago. Although very few prehistoric pods and pollen have been found in archaeological sites, a new technique has been developed to track and date the earliest uses of chiles. "We found that a widespread, but previously unidentified starch morphotype," writes Perry, "is derived from chile pepper fruits and is commonly preserved on artifacts." This microfossil was documented in seven archaeological sites ranging from the Bahamas to the Andes.

The starches were recovered from sediment samples, milling stones, and food residues from cooking vessels. The oldest positively identified starches were found at the sites of Loma Alta and Real Alta in southwestern Ecuador, and were dated at 6,000 years before the present (BP). Also found was evidence of maize (corn), squash, beans, and palms. But since Ecuador is not considered to be the center of domestication for any of the five domesticated species, "the presence of domesticated chiles within this early complex agricultural system indicates that these plants must have been domesticated elsewhere earlier than 6,000 years B. P. and brought into the region from either the north or the south."

The scientists noted that none of the microfossils contained starches typical of the wild species of *Capsicum*, so all of the chiles were grown by the Amerindians living at the sites. "The presence of domesticated plants used as condiments rather than as staple foods during the preceramic period indicates that sophisticated agriculture and complex cuisines arose early throughout the Americas and that the exploitation of maize, root crops, and chile peppers spread before the introduction of pottery," Perry notes. She adds: "Evidence from both macrobotanical and microbotanical remains indicates that once chile peppers became incorporated into the diet, they persisted." In addition to chile peppers, maize was also present at all seven sites. "Maize and chiles occur together from the onset of this record until European contact," she concludes, "and, thus, represent an ancient Neotropical plant food complex."

Because chiles cross-pollinate, hundreds of varieties of the five domesticated chile species were developed by humans over thousands of years in South and Central America. The color, size, and shape of the pods of these domesticated forms varied enormously. Ripe fruits could be red, orange, brown, yellow, or white. Their shapes could be round, conic, elongate, oblate, or bell-like, and their size could vary from the tiny fruits of chiltepíns or Tabascos to the large pods of the anchos and pasillas. But very little archaeological evidence existed to support these theories until the finds at Cerén.

AN EDUCATED GUESS

It was exciting to think that perhaps I had a window into the ancient chile domestication process. Because their seeds were collected, and the plants were growing in a courtyard, the chile plants at Cerén were obviously cultivated and were more than just "tolerated weeds." It was time to break out my metric ruler and start measuring seeds. I came up with the following table, ranked by seed width:

VARIETY	POD LENGTH	SEED WIDTH
ancho	12 cm	6 mm
serrano	7 cm	5 mm
jalapeño	6.5 cm	5 mm
de árbol	4.5 cm	5 mm
habanero	4.5 cm	4 mm
piquin	1.3 cm	4 mm
Cerén chile	?	3.5 mm
chiltepín	0.5 cm	3 mm

The first conclusion I reached was that the Cerén chiles were small podded. They certainly were not as large as anchos, whose seeds are twice the width of those of the Cerén chiles. They could, of course, have been chiltepíns, because the seeds were only half a millimeter wider than chiltepín seeds. But if they were somewhere between the size of chiltepíns and *piquins*, that would have made the pods about 1 centimeter long, less than half an inch. And since there is evidence that the chile pods had been hung up to dry with agave twine, that process would quickly dry the small-podded plants and their fruits.

The correlation between seed size and pod length is not exact. Note that the habanero, which is nine times the length of the chiltepín, has seeds only 1 millimeter wider. Also note that the de árbol variety, which is also 4.5 cm long, but much thinner, has seeds only 1 millimeter wider than the Cerén chiles. I believe that we are witnessing the early domestication process begun by the Mayan people. The complete domestication of chiles from chiltepíns to anchos and the development of many varieties would not happen until the Aztec culture of nearly a millennium after AD 595. This is my personal theory, and I am not a paleoethnobotanist, though sometimes I wish I had studied that discipline.

THE CUISINE OF CERÉN

In addition to the vegetable crops of corn, chiles, beans, maniocs, cacao, and squash, the archaeologists found evidence that the Cerén villagers also harvested wild avocados, palm fruits and nuts, and certain spices such as achiote, or annatto seeds. In fact, Dr. Sheets observes, "The villagers ate better and had a greater variety of foodstuff than their descendants. Traditional families today eat mostly corn and beans, with some rice, squash, and chiles, but rarely any meat. Cerén's residents ate deer and dog meat." They also consumed peccary, mud turtle, duck, and rodent, but deer was their primary meat. Fully 50 percent of the total bones found on the site belonged to white-tailed deer, and many of those deer were immature animals—giving rise to a very interesting theory.

Linda Brown, who wrote the 1996 Field Season Preliminary Report entitled *Household and Village Animal Use*, notes: "Cerén residents may have practiced some form of deer management. One of the deer procurement strategies the Cerén villagers may have utilized is 'garden hunting.' Garden hunting consists of allowing deer to browse in cultivated fields and household gardens where they can be hunted. While some vegetation is lost to browsing, the benefits include easy access to deer when needed." Expanding upon that theory, she writes:

> The ethnohistoric data make many references to the Maya partially taming white-tailed deer. Specifically, historical sources note that it was women who were responsible for taking in, semi-taming, and raising deer. [Diego de] Landa mentioned that women raise other domestic animals and let the deer suck their breasts, by which means they raise them and make them so tame that they never will go into the woods, although they take them and carry them through the woods and raise them there. Apparently, during historic times, there was a designated place in the woods where women would take deer to browse until they needed them. Scholars have argued that

pre-Columbian women may have raised deer, dogs, peccary, and fowl much like contemporary Maya women raise pigs and fowl for food, trade, and special occasion feasts. Perhaps the Cerén women raised dog, fowl (a duck was tethered inside the Household 1 bodega), and semi-tamed deer as a contribution to the domestic and ceremonial economy.

It is always a challenge for archaeologists to reconstruct ancient cuisines and cooking techniques. The Cerén villagers did not have metal utensils, but they did have fired ceramics that could be used to boil foods. They could grill over open flames and perhaps fry foods in ceramic pots using cottonseed oil or animal fat. They had obsidian knives that could cut as cleanly as metal. They had metates for grinding corn into flour and molcajetes for grinding fruits, vegetables, chiles, and spices together into sauces.

This was the cuisine—extended into the Aztec world—that existed in the New World before the Spanish and Portuguese arrived.

CAPSICUM-CONQUEROR CONTACT

Christopher Columbus "discovered" chile peppers in the West Indies on his first voyage to the New World. In his journal for 1493, he wrote, "Also there is much Ají, which is their pepper, and the people won't eat without it, for they find it very wholesome. One could load fifty caravels a year with it in Hispaniola." (A caravel was a small Spanish or Portuguese sailing vessel of the Middle Ages.)

Dr. Diego Chanca, the fleet physician for Columbus on his second voyage, wrote in his journal that the Indians seasoned maniocs and sweet potatoes with ají, and that it was one of their principal foods. Of course, both Columbus and his doctor believed that they had reached the Spice Islands, or East Indies. Not only did Columbus misname the Indians, he also mistook chiles for black pepper, thus giving them the inaccurate name "pepper." But he did one thing right—he transported chile seeds back to Europe after his second voyage, which began the chile conquest of the rest of the world.

Explorers who followed Columbus to the New World soon learned that chiles were an integral part of the Indians' culinary, medical, and religious lives. In 1526, just 34 years after Columbus's first excursion, El Capitán Gonzalo de Oviedo noted that on the Spanish Main, "Indians everywhere grow it [the chile] in gardens and farms with much diligence and attention because they eat it continuously with almost all their food."

Bernabé Cobo, a naturalist and historian who traveled throughout Central and South America in the early seventeenth century, estimated that there were at least 40 different varieties. He wrote: "Some [are] as large as limes or large plums; others, as small as pine nuts or even grains of wheat, and between the two extremes are many different sizes. No less variety is found in color . . . and the same difference is found in form and shape." He noted that in Peru, next to maize, ají was the plant most beloved of the Indians.

Chile peppers were such a novelty to the explorers that rumors were rampant about their medical properties. Wrote the Jesuit priest, poet, and historian José de Acosta in 1590, "Taken moderately, chile helps and comforts the stomach for digestion." The priest had undoubtedly heard about the reputed aphrodisiac qualities of chiles because he continued his description of chile with the following warning: "But if they take too much, it has bad effects, for of itself it is very hot, fuming, and pierces greatly, so the use thereof is prejudicial to the health of young folks, chiefly to the soul, for it provokes to lust." Despite the good father's suspicions, the only thing lustful about chiles was the desire that everyone, including the Spanish, had to devour them.

When the Spanish forces under Cortez arrived in Tenochtitlan (now Mexico City) in 1519, they were astounded by the size and complexity of the market at the great plaza of Tlatelolco. According to descriptions by Bernal Diaz del Castillo, it resembled a modern flea market, with thousands of vendors hawking every conceivable foodstuff and other products. The noise of the market could be heard three miles away, and some of the soldiers who had traveled to such places as Rome and Constantinople said it was the largest market they had ever seen. Every product had its own section of the market, and chiles were no exception; they were sold in the second aisle to the right. Sometimes chiles were used as a form of money to buy drinks or other small items.

Most of the chiles sold in the market had been collected as tribute, a form of taxation used by the Toltecs and Aztecs and later adopted by the Spanish. The payers of the tribute were the *macehuales*, the serfs or commoners; the collectors were Indian officials, or later on, Indian officials who worked for the Spanish. The tribute consisted of locally produced goods or crops that were commonly grown, and the tribute of each village was recorded in boxes on codices of drawn or painted pictographs.

According to many sources, chiles were one of the most common tribute items. The chiles were offered to the government in several different forms: as fresh or dried pods, as seed, in two-hundred-pound bundles, in willow baskets, and in Spanish bushels. After the chiles and the rest of the produce were moved to the capital, everything was stored in warehouses and closely guarded, and then sold. Chile peppers were considered to be the most valuable of the tributes.

One of the most famous tribute codices is the *Matrícula de tributos*, which is part of the *Mendocino Codex*. This codex was compiled for the first viceroy of New Spain, Antonio de Mendoza, who ordered it painted to help inform the Emperor Charles V of the wealth of what is now Mexico. Glyphs on the codex indicate the tribute paid to the Aztecs by conquered towns just before the Spanish conquest; the towns on one tribute list (in the area of what is now San Luis Potosí) gave 1,600 loads of dry chiles to the imperial throne each year!

The *Mendocino Codex* also reveals an early use of chile peppers in punishment. One pictograph shows a father punishing his 11-year-old son by forcing him to inhale smoke from roasting chiles. The same drawing shows a mother threatening her 6-year-old daughter with the same punishment. Today, the Popolocan Indians who live near Oaxaca punish their children in a similar manner.

Wherever they traveled in the New World, Spanish explorers, particularly non-soldiers, collected and transported chile seeds and thus further spread the different varieties. And not only did they adopt the chile as their own, the Spanish also imported foods that they combined with chiles and other native ingredients to create even more complex chile cuisines.

FEATURED CHILE PEPPER: CHILTEPÍN

Botanists believe that these wild chiles (*C. annuum* var. *glabriusculum*) are the closest surviving species to the earliest forms of chiles that developed in Bolivia and southern Brazil long before mankind arrived in the New World. The small size of their fruits was perfect for dissemination by birds, and the wild chiles spread all over South and Central America and up to what is now the United States border millennia before the domesticated varieties arrived. It is possible that they have the widest distribution of any wild chile variety; they range from Peru north to the Caribbean, Florida, and Louisiana, and west to Arizona.

There is a wide variation in pod shapes, from tiny ones the size and shape of BBs to elongated pods a half inch long. By contrast, domesticated piquins have much longer pods, up to three inches. The chiltepíns most prized in Mexico are spherical and measure five to eight millimeters in diameter. They are among the hottest chiles of the *annuum* species, measuring up to 100,000 shu.

The word *chiltepín* is believed to be derived from the Aztec-language (Nahuatl) combination word *chilli + tecpintl*, meaning "flea chile," an allusion to its sharp bite.

That word was altered to *chiltecpin*, then to the Spanish *chiltepín*, and finally Anglicized to *chilipiquin*, as the plant is known in Texas. In Sonora and southern Arizona, chiltepíns grow in microhabitats in the transition zone between mountain and desert, which receive as little as 10 inches of rain per year.

They grow beneath "nurse" trees such as mesquite, oak, and palmetto, which provide shelter from direct sunlight, heat, and frost. In the summer, there is higher humidity beneath the nurse trees, and legumes such as mesquite fix nitrogen in the soil—a perfect fertilizer for the chiltepíns. Nurse trees also protect the plant from grazing by cattle, sheep, goats, and deer. Chiltepíns planted in the open, without nurse trees, usually die from the effects of direct solar radiation.

Chiltepin pod in the author's garden. Photograph by Dave DeWitt

Although the chiltepín plant's average height is about four feet, there are reports of individual bushes growing 10 feet tall, living 25 to 30 years, and having stems as big around as a man's wrist. Chiltepíns are resistant to frost but lose their leaves in cold winter weather. New growth will sprout from the base of the plant if it is frozen back.

There is quite a bit of legend and lore associated with the fiery little pods. In earlier times, the Papago Indians of Arizona traditionally made annual pilgrimages into the Sierra Madre range of Mexico to gather chiltepíns. Dr. Gary Nabhan, formerly of Native Seeds/SEARCH in Tucson, discovered that the Tarahumara Indians of Chihuahua value the chiltepíns so much that they build stone walls around the bushes to protect them from goats. Besides using them to spice up food, Indians use chiltepíns for antilactation, the technique where nursing mothers put chiltepín powder on their nipples to wean babies. Chiltepíns are also an aid in childbirth because, when powdered and inhaled, they cause sneezing. And, of course, the hot chiles induce gustatory sweating, which cools off the body during hot weather.

In 1794, Padre Ignaz Pfefferkorn, a German Jesuit living in Sonora, described the wild chile pepper: "A kind of wild pepper which the inhabitants call *chiltipin* is found on many hills. It is placed unpulverized on the table in a salt cellar and each fancier takes as much of it as he believes he can eat. He pulverizes it with his fingers and mixes it with his food. The chiltipin is the best spice for soup, boiled peas, lentils, beans and the like."

Padre Pfefferkorn realized that chiltepíns are one of the few crops in the world that are harvested in the wild rather than cultivated. (Others are piñon nuts, Brazil nuts, and some wild rice.) This fact has led to concern for the preservation of the chiltepín bushes because the harvesters often pull up entire plants or break off branches. Dr. Nabhan believes that the chiltepín population is diminishing because of overharvesting and overgrazing. In Arizona, a chiltepín reserve has been established near Tumacacori at Rock Corral Canyon in the Coronado National Forest. Native Seeds/SEARCH has been granted a special-use permit from the National Forest Service to initiate permanent marking and mapping of plants, ecological studies, and a management-plan proposal.

YO SOY UN CHILTIPÍNERO

My amigo Antonio Heras swears that the motto of the Sonoran bus lines is "Better Dead Than Late," and I believe him. The smoke-belching buses were flying by us on curves marked by shrines commemorating the unfortunate drivers whose journeys through life had abruptly ended on this mountain road. We waved the buses on and cruised along at a safer speed to enjoy the spectacular vistas on the way to the valley of the *chiltepíneros*.

It was November 1990, the time of the Sonoran chiltepín harvest, yet the temperature was in the upper eighties. My wife, Mary Jane, and I had accepted the invitation of Antonio Heras to visit the home of his mother, Josefina, the "Chile Queen," who lives in the town of Cumpas. From there, we journeyed through the spectacular scenery of the foothills of the Sierra Madre range—chiltepín country. Our destination was the Rio Sonora Valley and the villages of La Aurora and Mazocahui. As we drove along, Antonio and I reminisced about our fascination with the wild chile pepper. During the early days of the *Chile Pepper* magazine, both of us had attended a symposium on wild chiles that was held in October 1988 at the Desert Botanical Garden in Phoenix. The leader of the conference was the ecologist Dr. Gary Nabhan, author of *Gathering the Desert*, director of Native Seeds/SEARCH, and an expert on chiltepíns. Other chile experts attending included Dr. W. Hardy Eshbaugh, a botanist from Miami University of Ohio; Dr. Jean Andrews, author of *Peppers: The Domesticated Capsicums*; and Cindy Baker of the Chicago Botanical Garden. The symposium on wild chiles was fascinating, and we even got to taste some chiltepín ice cream. But it was even more interesting to see the chiltepíneros in action two years later.

IN THE VILLAGE OF THE DAWN

The only way to drive to the Village of the Dawn (La Aurora) is to ford the Rio Sonora, which was no problem for Antonio's Jeep. The first thing we noticed about

the village was that nearly every house had thousands of brilliant red chiltepíns drying on white linen cloths in their front yards. We stopped at the modest house of veteran chiltepínero Pedro Osuna and were immediately greeted warmly and offered liquid refreshment. As Pedro measured out the chiltepíns he had collected for Antonio and Josefina, we asked him about the methods of the chiltepíneros.

He said that the Durans advanced him money so he could hire pickers and pay for expenses such as gasoline. Then he would drive the pickers to ranches where the bushes were numerous. He dropped the pickers off alongside the road, and they wandered through the rough cattle country handpicking the tiny pods. In a single day, a good picker could collect only six quarts of chiltepíns. At sunset, the pickers returned to the road, where Pedro met them. The ranchers who owned the land would later be compensated with a liter or so of pods.

Usually, the pods would be dried in the sun for about 10 days. But because that technique is lengthy and often results in the pods collecting dust, Antonio had built a solar dryer in back of Pedro's house. Air heated by a solar collector rose up a chimney through racks, with screens holding the fresh chiltepíns—a much more efficient method. Modern technology, based upon ancient, solar-passive principles, had arrived at the Village of the Dawn.

I asked Pedro how the harvest was going, and he said it was the best in more than a decade because the better-than-average rainfall had caused the bushes to set a great many fruits. Antonio added that during the drought of 1988, chiltepíns were so rare that there was no export crop. According to Pedro, factors other than rainfall also had an influence on the harvest—specifically, birds and insects. Mockingbirds, pyrrhuloxia (Mexican cardinals), and other species readily ate the pods as they turned red, but the real damage to the entire plant was caused by grasshoppers.

The total harvest in Sonora is difficult to estimate, but at least 20 tons of dried pods are collected and sold in an average year. Some chiltepíneros have suggested that in a wet year like 1990, 50 tons might be a better estimate. The total export to the United States is estimated at more than 6 tons a year, and the Durans account for much of that. As I watched Antonio and his mother weigh huge sacks of chiltepíns on the small scale in front of the market, I asked Antonio about prices.

He declined to tell me what he paid the chiltepíneros, but he offered a wealth of information about other pricing information. Between 1968 and 1990, the wholesale price of chiltepíns multiplied nearly tenfold. Between 1987 and 1990, the price nearly tripled, mostly because of the 1988 drought. Currently, chiltepíns are being sold in South Tucson in one-quarter-ounce packages for $2, which equates to a phenomenal $128 per pound. Thus, chiltepíns are the second most expensive spice in the world, after saffron.

Why do people in the United States lust after these tiny pods? Dr. Nabhan suggests that chiltepíns remind immigrants of their northern Mexico homeland and help them reinforce their Sonoran identity. Also, chiltepíns have traditional uses in Sonoran cuisine, as evidenced by the recipes we collected. In addition to spicing up Sonoran foods, they are an antioxidant and thus help preserve *carne seca*, the dried meat we call jerky. No wonder the Chile Queen and her son work hard to import many hundreds of pounds of pods.

After the sacks of chiltepíns were loaded into the Jeep, we were joined by *Arizona Republic* reporter Keith Rosenblum, who was writing a story on the chiltepíneros. We went for lunch in the nearby village of Mazocahui, passing signs reading "Se vende chiltepín" (chiltepíns for sale). At the rustic restaurant, which was really the living room of someone's house, we sat down for a fiery feast. Bowls of chiltepíns were on the table, and the extremely hot salsa *casera* was served with *carne adovada*, *carne machaca*, beans, and the superb extremely thin Sonoran flour tortillas.

Back in the town of Cumpas, loud salsa music enlivened the streets as if a fiesta were in progress. Josefina and her assistant Evalia prepared a wonderful chiltepín-spiced meal. We drank some *bacanora*, the magical Mexican moonshine, and dined on an elegant—and highly spiced—menu of Sonoran specialties. I felt inspired. After submerging myself in the chiltepín culture of Sonora, I was very comfortable in saying, "Yo soy un chiltepínero." I am a chiltepínero.

recipes

Based on the archaeological evidence, I have devised some recipes that reflect the main ingredients used in the cooking of the Mayas (from Cerén in particular), the Incas, and the Aztecs—adapted, of course, for modern kitchens. One of my basic theories about the history of cooking is that we should never underestimate our predecessors' culinary sophistication, so I cannot presume that as far back as 14 centuries ago the Mayas were preparing boring food. Especially since we know that they had chiles.

Spicy calabacitas. Prepared by Aaron Hill. Photograph by Douglas K. Hill.

SPICY CALABACITAS

yield 4 to 6 servings   *heat scale* medium

This recipe combines three Native American crops: squash, corn, and chiles. Although we don't know for sure, my theory is that the Cerén villagers would have known how to use green chiles. I have taken the liberty of substituting New Mexican chiles for the small Cerénean chiles, making a milder dish. The villagers, of course, would not have used butter, milk, or cheese but rather fat and water flavored with palm fruits.

½	cup chopped green New Mexican chiles, roasted, peeled, stems removed
3	zucchini squash, cubed
½	cup chopped onion
4	tablespoons butter or margarine
2	cups whole kernel corn
1	cup milk
½	cup grated Monterey Jack cheese

In a pan, sauté the squash and onion in the butter until the squash is tender.

Add the chiles, corn, and milk. Simmer the mixture for 15 to 20 minutes to blend the flavors. Add the cheese and heat until the cheese is melted.

XOCOLATL: ROYAL CHOCOLATE WITH CHILE

yield 1 serving   *heat scale* medium

Although this drink was served to royalty in the large Mayan cities, the discovery of chile in conjunction with cacao in Cerén indicates that even commoners knew how to make this concoction.

1½	cups water
¼	cup unsweetened cocoa powder (not instant hot-chocolate mix)
1	tablespoon honey

¼	teaspoon hot-chile powder, such as chiltepín
1	vanilla bean pod

In a pan, heat the water to boiling. Add the remaining ingredients and stir well. Serve immediately with the vanilla bean for garnish in the drink.

RED SNAPPER FILLETS

*Another dish that evolved from the Inca people, ceviche has fish or other seafood soaked in the juice of limes and lemons. The citric acid in the juice causes the proteins in the seafood to become denatured, or "cured," appearing to be cooked. Before the Spanish introduced limes and lemons to the New World, the juice of the rather sour Peruvian groundcherry (*Physalis peruviana*), also known as the cape gooseberry, was probably used. More than any other dish, ceviche is the* plato nacionál *(national dish) of Peru. Though the recipe given here makes use of one fish only, any number of seafood items including other fishes, scallops, shrimp, octopus, and crab may be used singly or in combination in preparing a ceviche. Peruvians like their ceviche fiery hot, so in the interest of authenticity, don't skimp on the diced chiles.*

1	pound red snapper fillet
	Juice of 8 limes
	Juice of 2 lemons
	Various Peruvian chile peppers; 2 minced habaneros make a good substitute
½	cup chopped fresh cilantro
1	large red onion, cut in julienned strips and then soaked in cold salted water
1	tablespoon salt
1	teaspoon fresh ground black pepper

Cut the snapper fillets into pieces about 1 inch long and ½ inch wide. Do not use pieces any larger than that, as they will not be properly cured by the citrus juices.

In a large stainless-steel bowl, marinate the fish in the lime and lemon juices. Cover and let sit for 1 hour.

Chop the chiles, removing any seeds, and soak the chiles in a bowl of cold water. Julienne the red onion and soak in another bowl of cold water.

Add the chiles and onion to the fish, mix well, and refrigerate for an hour before serving.

THE EARLIEST MOLE SAUCE

yield 2 ½ cups   *heat scale* medium

Why wouldn't the cooks of Cerén have developed sauces to serve over meats and veg-
etables? After all, there is evidence that curry mixtures were in existence thousands of
years ago in what is now India, and we have to assume that Native Americans exper-
imented with all available ingredients. Perhaps this mole sauce was served over stewed
duck meat, as ducks were one of the domesticated meat sources of the Cerén villagers.

4	tomatillos, husks removed	2	tablespoons medium-hot chile powder
1	tomato, toasted in a skillet and peeled	1	teaspoon achiote (annatto seeds)
½	teaspoon chile seeds	3	tablespoons vegetable oil
3	tablespoons pepitas (toasted pumpkin or squash seeds)	2	cups chicken broth
1	corn tortilla, torn into pieces	1	ounce Mexican or bittersweet chocolate

In a blender, combine the tomatillos, tomato, chile seeds, pepitas, tortilla, chile powder, and achiote to make a paste.

In a pan, heat the vegetable oil and fry the paste until fragrant, about 4 minutes, stirring constantly.

Add the chicken broth and the chocolate, and stir over medium heat until thickened to desired consistency.

THE GREAT MONTEZUMA

yield 4 servings   *heat scale* medium

Richard Sterling developed this recipe, which is his version of how the Spaniards might
have transformed Montezuma's favorite beverage with the addition of alcohol. He
commented: "Salud! Drink to the Old World and the New."

12 ounces hot chocolate made with unsweetened cocoa powder	2 tablespoons heavy cream
2 tablespoons honey	Cayenne powder and cinnamon sticks for garnish
½ teaspoon vanilla extract	Grated chocolate and dried red chiles for garnish (optional)
2 jiggers pepper vodka	

Combine the chocolate, honey, vanilla, and vodka in a small pitcher. Pour into two long-stemmed glasses or Irish coffee glasses. Float the cream on the tops of the two drinks. Dust with a pinch of cayenne pepper and garnish with cinnamon sticks, or dust with grated chocolate and garnish with dried red chiles. Cut them lengthwise and fix them to the edges of the glasses.

PEPITA-GRILLED VENISON CHOPS

yield 4 servings   *heat scale* medium

Here is a tasty grilled dish featuring native New World game, chiles, and tomatoes, plus pepitas—toasted pumpkin or squash seeds. Garlic is not native to the New World but is given here as a substitute for wild onions, which the people of Cerén would have known.

5 tablespoons pepitas	Puree all the ingredients, except the venison, in a blender. Paint the chops with this mixture and marinate at room temperature for an hour.
3 cloves garlic	
1 tablespoon red chile powder	
½ cup tomato paste	Grill the chops over a charcoal and piñon wood fire until done, basting with the remaining marinade.
¼ cup vegetable oil	
3 tablespoons lemon juice or vinegar	
4 thick-cut venison chops, or substitute thick lamb chops	

VENISON STEAK WITH JUNIPER BERRY AND FIERY RED CHILE SAUCE

yield 6 servings   *heat scale* medium

This recipe is by permission from Lois Ellen Frank, and it's taken from her book Foods of the Southwest Indian Nations (Ten Speed Press, 2002). Both the venison and the juniper berries are available from mail-order sources. The juice from wild grapes might have been available to the Mayas, but probably not wine. Lois has adapted this recipe for the modern kitchen.

THE SAUCE

1	tablespoon dried juniper berries
3	cups unsweetened dark grape juice or wine
2	bay leaves
1 ½	teaspoons dried thyme
2	shallots, peeled and coarsely chopped
2	cups beef stock

THE STEAKS

6	venison steaks, 8 to 10 ounces each
2	tablespoons olive oil
1	tablespoon salt
1	tablespoon freshly ground black pepper
4	whole dried chiles de árbol, seeds and stems removed, crushed

To make the sauce, wrap the juniper berries in a clean kitchen towel and crush them using a mallet. Remove them from the towel and place them in a saucepan with the grape juice or wine, bay leaves, thyme, and shallots. Simmer over medium heat for 20 to 25 minutes, until the liquid has been reduced to 1 cup. Add the stock, bring to a boil, then decrease the heat to medium and cook for another 15 minutes until the sauce has been reduced to 1 ½ cups. Strain the sauce through a fine sieve and keep it warm.

Brush the steaks on both sides with the olive oil and sprinkle with salt and pepper. Place the steaks on the grill and grill for 3 minutes, until they have charred marks. Rotate the steaks a half turn and grill for another 3 minutes. Flip the steaks over and grill for another 5 minutes until done as desired.

Ladle the sauce onto each plate, top with the steaks, pattern-side up, and sprinkle the crushed chiles over them.

CERÉN BEANS

yield 4 servings   *heat scale* medium

Three varieties of beans were found beneath the ash in the village kitchens of Cerén. Certainly they were boiled, and since they are bland, they were undoubtedly combined with other ingredients, including chiles and primitive tomatoes. The Cerén villagers would have used peccary fat for the lard and bacon, and of course they would not have had cumin. But they probably would have used spices such as Mexican oregano.

3	cups cooked pinto beans (either canned or simmered for hours until tender)	¾	cup Mexican chorizo sausage (not Spanish chorizo)
1	onion, minced	1	pound tomatoes, peeled, seeded, and chopped
2	tablespoons lard, or substitute vegetable oil	6	serrano chiles, stems removed, minced
5	slices bacon, minced	1	teaspoon cumin (or substitute Mexican oregano)

Sauté the beans and onion in the lard or oil for about 5 minutes, stirring constantly. In another skillet, sauté the bacon and chorizo together. Drain.

Combine the beans and onion with the drained bacon and chorizo in a pot, add the other ingredients, and simmer for 30 minutes.

TLATONILE

yield 4 to 6 servings   *heat scale* medium

A classic recipe descended from the Aztecs, tlatonile is a pipián from Jalcomulco, Vera-cruz. Pipiáns are spicy dishes from Mexico that utilize ground nuts or seeds. In Mexico, these are most often pumpkin or squash seeds. This recipe is from Susana Rodriguez and was collected by Kraig Kraft.

2	pounds pork or chicken (thighs and legs)
2	chayotes, or use yellow squash, sliced
8	ounces of hulled pumpkin seeds, toasted
1 ½	ounces of dried ground chile, preferably chile de árbol; Susana used a local variety called *chile puya*, a variety of de árbol
3	Roma tomatoes, halved
1	bunch epazote (a Mexican herb also known as wormweed or Mexican tea)
¼	cup cooked rice
	Salt to taste

Brown the pork or chicken in a stockpot. Add enough water to cover, add the chayote, and simmer until cooked.

Meanwhile, grind the pumpkin seeds until they form a thick paste. While the seeds that Susana used were quite high in oil and exuded oil when pressed, I had to add oil to my ground seeds at home.

Combine this paste with the dried ground chile, the salt, and a small amount of water.

Once the meat has cooked, add the halved tomatoes, the pumpkin-seed paste, and the epazote. Serve in bowls with a teaspoon of rice in the bottom.

STUFFED ROCOTOS (ROCOTO RELLENO)

yield 6 servings as an appetizer   *heat scale* hot

This recipe evolved from the Inca people and became a signature dish of Arequipa, a city spectacularly located in the Andes of southern Peru. Famous throughout the country, it has become a national dish, right behind ceviche and ají de gallina. The garlic and onions are post-Columbian crops, although the Incas may have used a few species of wild alliums occurring in the Andes, such as Allium juncifolium. The Peruvians typically accompany stuffed rocotos with beer, although a red wine is also appropriate. Note: This recipe requires advance preparation.

6	rocotos (large jalapeños may be used as a substitute)
2	tablespoons vegetable oil
1	medium onion, finely chopped
3	cloves garlic, minced
½	pound ground beef
½	teaspoon ground cumin
¼	cup pitted olives, chopped
1	teaspoon salt
2	teaspoons raisins
1	egg, lightly beaten
6	yellow potatoes, boiled and cut in half
1	cup grated mozzarella or Gruyere cheese
¼	cup milk
	Freshly ground black pepper to taste

One day prior to serving, cut the tops off the rocotos. The tops may be saved as a garnish. Remove all seeds and veins. Soak the rocotos for 24 hours in a bowl of water with 2 tablespoons salt, changing the water at least twice.

Heat the oil in a frying pan, add the onions, and cook until tender. Add the garlic and fry for 2 minutes. Add the meat and cumin, and fry until cooked. Add the olives, salt, raisins, and the beaten egg.

Stuff the rocotos with this mixture.

In a glass baking dish, arrange the rocotos and potatoes. Add the milk and arrange the cheese atop the rocotos.

Bake at 400 degrees F. for 40 minutes.

The Amazon Basin was the center of origin for the chinense species that spread throughout the Caribbean, but the oldest known chinense specimen ever found was a single intact pod that was discovered in Preceramic levels (6,500 BC) in Guitarrero Cave in coastal Peru. Such a discovery considerably predates the generally accepted time of chile pepper cultivation and suggests the possibility that the pod was introduced later to the archaeological site, or that by that date wild chinense pods had migrated far from the center of origin and had been collected by early hunter-gatherer civilizations.

Since both wild and domesticated forms of the Brazilian *chinense* exist today (there is some debate about the wild varieties), it follows that the species was domesticated much in the same manner as the *annuum* species was in Mexico. First, it was a tolerated weed with erect fruits. Then, as humans planted the seeds and tended the plants, there was a gradual evolution by human selection to larger, more pendant pods.

The domestication of the *chinense* species occurred around 2000 BC, and, according to ethnobotanist Barbara Pickersgill, "its domestication was probably connected with the development of agriculture in tropical forests. It seems reasonable to assume that *C. chinense* was domesticated east of the Andes by these tropical forest agriculturists, who were probably responsible for the domestication of manioc." She adds, wryly: "As a condiment, the chile pepper probably formed a welcome addition to any diet consisting largely of manioc starch." By about 1000 BC, domesticated *chinense* varieties had spread to the Pacific coast of Peru.

The cultivation of the *chinense* species produced many pod types and varieties. Bernabé Cobo, a naturalist who traveled throughout South America during the early seventeenth century, probably was the first European to study the *chinense* species. He estimated that there were at least 40 different pod types of the chiles: "Some [are] as large as limes or large plums; others, as small as pine nuts or even grains of wheat, and between the two extremes are many different sizes. No less variety is found in color . . . and the same difference is found in form and shape."

FEATURED PEPPERS: THE *CHINENSE* SPECIES IN THE ISLANDS

The dispersion of the domesticated *chinense* species into the Caribbean and Central America occurred in two different directions. Some *chinense* varieties spread into the isthmus from Colombia and eventually became common in Panama (as the

A breakfast nook on the cliffs of Negril, Jamaica. Photograph by Mary Jane Wilan. Used with permission.

ají chombo) and Guyana (as the "tiger tooth") and Costa Rica (where it was called the *panameño*). But apparently their spread north was halted before they reached the Yucatán Peninsula.

Meanwhile, during their great migrations, the ancestors of the Arawaks and Caribs transferred the *chinense* from the Amazon Basin through Venezuela and into the Caribbean, where pod types developed on nearly every island. The seeds were carried and cultivated by Native Americans as the *chinense* species hopped, skipped, and jumped around the West Indies, forming—seemingly on each island—specifically adapted pod types that are called "landraces" of the species. As we have seen, each landrace gained a name in each island or country, although the terms "Scotch bonnet" and "habanero" are used generically throughout the region. The pods of these landraces became the dominant spicy element of the Caribbean, firing up its cuisines—and its legends. Barbara Pickersgill believes that the habanero was "a historic introduction from the West Indies" into Yucatán, completing *chinense*'s island-hopping encirclement of the Caribbean Sea.

I will cover the habanero in detail later on in this chapter, but it is important here to address the circumstances that led to the development of what we now call "superhot" chile peppers in the two-island nation of Trinidad and Tobago (T&T). The fascinating fact about all these superhots is this: all the hottest chile peppers in the world originated in Trinidad and Tobago, including the 'Bhut Jolokia' that was transferred to India in 1854 when the governor of Trinidad, Lord George Francis Robert Harris, took the seeds to Madras when he became governor there (the full story is online at http://www.fieryfoodscentral.com/2010/11/05/lord-harris-the -ghost-pepper-governor/).. But how and why?

BASIC BREEDING STARTS WITH A MUTATION

Ever since the domestication of the five *Capsicum* species, human choice is the most important factor in the development of new chile varieties. Humans are selecting the plants to use in breeding because they have more useful variations than the other possible plants. Horticulturists call this "differential reproduction," and this term simply means that some parents will have more offspring than others because of human choice. Differential reproduction selects for more useful variations and against less useful variations. For example, in the development of the bell pepper from the poblano, pepper breeders were selecting for large size and reduced pungency, and they ended up with a very large pod with no pungency. And that entire

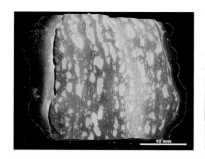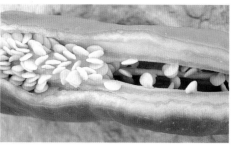

left Capsaicin sacs fluorescing on the interior pod wall of the 'Trinidad Moruga Scorpion.' Photograph by NMSU. Public domain.

right Note the yellow color near the seeds of this New Mexican chile. There is capsaicin in only two locations inside the chile— along the placental tissue. Photograph by New Mexico State University (NMSU). Public domain.

breeding project began with a mutation that added to the genetic diversity of the population. Breeders used the mutation to start breeding the bell pepper and, in successive grow-outs, selected the seeds from the largest and mildest pods until the bell was achieved. Using the bell pepper development as a guide, here is how I think the superhots of T&T were developed, sometime before 1854.

MUTATIONS HAPPENED AMONG THE ALREADY HOT PEPPERS OF T&T

The mutations were unplanned and unpredictable. They radically raised the level of pungency, and they added to the genetic diversity of T&T hot peppers. The mutation was discovered in 2016 by Dr. Peter Cooke of the New Mexico State University Core University Research Resources Laboratory. He managed to make the capsaicinoid sacs fluoresce in both jalapeños and 'Trinidad Moruga Scorpion' peppers and then examined the pods with an electron microscope. Dr. Paul Bosland, the famed chile breeder at New Mexico State University, explained, "There, you could see that the jalapeño was fluorescing on the placenta [the tissue to which the seeds are attached], while the superhots would fluoresce all over the [inner pod] wall. It's a very dramatic image to see. Right now we're assuming this is a genetic mutation in superhots because we've never seen this in wild chile peppers." Thus the superhots have more surface area for the capsaicinoid sacs than any other chile peppers.

ENVIRONMENTAL CONDITIONS (HUMAN CHOICE) MADE SOME OF THE MUTATIONS BENEFICIAL

People liked the hotter peppers and planted those seeds. People didn't like the milder peppers as much so they didn't plant them. Therefore, the plants with genes for superhot chiles had more offspring than the chiles with other parents. In time, this differential reproduction caused by breeders (human choice), that is, superhot peppers, became the norm in T&T.

Therefore, if this scenario is accurate, the more useful variation was the extremely high pungency of the newly developed varieties. Now there is one final question to answer: Why was the increased pungency such a useful variation? Considering food uses, in some cultures, the more capsaicin a pod contains, the more valuable it is. For example, if a person were preparing food for a feast, why buy seven chile pods if one would suffice to spice up all the food? Hence the name of one Trinidadian chile variety, 7-pot, which supposedly got its name from the ability of one pod to spice up seven kettles of pepper-pot stew. Given heat levels of one million Scoville Heat Units or more, it is perfectly conceivable that a single superhot pod, cut into seven sections, could accomplish this feat. Capsaicin in chile peppers is antibacterial and was used before refrigeration to reduce the spoilage of food, so the hotter the pepper, the greater its antibacterial powers.

In folk beliefs, the more pungent a chile pod, the more powerful it is in fighting evil. The East Indian population of Trinidad wraps seven red pepper pods with salt, onion skins, and garlic skins in paper and passes them seven times around a baby to remove *najar*, the evil eye, which is believed to cause unnecessary crying. Also, green chiles are dropped around the doorway of a house to keep away evil spirits. And in folk medicine, hot peppers have long been applied to wounds to prevent them from becoming infected, so the hotter the chile peppers, the better they would fight infection.

The story of superhot peppers does not end here. In chapter 7 I will examine how one variety of the superhots was transferred to India and over the years was thought to be native to that country. The 'Bhut Jolokia,' or ghost pepper, of course, was not native to India. In chapter 10, I discuss the enormous popularity of superhots with gardeners as these peppers became legendary in the United States.

A COLLISION OF CULTURES AND CUISINES

In the Caribbean, chile peppers are the dominant spice in a region filled with other spices such as ginger, nutmeg, mace, cloves, and allspice. Although there is little doubt that the Indians of the Caribbean Islands were cultivating and cooking with chile peppers for centuries before Columbus happened upon the hot fruits, they left little evidence of their cuisine. First, the Arawak Indians were wiped out by the ferocious Carib Indians, and then smallpox and swine flu, imported by European colonists, rendered the Caribs extinct. Survivors joined other tribes. So the main culinary influences upon the islands were from the Old World, with the exception of the chiles, which were adopted into the new foods and styles of cooking imported from Europe and Africa.

European influences in the Caribbean included Dutch, Spanish, English, and French styles of cooking that adopted native ingredients such as fruits, seafood, and of course, chiles. The arrival of slaves from West Africa and immigrants from India added even more exotic influences to the incredible mixture of cuisines that abounded in the Caribbean region. The combination of chiles with peanuts, for example, is typically both Peruvian and African (see chapter 6) but occurs commonly in Caribbean dishes such as groundnut soup. Many Indian-style curry dishes are found in the West Indies, particularly in Jamaica and Trinidad.

An old island adage says that the best Caribbean hot sauce is the one that burns a hole in the tablecloth. I've never seen that happen in all my trips to the Caribbean, but I'm certain that the earliest hot sauces in the region were made with the crushed *chinense* varieties. According to some sources, the Carib and Arawak Indians used pepper juice for seasoning, and after the "discovery" of chile peppers by Europeans, slave-ship captains combined pepper juice with palm oil, flour, and water to make a "slabber sauce" that was served over ground beans to the slaves aboard ship. The most basic hot sauces on the islands were made by soaking chopped Scotch bonnets in vinegar and then sprinkling the fiery vinegar on foods. Over the centuries, each island developed its own style of hot sauce by combining the crushed chiles with other ingredients such as mustard, fruits, or tomatoes. Homemade hot sauces are still common on the islands of the Caribbean. The sauces piquante and *chien* from Martinique and *ti-malice* from Haiti all combine shallots, lime juice, garlic, and the hottest *chinense* available. Puerto Rico has two hot sauces of note: one is called *pique* and is made with acidic Seville oranges and habaneros; the other is *sofrito*, which combines small piquins (bird peppers) with annatto seeds, cilantro, onions, garlic, and tomatoes. In Jamaica, Scotch bonnets are combined with the pulp and juices of mangoes, papayas, and tamarinds. The Virgin Islands has a concoction known as *asher*, which is a corruption of "limes ashore." It combines limes with habaneros, cloves, allspice, salt, vinegar, and garlic. This is one of the earliest cures for scurvy, which develops in humans from a lack of vitamin C.

The story goes that a poor woman discovered her kitchen was bare of the above ingredients except for chiles, so she decided all she could prepare for dinner was a soup made solely of habaneros and water. Her unsuspecting children ate one spoonful of the soup and then ran to the river to try to douse the heat, where they drank so much water that they drowned. Obviously, the apocryphal children were unaware that water is the least effective cooldown for chile heat—see chapter 8 for the best ones.

THE CONGO PEPPERS OF TRINIDAD AND TOBAGO

"Two unspoiled islands, one country—Trinidad and Tobago," pronounced Brian Kuei Tung, Minister of Trade, Industry, and Tourism. Mary Jane and I were sitting in his spacious high-rise office overlooking the Port of Spain harbor, and I was wearing long pants in honor of meeting a cabinet minister. "We don't allow logging, so the rain forests are intact. And we don't allow high-rise hotels to spoil our beaches."

Say what? Was I hearing this right? A country that actually was protecting its scenic beauty and not caving in to big business and developers? Unbelievable. And even more unbelievable was the fact that we were in Trinidad. That was the result of Dennis Hayes, who then worked for the Crossing Press in Freedom, California. He had selected me to be the principal author of *Callaloo, Calypso & Carnival: The Cuisines of Trinidad & Tobago*, so of course Mary Jane and I had to travel there to research what we would soon be writing about.

After island-hopping to Barbados and Grenada, our B-Wee (BWIA) flight landed at the Piarco International Airport outside of Port of Spain. My mind was asking the four most important questions for a visitor: Where do I sleep? Where do I eat? How do I get around? And where do I buy beer? Fortunately, all of those questions were soon answered. We were staying at the Kapok, a friendly hotel adjacent to the beautiful Queen's Park Savannah—a 200-acre park in the middle of the city. We were eating out twice a day, every day. Because of the narrow streets and crazed drivers in Port of Spain, we were taking taxis everywhere. And the local favorite beer, Carib, was available at corner markets and it was cheap. That was a good omen, I thought.

Our first full day there was Emancipation Day in August 1992, and nearly everything was closed for the holiday. But the Botanic Gardens near the Kapok were open, and as we strolled through the lush foliage, I thought, this is my kind of country. It's summer all year long. The phones work. There are palm trees and pepper plants, the language doesn't need constant translation, the food is great, and the literacy rate of the people is 97 percent.

While buying some Carib beer at a street-corner market a block from the Kapok, I spotted some fresh peppers that looked like gigantic red habaneros. "What do you call these?" I asked the clerk, and she said, "Congo peppers." Back at the hotel, I cut them open to save the seeds, and the pungent fumes were so strong that we were driven out of the room coughing and sneezing. It was the characteristic apricot aroma of the habanero, and the fumes were so powerful that even with the windows open and the air conditioning on high, we couldn't use the room for over an hour.

A congo pepper in Mary Jane's hand. Photograph by Dave DeWitt.

Later that afternoon in one of the few stores open I bought some locally published cookbooks and brushed up on the culinary history of T&T. I soon learned that the diversity of food on the islands was the result of one wave of immigrants after another. First, the Spanish occupied Trinidad and adopted many of the foods and cooking techniques of the indigenous Arawaks before they disappeared. Then the Spanish invited French immigration, and the French brought with them herbs, spices, and garlic—hallmarks of T&T cookery today. Accompanying the Frenchmen were African slaves who brought their own ingredients and cooking styles.

The British conquered Trinidad in 1797 and introduced breadfruit to feed the slaves, as well as tamarind from the East Indies. They also brought turnips and cabbage to Trinidad, two common vegetables in T&T markets today. After the abolition of slavery in 1838, more immigrants arrived to work in the sugarcane fields: the Portuguese, East Indians, and Chinese. Over the years, the immigrant foods became very popular in the country, and curries and chop suey were commonly served in homes and restaurants. Today, T&T has the most diverse cuisine of any of the Caribbean islands—and we dove into it right away with a meal of callaloo (an exquisite dasheen or taro-leaf soup) and grilled kingfish at the Café Savannah.

LIMING ABOUT

To "lime," according to a local dictionary of Trini slang, is "to pass the time in idle pleasure." It describes every possible form of indulgence except Carnival, which is more of a frantic than an idle pleasure. Liming is hangin' out, goofin' off, fishin', drivin', swimmin', boatin', picnickin', and generally just doing anything one wants to do. We were invited to lime about at a dinner party the next day at the home our host, Marie Permenter, shares with Vernon and Irene Montrichard, which overlooks a lovely bay. These three entrepreneurs founded the Royal Castle chain of spicy chicken and chips restaurants in 1968, then fought off the invasion of Kentucky Fried Chicken, and were currently setting sales records at 12 locations

in T&T. Trinidadians love chicken, and they especially love Royal Castle chicken, which is marinated in a special hot sauce of congo peppers and herbs before being fried.

At the party we met the cast of characters that Marie and Vernon had lined up to be our culinary guides. Mikey and Nancy Ramesar gave us lessons on East Indian cooking West Indian–style. Keith Nexar and Steve Mathura, directors of Advantage Advertising, the agency responsible for much of Royal Castle's success, set up interviews for us and even arranged our appearance on local television. Michael Coelho, marketing director of the Royal Castle chain, was our main guide and drove us all over Trinidad.

CONGO PEPPERS AND SHADOW BENNIE

On our first trip, Marie and Vernon took us to their pepper fields, where the congo peppers are grown for the Royal Castle hot sauce. In Trinidad, *congo* means anything large and powerful, and these varieties of *Capsicum chinense* lived up to their name.

We found some as large as lemons, and they had thicker walls that most of the habaneros we were familiar with. In 1992, we had never heard of superhot peppers and never saw any in the markets. No matter, though, because the congos were very hot, about 300,000 SHU. We also got a tour of their hot sauce factory.

Next, Michael located a four-wheel-drive Toyota and took us on back roads that led seemingly straight up the mountains. We were on our way to see the herb growers of Paramin, who farm Spanish and French thyme, plus other herbs, on the steep slopes. Since it rains nearly every day during the wet season, the herbs love the good drainage of the steep slopes. The herbs, which are sold in markets in Port of Spain, are also an ingredient in the Royal Castle hot sauce.

Along with Vernon, and Michael's wife, Danielle, we took a tour of the northern rain forests, with a stop along the way at Maracas Bay. That bay is the prime liming area for Port of Spain, and after a cooling dip in the surf, we descended on the roadside stands for some shark-and-bake. This dish features fried bread stuffed with tender shark, topped with congo-pepper hot sauce and another, dark green sauce they called "shadow bennie." The taste was strong, flavorful, and vaguely familiar. What herb was in it, we asked. "Shadow bennie" was all they knew.

The next few days flew by. With Michael as our guide, we dove into the food of T&T. At the Patraj Roti Shop in San Juan, we tasted nine different kinds of curried fillings for the roti bread—fish, beef, chicken, goat, conch, shrimp, liver, duck, and

Restaurant sign in San Juan, Trinidad. Photograph by Dave DeWitt.

"One bellyful don' fatten de hog," goes a proverb in Barbados, meaning that it takes a bit of an effort to achieve anything worthwhile. That saying applies to finding true Bajan food if you're staying at a resort or beach hotel, because they serve mostly American-style fare. So, to experience the wide range of fiery island delights, we had to desert the beach and meet the cooks, chefs, and sauce makers of Barbados.

potato. The fillings are wrapped in the bread or are served in bowls accompanied by torn-up bread called Buss-Up-Shut, which is slang for "burst up shirt," because the bread resembles torn-up cloth. The curry itself was not spicy, but the congo-pepper hot sauce served in squeeze bottles solved that problem.

Then it was time to go native. Michael turned us over to his friend, Johnny Nahous. Johnny, who is of Lebanese descent, owns Johnny's Food Haven, a restaurant that serves "native" food, or Creole food, as it's called there. On a typical day he serves stewed oxtail, curried crab and dumplings, callaloo, chicken pelau, Chinese marinated chicken, cow-heel soup, sautéed cassava, and at least four additional entrées. He has to have that many—on Fridays, Johnny sells 500 lunches.

Johnny took us on a tour of the bustling Central Market, where if you're not careful, you can get run over by a wheelbarrow full of cabbages. Vendors raised their prices when they saw the foreigners with him, but Johnny waved them off in disgust and pursued the bargains. The multiple displays of congo peppers were very impressive, being the most habaneros I had ever seen in one place—until I visited Yucatán, Mexico (see chapter 3). I also got a tour from Michael of the nearly vertical herb fields of Paramin. Those herbs were used by Johnny in many of his dishes.

Before we left T&T, we went down "de" islands again, this time on Vernon's boat to visit the resort islands between Trinidad and Venezuela. Later, we ate at more restaurants—including Ali Baba where we had a great Middle Eastern meal—and visited the pan yards, where the steel-drum bands were practicing for the upcoming Steelband Music Festival. And speaking of steel bands, even in August, six months before the festivities, much of the talk in T&T was about Carnival and how we hadn't really seen T&T unless we were there during that extravaganza of fetes, parades, masquerades, and calypso contests. After all, Trinidadian Peter Minshall had just designed the opening ceremony for the Olympics, our hosts reminded us, so imagine what he could do at Carnival!

Michael Coelho and the author in the herb fields of Paramin. Photograph by Mary Jane Wilan.

Callaloo, Calypso & Carnival: The Cuisines of Trinidad & Tobago was published by the Crossing Press in 1993. We returned to T&T in 1996 after a trip to Barbados.

GROUND PROVISIONS AND BONNEY PEPPERS

Our main guide to the culinary delights of this 122-square-mile island was Anne-Marie Whittaker, an energetic go-getter who markets food products under her brand, Native Treasures. With her help and the assistance of the Barbados Tourism Authority, and driver Emerson Clarke, we were able to conduct our whirlwind culinary exploration with maximum efficiency.

We began with a visit to Cheapside Market, a 100-year-old metal building that housed vendors both inside and outside. This market is a trip into the past, especially in Barbados with its fancy supermarkets. According to Anne-Marie, most of the locals were "too big-up to go to market," too full of their own self-importance to be seen buying "ground provisions": yams and sweet potatoes and vegetables such as cucumbers, tomatoes, okra, christophene (chayote squash), and eggplants. This was no tourist market—Mary Jane and I had the only white faces, and the closest thing to souvenirs were the bright red bonney peppers that appeared in nearly all the vendors' stalls.

The bonney pepper, a member of the same species as habaneros and Scotch bonnets, *Capsicum chinense*, closely resembles the congo pepper from nearby Trinidad. Fragrant and powerful, the bonney has a long and celebrated culinary history in Barbados. Richard Ligon, in his *A True and Exact History of the Island of Barbados* (1647), describes the two varieties of peppers he found on the island: "The one so like a child's corall, as not to be discerned at the distance of two paces, a crimson and scarlett mixt; the fruit about three inches long and shines more than the best pollisht corall. The other, of the same colour and glistening as much but shaped like a large button of a cloak; both of one and the same quality; both violently strong and growing on a little shrub not bigger than a gooseberry bush."

Anne-Marie was shopping for a picnic and she needed more than bonney peppers. We stopped by the stall of the one vendor who had seasoning peppers. Anne-Marie bought every one she had and ordered more, explaining that the vendor had carried the seasoning pepper seeds from St. Lucia and grew them in Barbados. The pods were identical to Trinidad seasoning peppers and Anne-Marie planned to use them in a seasoning paste for roasted pork.

At the stand of one grizzled elderly gentleman, I spotted a jar of small, thin peppers.

"Bird peppers?" I asked the vendor.

"Nigger peppers," insisted the vendor, who was a black man.

"Not a very polite term," I observed. The man just shrugged.

"They're bird peppers in Trinidad but nigger peppers here," explained Anne-Marie. "Nobody thinks anything about the word." Indeed. Later, I asked our driver, Emerson, and he just laughed. "Nigger peppers is what they are." I decided to drop the subject.

Inside the market were the meat vendors offering beef, pork, and what I took to be goat but was really black belly sheep, a common island farm animal and apparently a sheep that's adapted to 90 degrees and 90 percent humidity. At Nora's stand, we ate the traditional Saturday souse, which is pickled pork parts with cucumbers, bonney peppers, and other vegetables. I use the term "parts" because the cuts of pork used are generally the less desirable—the feet, facial meat, and other trimmings. Except for being overly fatty, the souse was delicious.

LIMIN' WITH THE LOCALS

There are no hot sauce factories in Barbados that offer an official tour but Anne-Marie was able to arrange visits to two facilities. "Factory" is an extravagant term for what is essentially hands-on manufacturing of the typical Bajan hot sauce that's bright yellow with dangerous red flecks of bonney pepper. At the Lottie's facility, about 14 workers sat around tables performing various necessary functions: cleaning bonney peppers, chopping onions, mixing herbs and spices, and applying labels to bottles of the finished products.

Jackie Heath, the owner of Lottie's, was in the middle of shipping a 55-gallon drum of hot sauce to the US, where it would be bottled as Spitfire Sauce. She revealed to us that she had switched careers in midstream, giving up selling insurance to become the producer of one of the island's best-known brands of hot sauces, seasonings, and fruit juices. Her mustard-based hot sauce is so popular that Jackie has part of each batch packed in 32-ounce bottles! She estimates that there are between six and eight firms manufacturing hot sauces in Barbados right now, and that probably a maximum of 100 acres of bonney peppers are under cultivation in many small plots to supply the hot sauce industry.

One of Jackie's competitors is Pat McClean, who runs L. G. Miller Import and Export, which manufactures and sells hot sauces and other products under the Windmill Products brand. Her father started the business in1965 with a home-made hot sauce recipe and soon they were producing 30 gallons of sauce a week. Nowadays, their capacity is about 2,000 gallons per week, and part of each batch is packed for competing brands. They also run special manufacturing for other Bajan food companies; for example, Pat bottles Anne-Marie's Native Treasures brand.

When we visited, the plant was down except for workers cleaning tamarind, but Pat showed us the modern, stainless-steel equipment and the stacked products produced from the last batches run: three versions of hot pepper sauce, two ketchups, a number of syrups, jams, and jellies, and the ever-present Bajan herb seasonings. Pat loaded us up with samples, and we staggered out to the car.

Ever the organizer, Anne-Marie had scheduled two sessions of "limin'." Now, to lime is essentially to relax and hang out with friends, which is easily done in friendly Barbados. One night, she and her husband, Charlie, took us to the fishing village of Oistins for a seafood feast. Numerous vendors prepared the day's catch, spiced up with the ubiquitous hot sauces. I opted for mahi-mahi at Bellamy's stand and received a succulent cut from near the backbone that tasted great with Anne-Marie's tamarind sauce, not to mention her nutmeg-dusted rum punch. We were joined by Mark and Kim and Noel and Andrea, and soon a spirited discussion resulted, during which we covered all the important subjects: Dole's chance to beat Clinton, Princess Di's affairs, the Chicago Bulls, and Mighty Gabby's calypso song about Lorena Bobbitt.

The limin' continued in full force on Sunday when a caravan of cars converged on Farley Hill and most of the crew from Oistins was joined by Jasmine and Frank, Norman the jokester, and Dennis for a rain-soaked picnic. Farley Hill is a landscaped national park and the ruins of a nineteenth-century plantation great house that was featured in the 1956 Harry Belafonte film, *Island in the Sun*. That would be before it burned down. Some 900 feet above the ocean, the ruins are constantly cooled by the trade winds, which brought squalls that kept us jumping back into the cars. Under the direction of Anne-Marie, we feasted on cabbage and bacon salad, roasted pork with Bajan seasoning, ackee and salt fish, Caribbean rice, coconut bread, black cake, and sweet potato–pineapple pie.

The only question we had was, could restaurant fare top this?

DINING FROM JERKIT TO SANDY LANE

Of course, it was our duty to eat at as many restaurants as possible. One thing we had not counted on was dining with birds. Since most of the restaurants are alfresco, dining with only a roof or umbrella over your head, the birds will readily help themselves to your food. They are nondescript but industrious sparrows and ravenous small grackles, jet black with brilliant yellow eyes. As we found out at breakfast at the Sandy Beach Island Resort, they are particularly fond of croissants.

There were several interesting restaurants near the Sandy Beach, where we enjoyed nice rooms and a great view of a truly sandy beach. At the tiny restaurant Jerkit on the Worthing Main Road, Al Knight and his son Ian told us that they went to Jamaica to study jerk technology and then changed the cooking style to meet Bajan tastes. The Bajans, as it turned out, would not eat crispy grilled pork. "They like their meat with gravy," explained Ian. So now they use typical jerk spices but stew the meat instead of smoke-grilling it as the Jamaicans do. The jerk chicken is grilled, however, because Bajans are accustomed to barbecued chicken done on a grill.

True local cuisine was the main menu at the Bonito Bar, in Bathsheba, on the wild east coast. Swimming is banned here but the site of the Barbados Surfing Championships is opposite the restaurant. Enid Worrell, former home-economics teacher and now owner and cook at the Bonito, was proud to inform us that her first name spelled backward is "dine," which was propitious considering the quality of her food.

I had to experience the Flying Fish, a Bajan specialty that's exquisite when slathered with the mustardy hot sauce. Mary Jane had the Creole Dolphin and our meals were accompanied by Fried Plantains and Breadfruit. Then Enid brought us her pride and joy, corned peppers. She described this use of bonney peppers in her thesis, "Local Nutritional Satisfying Foods": "These peppers were 'corned' with vinegar and salt after extracting the seeds to reduce the strength of their flavors and these pickled peppers were stored for future use, when the fresh ones became scarce."

Continuing our search for local food, we tried with great delight the Planter's Buffet at Brown Sugar in Bridgetown. This classy, open-air restaurant had mahogany accents and delightful prints of the early days of sugar production and colonial Bridgetown on the walls. The buffet included Creole Eggplant, Pepperpot, Fried Flying Fish (again), Creole Okra, Saffron Rice, and Gooseberry Tart. The pepper pot, with its sweet and spicy slow-cooked meat was particularly memorable.

The Waterfront Café alongside the Careenage, in downtown Bridgetown, took the worship of local flying fish to the next logical step with melts: flying-fish roe that's battered and fried. I loved shad roe when I lived in Virginia, but this roe was much milder and tasted more like a delicious fried clam. It was washed down with the local island beer, Banks.

The Waterfront's owner, energetic Susan Walcott, recognized Emerson and quickly pried out of us our purpose for hiring a Taxi Driver of the Year. In the true spirit of Mary Jane's philosophy that "it's a small world and you gotta be good all the time," Susan, hearing we were from New Mexico, said that a famous musician from Santa Fe was having lunch on the patio. A few minutes later, jazz great Herbie Mann and his wife, Janeal Arison, dropped by our table to introduce themselves. Herbie was in Barbados for a concert and was dining at the Waterfront because it was the main jazz bar on the island.

Speaking of musicians, we were fortunate enough to interview Eddy Grant, best known to North Americans for his hit reggae songs "Romancing the Stone," "Electric Avenue," and "Baby Come Back," but who now is becoming famous for his efforts to preserve the history of calypso music. He is planning to open a calypso museum in Barbados.

On our last day on the island, we went from the ridiculous to the sublime. We flew back from a short visit to Trinidad on a Sunday around noon, and not only was it too early to check into the hotel but very few restaurants were open for lunch. Jerkit was closed and we eschewed the fast food of Chefette, so we ended up at Bubba's Sports Bar in Worthing, eating hamburgers and watching Germany beat the Czech Republic in soccer. We felt a bit guilty, but hey, it was all part of the Bajan experience. And the burgers weren't half bad!

What a reversal for dinner! I changed from shorts and T-shirt into a coat and tie, and Emerson drove us to the fanciest resort on the island, the Sandy Lane, where the room rates start at $800 a night. We were the guests of Executive Chef Hans Schweitzer, who had led the Barbados team of chefs to victory in the most recent Caribbean Culinary Classic.

The Sandy Lane was extremely classy and for a moment I worried about my garish chile pepper tie. But Hans professed to love it as he greeted us and kissed Mary Jane on both cheeks. Swiss chefs must do that in Barbados, I thought.

Dining in a covered verandah open to the gentle breeze, we could hear the soft sound of the surf and gaze on the softly lit tropical foliage below us. It was quite romantic, and fortunately, the Sandy Lane management had thoughtfully provided netting to keep out the grackles. Chef Hans himself brought out the sinfully rich foie gras, imported from—where else?—Long Island, New York.

As if that weren't overkill, we shared a large portion of Lobster Ratatouille that was extraordinary. Then it was time to order the main course and there it was! Oven-Roasted Leg of Black Belly Sheep with Yams and Local Vegetables. Mary Jane opted for the Gently Fried Dolphin with Pommes Duchess and Tomato Basil Fondue. The sheep was lean and tasty, much like a cross between lamb and venison. Chef Hans's food was every bit as elegant as the venue. When we return to Barbados, we're thinking about reserving the Sandy Lane Penthouse Suite at $2,200 a day and staying for as long as we can afford: about four hours.

Because of sugarcane and rum, Barbados became the wealthiest European colony in the Caribbean. It's still wealthy. During high tourist season years ago, two Concorde flights a day from London landed at Grantley Adams International Airport. And because none of the other powers in the Caribbean—Spain, France, or Holland—ever captured it, Barbados has remained staunchly British in attitude and custom. The literacy rate is 95 percent, and you don't see the shantytowns, grinding poverty, and crime I've witnessed in Montego Bay and Port of Spain. Even the money is easy: two Barbados dollars for one American. The Bajans speak English clearly, have a great sense of humor, and love sports and hot and spicy food. What more could you want from an island paradise? Oh yeah, the beaches are perfect too.

The beach at the Sandy Beach Resort, where we stayed in Barbados. Photograph courtesy of the Barbados Tourism Authority.

CHAPTER TWO

JAMAICA: SCOTCH BONNETS AND COUNTRY PEPPERS

"In Jamaica, much use is made of fresh peppers," writes Norma Benghiat, author of *Traditional Jamaican Cookery*, "the most highly esteemed hot pepper being the 'Scotch bonnet,' which has a wonderful perfume and flavour." She adds, tantalizingly: "In recent times a Scotch bonnet pepper has been developed which retains the aroma and flavour, but is not hot." According to one source, this pepper, like the one in Trinidad, is also called "seasoning pepper," and is a pepper that is mildly pungent and remains green, never maturing to orange or red.

We tried to track down such a pepper during several trips to Jamaica, and at first we thought we had found it: the "country pepper," as it's called. But the more we asked people to distinguish among the varieties, the more we became caught up in a typically confusing pepper nomenclature controversy.

According to vendor Bernice Campbell in the Ocho Rios Market, country peppers are more elongated than Scotch bonnets and have more flavor. With a typical pepper contrariness, cook Betty Wilson disagreed. While serving Dave and Mary Jane fricasseed chicken and grilled parrot fish at a streamside picnic on

Bernice Campbell in the market at Ocho Rios, Jamaica. Photograph by Dave DeWitt.

Jamaican peppers from the book *Jamaican Food*; illustration by Rev. John Lindsay, 1767. Public domain.

the Rio Grande near Port Antonio, she claimed that Scotch bonnets are not as hot as country peppers but are more "flavored."

Our room attendant at Ciboney Resort, Carol Burrell, insisted that no, Scotch bonnets were hotter than country peppers. Habanero grower Graham Jacks wrote to us: "One of these country peppers is a deep brownish purple when ripe, and is truly ferociously hot; much hotter than the Scotch bonnet."

To add to the confusion, a variety called "Jamaican hot" occasionally appears in pepper literature. Author and chef Mark Miller, in his guide, *The Great Chile Book*, describes it as "smaller than the habanero but similar in shape." It is possible that this variety is the same as the "West Indian Hot" mentioned by Jean Andrews, but pepper importer Joe Litwin told us that the "hots" are generic terms used in the United States but not in Jamaica.

According to Joe, who imports Jamaican peppers through his KAL International Company, there are two kinds of Scotch bonnet: one is green that matures to yellow; it is very common and is called Scotch bonnet. The term "country pepper" is broadly used for red peppers, which have the same shape as the yellow ones. Large red habanero-shaped pods are also called country pepper and are probably congo-pepper imports from Trinidad. I am still very confused about country peppers, seasoning peppers, and Jamaica hots.

Joe Litwin, incidentally, started growing Scotch bonnets in Jamaica in 1991; he had previously cultivated organic sugarcane. He has 25 acres under cultivation in various parts of Jamaica and he also utilizes contract fields. There is no way to estimate total Jamaican production, Joe told me, but his company imports the fresh pods into the United States at the rate of 3,000–4,000 pounds a week. And because of fears of drug loads being smuggled along with the peppers, Joe or one of his employees personally oversees the loading of every shipment of Scotch bonnets onto the plane. He also manufactures a line of products under the Jabeba House brand, including Scotch bonnet hot sauces in red and yellow, and jerk sauce.

Jamaican jerk sauces are a combination of spices and Scotch bonnet chiles used as a marinade and baste for grilled meats. The word "jerk" is thought to have origi-

nated from the word *ch?arki* (the question mark is part of the word), a Quechua term from Peru. The Spanish converted the term to *charqui*, meaning jerked or dried meat, which in English became known as "jerk" and "jerky."

The technique of jerking was originated by the Maroons, Jamaican slaves who escaped from the British during the invasion of 1655 and hid in the maze of jungles and limestone sinkholes known as the Cockpit Country. The Maroons seasoned the pork and cooked it until it was dry and would preserve well in the humidity of the tropics. During the twentieth century, the technique gained enormous popularity in Jamaica, and today "jerk pork shacks" are commonly found all over Jamaica. The method has evolved, however, and the pork is no longer overcooked. In addition to pork, heavily spiced chicken, fish, and beef are grilled to juicy perfection. Today there are dozens of brands of jerk sauces manufactured in Jamaica and the United States.

In addition to their use in hot pepper sauces and jerk sauces, Scotch bonnets are also pickled whole and in crushed form. In cooking, yellow Scotch bonnets are used with escovitch fish, which are fillets cooked with the pepper slices in vinegar, lime juice, and pimento (allspice). The whole pods are often floated in stews or stewed dishes such as oxtail soup, curry goat, fricasseed chicken, and stew peas and rice, and are removed just before serving. Cooks take care not to let the pods burst or the meal may be too hot to eat!

Scotch bonnet peppers on thyme. Photographer unknown. This work has been released worldwide into the public domain by its author, Microdac, at English Wikipedia.

BELIZE AND YUCATÁN

In 1988, Mary Jane and I teamed up with Nancy and Jeff Gerlach and traveled to the Caribbean country of Belize to investigate habanero usage, and we soon became fascinated by the extremely hot sauces produced there utilizing habanero chiles—including Habanero Five Drops, Pica Rico, Hi-Taste, and Melinda's. We hired a small plane with a pilot and flew to the tiny town of Melinda in the foothills of the Maya Mountains in the southern part of Belize and met Marie and Gerry Sharp, who have a hot sauce–bottling operation.

Marie Sharp began bottling Melinda's Hot Sauce in 1983 after she became frustrated with the local produce markets. A lover of habanero chiles, she had grown

A bowl of habaneros. Photograph by Dave DeWitt.

about a hundred plants among citrus groves on the Sharp's 400-acre plantation. After the initial harvest, she carried the chiles to the local market, where buyers insulted her by offering one dollar Belize (fifty cents US currency) for a gallon of pods.

"I will not give away my peppers," Marie vowed, and from that point on she knew that a bottled sauce was the answer to marketing the habaneros. But there was one problem—her friends told her that the other habanero sauces were so hot that a single bottle often lasted six months or more. Since she wanted her customers to buy more than two bottles of sauce a year, Marie experimented with numerous recipes until she found one with more flavor and less heat than the competition.

Next it was necessary to find a dependable source for the habanero chiles, since in Belize they are grown only in limited quantities for the local market or under contract to other sauce producers. The Sharps contacted various growers and began horticultural experimentation with the habaneros, which, like other peppers, are susceptible to phytophthora wilt and viral diseases in the tropics, where the rainfall can be 100 inches per year or more.

In order to standardize the color in their habaneros, which can vary from orange to purple at maturity, only the reddest pods are selected, and those seeds are spaced for plants three feet apart in rows four feet apart. The habanero plants grow about one year before producing pods and reach a height of four feet or more. They are perennial and produce pods constantly for about three years before yields are reduced. Then the plants are removed and the rows replanted with seeds from the reddest pods available. In 1988, the Sharps had about five acres of habaneros under cultivation but expected to double that as export demand for Melinda's sauce increased. It takes about seven pounds of habaneros to produce about five gallons of hot sauce.

Marie sold the US rights to Melinda's Hot Sauce to the Figueroa Brothers, who came out with numerous hot sauces with the same brand name. Then Marie renamed her sauce Marie Sharp's Hot Sauce for sales in the United States.

HABANEROS IN YUCATÁN

The story of the habanero in Yucatán has as much to do with distinctions of class as it does with heat and aroma. The habanero is beloved by the indigenous Mayas, who look down their noses at jalapeños and serranos. But on the other hand, so the story goes, the Mexicans of European descent dislike the habanero and regard it as a lowly Mayan pepper with too much perfume. Amal Naj, who traveled in Yucatán while researching his book *Peppers*, notes: "I quickly sensed that the habanero in a way symbolized for the Maya their fierce independence within Mexico and that the jalapeño symbolized the European Mexican, the invader." In reality, of course, the jalapeño is probably the older pepper variety in Mexico, since it was developed in prehistoric times; many experts believe that the habanero is a fairly recent introduction.

In modern Mayan communities, backyard habanero plots are associated with nearly every household, where they often grow as perennial plants. There is some commercial growing; about 500 farmers grow habaneros on a scant 600 acres in the Mexican part of the Yucatán Peninsula. About 2,500 tons of fresh pods are harvested each year, and 75 percent of that is used in fresh form, mostly combined into a salsa with lime juice and salt as the salsa *xnipec*. Twenty-two percent of the crop is processed into sauces and the remaining 3 percent is used for seed. The pods are graded according to weight, with the first category weighing over 10 grams, the second 7.5 to 10 grams, and the third 5.0 to 7.5 grams.

More than a decade ago, I spoke at a habanero conference in Mérida hosted by Dr. Tomas Gonzalez Estrada, who then was a researcher and habanero breeder at the Scientific Research Center of Yucatán (CICY). He drove us to various habanero fields and processing plants, not to mention some great restaurants specializing in habanero dishes. He told me that the habanero pepper is one of the main agriculture commodities grown in the Yucatán Peninsula. Usually, its pods are sold fresh; however, the current demand for high-quality habanero dried pods, powder, and mash exceeds the supply, and this has resulted in a rush to grow more habaneros in the US, Central and South America, and the Caribbean. Pod quality in terms of color, aroma, flavor, and pungency is very important for this crop. The habanero pepper grown in Yucatán has an international reputation for being a high-quality hot pepper with a bright orange color, high pungency with a special flavor, a typical aroma, and a long shelf life. This is what the growers and processors are trying to preserve in Yucatán today.

And the story of the habanero doesn't end here either. In chapter 10, I reveal the habanero's one brief shining moment when it was known as the hottest chile pepper in the world.

JOHNNY'S FOOD HAVEN PEPPER SAUCE

yield 2 cups   *heat scale* extremely hot

The motto at Johnny's Food Haven is "Trinidad home cooking away from home." Johnny serves his food cafeteria-style—one of only two or three restaurants to do so in Trinidad.

5	congo peppers (habaneros) or as many as can be stuffed into 1 cup
1	cup water
½	teaspoon salt
1	onion, minced
2	cloves garlic, minced
¼	cup shadow bennie (*culantro*), or substitute cilantro, minced

Puree the peppers with the water in a blender. Add the remaining ingredients and let the mixture sit for at least an hour to blend the flavors. Serve with grilled meats, poultry, or fish.

variation Add cooked and pureed pumpkin (Hubbard squash) or carrots to make the sauce milder.

CALLALOO

yield 8 to 10 servings   *heat scale* varies

This remarkable bright green soup is often called "the national dish of T&T." As prepared by chefs Keith Toby and Irvine Jackson of the Café Savannah, it usually features callaloo (taro leaves or dasheen), but spinach is an excellent substitute. Use coconut milk, not the canned, sickly sweet coconut cream used in drinks.

3	bundles callaloo or 3 bunches fresh spinach, washed, tough ribs removed, coarsely chopped
4	cups coconut milk (made by soaking 4 cups grated coconut in 4 cups of hot water for a ½ hour, then straining it)
2	cups milk
2	cloves garlic, minced
2	medium onions, chopped
1	bunch scallions, chopped
¼	pound pumpkin or Hubbard squash, peeled and coarsely chopped
¼	pound butter
	Salt and pepper to taste
	Habanero hot sauce to taste

In a stockpot or soup pot, combine all the ingredients and boil for 4 minutes. Reduce the heat and simmer for 40 minutes. If too thick, add more milk. Remove from the heat, cool, and puree in a blender in small batches. Reheat the soup and serve.

variation Add 2 cups of cooked crab meat to the finished callaloo.

ROYAL CASTLE FRIED CHICKEN

yield 3 to 4 servings   *heat scale* medium

This marinated chicken was available all over Trinidad at the Royal Castle restaurants, and we've duplicated it here for people not able to visit Trinidad. Marie Permenter serves it with a sweet coleslaw and french fries (called "chips," of course). We munched on it while driving all over Trinidad.

1	chicken, cut up into 6 pieces	1	egg, beaten
1	bottle Trinidad habanero sauce (available at gourmet shops and by mail order), or more to taste		Flour for dredging
			Oil for frying (soy or canola)
2	tablespoons water		

Arrange the chicken in a glass baking dish and pour the sauce over it. Sprinkle the water over the top and marinate the chicken overnight in the refrigerator.

Remove the chicken from the marinade and let it drain in a colander. Dip the pieces in the egg and then place them in a large plastic bag filled with the flour. Shake the bag to coat all the pieces, and then fry them in the oil, saving the breasts until last since they will take less time. The legs and thighs will take about 8 minutes per side. Do not crowd the chicken, and fry it in two batches if necessary.

Drain the chicken on paper towels and serve immediately with additional habanero sauce.

RAMESAR CURRIED MANGO

yield 6 to 8 servings as a side dish   *heat scale* mild

This recipe is from our cooking lesson with Nancy Ramesar. She includes the mango seeds as part of the recipe because, as she says, it's great to pick them up and suck the flavor off them. Nancy uses the famous Chief brand Amchar Massala, but a good substitute is to toast 6 tablespoons of coriander seeds, 1 teaspoon of fenugreek seeds, 2 teaspoons of fennel seeds, 1 teaspoon of mustard seeds, and 1 ½ teaspoons of cumin seeds, and grind them all together.

4	green mangos, only about half ripe	2	cloves garlic, mashed
2	tablespoons vegetable oil	2	tablespoons Amchar Massala or commercial curry powder
1	cup water		

Scrub the mangoes thoroughly, leave the skins on, and cut into 2-inch slices, leaving some mango meat on the seeds.

Heat the oil in a large, heavy casserole. Add the mashed garlic cloves, water, and masala, and cook for 2 to 3 minutes on medium heat.

Add the mangoes and stir to coat them with the mixture. Reduce the heat, cover, and simmer until tender, about 30 to 40 minutes.

Check the mixture about halfway through the cooking and add more water if it is dry. Taste the mixture when it's done, and if it's too sour, add 1 teaspoon of sugar.

THE PRIME MINISTER'S HOT SAUCE

yield about 2 cups   *heat scale* hot

Here is the hot recipe of the famous Errol W. Barrow, who was prime minister of Barbados from 1961 to 1976 and again from 1986 until his death in 1987. He was also an accomplished cook and published Privilege: Cooking in the Caribbean (Macmillan Caribbean) in 1988. He notes: "Pepper sauce recipes can be adjusted to suit individual tastes: green papaya, green mango may also be used." We have modified this recipe slightly for the food-processor-enhanced kitchen.

6	large bonney peppers, seeds and stems removed, chopped	1	tablespoon white vinegar
		1	tablespoon vegetable oil
1	large onion, coarsely chopped	½	cup chopped carrots
2	small cloves garlic	1	cup water
1	tablespoon mustard		Salt and pepper to taste

Combine all ingredients in a saucepan and boil for about 15 minutes. Adjust the consistency with water. Puree in a food processor or blender and bottle in sterilized bottles.

BAJAN SEASONING

yield about 2 to 3 cups   *heat scale* hot

This version of the famous island seasoning is from Ann Marie Whittaker, who notes: "This is found in almost every home and is the secret to the success for many mouth-watering Bajan dishes." One of the favorite uses is to place it between the meat and skin of chicken pieces before grilling, baking, or frying. Note: This recipe requires advance preparation.

2	large onions, peeled and coarsely chopped	2	ounces fresh parsley
		2	ounces fresh marjoram
10	green onions, white parts only, coarsely chopped	1 ½	cups vinegar
		2	tablespoons Worcestershire sauce
8	garlic cloves, peeled	1	teaspoon ground cloves
4	bonney peppers, seeds and stems removed, or substitute habaneros	¼	teaspoon black pepper
2	ounces fresh thyme	3	tablespoons salt

In a food processor, combine the onions, green onion, garlic, and bonney peppers, and process to a coarse paste.

Remove the leaves from the stems of the thyme, parsley, and marjoram. Place the leaves and the vinegar in a food processor or blender and liquefy.

Combine the onion paste, vinegar mixture, and the remaining ingredients in a bowl, and mix well. Cover, transfer to the refrigerator, and allow to sit for 1 week before using. The seasoning will keep in the refrigerator for at least 6 months.

ENID WORRELL'S CORNED BONNEY PEPPERS

yield 1 pint   *heat scale* hot

In tiny Bathsheba on the wild Atlantic coast of Barbados, Enid Worrell creates some of the best Bajan cuisine at her establishment, the Bonito Bar and Restaurant. She was kind enough to give us her recipe for corned—or pickled—bonney peppers. The vinegar acquires the heat of the peppers, and then it's sprinkled over fish or curries. The pickled peppers are chopped up and used when fresh ones are not available. Note: This recipe requires advance preparation.

1	pint fresh red bonney peppers, or substitute habaneros, stems removed, left whole
1	tablespoon vegetable oil
1	teaspoon salt
1	tablespoon rum
	White vinegar to cover

Place the peppers in a 1-pint jar. Add the vegetable oil, salt, and rum, then add the vinegar to cover all. Shake vigorously. Allow the peppers to pickle for at least 2 weeks before using. As the vinegar is used, replace it with fresh vinegar.

CREOLE PUMPKIN SOUP

yield 6 servings   *heat scale* medium

Here is a classic Caribbean soup, as served at the Sandy Beach Resort. Be sure to use a mustard-based Bajan sauce such as Windmill or Lottie's. Remember that pumpkin in the Caribbean is winter squash, such as Hubbard.

2	tablespoons vegetable oil	5	cups chicken stock
1	medium onion, diced	5	cups chopped Hubbard squash
3	cloves garlic, minced	½	cup butter
2	medium carrots, diced	1	cup cream
3	tablespoons brown sugar	3	tablespoons fresh lime juice
1	teaspoon ground nutmeg	2	tablespoons Bajan hot sauce

In a large pot, heat the vegetable oil and sauté the onion, garlic, and carrots until the carrots are soft. Stir in the sugar and nutmeg.

Add the chicken stock and squash, and cook until the squash is soft. Transfer the mixture to a food processor or blender and puree until smooth. Return to the pot, add the butter, cream, lime juice, and hot sauce. Heat, stir well, and serve.

FRIED FLYING FISH

yield 4 servings   *heat scale* varies

There are a great number of variations on this favorite Bajan specialty. This is probably the favorite version, as described in John Lake's book, The Culinary Heritage of Barbados. Flying fish is sometimes found frozen in Florida markets; if it's not available, substitute any mild white fish, such as flounder.

8	small flying-fish fillets
	Bajan seasoning as needed (see recipe)
2	eggs, beaten
	Bread crumbs and flour, mixed
½	cup butter
	Lime slices and parsley for garnish
	Bajan hot sauce, such as Windmill or Lottie's

Rub the fillets with the Bajan seasoning, then dip them in the beaten eggs, then in the bread crumbs and flour. Fry the fillets in the butter until lightly browned, turning once.

Serve garnished with the lime slices and parsley. Sprinkle hot sauce over the fillets to taste.

JAMAICAN JERK PORK

yield 6 or more servings   *heat scale* medium-hot

The "jerk" in jerk pork is a spice mixture that was used to preserve meat before refrigeration. It was developed by the Arawak Indians and later refined in Jamaica by runaway slaves known as Maroons. These days, the spices are used to season meats for barbecue and to tenderize rather than to preserve. An inexpensive smoker or a covered grill can be substituted for the traditional jerk pit and is a lot easier than digging a pit in your yard. Note: This recipe requires advance preparation.

PASTE

3 to 4 Scotch bonnet chiles, stems and seeds removed, chopped

¼ cup chopped green onions, including some of the greens

3 tablespoons crushed allspice (pimiento) berries, or substitute 2 teaspoons ground berries

3 tablespoons fresh thyme

3 cloves garlic

2 tablespoons grated ginger

2 tablespoons lime juice, fresh preferred

2 tablespoons red wine vinegar

2 bay leaves

3 teaspoons freshly ground black pepper

2 teaspoons ground cardamom

1 teaspoon ground cinnamon

1 teaspoon ground nutmeg

1 teaspoon salt

3 to 4 tablespoons vegetable oil

1 3- to 4-pound pork butt or loin roast

To make the jerk paste, either pound the ingredients together using a mortar and pestle or place them in a blender or food processor, adding the oil to make a paste.

Place the roast, fat side down, in a nonreactive pan. Make slashes in the pork about 1 ½ to 2 inches apart and almost through the roast. Rub the jerk over the meat, making sure to get it thoroughly into the slashes. Cover with plastic wrap and marinate in the refrigerator overnight.

Remove the pork and bring it to room temperature.

Prepare either the grill or smoker. If using a grill, be sure to use a pan under the pork to catch the drippings. Smoke the pork for about 2 to 3 hours, turning the roast every 30 minutes to ensure even browning. Cook until a meat thermometer inserted into the thickest part registers 150 degrees F.

Variations: Substitute lamb chops, chicken, or rib steaks for the pork.

Latin America is an enigma when it comes to chile peppers. Since the fiery fruits originated and proliferated there for thousands of years before the Spanish arrived, it would stand to reason that chiles would have permeated all of the cuisines of this vast area. Yet in South America, Peru is hot while Venezuela is not.

Thus there are definite pockets of heat scattered about Latin America, especially in those countries where the indigenous population had a greater influence on the cuisine than the European settlers. Generally speaking, these pockets are the regions where the great civilizations of the Incas, Mayas, and Aztecs arose: Peru and adjoining Andean countries, Yucatán, Central America, and Mexico.

It is in these four areas that the peoples' fanatic fondness for chile peppers created what I call a "fiery cuisine." This is not to say that chiles do not appear in other regions; they do, but only sporadically at best. Countries such as Argentina and Chile have some wonderful chile-spiced dishes, but true fiery cuisines have not evolved.

The arrival of Europeans greatly assisted the development of the chile-dominated cuisines of the New World. It is difficult to imagine the cuisines of the Americas today without the foods introduced by the Spanish, Portuguese, and Africans: grains such as rice, oats, and wheat; fruits such as apples, peaches, mangoes, limes, oranges, olives, bananas, and new varieties of grapes; meats such as chicken, beef, pork, and lamb; vegetables such as onions, garlic, carrots, okra, and lettuce; and spices such as cumin, black pepper, cinnamon, mustard, and horseradish.

These new foods were adopted by the indigenous civilizations in varying degrees depending upon region, climate, and local preference. In many cases—especially with the grains, meats, vegetables, and spices—they were combined with chile peppers for the first time in history.

THE LEGACY OF THE INCAS

It is ironic that the chile cuisines of the countries of South America, where the chile pepper originated, are not as complex as those of Mexico, or even Thailand, for that matter. The people of the Andean region of Peru, Ecuador, and Bolivia still eat basically Incan food that has been only slightly modified by the meats and

A colorfully painted chicken bus roars down a street in Antigua,
under the towering majesty of the Agua Volcano, Antigua, Guatemala.
Photograph by Paul Ross. Used with permission.

vegetables introduced by the Spanish. But despite the basic nature of the cuisine of this region, chiles are used extensively, and they are among the hottest in the world.

There are several chiles of choice in the Andes, where they are generically called "ají" or "uchu." The first and foremost chile is the specific ají, *Capsicum baccatum*, which is often called "ají amarillo" because of its yellow fruits. One variety of ají, *puca-uchu*, grows on a vine-like plant in home gardens because ajís are rarely commercially cultivated in South America.

Another favorite chile in the Andes is *rocotillo*, a variety of *Capsicum chinense* and a close relative of the habanero—though it is considerably milder. It is used in a similar manner to bells and is sometime called a squash pepper. Such terminology is confusing because there is a variety of *Capsicum annuum* called tomato or squash that is cultivated in the United States. The rocotillo is served fresh as a condiment or garnish, cooked with beans and stews, or spread over grilled meat.

Another species, *Capsicum pubescens*, is beloved in the region and is called "rocoto." The cherrylike pods of the rocoto are as dangerously hot as the ajís. In fact, they are so pungent that there is a Peruvian expression about them, *llevanta muertos*, meaning they are hot enough to raise the dead.

In addition to their culinary uses, the various South American chiles are employed in other ways. Mothers who are descendants of the Incas in Peru coat their nipples with chile juice or powder to discourage their babies from suckling during the weaning process. Perhaps the oddest usage of the ajís is in southern Colombia, where Indians mix powdered chile with cocaine before snorting it. Supposedly, the chile increases the mucus secretions and somehow heightens the stimulating properties of the drug. Both practices sound remarkably painful, especially considering the pungency of most South American chiles, and neither is recommended. However, they do give an indication of just how pervasive chiles are in Andean culture.

Such pervasiveness is also illustrated by the reputation of certain cities for having particularly fiery cuisines. Arequipa, in southern Peru, is probably the hottest food city in South America and is in the competition for the title of hottest city in the world. There, the dishes are so hot that restaurants in Lima list menu items as *arequipeño*, meaning they are from Arequipa and diners should use caution when eating them.

Some examples of fiery dishes from Arequipa include *ocopa*, potatoes covered with a hot cheese and peanut sauce plus a yellow ají chile paste; rocoto chiles stuffed with cheese or sausage; and *papas a la huancaína*, another dish with an ají-spiced cheese sauce. The use of peanuts in hot-chile dishes in Arequipa is interesting because it anticipates some African dishes with similar ingredients. The peanut, like the chile pepper, is a native of South America (a similar nut, the Bambarra groundnut, is a native of Africa) and has been found in Peruvian mummy graves in Ancón. The combination of the two is a classic example of the addition of chile to spice up an essentially bland food.

In the Andes, ajís or ají salsas are used to add heat to other bland foods such as potatoes and maniocs. There are several kinds of ají salsas, but the most important of them is *ají molida*, which is prepared by mixing the fresh chiles with ground herbs, onions, and water. On the coast, Peruvian fishermen mix the ajís with olives, olive oil, and chopped onions, or add them to raw fish to create ceviche, a dish that now appears, with variations, all over the world.

Other Andean dishes also demonstrate the influences of both the Spanish and Incan cultures. Chickens spiced with ajís reflect the combination of native chiles with European-introduced chickens. It is probable that a pre-Columbian version of this dish combined the chiles with birds such as the macuca, a large jungle fowl. Another meat commonly raised and eaten in the Andes with chiles is the cui, or guinea pig.

In Chile, various sauces are used to spice up bean, potato, and chicken dishes. One simple sauce is *color*, which is made by sautéing garlic, paprika, and dried red chiles in cooking oil. Its name alludes to its bright red-orange—well—color. Another sauce is *pebre*, which combines a red chile paste with olive oil, vinegar, cilantro, onions, and garlic.

In other parts of South America, where European influences had a greater impact upon the cuisines, chile peppers are combined with a wider variety of Old World foods.

BRAZIL AND BEYOND

The chiltepín (*C. annuum* var. *glabriusculum*) is generally thought to be the "wild progenitor" of the rest of the *annuum* species. Put another way, the undomesticated and primitive chiltepíns are the original genetic material from which the cultivated varieties we know today evolved through human selection. Since the *annuum* species has a wild progenitor, it makes sense that the *chinense* species would have one too. The trouble is, no one's certain of this. "So far the wild progenitor has not been discovered," states J. W. Purseglove in his book *Spices*, volume 2.

But maybe it has been discovered. Just as there are people who collect stamps or trading cards, there are professionals and hobbyists who collect seeds. Chile seeds, to be more specific, and *chinense* seeds, to narrow the focus even further. Jim

Brazilian bird pepper in the author's garden. Photograph by Dave DeWitt.

Ault is such a person. At Longwood Gardens in Kennett Square, Pennsylvania, he maintains a collection of about a hundred *Capsicum* accessions (varieties) of which forty are *chinense*. His offer to swap seeds with me in 1993 was gratefully accepted, and I sent off seeds that I had collected in Trinidad and Costa Rica. Jim was generous in return, sending me six *chinense* varieties from Africa, Bolivia, Peru, Cuba, and Brazil.

I already had two Brazilian *chinense* varieties in my collection, so I felt that the plants from Jim's seeds would make an interesting comparison. As usual, the specimen of Jim's unnamed Brazilian *chinense* that was planted in the garden did poorly, but its counterpart flourished in a large pot, growing two feet tall and two and a half feet wide. The leaves, though only an inch long, had the characteristic "crinkled" aspect found in the *chinense* species and the fruits ranged from one to three per node. And what fruits they were!

Instead of the familiar lantern shape of many *chinense* peppers, these were spherical, erect pods about one-quarter inch wide. It was the smallest-podded *chinense* I'd ever encountered. The pods' resemblance to the Sonoran chiltepíns' was startling; held up side by side, they were nearly identical—with one exception. Instead of being red, the mature Brazilian pods were bright yellow. I performed the smell test by cutting a pod in half and there it was, the unmistakable apricot-like aroma of the *chinense*. It was so pungent that when I held it close to the nose, I was convulsed by fits of sneezing. I noticed that the pods were not easily deciduous; in other words, they did not separate easily from the calyx—just like the chiltepín pods. The tiny yellow pods are called *pimenta do cheiro*. It's a variety with a number of variant spellings, including *pimento de cheiro*. It is also called the Brazilian bird pepper.

"The Amazon basin supports the world's largest number of habanero [*chinense*] varieties," notes Jessica Harris, the author of *Tasting Brazil*. "These chiles appear in a variety of ways in Brazilian cooking, particularly that of the northeastern region. They are chopped and put into homemade sauces and pickled and show up on the table as condiments."

When Columbus first explored the Caribbean islands in 1492, there's a good chance that the first chile pepper he encountered was a Scotch bonnet or its cousin. After all, long before Columbus arrived, the *chinense* had spread throughout the islands, presumably by ancestors of the Arawaks and Caribs. So it would not be surprising to learn that Columbus misnamed the pod "pimiento" (pepper) right after biting into a *chinense*.

According to Jean Andrews, "After 1493, peppers from the West Indies were available to the Portuguese for transport to their western African colonies." Brazilian peppers were available by 1508, when Portugal colonized Brazil. After sugarcane was introduced into Brazil in 1532, there was a great need for slave labor. Considerable trade sprang up between Portuguese colonies in Angola and Mozambique and across the Atlantic in Pernambuco, Brazil. It is believed that this trade introduced New World peppers into Africa, especially the *chinense* and *frutescens* species.

COLLIDING CULTURES AND CUISINES

After the Andean region, chiles are most prevalent in Brazilian cookery and occur in many dishes. The popularity of chiles in Brazil is the result of three factors: the prevalence of chiles in the Amazon Basin, their combination with foods introduced by the Portuguese, and the fact that the first African slaves readily adopted the native chiles.

Most probably, the habaneros found today in the Caribbean Islands and Central America migrated from the Amazon region. However, they are not the only chiles in the region. Varieties of both *C. annuum* and *C. frutescens*, the Tabasco type, also appear in Brazil, and pickled Tabascos are often called for in Brazilian dishes. One type of *frutescens* in Brazil is known as the malagueta pepper, and it is quite similar to Tabasco chiles (see the introduction for a photograph).

Brazilian cuisine was influenced more by African sources than its own native Indian tribes. In colonial times, the Portuguese were totally dependent upon African cooks, who began as slaves and utilized both Brazilian and West African foods. A good example of such cooking is *vatapá de camarão e peixe*, a Bahian dish that combines shrimp, chiles, coconut, peanuts, ginger, and tomatoes. In the coastal city of Salvador de Bahia, the dish is very spicy, with either dried or fresh chiles added. In more tourist-influenced areas such as Rio de Janeiro, vatapá is generally much blander.

Salsa carioca is a Brazilian variation on Mexican guacamole, featuring the ever-popular and native avocado, a Tabasco-type sauce, tomatoes, eggs, and hot chiles. Also popular in Brazil are the *moquecas*, or native stews. Other Brazilian dishes are often seasoned Caribbean-style with hot sauces. One such sauce is *molho de pimenta e limão*, which combines habanero chiles with limes.

In southern Brazil and northern Argentina, spicy barbecues called "churrascos" are enormously popular, especially where large cattle ranches are located. Beef cuts and sausages are marinated in various chile barbecue sauces and are then skewered

on large "swords" and grilled. Some cuts of meat are drenched in sauces, wrapped in papaya leaves, and buried in hot coals. The papaya leaves contain papain, which tenderizes the meat.

MOVING NORTH

Central America also has its pockets of heat. As is true of South America and the Caribbean, some countries have embraced chile peppers with more fervor than others. Panama and Costa Rica, for example, have some spicy dishes, but the overall cuisine is not as spicy as that of Belize or Guatemala. Perhaps because of its Mayan heritage, Guatemala has a fiery cuisine second only to Mexico in terms of chile usage.

The most popular chile in Guatemala is the chile de Cobán, a variety of piquin with round to slightly elongated pods that are smoke-dried over wood and have a powerful smoky taste. *Jocón* is a perfect example of a Mayan recipe that has resisted European influences; the only non–New World ingredients are the garlic, onions, and chicken. The Mayas, of course, would have substituted duck or turkey for the chicken. Another Central American dish from the Yucatán Peninsula features chiles combined with black beans in black-bean soup.

The Old World influence was greater in Mexico than Central America, and the arrival of the Spanish in Mexico had a profound effect on the cuisine of the country. The Old World foodstuffs the explorers brought with them soon transformed the eating habits of the Indians. However, the Aztecs and their descendants did not give up their beloved staples such as chiles, beans, squash, corn, and chocolate; they combined them with the new imports and thus created the basis for the Mexican cuisines of today.

Throughout the centuries, an astonishing variety in Mexican cooking developed as a result of geography. From the Yucatán Peninsula, Mexico stretches over 2,000 miles to the deserts of the North, so the length and size of Mexico, combined with the fact that mountain ranges separate the various regions, led to the development of isolated regional cuisines. This geographical variety is the reason that the cooking of tropical Yucatán differs significantly from that of the deserts of Chihuahua and Sonora.

One common factor, though, in Mexican cookery is the prevalence of chile peppers. Unlike South America, where chiles are still consumed mostly by the Indian population, in Mexico everyone fell in love with the pungent pods. Chile peppers

are Mexico's most important vegetable crop; they are grown all over the country from the Pacific and Gulf coasts to mountainous regions with an altitude above 8,000 feet. Approximately 200,000 acres of cultivated land produce 500,000 tons of fresh pods and 30,000 tons of dry pods. Although over 10 different varieties are grown or collected in Mexico, anchos/poblanos, serranos, 'Mirasol' peppers, and jalapeños account for 75 percent of the crop. In 1988 Mexico exported 2,529 metric tons of fresh or dried chiles worth $4.6 million into the United States. By 2008, that number had increased to 177,565 metric tons, thanks to the North American Free Trade Agreement. In the northern state of Chihuahua, New Mexican cultivars such as 'NuMex Heritage 6-4' are grown in great quantities and are imported into New Mexico because New Mexican farmers cannot grow enough pods to satisfy the demands of consumers.

In 1985, each Mexican consumed about 14 pounds of green chile and nearly 2 pounds of dried chile. In fact, the Mexicans eat more chile per capita than onions

Cobán chiles in the author's garden. Photograph by Dave DeWitt.

or tomatoes. The favorite chiles are about evenly divided between those harvested fresh and those utilized in the dry form.

The serranos and jalapeños are grown for processing and the fresh market, where they are the chiles of choice for salsas. Over 90 percent of the serrano crop is used fresh in homemade salsas such as *pico de gallo*, which is known by quite a few other names. Serranos are also used in a popular cooked sauce, tomatillo sauce.

About 60 percent of the jalapeño crop is processed, either by canning or pickling, or by making commercial salsas. Of the remainder, 20 percent is used fresh and 20 percent is used in the production of chipotles, the smoked and dried form of the jalapeño.

The use of another favorite Mexican chile, the ancho/poblano, is equally divided between fresh (poblano) and dried (ancho). Some Mexican chiles, such as pasilla, 'Mirasol,' and de árbol are used almost exclusively in the dried form as the basis for a number of cooked sauces. These sauces, which are nearly identical to those in the American Southwest, are discussed in chapter 4—except for the moles.

The word *mole* means "mixture" in Spanish, as in guacamole, a mixture of vegetables (*guaca*). The word used by itself embraces a vast number of sauces utilizing every imaginable combination of meats, vegetables, spices, and flavorings—sometimes up to three dozen different ingredients.

In Mexico today, cooks who specialize in moles are termed *moleros*, and they even have their own competition, the National Mole Fair held every year in October at the town of San Pedro Atocpan, just south of Mexico City. At the fair, thousands of people sample hundreds of different moles created by restaurateurs and mole wholesalers. This fair is the Mexican equivalent of chili con carne cookoffs in the United States; the moleros take great pride in their fiery creations and consider each mole a work of art in the same way that chili-cookoff chefs regard their chili con carne. Their recipes are family secrets not to be revealed to others under any circumstances. Often the preparation of a family mole recipe takes as long as three days.

The color of a particular mole depends mostly upon the varieties of chiles utilized.

Serrano chiles in the Mercado de la Merced, Mexico City. Photograph by Dave DeWitt.

A green mole consists mostly of poblano chiles while a red mole could contain three or four different varieties of dried red chiles, such as chiles de árbol or cascabels. The brown and black moles owe their color to pasillas and anchos, both of which are often called *chile negro* because of their dark hues when dried.

Other than chiles, there are literally dozens of other ingredients added to the various moles, including almonds, anise, bananas, chocolate, cinnamon, cilantro, cloves, coconut, garlic, onions, peanuts, peppercorns, piñons, pumpkin seeds, raisins, sesame seeds, toasted bread, tomatillos, tomatoes, tortillas, and walnuts. Undoubtedly, some moleros add coriander, cumin, epazote, oregano, thyme, and other spices to their moles.

On the basis of the devotion of its people to the fiery chiles used in their moles, it is evident that San Pedro Atocpan is also in the running to be named the hottest city in the world. No wonder—it is located in the state of Puebla, renowned for the most famous mole of all, mole poblano.

This is the sauce traditionally served on special occasions such as Christmas, and it combines chiles and chocolate, a popular and revered food of the Aztecs.

One of the mole vendors at the Feria de Mole in San Pedro Atocpan, D.F. Photograph by Alejandro Linares Garcia. Wikimedia. GNU Free Documentation License, Version 1.2.

Moctezuma's court consumed 50 jugs of chile-laced hot chocolate a day, and warriors drank it to soothe their nerves before going into battle. However, the story of how chocolate was combined with chile sauces does not involve warriors but rather nuns.

Legend holds that mole poblano was invented in the sixteenth century by the nuns of the convent of Santa Rosa in the city of Puebla. It seems that the archbishop was coming to visit, and the nuns were worried because they had no food elegant enough to serve someone of his eminence. So they prayed for guidance and one of the nuns had a vision. She directed that everyone in the convent should begin chopping and grinding everything edible from the kitchen. Into a pot went chiles, tomatoes, nuts, sugar, tortillas, bananas, raisins, garlic, avocados, and dozens of herbs and spices. The final ingredient was the magic one: chocolate. Then the nuns slaughtered their only turkey, cooked it, and served it with the mole sauce to the archbishop, who declared it the finest dish he had ever tasted.

It is a nice story, but more likely, mole was invented by the Aztecs long before the Spaniards arrived. Since chocolate was reserved for Aztec royalty, the military nobility, and religious officials, perhaps Aztec serving girls at the convent gave a royal recipe to the nuns so they could honor their royalty, the archbishop. At any rate, the recipe for mole poblano was rescued from oblivion and became a holiday favorite. Another popular holiday chile dish unites chiles and walnuts and is called *chiles en nogada*.

Visitors to Mexico are often surprised to discover that chiles and seafood often appear in the same dish. Chile aficionados realize, however, that dishes such as shrimp in adobo sauce merely reflect a culinary tradition thousands of years old. Chiles both spice up usually bland fish and also assist in the preservation process. Huachinango a la Vera Cruz is a perfect example of the elegance of some of these chile-seafood dishes. It is considered to be the signature dish of the state of Veracruz. Traditionally, a whole red snapper is cleaned, the scales are removed, and then it is marinated in lime juice, salt, pepper, nutmeg, and garlic. A sauce is created using onions, garlic, tomato, jalapeños, olives, and herbs, and the fish is baked in the sauce until tender.

Although chiles are grown and consumed all over Mexico, they are particularly evident in the cooking of northern Mexico, which is termed "norteño-style" Mexican food, or the food of La Frontera, the frontier. In fact, in Mexico City the fiery cooking of the states of Chihuahua and Sonora is termed *platillos popular* on both sides of the border. The lore of Mexican cuisine holds that Norteño-style cooking is the hottest of them all, and that level of heat is a tradition that migrated to the American Southwest.

IN SEARCH OF HOT STUFF IN COSTA RICA

In September 1992, the DeWitts and Gerlachs joined forces once again to invade a Central American country—ostensibly for a vacation, and this time Costa Rica was the target. It was the first trip together for the DeWitts and Gerlachs since we took on Belize, and we planned, as usual, to eat our way across the country.

But our friends all cautioned us that the food in Costa Rica was bland! We ignored the warning, believing that travelers can find hot and spicy food in virtually any country in the world. It was only a matter of time, we figured, before we uncovered some really fiery dishes. That matter of time turned out to be longer than we ever imagined.

Escazú and Arlene Too

San José, the capital, was our first stop, and from the comfortable Aparthotel Maria Alexandra in the suburb of Escazú, we set out to taste the local cuisine. It didn't take long to figure out that although the local Tico food was tasty, it was also rather, well, bland—like the hearts-of-palm salad, for example, or the *gallo pinto*, the local name for rice and beans. The homemade corn and flour tortillas were excellent too, but whatever filled them had no bite. We decided to ask an expert about the local food.

We were fortunate to meet one of Costa Rica's premier chefs, Arlene Lutz, who is also a restaurateur and the star of *La hora de Arlene*, a televised cooking show that is shown in both Costa Rica and Guatemala. All this from a woman who didn't know how to cook when she got married! Because of a strong desire to be "the best cook she could be," Arlene went first to New York to study at the Waldorf Astoria. Over the years she continued to hone her cooking skills at the Cordon Bleu School in Paris and Bon Appetit in Los Angeles. So when the opportunity arose for a locally produced TV show, she had all the culinary skills necessary. Arlene is extremely proud of her heritage and promotes Costa Rican cooking whenever possible, but her *La hora de Arlene* showcases all types of cuisines. And, in the show's 21 years, she has never repeated a recipe!

We met up with Arlene at her restaurant, named Arlene's, of course. The menu, offering dishes from around the world, reflects her varied culinary interests, and every Sunday the restaurant has a "theme buffet" featuring foods from a different country. After we enjoyed a wonderful meal and a delightful after-dinner discussion with Arlene, she invited us to return for a typical Costa Rican meal that she would prepare just for us!

That special evening began on a good note: We quickly hailed a cab in the pour-

A waterfall in
Costa Rica.
Photograph by
Mary Jane Wilan.

ing rain and made it to the restaurant before we got soaking wet. A separate table had been set for us using gaily decorated tin dishes that are commonly used in the countryside, and next to us was a buffet table with lovely floral arrangements of bird of paradise and flowering ginger. After each dish was served during the meal, the remainder was placed on the buffet table, so by the end of the meal a beautiful display of Costa Rican food had been assembled.

The banquet began with a hearts-of-palm salad and was followed by a sweet-potato soup flavored with a hint of orange. Next was a plate of the unusual pejibaye or *pipas*, which are fruits of the same palm tree that yields hearts of palm. These very popular starchy fruits are boiled with herbs and served garnished with mayonnaise, and are definitely an acquired taste.

The entrée of tongue in white wine and prunes was from a recipe handed down to Arlene by her grandmother. It was surprisingly tender and flavorful, and even those of us who didn't think we would like tongue came back for seconds. We were then served Spanish rice, the only familiar recipe on the menu, and chayote and corn. Dessert was a wide array of local fruits including melons, oranges, the unusual red and fuzzy mangosteens, and armored cherimoyas with their custard-like taste—a refreshing end to a wonderful meal that lacked only chiles.

Our conclusion after a few days in San José: Our friends had been right. If ever there was a cuisine that needed chile peppers, it was Costa Rica's. We just had to dig deeper. It was time to split up and search the coasts. Mary Jane and I headed to the Pacific Coast while Nancy and Jeff were Caribbean-bound.

Questions in Quepos

Mary Jane and I were stuck in the tiny town of Parrita while I asked the gas-station attendant my first question in flawless, first grade–level Spanish: "Donde está Quepos?"

The attendant pointed to the rickety, single-lane bridge that angled across a dark, raging river, and to the dirt trail beyond that passed for a road.

"Á Quepos," he said. To Quepos.

"¿Verdad?" asked a skeptical me. The truth?

"Sí," assured the attendant, pointing again. "Quepos."

"Gracias. Let's beat that bus to the bridge!" I yelled, peeling gravel.

"Arrrrgh!" screamed Mary Jane. "We're going to die!"

Not to worry—I was just kidding about the bus. The bridge held up, and the road was not really all that bad—mostly rutted and full of gravel—but Mary Jane was still afraid I'd drive off the edge and into a crocodile-infested river.

Fifteen bone-thumping miles later, we arrived at Quepos—and the roads were worse! Huge potholes resembling Serbian mortar craters caused drivers to weave about as if under the influence of an exotic tropical drug, and the maximum speed through the former banana port was about five miles an hour. We found the sign indicating Manuel Antonio National Park and took a much better road to the top of a mountain, where the string of small hotels began. Some were perched atop the mountain, overlooking the spectacular view of three beaches and numerous dramatic islands, and others were beachfront establishments. We choose La Arboleda, on the beach, partially because of the reasonable price and partially because it had its own miniature zoo, complete with deer, agoutis, and parrots. After checking in, we began our exploration.

Quepos is just being discovered as a tourist destination, so it is relatively unspoiled. There are only about 250 beds in about two dozen hotels and guesthouses, and most of the tourists fly into the small airport from San José. The lovely beaches and the national park are the main attractions, but a golf course and 17 hotel projects were under construction then, so I knew it wouldn't be long until Quepos resembled a miniature Acapulco. Locals worry that such development, along with 150,000 visitors annually, will harm the national park and its profusion of birds, monkeys, iguanas, and other wildlife.

One resort that blended perfectly into the environment was La Mariposa, which overlooks the national park and its three beaches. It was built in 1997 by David Tucker and Garth Kistler, two renegade businessmen from Atlanta who gave up the executive life and took an enormous risk when they bought five acres in the middle of the jungle.

We sat with David Tucker on the terrace while the Mariposa cat bonked our legs, and David described the tedious process of construction, which required the Spanish colonial resort to be earthquake proof. It took them nearly 20 years to build the resort to its current dramatic, airy, and beautiful ambience.

We were his guests for dinner, and the food—which he called "standard continental fare"—was excellent. We had baked snapper with a cream and wine sauce, chicken dominical (marinated in lemon juice and rum), and beef roulades. It certainly wasn't Tico food, but it had one thing in common with it: no heat. David provides the local *chilero* hot sauce, but that's it for pungency in Quepos. He did give us his chef's recipe for gallo pinto, and that does have something of a bite.

David mentioned that one of his employees, Leo Godinez, was a naturalist who gave "backwoods" tours of Manuel Antonio National Park, so the next morning at six we met Leo and drove down to the park. Within minutes, Leo had leaped into a stream and caught a three-foot male iguana with his bare hands. I wanted to take it home with us, but Mary Jane said it would never clear customs. The park tour was fascinating, and we saw many varieties of birds (Costa Rica has one-tenth of the world's species, more than 850) and butterflies (more species than in all of Africa). Also making an appearance were sloths (very slow) and Jesus Christ lizards (very fast) that literally run across the surface of the water.

Then the rains came, an intense downpour that made me worry about the condition of the road to Parrita. But we put such negative thoughts out of our mind while dining—safe from the rain under the thatched roof of Karola's Restaurant, and listening to CDs of the guitar music of Ottmar Liebert and Carlos Santana—eating swordfish, shrimp, and yellowfin tuna that were fresh and delicious but, you guessed it, bland.

It was still raining the next morning when we threaded our way through the Quepos potholes and found ourselves on the dreaded road to Parrita, which was slick with mud. It was crocodile weather for sure. Only my great driving ability and superb sense of timing got us safely back to San José.

"Make that blind, dumb luck," corrected Mary Jane. It was only after we returned to the States that we read in *Conde Nast Traveler*, "Only the brave actually drive from San José to Quepos."

Rica Red to the Rescue

Back in Escazú, we hooked up with Stuart Jeffrey and Cody Jordan of Quetzal Foods International Corporation, who promised to prove that at least some parts of Costa Rica were hot and spicy. They should know since they have the largest habanero plantation in Central America.

With Stuart and Cody as our guides, and with Stuart's friend Brenda, we journeyed to Turrialba to meet with the researchers at CATIE (Centro Agronómico Tropical de Investigación y Enseñanza), who had assisted in the habanero project. At CATIE, we met with chile expert Jorge Morera, who told us about their collection of *Capsicum* seeds, which are kept below zero in a huge cryogenic storage facility (read: freezer).

"We have somewhere between 1,500 and 2,000 different accessions," he told us, "of which 660 have been characterized." Translated, that means 660 varieties have been grown out, identified as to species and pod type, and their characteristics recorded. Morera also said that unlike in the past, when coffee and bananas received all the attention, CATIE was now emphasizing cacao, tropical fruits, squash, and chile peppers in its programs to assist farmers. He told us that the main pepper

crops in Costa Rica were jalapeños, cayennes, Tabascos, and bells—until Quetzal Foods began their Rica red operation.

Later, with Melena as our driver, and Ricardo Quieros from the University of Costa Rica as our guide, we drove north toward the habanero fields. It was a long drive over mountain roads with hairpin curves and spectacular vistas, and we made several interesting stops along the way.

First we visited two palmito (hearts of palm) processing factories, where palm stems are peeled, cut, and processed into tender cylinders about an inch wide and five inches long. According to Nancy, Costa Rican hearts of palm are much tastier than their Brazilian counterparts, and Ricardo told us that Costa Rica was starting to challenge Brazil in production and export. Next we stopped at a black-pepper farm, walked through the fields of rather bizarre-looking vines

Black pepper vines growing on poles. Photograph by Dave DeWitt.

growing on posts, and tasted some peppercorns, which were quite pungent.

After an evening of relaxation at the Tilajari Hotel Resort, within sight of the highly active Arenal Volcano, we continued our journey north, and Stuart and Cody explained how they started growing habaneros in Costa Rica. Their story was a classic tale of determination and problem solving. It all began in 1984, when Stuart, who had been an agronomist working with kiwi fruit, began growing habaneros in New Orleans from seeds he brought back from his native Belize. His fascination with the fiery and tasty habaneros led to dreams of producing habanero products, but he needed adequate production. He investigated buying a couple of sauce plants in Belize, but they were just too small to be feasible.

By this time he had contacted his longtime friend Cody and had sent him a sauce he had concocted from his backyard habaneros, as well as from dried pods and powder. Cody took these fledgling products around Dallas to restaurants and spice companies. Although no one had ever heard of habaneros, the response was overwhelming. One restaurant wanted a hundred cases of hot sauce immediately. One spice company placed an order for two million pounds of habanero powder! It was obvious they could not fill those orders from Stuart's backyard garden, but it was also apparent that they had to locate massive amounts of habaneros. But where?

Stuart and Cody began searching the Caribbean and Central America for the ideal spot to find (or grow) massive quantities of habaneros. Some were grown in the Yucatán Peninsula of Mexico, but that crop was consumed locally and was not exported. They explored Guatemala, Honduras, the Dominican Republic, Dominica, and Jamaica, and found the same situation everywhere—small plots with limited commercial habanero production. In 1985, somewhat discouraged but not giving up, they posted bulletins with the Foreign Agricultural Service of us Embassies in Central America: "Pepper growers wanted!"

Finally, a response came from Ricardo Quieros of the University of Costa Rica. He could help them, he wrote, and his family had grown peppers for many years. That was the break Stuart and Cody needed. They rushed to Costa Rica and inspected Ricardo's 10 acres of a Panama-cayenne cross. Ricardo told them it was not a true habanero but that one could be developed.

The next few years were devoted to developing the Rica red variety of habanero and determining where to grow it. Ricardo collected seeds from 22 varieties of Panama peppers being grown on two small plots in Limón and planted them on sites all around the country—isolated, of course, from other varieties of peppers. From those planting, Ricardo selected 6 strains that had desirable qualities: large, round pods, bright red color, high heat, and disease resistance. These strains were again planted around the country, and the seeds from the best pods were collected. Finally, after four years, Ricardo had the Rica red variety breeding true more than 90 percent of the time and had determined the ideal spot to grow it. The location was the northernmost town in Costa Rica and it is called, appropriately enough, Los Chiles.

We were greeted there by rain again, a portion of the 120 inches the region receives annually, and the "road" to the chile fields was so muddy we all had to cram into a four-wheel-drive truck to get there. But once we arrived, we were astounded. Spread out before us were more than 200 acres of Rica red habaneros growing between rows of young orange trees. The plants ranged in size from a few inches tall (recently planted) to monsters nearly seven feet high! The latter plants were two years old, had been pruned back after the first year, and were still producing

A Rica red habanero in the rain in Los Chiles. Photograph by Dave DeWitt.

well—some had over a hundred pods on them. They were grown on gentle slopes for good drainage, and the crop was amazingly healthy. Perhaps 1 in 30 or 40 plants was bare of leaves and fruit, but there had had been no time to identify the problem because the others were producing bumper yields of fruit.

Stuart and Cody estimate that they and their Costa Rican partners have invested about $1.5 million in the Rica-red habanero operation, creating jobs for the locals and hot pods for American consumers in the process. The Rica red habaneros are fermented in mash form in a plant at the site, and the mash is sold to Louisiana hot sauce manufacturers to spice up their cayenne sauces.

We had finally found the hot stuff in Costa Rica!

SPICY ADVENTURES IN MEXICO

I've visited Mexico more times than any other country in the world. I haven't kept count but certainly more than 50 trips. The most memorable excursion there was an extended trip covering four locations where we shot video for a documentary entitled *Heat Up Your Life*, which was produced by Patrick Holian and myself. At the time, Patrick, a good friend, was a videographer and producer at New Mexico State University. Accompanying us as a facilitator and translator was José Marmolejo, another good friend of ours.

I remember the elegant restaurants and highly creative chefs of Mexico City because that was the first time I ever ate *huitlacoche*, which is a fungus that attacks ears of corn. It is a fascinating food. The fungus infects all parts of the ear by invading its ovaries. The infection causes the corn kernels to swell up into tumorlike galls, whose tissues, texture, and appearance are mushroomlike. It is usually made into a sauce, and the chef who served it to us had spiced it up with chile powder and ladled it over a small grilled beefsteak.

Mexico City offered another quite interesting dish, *enchiladas suizas*, or "Swiss enchiladas," a cheesy, creamy concoction that originated at a Sanborns Café in Mexico City in 1950. Its name alludes to the copious amounts of dairy contained in it, usually a cup of sour cream combined with a cup and a half of queso Oaxaca, a very rich cheese from the city of Oaxaca. Since the sour cream and cheese will

cut the heat of the chiles, most recipes call for two or three serrano chiles and two poblano chiles.

In one of our cooking segments, in order to learn how chiles had influenced Mexican cuisine in the centuries since the Spanish conquest, I accepted the invitation of Lula Bertán, a food expert and television star. She told me that she would prepare a number of chile-oriented dishes for me, and I was eager to see them. My favorite dish she prepared was stuffed jalapeño rings. To make the batter, she combined one cup of flour, one tablespoon baking powder, one tablespoon salt, and about a half cup of milk.

With a whisk, she stirred it until thick. Lula explains the next steps:

> To fry jalapeños, you take the seeds out and then you dip the rings in the
> batter, and right away in the oil. And then you wait for them to get a very
> nice brown . . . light brown, okay. And then you just take them out and
> place them on paper towels. Once you have them fried, crispy and good, you
> are going to stuff them with a mixture of cream cheese and chorizo. You
> know chorizo is our Mexican sausage, very spicy, lots of chiles in it. What
> we are going to do is just mix the two of them and have a very nice mixture
> and then we are just going to put this on top. This is the way to serve them,
> real hot so that the chile and the chorizo blend very well.

What do Mexicans do when they want to escape the noise and bustle of the big city? They go to the beach, that's what they do. And we followed their lead to one of the greatest resorts in the world—Cancún. There, at the Ritz-Carlton Hotel, we met up with chef John Gray—on the beach with a grill and a seven-pound red snapper. He was going to prepare *tikin xik*, pronounced "teekin sheek," a marinated and grilled whole fish.

First, John prepared the red achiote marinade, which is made from a paste consisting of annatto seeds, oregano, and garlic. This is a very simple blender recipe: add the achiote paste, two ounces of lemon juice, orange juice (preferably bitter orange), a little white vinegar, two large cloves of fresh garlic, a half cup of water, some slices of onion, and a little salt.

He basted the fish with the marinade and then described the next step: "We simply layered the fish with some of the thin slices of onion, fresh tomatoes and the *xcatic* pepper. We are laying it on the banana leaves to protect it from the fire a little bit, so that it doesn't actually burn the fish. Because we just want it to steam in the banana leaves." I was blown away by both the dramatic appearance of the fish and its superb flavor.

In the southern state of Oaxaca, we needed a person to explain the seven moles that are so famous there, and found Susana Trilling, owner of the Seasons of My Heart Cooking School. She was going to show us how to make the most famous mole of the region, *mole negro oaxaqueño*, and first she told me about the chiles in the dish.

"We're going to use chilhuacle negro, a chile especially from Oaxaca, pasilla Mexicana, which is a chile from Zacatecas, Mexico, mulato negro or ancho negro, chile guajillo and also the chipotle meco, which is a type of seedless chipotle."

The chiles are all fried in lard and then added to the following ingredients, as I describe in my script:

Susana adds the pureed tomatoes and tomatillos . . . the grilled onion and garlic mixture . . . the nut mixture that Paula prepared on the metate . . . the bread, plantains, and raisins mixed with the toasted cloves, black pepper, and cinnamon . . . the blackened chile seeds . . . and even more interesting ingredients, such as . . . flame-toasted avocado leaves . . . and some semi-sweet chocolate ground from beans in the molinas—or mills—in the markets of Oaxaca.

I almost accomplished my goal of tasting all seven Oaxacan moles while I was there, missing only two of them. The ones I tasted (I loved them all) were the black mole from Susana; *mole coloradito*, a brown mole with chocolate; *mole manchamanteles* (the tablecloth-staining mole); *chichilo oaxaqueño* (Oaxacan chichilo), a beef stock–based mole; and *mole amarillo* (yellow mole). The two I missed were green and red: *mole verde* and *mole rojo*.

Space limitations prevent me from sharing the stories of the people we met and the dishes devoured in Ciudad Juárez, Chihuahua; the great times in Baja California Sur at the Hotel California; and the spicy seafood of Puerta Vallarta, Guaymas, and Isla Mujeres. But I have a hunch that readers now understand the Mexicans' love affair with chile peppers.

FEATURED CHILE PEPPERS

Ancho/Poblano

This chile is a pod type of the *annuum* species. The name ancho means wide, an allusion to the broad, flat, heart-shaped pods in the dried form. The fresh pod is called poblano.

Anchos are multiple stemmed and compact to semi-erect, semi-woody, and about 25 inches high. The leaves are dark green and shiny, approximately 4 inches long and 2 ½ inches wide, and the corollas are off-white and appear at every node. The flowering period begins 50 days after sowing and continues until the first frost. The pods are pendant, vary between 3 to 6 inches long, and 2 to 3 inches wide, are conical or truncated, and have indented shoulders. Immature pods are dark green, maturing to either red or brown, and the dried pods are a very dark reddish brown, nearly black. They are fairly mild, ranging from 1,000 to 1,500 SHU.

Red poblano pod. Photograph by Harald Zoschke. Used with permission.

This variety is one of the most popular peppers grown in Mexico, where about 37,000 acres of it are under cultivation. The ancho/poblano varieties grow well in the US but only about 150 acres are planted. Growers in the eastern US reported that their plants grown in Wharton, New Jersey, topped 4 feet and needed to be staked to keep them from toppling over. These plants produced well, but the pods never matured to the red stage before the end of the growing season. The usual growing period is 100 to 120 days, and the yield is about 15 pods per plant, although there are reports of up to 30 pods per plant.

Fresh poblanos are roasted and peeled, then preserved by canning or freezing. They are often stuffed to make chiles rellenos. The dried pods can be stored in airtight containers for months, or they can be ground into a powder. Anchos are commonly used in sauces called moles.

Jalapeño

This chile was named after the city of Xalapa in Veracruz, Mexico, where it is no longer commercially grown. This chile pepper is a pod type of *Capsicum annuum*. Jalapeños usually grow from 2 ½ to 3 feet tall. Jalapeños have a compact single stem or upright multibranched spreading habit. The leaves are light to dark green and measure about 3 inches long and 2 inches wide. The flower corollas are white with no spots. The pods, which are conical and cylindrical, are pendant and measure about 2 to 3 inches long and 1 inch wide. They are green (occasionally sunlight will cause purpling), maturing to red, and measure between 2,500 and 10,000 SHU. The brown streaks, or "corking," on the pods are desirable in Mexico but not so in the US.

In Mexico, commercial cultivation measures approximately 40,000 acres in three main agricultural zones: the Lower Papaloapan River Valley in the states of Veracruz and Oaxaca, northern Veracruz, and the area around Delicias, Chihuahua. The later region grows the American jalapeños, which are processed and exported into the US. Approximately 60 percent of the Mexican jalapeño crop is used for processing, 20 percent for fresh consumption, and 20 percent in production of chipotle chiles, smoked jalapeños.

In the United States, approximately 5,500 acres are under cultivation, with Texas the leading state for jalapeño production, followed by New Mexico. Home gardeners should remember that the US varieties of jalapeños flourish better in semiarid climates—ones with dry air combined with irrigation. If jalapeños are planted in hot and humid zones in the US during the summer, the yield decreases, and so Mexican varieties should be grown. The growing period is 70 to 80 days, and the yield is about 25 to 35 pods per plant. Recommended Mexican varieties are *típico* and *peludo*; recommended US varieties are early jalapeño (hot) and 'TAM Mild Jalapeño I.'

Jalapeños are one of the most famous chile peppers. They are instantly recognizable and a considerable mythology has sprung up about them, particularly in Texas. The impetus for the popularity of jalapeños starts from a combination of their unique taste, their heat, and their continued use as a snack food.

In 1956, *Newsweek* magazine published a story on a pepper-eating contest held in the Bayou Teche country of Louisiana, near the home of the famous Tabasco Sauce. The article rated the jalapeño as "the hottest pepper known," more fiery than the "green

Green and red jalapeño pods. Photograph by Harald Zoschke. Used with permission.

tabasco" or "red cayenne." Thus the Tex-Mex chile was launched as the perfectly pungent pepper for jalapeño-eating contests, which have proliferated all over the country.

Many jalapeños are used straight out of the garden in salsas. Others are pickled in escabeche and sold to restaurants and food services for sale in their salad bars. Jalapeños are processed as "nacho slices," and "nacho rings" that are served over nachos, one of the most popular snack foods in arenas and ball parks. Jalapeños are commonly used in commercial salsas and picante sauces, which make up a large percentage of the imports from Mexico.

PICO DE GALLO SALSA

yield 6 servings   *heat scale* medium

This universal salsa—also known as salsa fria, salsa cruda, salsa fresca, salsa Mexicana, and salsa picante—is served all over Mexico and often shows up with nontraditional ingredients such as canned tomatoes, bell peppers, or spices like oregano. Here is the most authentic version. Remember that everything in it should be as fresh as possible, and the vegetables must be hand-chopped. Never, never use a blender or food processor. Pico de gallo ("rooster's beak" for its "sharpness") is best when the tomatoes come from the garden, not from the supermarket. It can be used as a dip for chips, or for spicing up fajitas and other Southwestern specialties. Note: It requires advance preparation and will keep for only a day or two in the refrigerator.

4 serrano or jalapeño chiles, seeds and stems removed, chopped fine (or more for a hotter salsa)	1 medium onion, chopped fine
	¼ cup minced fresh cilantro
2 large ripe tomatoes, finely chopped	2 tablespoons vinegar
	2 tablespoons vegetable oil

Combine all ingredients in a large bowl, mix well, and let the salsa sit, covered, for at least an hour to blend the flavors.

PERUVIAN MIXED SEAFOOD CEVICHE

yield 4 servings   *heat scale* medium

This particular ceviche is spicy because of the addition of a fair number of crushed ajís or whatever dried chiles you have available. The use of corn and sweet potatoes signals this dish as being very typically Peruvian. Serve it as an entrée for lunch or dinner on those hot and sweltering days of summer. Note: This recipe requires advance preparation.

¾ cup fresh lime juice

¾ cup fresh lemon juice

3 dried ají chiles, seeds and stems removed, crushed in a mortar, or substitute 2 New Mexican chiles (mild) or 6 piquins (hot)

1 clove garlic, minced

1 large red onion, sliced paper thin

1 teaspoon salt

¼ teaspoon freshly ground black pepper

½ pound white fish fillets, such as catfish, cut into 1-inch pieces

1 pound cleaned shellfish (clams, oysters, mussels, or a mix)

1 teaspoon paprika (optional)

1 tablespoon chopped fresh parsley, Italian preferred

3 sweet potatoes, peeled and cut into 1-inch-thick slices

3 ears of fresh corn, cleaned and cut into 2-inch-thick slices

4 Bibb lettuce leaves

Combine all the ingredients except the potatoes, corn, and lettuce in a large ceramic bowl, mix well, cover tightly, and refrigerate for 3 to 5 hours. If the citrus juice doesn't cover the fish, add more.

Just before serving, bring a large pot of salted water to a boil, and drop in the sweet potatoes and boil for 10 minutes. Then add the rounds of corn to the pot and boil for another 10 minutes. Drain the vegetables thoroughly.

Drain the fish in a colander to remove the marinade, and arrange the fish on the lettuce on 4 dinner plates. Garnish with the sweet potatoes and the rounds of corn.

CARNE EN JOCÓN
(BEEF IN TOMATO AND CHILE SAUCE)

yield 6 servings   *heat scale* medium

This spicy beef dish is found throughout Guatemala; it is a famous and traditional favorite that is usually served with hot cooked rice. Mexican green tomatoes, called tomatillos, are available at Latin American markets and even in some chain supermarkets. The tomatillos add an interesting taste dimension with a hint of lemon and herbs.

3 to 4 tablespoons vegetable oil

1   cup chopped onion

2   cloves garlic, minced

1   bell pepper, seeded and chopped

2   fresh jalapeño chiles, seeds and stems removed, chopped

3   pounds boneless beef, cut into 1-inch cubes

½   teaspoon salt

¼   teaspoon freshly ground black pepper

10   ounces fresh tomatillos, husks removed, and diced; or substitute a 10-ounce can of tomatillos

3   tomatoes, peeled and chopped

1   bay leaf

¼   teaspoon ground cloves

1   teaspoon oregano

¾   cup beef stock

2   tortillas

Water for soaking

Heat the oil in a heavy casserole and sauté the onion, garlic, and the peppers. Push the mixture to one side of the casserole, and add the beef and brown it lightly. Mix the meat and the sautéed onion, and add the remaining ingredients, except the tortillas and water.

Bring the mixture to a boil, reduce the heat to a simmer, cover, and gently simmer for 2 hours.

Soak the tortillas in cold water for a few minutes. Squeeze the water out and finely crumble the tortillas into the beef. Stir the crumbled tortillas into the beef and simmer for a few minutes until the meat mixture thickens.

CHILES ANCHOS CAPONES
(STUFFED SEEDLESS ANCHO CHILES)

yield 8 servings   *heat scale* medium

The word capon translates as "castrated" but in this case merely means seedless. Yes, dried chiles such as anchos and pasillas can be stuffed, but they must be softened in hot water first. They have an entirely different flavor than their greener, more vegetable-like versions. Lula Bertán served this dish to me in Mexico City during the shooting of episode 3 of my video documentary, Heat Up Your Life. It's on YouTube. Unfortunately, that particular cooking sequence was cut in the final edit of the show, but Lula cooks several other dishes.

10	ancho chiles
1	quart hot water
2	pounds *queso añejo* or Romano cheese, grated
8	cups chicken stock
3	cups small green onions, without the green ends
1	cup pork lard, or substitute vegetable oil
¼	cup flour
	Salt to taste

In a dry skillet, lightly toast the ancho chiles without burning them. Soak the chiles for 5 minutes in hot water to soften them, then drain and dry them. With a knife, make a slit in the side of each pod and deseed it. Stuff the chiles with the cheese and set aside. You can tie them to keep the stuffing from falling out if you wish.

Heat the chicken stock and boil the green onions for 3 minutes. Remove the onions from the stock and set both aside.

Heat the lard until lightly smoking. Fry the chiles on both sides, starting on the open side. Remove the chiles from the oil and drain on paper towels. Fry the green onions in the lard. Remove and set aside. Add the flour to the lard and stir until completely mixed without letting the mixture turn brown. Pour the chicken stock in the pan and stir until no more lumps are seen. Simmer the sauce to thicken for 5 minutes while stirring. Add the chiles and let simmer 2 more minutes. The sauce should be smooth but not too thick. Add stock if necessary. Serve the chiles immediately with some green onions on the side.

COCHINITA PIBIL
(PORK COOKED BY THE PIBIL METHOD)

yield 4 to 6 servings   *heat scale* mild

This pre-Columbian dish is probably the best-known food of the Mayas, according to Jeff and Nancy Gerlach, who collected this recipe on one of their many trips to Yucatán. It is one of the most popular entrées of this area and is on virtually every menu. This dish is traditionally served with warmed corn tortillas, black beans, cebollas encuridas (marinated onions), and habanero salsa. Note: Advance preparation is required.

10	whole black peppercorns
¼	teaspoon cumin seeds
5	cloves garlic
3	tablespoons *recado rojo*, or substitute achiote paste (both available from online sources)
1	teaspoon dried Mexican oregano
2	bay leaves
⅓	cup bitter orange juice, or substitute ⅓ cup lime juice, fresh preferred
2	pounds lean pork, cut into 1 ½–inch cubes
	Banana leaves or aluminum foil
3	xcatic chiles, stems and seeds removed, cut in strips; or substitute banana or yellow wax hot chiles
1	large purple onion, sliced

Place the peppercorns and cumin seeds in a spice or coffee grinder and process to a fine powder. Add the garlic and grind again.

In a bowl, combine the spice mixture, recado rojo, oregano, bay leaves, and orange juice. Pour the marinade over the pork and marinate for 3 hours or overnight.

Cut the banana leaves in pieces to fit a roasting pan. Soften the leaves by passing them over a gas flame or by holding them over an electric burner for several seconds until the leaves begin to turn light green. Remove the center ribs from the leaves and use for tying. Lay a couple of these ribs—that are long enough to tie around the pork—along the bottom of the pan. Line the pan with the banana leaves or foil.

Place the pork, including the marinade, on the leaves, and top with the chiles and onion. Fold the banana leaves over and tie with the strings. Cover the pan and bake in the oven at 325 degrees F. for 1 ½ hours.

SALSA DE MOLE POBLANO
(CLASSIC MOLE POBLANO SAUCE)

yield about 2 cups   *heat scale* medium

*This subtle blend of chocolate and chile is from Puebla, where it is known as the
"national dish of Mexico" when it is served over turkey. This sauce adds life to any
kind of poultry, from roasted game hens to a simple grilled chicken breast. It is
also excellent as a sauce over chicken enchiladas.*

4 dried pasilla chiles, seeds and stems removed	½ corn tortilla, torn into pieces
	¼ cup raisins
4 dried red guajillo or New Mexican chiles, seeds and stems removed	¼ teaspoon ground cloves
	¼ teaspoon ground cinnamon
1 medium onion, chopped	¼ teaspoon ground coriander
2 cloves garlic, chopped	
2 medium tomatoes, peeled and seeds removed, chopped	3 tablespoons shortening or vegetable oil
2 tablespoons sesame seeds	1 cup chicken broth
½ cup almonds	1 ounce bitter chocolate (or more to taste)

Combine the chiles, onion, garlic, tomatoes, 1 tablespoon of the sesame seeds, almonds,
tortilla, raisins, cloves, cinnamon, and coriander.

Puree small amounts of this mixture in a blender until smooth.

Melt the shortening in a skillet and sauté the puree for 10 minutes, stirring frequently. Add
the chicken broth and chocolate, and cook over a very low heat for 45 minutes. The sauce
should be very thick. The remaining sesame seeds are used as a garnish, sprinkled over
the finished dish.

In colonial America, chiles were grown by Thomas Jefferson, who was given seeds by other American gardeners and planted them at his various plantations, including Monticello. When I visited Monticello in 2011 to give a talk about my book *The Founding Foodies*, I discussed Jefferson's fondness for peppers with Peter J. Hatch, the director emeritus of gardens and grounds for the Thomas Jefferson Foundation. Hatch was responsible for the maintenance, interpretation, and restoration of the 2,400-acre landscape at Monticello from 1977 to 2012. He writes in his book *"A Rich Spot of Earth": Thomas Jefferson's Revolutionary Garden at Monticello*:

> Jefferson grew various forms of Bells, Bullnose, sweet, and cayenne pepper (*Capsicum annuum*), as well as Texas bird pepper (*Capsicum annuum* var. *glabriusculum*). His documented sowing of cayenne pepper seed at Shadwell in 1767 is one of the earliest references to this form of Capsicum in North America. Later, in the 1812 "Calendar," "Major," "cayenne," and "Bullnose" (marked by a crinkled, noselike appendage on the blossom end) were planted in adjacent rows in square IX. The Texas bird pepper, obtained from Dr. Samuel Brown of Natchez through acquaintances near San Antonio, was among Jefferson's most exciting introductions. Jefferson planted bird pepper seed in the garden and with a dibble in flowerpots, and relayed the seed to Bernard McMahon in 1813. Green (also called "Bell" and "Bullnose") peppers appear in the Jefferson family manuscripts as additions to tomato pickles and gumbo soup, while cayenne peppers were added to Virginia Randolph Trist's tomato soup and Septimia Meikleham's salad dressing. The Monticello family physician, Dr. Dunglison, prescribed a red pepper gargle to relieve the sore throats of Jefferson's granddaughters. Culinary historian Karen Hess called the use of hot peppers in traditional Virginia cooking "highly skilled and discrete."

George Washington grew "bird peppers" at Mount Vernon, along with other experimental plants such as palmettos and guinea grass. But chiles never really became popular on the East Coast. They were, however, adopted with great fervor in Louisiana by way of Mexico.

Jefferson's garden at Monticello.
Photograph by Dave DeWitt.

A BRIEF HISTORY OF TABASCO® SAUCE

While the early settlers of the Southwest were growing New Mexican–type chiles and cooking enchiladas, Mexicans were developing and cultivating many different strains of capsicums. One such strain, *Capsicum frutescens*, was grown near the port of Tabasco on the Gulf of Mexico, which had regular trade with New Orleans. During the US war with Mexico, American soldiers captured the port of Tabasco (which is now called San Juan Batista) in July 1847.

Although exact details are lacking, historians believe that chiles were imported into New Orleans by soldiers returning to that city for treatment of various tropical diseases. Somehow, seeds were transferred to a prominent banker and legislator, Colonel Maunsell White. By 1849, White was cultivating the chiles, which were then spelled "Tobasco," on his Deer Range Plantation. That year, the *New Orleans Daily Delta* printed a letter from a visitor to White's plantation who reported, "I must not omit to notice the Colonel's pepper patch, which is two acres in extent, all planted with a new species of red pepper, which Colonel White has introduced into this country, called Tobasco red pepper. The Colonel attributes the admirable health of his hands to the free use of this pepper."

Colonel White manufactured the first hot sauce from the Tobasco chiles and advertised bottles of it for sale in 1859. About this time, he gave some chiles and his sauce recipe to a friend named Edmund McIlhenny, who promptly planted the seeds on his plantation on Avery Island. McIlhenny's horticultural enterprise was interrupted by the Civil War and invading Union troops from captured New Orleans. In 1863, McIlhenny and his family abandoned their Avery Island plantation to take refuge in San Antonio, Texas.

When the McIlhenny family returned to Avery Island in 1865, they found their plantation destroyed and their sugarcane fields in ruin. However, a few volunteer chile plants still survived, providing enough seeds for McIlhenny to rebuild his pepper patch. Gradually, his yield of pods increased to the point where he could experiment with his sauce recipe, in which mashed chiles were strained and the resulting juice was mixed with vinegar and salt and aged in 50-gallon white-oak barrels. In 1868, McIlhenny packaged his aged sauce in 350 used cologne bottles and sent them as samples to likely wholesalers. The sauce was so popular that orders poured in for thousands of bottles priced at a dollar each wholesale.

In 1870, McIlhenny obtained a patent on his Tabasco (as it was now spelled) brand hot pepper sauce, and by 1872 he had opened an office in London to handle the European market. The increasing demand for Tabasco Sauce caused changes in the packaging of the product as the corked bottles sealed with green wax were replaced by bottles with metal tops. In 1885, the product won a gold medal for excellence at the World's Industrial and Cotton Centennial Exposition in New Orleans. By 1886, completion of the nationwide railway network greatly assisted the distribution of Tabasco Sauce.

After the death of Edmund McIlhenny in 1890, the family business was turned over to his son John, who immediately inherited trouble in the form of a crop failure. John attempted to locate Tabasco chiles in Mexico but could not find any grower to meet his specifications. Fortunately, his father had stored sufficient reserves of pepper mash, so the family business weathered the crisis. However, that experience taught the family not to depend solely upon Tabasco chiles grown in Louisiana. Today, Tabascos chiles are grown under contract in Colombia and other Central and South American countries, and the mash is imported into the United States in barrels.

John McIlhenny was quite a promoter and traveled all over the country promoting his family's sauce. "I had bill posters prepared," he once said, "and had large wooden signs in the fields near the cities. I had an opera troupe playing a light opera. At different times I had certain cities canvassed by drummers, in a house-to-house canvass. I had exhibits in food expositions, with demonstrators attached. I gave away many thousands of circulars and folders, and miniature bottles of Tabasco pepper sauce."

All of this promotion did not go unnoticed by the competition. In 1898, another Louisiana entrepreneur named B. F. Trappey, a former employee of the McIlhenny company, began growing Tabasco chiles from Avery Island seeds. He founded the company B. F. Trappey and Sons and began producing his own sauce, which was also called "Tabasco." The McIlhenny family eventually responded to this challenge by receiving a trademark for their Tabasco brand in 1906. The two companies competed with identically named sauces until 1929, when the McIlhenny family won a trademark-infringement suit against the Trappeys. From that time on, only the McIlhenny sauce could be called "Tabasco," and competitors were reduced to merely including Tabasco chiles in their list of ingredients.

I wanted to know precisely how Tabasco® Sauce was made. So on a shoot for *Heat Up Your Life*, I traveled with our crew to Avery Island, Louisiana, where I interviewed Paul McIlhenny, president of the McIlhenny Company and the great-grandson of its founder, Edmund McIlhenny.

DAVE: Paul, tell me exactly how Tabasco® Sauce is made.

PAUL: The day the peppers are harvested—and of course it is just the bright red juicy peppers. We grind them up with 8 percent salt, really Avery Island salt, coarse ground salt, and that mash then actively ferments or works for about 30 to 60 days. It is not a fermentation like in the production of alcohol, but it is a fermentation. Then the mash stays in the barrels for three years. We bring the mash here to Avery Island and finish the aging here. After the aging, we clean off the oxidized mash from the top, and we inspect each barrel. We take the aged, drained, inspected mash, which is what this is here. We add very strong 100-grain vinegar, mix it slowly for four weeks, and then extract or strain off the seeds and skins.

DAVE: How many peppers do you think went into that one scoop there?

PAUL: Well, an awful lot, a lot more than you think. Because we take the seeds and the skins out, and that is a large amount of the bulk. It takes a lot of peppers to make a two-ounce bottle of Tabasco® Sauce. And our brand name is probably one of the most famous brand names all over the world. Like Coca-Cola®, Ford®, Xerox®, it is a trademark that is easily recognized not only here but all over the globe. We print our cartons in 19 foreign languages and we sell to more than 100 foreign countries.

The author and Paul McIlhenny at Avery Island, Louisiana.

After the interview, Paul was kind enough to prepare a crawfish boil for our cast and crew in the backyard of the colonial-style Marsh House, where we were staying.

The rise of Louisiana hot sauces greatly influenced the two related cuisines in the area, Creole and Cajun. The Creoles are descendants of the original French settlers of Louisiana, while the Cajuns are descended from French-speaking immigrants from Nova Scotia, which was originally called Acadia. (The term Cajun is a corrupt form of Acadian.) Although Creole cooking is basically a localized urban version of French cooking, and Cajun cuisine is a countrified mélange of French, African, and Indian cooking, both styles share similar ingredients and recipes.

Some food historians speculate that Creole and Cajun food was first spiced up by cayenne chiles brought from Africa by slaves and grown in plantation gardens but never commercially cultivated until the twentieth century. Today, both cayenne and Tabasco chiles are grown in Louisiana, but not in great amounts—only about 230 acres of chiles are cultivated in the state, and much of that is Tabascos grown for their seeds. However, imported cayenne powder, locally bottled cayenne hot sauces, and many brands of Tabasco-based hot sauces are readily available to spice up Cajun and Creole dishes.

So if you're versed on Louisiana history and culture, then all you really need to know is that Creole cuisine uses tomatoes and proper Cajun food does not. A vastly simplified way to describe the two cuisines is to deem Creole cuisine as a little higher brow, or more aristocratic, than Cajun. Due to the abundance of time and resources, the dishes employ an array of spices from various regions, used in

creamy soups and sauces. A remoulade sauce, for example, which consists of nearly a dozen ingredients, would not typically be found in Cajun kitchens. Creole cuisine has a bit more variety because of the easier access Creoles had to exotic ingredients, and because of the wide mix of cultures that contributed to the cuisine. That's why you find tomatoes in Creole jambalaya and not in Cajun jambalaya, or why a lot of times you find a Creole roux made with butter and flour while a Cajun roux is made with oil and flour.

The primary Creole dishes include gumbo, the stew-like soup of Louisiana. The name "gumbo" comes from the West African term for okra, *gombo*. Okra is used as a thickening agent and for its distinct flavor. A *filé gumbo* is thickened with dried sassafras leaves after the stew has finished cooking. Jambalaya, derived from the Spanish dish paella, contains rice, some sort of meat (chicken or beef) or seafood (shrimp or crawfish), green peppers, onions, celery, tomatoes, and hot chile peppers. Shrimp Creole is a favorite of Creole cuisine and is made with shrimp, tomatoes, onions, bell peppers, celery, garlic, and cayenne pepper. Red beans and rice is one of the most common dishes found in New Orleans. The red beans arrived with white French Creoles from Haiti, and the combination of the beans with rice has a strong Caribbean influence.

Popular Cajun dishes include étouffée, a seafood stew served over rice. It's a staple Cajun dish on the menu, and during the spring crawfish season, fresh crawfish are used, and at other times of year, frozen crawfish or shrimp. Boudin is a spicy pork sausage made with green onions and rice. The "boudin balls" are battered and deep-fried, and feature bite-sized pieces of sausage. A crawfish or shrimp boil is a spicy one-pot dish made for festivals, parties, and events, including restaurant meals to mark the start of crawfish season.

Another Cajun favorite is alligator, and I learned how to prepare it when I visited the beautifully restored Acadian Village near Lafayette where we did a shoot for *Heat Up Your Life*. I met up with chef Scott Landry, who hails from Lake Charles. He agreed to cook some of his favorite native dishes—outside, just to show us how easy it is. He made crawfish étouffée, chicken and sausage jambalaya, and one of his favorite foods from a nearby bayou. Using a skillet on a gas grill and some homemade hot sauce and a few vegetables, here's how he did it.

SCOTT: What we are going to do right now is we are going to season this alligator up that we caught and we are going to put that Byron seasoning on there. Remember, you have got to season that. It doesn't have to be long that you season that—10 minutes, 15 minutes, that is all. Byron

seasoning, some habaneros and cayenne peppers, it is a little bit of everything. It's a brand-new bottle, so if you don't mind, I am going to—not,
I didn't have to use my teeth. You know, God gave you can openers, you
just open your mouth like that.

Anyway, I am going to put that in there. You can't put that in there
like that—you have to put that in there like this. Put you a lot, boy that
smells good. Then I am going to sprinkle this all around in there. I am
going to use my knife to move that all around. This is going to be hot for
you people up north, but not too hot for us down here. Then I am going
to put some parsley and some onion, then I am going to use these red
and yellow bell peppers. Do you know what the difference is? One is rip-
er than the other.

The most important thing to remember in alligator is to cut all that fat
off, because that fat is oh man that is nasty. I'm going to tell you that if
you don't have no alligator at your grocery store, I don't think you might
get that, but in Lake Charles we get that. If you don't, use some chicken.
What I want to tell you about this dish is, alligator, if you cook it too
long, it is like rubber on your feet. You don't have to do that if you want.
My wife—you know that I used to have a wife, but she left me one time.

She is the best housekeeper that I have ever met. I married her and when I left, she kept the house. It is just one of those things, you just can't understand that.

You know alligator, everyone wants to know what it tastes like. I told some men the other day when I was in Florida that it tastes a little bit like manatee or eagle, but don't cook that. Oh, they will get on your case, but it makes a pretty good gumbo. And you stir all that up and you have the colors in there. If you want, you can put your hand in there and tear it up before it gets too hot. If it is too hot, the sauce that I am cooking with is pretty hot, you just add a little water.

As you can see, it don't take long to cook this. You don't want to overcook this because it will be too chewy, and you don't want any fat because it will be rancid. I got this dish all done here. Get these onions cooked down a little bit, it would be fine.

DAVE: It smells great.

SCOTT: Let's try a little of this alligator now.

DAVE: Do alligators eat crawfish?

SCOTT: They eat anything that don't eat them first.

DAVE: That's good, that's spicy.

SCOTT: It'll make you grow up big and strong.

DAVE: Alligator's kinda hard to find in New Mexico, but I guess it's good here.

SCOTT: You can make it with anything you want.

We do have alligators in the markets in New Mexico—alligator pears, that is, or avocados.

CHILES IN SOUTHWESTERN CUISINES

When I wrote the book *The Southwest Table* (Lyons Press, 2011), the first thing I had to do was define the term Southwest. Since everyone agrees that New Mexico and Arizona are in the Southwest, I started there, but eliminated California (Far West) and Oklahoma (Midwest). But what about Texas? I finally decided that Southwest Texas, including the cities of Austin, San Antonio, and El Paso, was in the Southwest, but the rest of the state was not. I also eliminated Colorado from the Southwest in that book, but for the purposes of this book, considering the growing popularity of 'Pueblo' chiles, I am including southern Colorado in the Southwest. So, the term Southwest consists of New Mexico, Arizona, southwest Texas, and southern Colorado. Let's move east to west when discussing these chile-based cuisines.

THE "NATIONAL DISH" OF TEXAS

Perhaps the most famous Tex-Mex creation is that bowl o' red, chili con carne, a dish that most writers on the subject say did *not* originate in Mexico. Even Mexico disclaims chili; the *Diccionario de mejicanismos*, a Mexican dictionary published in 1959, defines it as "A detestable food passing itself off as Mexican and sold from Texas to New York City."

Despite such protestations, the combination of meat and chile peppers in stew-like concoctions is not uncommon in Mexican cooking. Mexican *caldillos* (thick soups or stews) and adobos (thick sauces) often resemble chili con carne in both appearance and taste because they all use similar ingredients: various types of chiles combined with meat (usually beef), onions, garlic, cumin, and occasionally tomatoes.

E. De Grolyer, a scholar and chili aficionado, believes that Texas chili con carne had its origins as the "pemmican of the Southwest" in the late 1840s. According to De Grolyer, Texans pounded together dried beef, beef fat, chile peppers, and salt to make trail food for the long ride out to San Francisco and the gold fields. The concentrated, dried mixture was then boiled in pots along the trail as sort of an "instant chili."

Chili con carne.
Photograph by
Wes Naman.
Work for hire.

A variation on this theory holds that cowboys invented chili while driving cattle along the lengthy and lonely trails. Supposedly, range cooks planted oregano, chiles, and onions among patches of mesquite to protect them from foraging cattle. The next time they passed along the same trail, they would collect the spices, combine them with beef (what else?), and make a dish called "trail drive chili." Undoubtedly, the chiles used with the earliest incarnations of chili con carne were the chiltepíns, called chilipiquins in Texas, which grow wild on bushes—particularly in the southern part of the state.

Probably the most likely explanation for the origin of chili con carne in Texas comes from the heritage of Mexican food combined with the rigors of life on the Texas frontier. Most historians agree that the earliest written description of chili came from J. C. Clopper, who lived near Houston. He wrote of visiting San Antonio in 1828: "When they [poor families of San Antonio] have to pay for their meat in the market, a very little is made to suffice for the family; it is generally cut into a kind of hash with nearly as many peppers as there are pieces of meat—this is all stewed together."

Except for this one quote, which does not mention the dish by name, historians of heat can find no documented evidence of chili in Texas before 1880. Around that time in San Antonio, a municipal market—El Mercado—was operating in Military Plaza. Historian Charles Ramsdell notes that "the first rickety chili stands were set up in this marketplace, with the bowls of red sold by women who were called 'chili queens.'"

The fame of chili con carne began to spread, and the dish soon became a major tourist attraction, making its appearance in Mexican restaurants all over Texas— and elsewhere. The first known recipe appeared in 1880 in *Mrs. Owens' Cook Book*. She got it all wrong, of course, referring to the bowl o' red as "the national dish of Mexico," and added ham, carrots, celery, and cloves to it.

At the World's Fair in Chicago in 1893, a bowl o' red was available at the San Antonio Chili Stand, and in 1896, the first US Army recipe appeared in *The Manual for Army Cooks*. Incidentally, Army chili contained both rice and onions. Given the popularity of the dish, some commercialization of it was inevitable. In 1898, William Gebhardt of New Braunfels, Texas, produced the first chili powder and began canning his chili con carne, Gebhardt Eagle. By 1918, Walker Austex was producing 45,000 cans a day of Walker's Red Hot Chile Con Carne and 15,000 cans a day of Mexene Chili Powder.

The chili queens were banned from San Antonio in 1937 for health reasons— public officials objected to flies and poorly washed dishes. They were restored by

Mayor Maury Maverick (a real name) in 1939, but their stands were closed again shortly after the start of World War II. Texans, however, have never forgotten their culinary heritage, and in 1977 the Texas legislature proclaimed chili con carne to be the "Official Texas State Dish." Incidentally, in 1993, the Illinois State Senate passed a resolution proclaiming that Illinois was to be the "Chilli [sic] Capital of the Civilized World," a move that outraged Texans.

Today there is a movement afoot by the International Chili Society (in California, of all places!) to have Congress name chili as the official national dish, but the idea isn't new. In the mid-1970s, Craig Claiborne wrote, "We thought for years that if there's such a thing as a national American dish, it isn't apple pie, it's chili con carne. . . . In one form or another, chili in America knows no regional boundaries. North, South, East, and West, almost every man, woman, and child has a favorite recipe."

Chili con carne is still enormously popular in Texas and other states, and huge chili cookoffs are held. Teams of cooks use highly guarded secret recipes to compete for thousands of dollars in prizes while having a good ol' time partying. Some traditionalists, however, scorn the cookoff-style chili con carne as too elaborate and are promoting a return to the classic "keep it simple, stupid" café-style chili.

Sam Pendergrast of Abilene is such a purist, and in his landmark article, "Requiem for Texas Chili," which appeared in *Chile Pepper* magazine in 1989, he notes: "I have a theory that real chili is such a basic, functional dish that anyone can make it from the basic ingredients—rough meat, chile peppers, and a few common spices available to hungry individuals—and they'll come up with pretty much the same kind of recipe that was for most of a century a staple of Texas tables. So all we have to do to get back to real chili is to get rid of the elitist nonsense."

THE ADVENT OF TEX-MEX

Throughout the Southwest, each state has its own version of what is called Mexican cooking. With a few exceptions, the same basic dishes—enchiladas, tacos, and the like—have become very popular, but they do not truly represent the cooking of Mexico. Rather, they have become Mexican American versions of cooking borrowed from the northern states of Mexico—versions that developed when our states were a part of Mexico—but these dishes evolved in their own directions, based on regional ingredients and cooking styles.

The first Mexican restaurant to open in Texas was the Old Borunda Café in Marfa in 1887, closely followed by the Original Mexican Restaurant in San Antonio in

1900. Restaurants had a great influence on the development of Tex-Mex cooking. As Texas food writer Richard West explains, "The standard Tex-Mex foods (tacos, enchiladas, rice, refried beans, and tamales)—and newer editions, like *chiles rellenos*, *burritos*, *flautas*, and *chalupas*—existed in Mexico before they came here. What Texas restaurant cooks did was to throw them together and label them Combination Dinner, Señorita Dinner, and the hallowed Number One. In so doing, they took a few ethnic liberties and time-saving short cuts. For example: Tex-Mex tacos as we know them contain ground, instead of shredded, meat. And chile gravy is most often out of the can, instead of being made fresh with *chiles anchos* and special spices."

The chile peppers most commonly used in homemade Tex-Mex cuisine are the poblanos from Mexico (and their dried version, anchos), which are tasty and mild, the fresh ones usually served relleno-style; the serranos for fresh salsas; the chilipiquins (chiltepíns) for soups and stews; and, of course, the ubiquitous jalapeño. This fat and fiery pepper is popular everywhere and is served raw, pickled, stuffed, or chopped up in salsas, and is even utilized in cooked sauces for topping enchiladas and huevos rancheros, which are served with fried eggs and *salsa ranchera* over corn or wheat tortillas.

However, the Texans' love of jalapeños has waned in recent years and the cause rests with chile breeders from Texas A&M University. The 'TAM Mild Jalapeño I' pepper plant is a mild cultivar of the jalapeño pepper developed at Texas A&M University in the early 2000s. It was much milder and larger than the traditional jalapeños, and genes of this mild pepper entered the general jalapeño pool. Cross-breeding caused the gene pool to become overall larger and milder, with some individual pods reaching six inches long. Food expert Sharon Hudgins reports that, 15 to 20 years ago, she spoke with Texas chefs who had given up on using these mild jalapeños and had switched to serrano chiles.

New Mexican chiles are now making an appearance in Tex-Mex cooking, especially in the dried red form. For example, Chuy's restaurant chain in Austin now brings in more than 10,000 pounds of fresh green New Mexican chiles from Hatch, New Mexico, and has a roasting and peeling fiesta; and the Central Market locations in Dallas, Ft. Worth, Austin, and Houston have Hatch Chile Fiestas where they sell and roast Hatch chiles, and hire cooks like me to give cooking demonstrations.

No discussion of Texas food would be complete without mentioning beans. They are cooked in many different ways and are served with all the major Texas food groups: barbecue, chili, and Tex-Mex. One of the greatest celebrators of Texas beans was the famous author, professor, and naturalist, J. Frank Dobie. "A lot of people want chili with their beans," he wrote in the 1949 Niemann-Marcus

Hatch chiles in the Central Market, Austin. Photograph by Dave DeWitt.

book, *The Flavor of Texas*. "Chili disguises the bean just as too much barbecue sauce destroys the delectability of good meat. For me, chili simply ruins good beans, although I do like a few chilipiquins cooked with them. I believe, however, that the chilipiquins make a better addition after the beans are cooked. I add about three to a plate of beans and mash them up in the plate along with a suitable amount of fresh onion. A meat eater could live on beans and never miss meat. When a Mexican laborer is unable to lift a heavy weight, his companions say he 'lacks frijoles.' As you may deduce, I am a kind of frijole man. On the oldtime ranches of the border country, where I grew up, frijoles were about as regular as bread and in some households they still are."

Today, Texas cuisine is somewhat of a melting pot, a tossed-salad kind of cooking, with many different influences vying for top honors. In addition to the cooking styles covered above, Texas is influenced greatly by Gulf Coast and Louisiana cooking, Southern cooking (particularly in eastern Texas), Midwestern styles, and even New Mexican cuisine in West Texas. One of the great things about traveling through Texas is the opportunity to sample a wide variety of Southwestern cooking.

NEW MEXICO AND THE UBIQUITOUS CHILE

According to many accounts, chile peppers were introduced into what is now the US by Capitán General Juan de Oñate, the founder of Santa Fe, in 1598. However, they may have been introduced to the Pueblo Indians of New Mexico by the Antonio Espejo expedition of 1582–1583. Baltasar Obregón, one of the members of the expedition, claimed: "They have no chile, but the natives were given some seed to plant." By 1601, chiles were not on the list of Indian crops, according to colonist Francisco de Valverde, who also complained that mice were a pest who ate chile pods off the plants in the field.

After the Spanish began settlement, the cultivation of chile peppers exploded, and they were grown all over New Mexico. It is likely that many different varieties were cultivated, including early forms of jalapeños, serranos, anchos, and pasillas. But one variety that adapted particularly well to New Mexico was a long green chile that turned red in the fall. Formerly called Anaheim because of its transfer to California around 1900, the New Mexican chile was cultivated for hundreds of years in the region with such dedication that several landraces developed. These landraces, called Chimayo and Española, are varieties that adapted to particular environments and are still planted today in the same fields they were grown in centuries ago; they constitute a small but distinct part of tons of pods produced each year in New Mexico.

In 1846, William Emory, chief engineer of the Army's Topographic Unit, was surveying the New Mexico landscape and its customs. He described a meal eaten by people in Bernalillo, just north of Albuquerque: "Roast chicken, stuffed with onions; then mutton, boiled with onions; then followed various other dishes, all dressed with the everlasting onion; and the whole terminated by chile, the glory of New Mexico."

Chile field and mesa, Doña Ana County. Photograph by Paul W. Bosland. Used with permission.

Emory went on to relate his experience with chiles: "Chile the Mexicans consider the chef-d'oeuvre of the cuisine, and seem really to revel in it; but the first mouthful brought the tears trickling down my cheeks, very much to the amusement of the spectators with their leather-lined throats. It was red pepper, stuffed with minced meat."

All of the primary dishes in New Mexico cuisine contain chile peppers: sauces, stews, carne adovada, enchiladas, posole, tamales, huevos rancheros, and many combination vegetable dishes. The intense use of chiles as a food rather than just as a spice or condiment is what differentiates New Mexican cuisine from that of Texas or Arizona. In neighboring states, chile powders are used as a seasoning for beef or chicken broth-based "chili gravies," which are thickened with flour or cornstarch before they are added to, say, enchiladas. In New Mexico, the sauces are made from pure chiles and are thickened by reducing the crushed or pureed pods.

New Mexico chile *sauces* are cooked and pureed, while *salsas* utilize fresh ingredients and are uncooked. Debates rage over whether tomatoes are used in cooked sauces such as red chile sauce for enchiladas. Despite the recipes in numerous cookbooks (none of whose authors live in New Mexico), traditional cooked red sauces do *not* contain tomatoes, though uncooked salsas do.

Carne adovada, pork marinated in red chiles and then baked, is one of the most popular New Mexican entrées. Another is enchiladas; in fact, there are so many variations on enchiladas that cooks soon determine their favorites through experimentation.

New Mexicans love chile peppers so much that they have become the de facto state symbol. Houses are adorned with strings of dried red chiles, called *ristras*. Images of the pods are emblazoned on signs, T-shirts, coffee mugs, posters, windsocks, and even underwear. In the late summer and early fall, the aroma of roasting chiles fills the air all over the state and produces a state of bliss for chileheads.

A la primera cocinera se le va un chile entero, goes one old Spanish *dicho*, "To the best lady cook goes the whole chile."

The chile was recognized as a New Mexico State Vegetable, but in reality it is a fruit. The other State Vegetable, the pinto bean, is a legume, not a vegetable!

In New Mexico, Santa Fe is not only the political capital; it is also the culinary capital of the state. Because of its popularity with tourists, hundreds of restaurants serve up an eclectic variety of world cuisines. As one can imagine, chile peppers play an important role in the dishes served in most of these restaurants. I spoke with Mark Miller who is a chef, a chile expert, a culinary anthropologist, and the founder of the famous Coyote Café. He said,

Chile is probably the quintessential American food product. I think that probably when you create an environment in which chile is being used, you have to look at the American traditions that it comes from and you have to be sensitive and respectful of those traditions. Chiles for me are not just Mexican or Southwestern or Tex-Mex, or New Mexican, or modern Southwestern, they are one of the most important culinary traditions in America. This is one of the products that every single person who eats or cooks in America should know about and use.

COLORADO'S 'PUEBLO' CHILES

They've got their own growers association. They have a festival of their own: the Chile and Frijoles Festival. They have their own supermarkets: Colorado Whole Foods Market locations dumped Hatch chiles and replaced them with 'Pueblo' chiles. And Governor John Hickenlooper has even designated the last Saturday of the Colorado State Fair as Pueblo Chile Day.

That's called Getting Famous Fast. Although a type of 'Mirasol' chile has been grown in the Pueblo area for more than a hundred years, the current craze for the 'Pueblo' chile began in 1992. That's when Dr. Michael Bartolo, an extension vegetable crops specialist and associate professor at Colorado State University's Arkansas Valley Research Center, obtained a plant of a strain of 'Pueblo' chile from his uncle, Harry Mosco, a farmer on the Saint Charles Mesa, east of Pueblo. Bartolo writes, "Seed from that original plant was subsequently sown in 1995. In 1995, a single plant was then selected out of that population. The single plant selection process was repeated for three more years (1996–1998). In 1999–2004, the seed from selected uniform plants was bulked for testing at Colorado State University's Arkansas Valley Research Center (AVRC) in Rocky Ford, Colorado." In 2005, Arkansas Valley growers first planted the 'Mosco' cultivar Bartolo developed. Today, 'Mosco' is one of the most popular cultivars grown in and around the Pueblo area.

Readers should note that the 'Pueblo' chile grown in Colorado is completely different from the New Mexican 'Pueblo' cultivar. And interestingly, although Coloradans declare that the 'Pueblo' chile is superior to the Hatch chile, their 'Pueblo' chile has a strong New Mexican connection. According to Bartolo, "The Pueblo chile is characterized by the upright growth habit of the pepper. Hence the name Mira Sol, which translates as looking at the sun." He adds that the 'Pueblo' chile originated in Mexico and was brought into the United States as a 'Mirasol' around 1910, and was improved by horticulturist Fabian Garcia, a chile pepper

Pueblo chile peppers. Photograph by Joze Macek. Dreamstime Stock Photos.

researcher at what is now New Mexico State University. From there, the pepper somehow made its way into southern Colorado, where farmers grew it haphazardly until Bartolo began to improve the crop by using classic crop-breeding techniques.

The Plants and Pods

The growth habit of the 'Pueblo' chile is lower and more branching than the typical Anaheim and 'Mirasol' peppers. The fruit grows in an upright position but may bend downward as the pods reach full maturity and weight. The 'Mosco' has thick fruit walls and high yield potential. It is more pungent than a typical Anaheim-type pepper, having an estimated pungency of 5,000 to 6,000 SHU, or five to six times the pungency of a 'NuMex Heritage 6-4' pod, better known as a Hatch. The 'Mosco' fruits are broad shouldered, taper to a point at the end, and measure five to six inches in length. The pods start green and mature to a bright red. Bartolo believes that the red 'Mosco' chile is a bit sweeter with a subtler heat than the green. The 'Mosco' cultivar is an excellent roasting chile, green or red.

And that's what convinced Steve Lunzer, regional coordinator at Whole Foods Market, to replace Hatch chiles with those from Pueblo in 2015. He said, "The Pueblo chile has been overlooked. I'm a huge green chile fanatic myself. I also quickly realized that Pueblo has a more intense flavor, thicker meat on the peppers, and are much better for roasting." He announced that Whole Foods plans to put 125,000 pounds of 'Pueblo' chiles throughout most of the Rocky Mountain region, including Colorado, Kansas, Idaho, and Utah.

Notions for Promotions

The Whole Foods Market's acceptance of the 'Pueblo' chile was a breakthrough for the southern Colorado chile industry and was the result of an intense collaboration of resources. First, because of marijuana legalization and taxation starting in 2013, the state of Colorado is awash with really green money. Next came some agricultural grants, the founding of the Pueblo Chile Growers Association, and then a trademark, a logo, a branding campaign, and agritourism with a road map for chileheads who want to visit the green chile farms in Pueblo County and get their fix right from the source.

What does your car need for traversing the highways on the chilehead roadmap? A 'Pueblo' chile-pepper license plate, obviously. The idea of a 'Pueblo' chile–group special license plate occurred during a casual conversation between state representative Daneya Esgar and Pueblo county commissioner Buffie McFadyen. "We want to make sure that all of Colorado knows that Pueblo Chile is our chile. Pueblo Chile is Colorado's Chile, and eventually will be the leading brand of chile across the United States," Representative Esgar said in a press conference—revealing a mock-up of what the license plate could look like—at the Pueblo Chile and Frijoles Festival on Friday, September 23, 2016.

For the past 22 years, 'Pueblo' chiles have been taking over Pueblo for an entire weekend during the annual Pueblo Chile and Frijoles Festival. In 2016, the festival filled up Pueblo's Union Avenue Historic Commercial District with booths for 'Pueblo' chiles and related foodstuffs. It ran for a half mile, passing the Riverwalk and the headquarters of the Professional Bull Riders Association. More than 40 music acts filled four entertainment tents, playing rock, folk, R&B, blues, and pop, and about 50 food vendors sold green chile–infused treats, ranging from Hopscotch Bakery's chile shortbread to O'Hara's green chile jam. Another booth sold "green chile ice cream sundaes" with green chile–infused chocolate and raspberry toppings. There were also competitions to see who could produce the best individual and commercial green chile dishes.

The highlight of the festival began at nightfall when chile roasters lit up the street as flames from the propane burners blackened the chiles. Farms outside of Pueblo brought in thousands of bushels of green chiles and roasted them in homemade cylindrical metal roasters that seemed to glow in the dark. The Pueblo Chamber of Commerce reported that the 2016 Chile and Frijoles Festival set attendance records. An estimated 140,000 to 150,000 people came to Pueblo for the three-day event.

Chris Markuson, director of economic development for Pueblo County, predicts a healthy economic benefit from all the new strategies that have been developed to promote 'Pueblo' chiles. "We're estimating the annual increased economic impact [of the 'Pueblo' green chile market] will be $1.1 million in 2015, and that growth rate will increase by 9.4 percent every year." Arkansas Valley chile growers took their passion for chiles a step further by trademarking and launching the Pueblo Chile brand in 2015. Markuson also thought that the trademarking could help solve a problem. "People were bringing chiles from New Mexico to Colorado and passing them off as Pueblo chiles," he said. "We wanted to make sure that was not what happens."

The Battle of the Neighboring Chile States

"The mirasol lifts its head toward the sun," bragged a proud worker from Musso Farms, one of the biggest chile growers in Pueblo County; "Hatch chile hangs its head down to the earth." Daniel Archuleta, a NASA engineer, countered comments like that in a Facebook post. "I have lived in both Colorado and New Mexico," he wrote, "and let me tell you, New Mexicans are chile purists. Colorado chile, even when they use New Mexican peppers, is like taking the best scotch you can buy and mixing it with cocaine."

In 2014, when the Denver Broncos were heading to the Super Bowl, Denver mayor Michael Hancock made a bet with the mayor of Seattle that included skis, a hoodie, and some of Denver's "amazing green chile" that was grown near Pueblo. The response from New Mexico was immediate. Katie Goetz, a spokeswoman for the New Mexico Department of Agriculture insisted: "We are the chile state." The governor of New Mexico, Susana Martinez, said, "Although New Mexico doesn't have an NFL team, we definitely win the Super Bowl of green chile every single year. Our green chile, whether from Hatch or Chimayo or anywhere else in the state, is our state's Lombardi Trophy."

Are 'Pueblo' chiles the beginning of the end for Hatch chiles? Don't count on it.

ARIZONA: DOMESTICATING THE DESERT

The Spanish had already settled New Mexico for a century before they undertook the taming of the Sonoran Desert near what is now Tucson. It wasn't until 1700 that the Jesuit priest Padre Eusebio Francisco Kino founded the San Xavier del Bac Mission, said to be the finest example of mission architecture in the United States. Kino spent the last 24 years of his life on a missionary tour of Sonora and Arizona that covered 75,000 miles and resulted in the founding of 73 *vistas* (local churches) and 29 missions. In addition to converting the Native Americans to Christianity, Kino—and the Spanish settlers who followed after his death in 1711—introduced cattle, sheep, goats, horses, mules, and chickens into Arizona. Additionally, the Spanish planted wheat, barley, grapes, onions, garlic, cabbage, lettuce, carrots, peaches, apricots, pomegranates, figs, pears, peaches, quinces, and mulberries.

Chile peppers were probably introduced about this time as well, though any records about them appear to be lost. We do know that in 1776, as the eastern colonies were fighting for their independence from England, Fray Pedro Font was describing the agriculture and food of the Spanish settlers of the desert in his diary: "They plant with a stick and grow maize, beans, squash, and chiles. With their fingers, they eat tortillas and beans, chiles, and tomatoes. They begin their day hours before breakfast, stopping about 10 a.m. for maize cereal, sweet with honey or hot with red pepper. The main meal is in the early afternoon, usually tortillas, beans, and salsa. On special occasions, bits of meat in cornmeal are steamed in husks."

Font's description of tamales is still accurate today, and despite the introduction of European foods into Arizona, the Spanish padres were quite aware of the native plants growing around them. In 1794, the improbably named missionary Ignaz Pfefferkorn described his encounter with the wild chile, the chiltepín: "After the first mouthful the tears started to come. I could not say a word and believed I had hellfire in my mouth. However, one does become accustomed to it after frequent bold victories, so that with time the dish becomes tolerable and finally very agreeable."

Sonoran Style

Unlike the food in New Mexico and Texas, "Mexican" cooking was not well established in Arizona until much later in time. Whatever Mexican cuisine had been established there was wiped out in the early 1800s and did not reappear until the immigration from Mexico began later in the century. In fact, as late as 1880, the Mexican American population of Arizona was fewer than 10,000 people. Thus, Arizona versions of norteño cookery were developed at least two centuries after New Mexicans were growing and eating their heavily spiced versions.

Generally speaking, Arizona cuisine is not as fiery as that of New Mexico or Texas; the chiles used most are mild New Mexican types, and many Sonoran recipes call for no chiles at all. Mexican poblanos and dried anchos are surprisingly uncommon except in heavily Hispanic neighborhoods. These general rules are often contradicted when the fiery chiltepín enters the picture. This progenitor of the modern chile pepper grows wild in Sonora and southern Arizona on perennial bushes, as in Texas. The red berry-like pods are harvested and dried and then crushed and sprinkled over soups, stews, and salsas.

However, as is true for the entire country, jalapeños and the hotter New Mexican varieties are steadily invading Arizona. Growers are increasing the size of fields, and more of the fiery fruits are being imported from New Mexico. Jalapeños, chipotles, and serranos are also being imported from Mexico, so, as with the rest of the country, Arizona is starting to heat up.

Perhaps the most basic Sonoran-style dish is *machaca*, which evolved from carne seca. These days, the words are used interchangeably in Arizona, but they are actually two different things. In frontier times, dried beef was rehydrated, then allowed to stew with chiles and tomatoes until it fell apart. These days, since it is no longer necessary to dry meat, machaca is simply meat that is stewed, again with chiles and tomatoes, until it can be shredded (the Spanish verb *machacar* means "to pound"). The shredded meat is then used to stuff *burros*, as burritos are called in Arizona.

Another basic Sonoran-style dish is chiles rellenos, such as in this recipe from the *Bazar Cook Book*, published in 1909 by the Ladies' Aid Society of Tucson's First Congregational Church: "Take green chile peppers, roast on top of the stove, roll in cloth to steam until cold, then peel (after being steamed in this way, the skins are easily removed). Cut off tops. Scoop out carefully to remove the seeds and veins and fill with mixture made of grated Mexican cheese, chopped olives, chopped onion. Dip in egg and cracker meal and fry in hot lard as you would oysters. Serve hot."

In Arizona, huevos rancheros are surprisingly served Texas-style, with fried eggs served over wheat or corn tortillas and then smothered in a mild ranchero sauce that often contains tomatoes. There are at least three different styles of "Sonoran-style" enchiladas served in the state. One version, prepared around Douglas where most of the New Mexican types of chiles are grown, is similar to New Mexican enchiladas in that it uses a chile sauce rather than a gravy. Another is more like the Tex-Mex enchiladas, and a third has been moved virtually intact from Sonora.

In the westernmost part of the Southwest, wheat tortillas are more popular than corn, primarily because farmers in both Sonora and Arizona grow more wheat than corn. These tortillas are usually quite large—as much as 16 inches across—and are stuffed with meat, beans, and cheese, and called burros, which are more popular than enchiladas.

Perhaps the most famous Arizona specialty dish is the chimichanga, a dish whose name is translatable only as "thing-a-ma-jig." It is a burrito (usually stuffed with beans or ground meat, chiles, and cheese) that is deep-fat fried and served with guacamole and a pico de gallo–type salsa.

Anne Lindsay Greer, an expert on Southwestern cuisine, observes of Arizona food: "Though 'Sonoran style' is the popular term used to describe this food, fast-food chains have had a devastating effect on the regional idiom, particularly in the western part of the state. 'Authentic' Sonoran style is more likely to be found around Tucson, where the peasant roots of the cuisine are still a source of pride."

FEATURED CHILE PEPPER: NEW MEXICAN

For nearly a century, confusion has reigned over the proper name for the long green varieties of chiles that turn red in the fall. Originally, they were developed and grown in New Mexico; however, seeds were transported to California during the early part of this century and the pod type was given the name Anaheim.

Since few—if any—chiles are grown near Anaheim these days, it makes little sense to use that name to describe them. Chile experts at New Mexico State University made a decision to use a more accurate descriptive term. Hence, the name of this type is now New Mexican. Varieties within this type will include "Anaheims," California strains, and the numerous New Mexico–grown cultivars such as 'Big Jim,' 'NuMex Heritage 6-4,' and 'Española Improved.' To put it simply, the Anaheim has been reduced from a pod type to a variety, and the pod type has been renamed New Mexican.

Since there are significant differences among New Mexican varieties, what follows is a description of the most commonly grown cultivar, 'NuMex Heritage 6-4.' The plant measures between 20 and 30 inches high, has an intermediate number of stems, and its habit varies between prostrate and compact. Corolla color is white with no spots. The leaves are ovate, medium green in color, fairly smooth, and approximately 3 inches long and 2 inches wide. The fruit is smooth, elongate, and pendant, measures between 6 and 7 inches in length, and is bluntly pointed. New Mexican varieties vary between 100 and 10,000 SHU. However, most New Mexican varieties are in the 500–2,500 range.

While Emilio Ortega was growing chiles near Anaheim, development and improvement of the modern cultivars began in New Mexico. In 1907, Fabian Garcia, director of the New Mexico Agricultural Experiment Station, developed the 'No. 9' or 'College 9' cultivar and succeeded in his goal of standardizing chiles into recognizable cultivars so that farmers could know precisely what they were growing. By 1950, the 'No. 9' cultivar had been crossed with larger

cultivars to produce 'New Mexico No. 6-4,' the most popular cultivar of the New Mexican type ever released.

In New Mexico, Arizona, California, and parts of Texas, the New Mexican cultivars are the principal chile peppers used in the American versions of Mexican cooking. Although the names of the dishes may be similar, the styles of cooking and tastes are quite different. In New Mexico, red or green chiles can appear in every meal and in every dish imaginable: drinks, salsas, sauces, salads, stews, roasts, casseroles, vegetables, dressings, candies, and desserts.

THE NUMEX CHILES OF NEW MEXICO STATE UNIVERSITY

My good friend Harald Zoschke assembled this montage of chile cultivars developed by the Department of Plant and Environmental Sciences at NMSU.

1 *NuMex Suave Orange* and **2** *NuMex Suave Red* These two mildly pungent habanero-type chiles were released in 2004.

3 *NuMex Mirasol* Released in 1993, this chile type is called 'Mirasol' because the fruits are erect and point to the sun. It is an ornamental; for instance, in the Southwestern United States, wreaths made with chiles are a popular tourist product.

4 *NuMex Las Cruces Cayenne* This is a high-yielding, high-heat cayenne pepper with a maturity similar to that of 'Large Red Thick,' an early maturing cayenne cultivar. Released in 2010, it helps farmers who supply cayenne mash to the Louisiana cayenne hot sauce manufacturers.

5 *NuMex Heritage Big Jim* Released in 2013, this cultivar has superior flavor, a uniform and higher heat level, greater plant and pod uniformity, and higher yield as compared with its earlier version. It is the largest NuMex chile cultivar grown in the state.

The Myth of Hatch Chiles

The mating of the words "Hatch" and "chile" first occurred publicly nearly 30 years ago when the village of Hatch launched the first Hatch Chile Festival. The second mating of the two words occurred when the Hatch Chile Company began producing and selling enchilada sauce under the trademark Hatch Chile Co.® in 1995. (Note: A prior usage connecting Hatch and processed jalapeño peppers under the trademark Hatch Select® first occurred in 1988.)

The constant linking of the two words "Hatch" and "chile" over nearly 30 years has led consumers to believe that there is a horticultural variety of unprocessed chiles known as Hatch. I've been asked repeatedly if I think that the best chile from New Mexico is the Hatch variety. I always reply that's there's no such thing as a Hatch chile.

I believe that "Hatch Chile" is now a marketing term for unprocessed chile peppers grown in New Mexico and should not be controlled by any particular organization by way of a certification mark.

NuMex chiles. Photograph by Harald Zoschke.

1 NuMex Suave Orange

2 NuMex Suave Red

3 NuMex Mirasol

4 NuMex Las Cruces Cayenne

5 NuMex Heritage Big Jim

6 NuMex Heritage 6-4

7 NuMex Orange Spice

11 NuMex Bailey Piquin

8 NuMex Centennial

9 NuMex Twilight

10 NuMex Sunglo

12 NuMex Piñata

6 *NuMex Heritage 6-4* The name was chosen to distinguish the new select-ed cultivar from the original cultivar, 'New Mexico No. 6-4,' while retaining its association. 'NuMex Heritage 6-4' has superior flavor compared with the orig-inally grown, standard green chile pepper. This is the cultivar most commonly grown by farmers in New Mexico.

7 *NuMex Orange Spice* Released in 2015, 'NuMex Lemon Spice,' 'NuMex Orange Spice,' and 'NuMex Pumpkin Spice' jalapeños provide unique mature fruit colors—yellow, orange, and pumpkin orange, respectively—which are not currently available in any other jalapeño variety in the marketplace.

8 *NuMex Centennial* Released in 1994 to honor the 100th-year anniversary of the university, 'NuMex Centennial' and **9** *NuMex Twilight* are piquin-type ornamental chiles. These compact plants were developed for growing in small containers, but they are suitable for cultivation in a formal garden bed.

10 *NuMex Sunglo* is an ornamental de árbol–type chile. This chile is unique in providing a source, as well as alternative colors, for making mini-ristras and chile wreaths. It was released in 1991.

11 *NuMex Bailey Piquin* New Mexico State University's Chile Pepper Breeding Program (CPBP) released this machine-harvestable piquin-type chile pepper in 1991. It was named in honor of Alton L. Bailey, New Mexico State University Extension Vegetable Specialist Emeritus, a valuable cooperator with the CPBP, who actively helped evaluate this selection.

12 *NuMex Piñata* This jalapeño is unique in the range of colors it expresses during fruit ripening; it is the only known jalapeño cultivar that changes in color from light green to yellow to orange and finally to red as it ripens. That was the result of a spontaneous genetic mutation. It was released in 1998.

recipes

CHILES RELLENOS CLÁSICOS
(CLASSIC STUFFED CHILES)

yield 4 servings   *heat scale* medium

The 'Big Jim' cultivar of New Mexican chile makes excellent chiles rellenos (stuffed chiles) because the pods are large and meaty, but any of the New Mexican varieties will work well in this recipe. Top these chiles rellenos with either a Classic New Mexico Green Chile Sauce or a Classic New Mexico Red Chile Sauce. Serve with shredded lettuce and guacamole, Spanish rice, and refried beans.

4 green New Mexican chiles, roasted, peeled, with stems left on	3 tablespoons flour
Cheddar cheese or Monterey Jack, cut in sticks	1 tablespoon water
Flour for dredging in a large bowl	¼ teaspoon salt
3 eggs, separated	Vegetable oil for frying
	Chile sauce for topping

Make a slit in the side of each chile and stuff the chiles with the cheese sticks. Dredge the chiles in the flour.

Beat the egg whites until they form stiff peaks.

Beat the yolks with the water, flour, and salt until thick and creamy. Fold the yolks into the whites.

Dip the chiles in the mixture and fry in 2 to 3 inches of oil until they are a golden brown. Serve topped with the chile sauce.

CLASSIC NEW MEXICO RED CHILE SAUCE

yield about 3 cups   *heat scale* medium

This basic sauce can be used in any recipe calling for a red sauce—either traditional Mexican or New Southwestern versions of beans, tacos, tamales, and enchiladas.

10 to 12 dried whole red New Mexican chiles

1   large onion, chopped

3   cloves garlic, chopped

3   cups water

Place the chiles on a baking pan and put in a 250-degree F. oven for about 10 to 15 minutes or until the chiles smell like they are toasted, taking care not to let them burn. Remove the stems and seeds and crumble them into a saucepan.

Add the remaining ingredients, bring to a boil, reduce the heat, and simmer for 20 to 30 minutes.

Puree the mixture in a blender until smooth and strain if necessary. If the sauce is too thin, place it back on the stove and simmer until it is reduced to the desired consistency.

LOUISIANA CRAWFISH BOIL

yield 8 to 10 servings   *heat scale* medium

When our video crew traveled to Avery Island to shoot footage about Tabasco Sauce for Heat Up Your Life, Paul McIlhenny put us up at the Marsh House and personally prepared a crawfish boil for us in the backyard. If you can't find crawfish, substitute shrimp or crab. (See the photo on page 102.)

10 gallons water	1 tablespoon black peppercorns
10 bay leaves	1 teaspoon whole cloves
½ cup salt	4 large potatoes, quartered
¾ cup ground red chile pepper	4 ears of corn, quartered
¼ cup whole allspice	4 celery ribs, quartered
2 tablespoons mustard seeds	3 medium-size onions, halved
1 tablespoon coriander seeds	3 garlic bulbs, halved crosswise
1 tablespoon dill seeds	5 pounds crawfish
1 tablespoon red pepper flakes	Tabasco Sauce to taste

Bring the water to a boil in a 19-quart stockpot over high heat. Add bay leaves and all the ingredients, except the crawfish, to the water. Return to a rolling boil.

Reduce heat to medium, and cook, uncovered, 30 minutes.

Add the crawfish. Bring to a rolling boil over high heat; cook 5 minutes.

Remove stockpot from heat; let stand 30 minutes. (For spicier crawfish, let stand 45 minutes.)

Drain the crawfish. Serve on large platters or newspaper. Add Tabasco Sauce as needed.

CHILI QUEEN'S CHILI

yield 6 to 8 servings   *heat scale* medium

According to legend, this is one of the San Antonio chili queens' original recipes. Some changes have been made in order to take advantage of modern ingredients. Never cook beans with chiles and meat! Serve them as a separate dish if you must.

2	pounds beef shoulder, cut into ½-inch cubes
1	pound pork shoulder, cut into ½-inch cubes
	Flour for dredging
¼	cup suet
¼	cup lard
1	quart water
4	ancho chiles, stems and seeds removed, chopped fine
1	serrano chile, stems and seeds removed, chopped fine
6	dried red chiles, stems and seeds removed, chopped fine
3	medium onions, chopped
6	cloves garlic, minced
1	tablespoon cumin seeds, freshly ground
2	tablespoons Mexican oregano
	Salt to taste

In a bowl, lightly flour the beef and pork cubes. Quickly cook them in the suet and pork fat, in a pot, stirring often. Add the onions and garlic, and sauté until they are tender and limp. Add the water to the mixture and simmer for 1 hour.

Grind the chiles in a molcajete or blender. Add to the meat mixture. Add the remaining ingredients and simmer for an additional 2 hours. Skim off the fat.

variations Spices such as cumin, coriander, and Mexican oregano may be added to taste. Some versions of this sauce call for the onion and garlic to be sautéed in lard—or vegetable oil, these days—before the chiles and water are added.

CLASSIC NEW MEXICO GREEN CHILE SAUCE

yield about 2 cups   *heat scale* medium

This all-purpose sauce recipe is from the southern part of New Mexico, where green chile is the number one food crop and is used more commonly than the red form. It is used with enchiladas and is often served over scrambled eggs.

1	small onion, chopped
2	cloves garlic, minced (optional)
2	tablespoons vegetable oil
6	green New Mexican chiles, roasted, peeled, seeds and stems removed, chopped
½	teaspoon ground cumin
2	cups chicken broth or water

In a pan, sauté the onion and garlic in 2 tablespoons of oil until soft.

Add the chile, cumin, and water, and simmer for ½ hour. The sauce may be pureed in a blender to the desired consistency.

variations To thicken the sauce, make a roux by sautéing 1 tablespoon flour in 1 tablespoon vegetable oil, taking care not to let it burn. Slowly stir the roux into the sauce and cook to the desired thickness. Ground coriander and Mexican oregano may be added to taste. For added heat, add more New Mexican chiles or a serrano or two.

GREEN CORN TAMALES

yield 20 or more tamales   *heat scale* mild

The "green" in this favorite Arizona tamal refers both to the green chiles and the fresh, or "green," corn used in the filling. Tamales are usually a seasonal dish that is prepared in the summer and early fall, when fresh corn is available. This recipe is from Poncho's on South Central in Phoenix and is delicious as a side dish.

3	cups corn masa
¾	cup lard or shortening
½	teaspoon baking powder
	Pinch of salt
1 ½	cups green chile cut into thin strips
1 ½	cups grated longhorn cheese
3	cups freshly cooked white corn, pureed in a blender
20	or more corn husks, rinsed

In a bowl, combine the masa, lard, baking powder, and salt, and thoroughly mix until the dough is very fluffy. Add the remaining ingredients except the corn husks and mix again, taking care not to crush the chile strips. Let the mixture sit for at least 10 minutes.

Place a large spoonful of the mixture on a corn husk, roll up, and tie each end in a bow with a thin sliver of corn husk.

Place the tamales in a steamer and steam over medium heat for about an hour.

To serve, place the tamales on a plate and allow the guests to unwrap their own.

Shortly after Christopher Columbus brought back the first chile pods with seeds from the West Indies on his second voyage, the word was out about the pungent pods. Peter Martyr, a cleric in the service of the Spanish court at Barcelona, wrote in 1493 that the new hot pepper was called "caribe, meaning sharp and strong," and that "when it is used, there is no need of black pepper." From that point on, chiles spread like wildfire across the globe.

At any time after 1493, chile seeds from the West Indies were available to the Spanish and Portuguese for transmittal to ports anywhere along their trade routes. Spanish and Portuguese ships returning home were not only loaded with gold and silver; they also carried packets of the seeds of the New World plants that were destined for monastery gardens. Monks and amateur botanists carefully cultivated the capsicums and provided seeds to other collectors in Europe.

In 1494, papal bulls of demarcation divided the world into Spanish and Portuguese spheres of influence; Portugal controlled Africa and Brazil, while Spain effectively ruled the remainder of the colonies of the New World. Thus Spanish and Portuguese traders, setting out from both the Iberian Peninsula and the major colonies of these two nations, used their extensive trade routes to spread chiles throughout the Eastern Hemisphere.

IN SEARCH OF A EUROPEAN CHILE CUISINE

Considering the fact that chiles arrived so early in Spain and Portugal, it is something of a mystery that these countries never became hotbeds of fiery cuisines. Why did Spaniards and Portuguese in the New World fall in love with chiles while their countrymen back home virtually ignored them? The most probable answer is that the colonists were literally inundated by chiles and chile dishes; in Spain and Portugal the seeds were scarce, the pods were rare and exotic, and cultivation was not extensive.

Although the Spanish and Portuguese never embraced chiles with the fervor of other cultures, a few fiery foods caught on and are still served today on the Iberian Peninsula. The spicy Spanish paprika called *pimentón picante* is the foundation of many of the spicy foods of Spain. Food historian Sharon Hudgins notes: "In 1893, when the Spanish gastronome Ángel Muro published his first edition of *El practicón*—Spain's nineteenth-century equivalent of *The Joy of Cooking*—he referred to both sweet and hot pimentón. Muro claimed that paprika had 'become, for almost

Chile greenhouse of the late Mario Dadomo at the Azienda Agraria Sperimentale Stuard in Parma, Italy. Photograph by Dave DeWitt.

all the inhabitants of Spain, but primarily for those of [the region of] Old Castile, an article of prime necessity, like salt and vinegar.' He went on to say that in Old Castile 'not a single food is put on the table that is not seasoned with sweet or hot paprika.' He also pointed out that large amounts of paprika were consumed in the region of Extremadura, not only as an ingredient in cooked dishes but also as an element in preserving the many types of chorizos (pork sausages) produced in that part of Spain."

Pimentón de La Vera—a smoked paprika from La Vera region of Extremadura—was the first paprika to earn a *denominación de origen* designation, or "protected name status," in Spain, ensuring that only the special paprika produced there could bear that title. The hot type is used in winter soups and Galician *pulpo*, or octopus. The octopus is boiled and sliced, then sprinkled with olive oil, salt, and hot pimentón powder. Interestingly, there are recipes for chorizo and potato stews that utilize all three of the types of pimentón. Substitutions for pimentón include hot paprika and New Mexican ground red chile, but for a better approximation of the smokiness of the pimentón, mix in some ground chipotle chile. Conversely, hot pimentón can be substituted for any recipe calling for paprika or ground red chile. Chili con carne enthusiasts should experiment with pimentón in their never-ending quest to improve their chili.

Sharon Hudgins also wrote about *pimientos de padrón*, a favorite tapa in many Spanish bars. "These are fresh whole green peppers from the region of Galicia, which

are quickly fried in olive oil, then sprinkled with coarse sea salt. As the bartender will warn you, '*Unos pican y otros non*' (some are hot and the others are not), but until you bite into them, you don't know which of those little green peppers is going to blow your taste buds away." My wife and I tried these in a bar in Torremolinos, outside of Málaga, and they were exactly as the bartender described them.

In Portugal, the *piri-piri* is the pepper of choice. Food writer Blaise Lawrence explains: "*Piri-piri* means 'pepper-pepper' in Swahili, the pan-African language, and sometimes the chile is called 'pili-pili.' It is a generic term that can apply to any member of the *Capsicum* genus, but in Portugal it specifically refers to a small-fruited variety that resembles a piquin. The question is: how did it get to Portugal? The answer is ironic because after Columbus brought back chile seeds to the Iberian Peninsula on his second voyage to the New World, Portuguese traders carried the seeds to their African colonies of Angola and Mozambique. Soon, spread by birds, traders, and farmers, chiles conquered all of Africa and became an inexpensive way for people to spice up their bland foods. Sometime during this process, traders took small, hot pods back to Portugal where they were called *piri-piri*, the Swahili term."

In Portugal, there are dozens of piri-piri sauces and the same pepper spices up *molhos* (salsas), *caldos* (soups), tuna pâté, and *cataplana*, a signature dish that is named after the wok-like copper pressure cooker in which it is prepared. There are several variations of this classic dish, but it usually has clams and spicy Portuguese sausage in it.

Perhaps the most unusual Portuguese dish is *enguias*, which are baby eels boiled in olive oil and water with chiles and garlic.

ENGLAND'S CURRIES

The first meal on our European chile pepper trip was deliciously spicy. After we landed in London, we dropped in on Sanjay and Reena Anand, who are producers of elaborate Asian weddings. Because we had traveled with them in India, they knew we loved fired-up food, so they treated us to an Indian brunch to ease our jet lag. Their cook prepared unusual chapaties, a round flatbread, with a variety of ingredients such as potatoes, cauliflower, and green onions. They were served with a marvelous yogurt and a fiery mango pickle with small hot red chiles (or *chillies*, as they spell it there). The brunch climaxed with a medium-hot curried lamb that set the tone of our European tour: it was the first of many curries with no turmeric, and it suggested the oncoming food theme of the trip—the food of the former colonies heating up the former colonial powers.

After brunch, we were picked up by Pat and Dominique Chapman, who were determined to show us as much of rural England as possible in six days. Pat is one of England's foremost food experts, and he is called the "King of Curries" there because he has authored dozens of books on the subjects of curries and other Indian foods. On our way to Stonehenge, he railed about what was happening to English food. On one hand, it was great that thousands of Indian, Bangladeshi, and other Asian restaurants had opened in the UK over the past 30 years. On the other hand, British traditional pub grub was turning into mass-marketed, predictable slop as large corporations took over individual pubs, made them part of their chains, and then standardized the food. The meals are now partially prepared in a central location and shipped to the various pub locations, where they are assembled by "deskilled chefs" according to the formula of the central office of a chain like Beefeaters. I am not making up the term "deskilled chef"—it is precisely what the words imply, and I cannot imagine anyone putting it on his or her résumé.

The Feast of Bath

Then it was on to Bath, but we got caught up in the traffic headed toward the huge Glastonbury Festival, an outdoor rock concert attracting more than 100,000 fans, so after we stopped dead in our tracks and didn't move for 20 minutes, Pat had to pull out his maps and make some radical detours. Along the way, signs read "Concealed Entrance," and I was certain that some sort of weird hay cutter would

Traders at a market stall selling curry and varieties of cooked foods at Camden Market, London. Photograph by Alena Kravchenko. iStock.

pull out in front of us. But the detour was worth it, for in Bath we were treated to one of the spiciest and most delicious meals of the entire trip, at the Eastern Eye.

Let me set the scene: The restaurant, owned by Shuhan and A. H. Choudhury, is set in an elegant Georgian mansion built in 1824. It has enormous round skylights and a sumptuous interior. And the food! Because Pat is the author of the *Good Curry Guide*, which rates the UK curry restaurants, he is quite a celebrity and always an honored guest. As such, he is not allowed to order dinner. The owners always order for him so that he will always have their premier dishes. This time, the four of us dined on samosas, pastries filled with vegetables; *seekh kebab*, highly spiced minced lamb grilled in a tandoori oven; *Dhaka* chicken roll, marinated and fried chicken; and chicken *hariyali*, a Nepalese dish also cooked in a tandoori oven. Those were just the starters.

Then we graduated to chicken *jalfrazy*, which was sautéed in fresh chile and tomatoes; Bengali king prawn masala; chicken tikka masala, marinated in yogurt and then barbecued; and *ayre tarkari*, a Bangladeshi fish served in a very spicy sauce. Those were just the chef's recommendations. Served along with all these delicious entrées were the vegetarian accompaniments: *navrattan pilau*, the nutty and fruity spiced rice; mushroom *bhaji* (sautéed); eggplant bhaji (also sautéed); and *saag ponir*, homemade Indian cheese cooked with spinach with a touch of spice and fresh cream. Although the final accompaniment contained no chile, it was one of the best dishes we tasted that night.

For dessert, we were treated to the liqueur called *paan*, which is made from the leaf of the *Piper* genus. Specifically, this pepper leaf is *Piper betle*, so named because it is used to wrap the betel nut, the mildly euphoric, habit-forming substance that is chewed all over the subcontinent. The liqueur paan smelled and tasted like an exotic flower. It is a digestive with spiritual values symbolic of love, friendship, and respect. We certainly felt that way after the wonderful feast of Bath.

The Banquet at Jaipur and the Malaysian Satis House

The restaurant known simply as Jaipur is located in the city of Milton Keynes and is owned by Mr. Ahad, known simply as Ahad, another person who was on our tour of India with Pat and Dominique Chapman. He greeted us effusively, ordered up drinks (our choice), seated us, and proceeded to have his waiters bring out a banquet: his choice, of course. That turned out to be Bengal *niramesh*, spiced mixed vegetables; *aachari ghost*, pickled lamb; king prawns; tandoori lamb chops; lamb tikka masala; yellow lentils with fried garlic; swordfish curry; and lamb shank curry. The banquet was superb—but was it better than the Feast of Bath? I'll be diplomatic and say they were equal, and both were superior to most of the dishes we were served in India.

We motored on to the little town of Yoxford in Suffolk, where Chris and Chiu Blackmore own a combination bed and breakfast (seven rooms) and Malaysian restaurant. The Satis House, as it's called, dates from the early 1800s, and Charles Dickens was a friend of the family who owned the house between 1812 and 1878. In *Great Expectations*, Dickens writes: "'Satis House,' said Pip, 'that's a curious name.' 'It's Greek, Latin, or Hebrew, maybe all three,' she replied. 'It means that whoever lives in the house could wish for nothing more.'"

That was certainly the case for our third former-colony feast. Malaya, of course, was a British colony, and once again we were treated to an example of how the

Jaipur Restaurant in Milton Keynes. Photograph by Mary Jane Wilan.

former colonies are heating up the Brits. Under the direction of Chiu, Pat and Dominique, Tony and Jenny Stockman (who also went on the India trip), and Mary Jane and I were treated to appetizers consisting of various satays, skewered meats; pork ribs marinated in plums and hoisin sauce; stir-fried vegetables with garlic; lamb with black pepper, an intensely flavored dish that was fiery hot yet without chiles; and beef penang, a curry-like dish that was hot with chiles. Once again the former colony was striking back at the colonial power and overpowering us with its spices.

FIERY FRANCE

Some varieties of chile peppers are given treasured status in certain regions of the world, where they are celebrated in art, legend, the kitchen, and festivals. Paprika has such status in Hungary, the jalapeño in Laredo, Texas, and the mole varieties ancho and pasilla in central Mexico. The New Mexican varieties are worshiped from Taos to Las Cruces, and from Gallup to Tucumcari in the Land of Enchantment. But a little-known chile is acclaimed in—of all places—southwestern France, where it has gained controlled-name status, much like Champagne sparkling wine and Roquefort cheese. That chile is *piment d'Espelette*, or the Espelette pepper, and it has become a cultural and culinary icon in that part of Basque country.

When Columbus brought chile peppers to Europe from the Caribbean after his second voyage in 1493, they were first grown in monastery gardens in Spain and

Portugal as curiosities. But soon the word got out that the pungent pods were a reasonable and cheap substitute for black pepper, which was so expensive that it had been used as currency in some countries. So the best thing about chiles—in addition to their heat and flavor—was that they did not have to be imported from India; anyone could grow them as annuals in temperate climates.

Carried by Spanish and Portuguese explorers, numerous varieties of chiles quickly spread throughout the Mediterranean region, Africa, and the rest of the Eastern Hemisphere, where they permanently spiced up world cuisines such as those of India, Southeast Asia, and China.

In France, however, chiles were established as a tradition in just one region: the Nive Valley in the Southwest, and especially in the village of Espelette to the south. It is believed that chiles were introduced into the Nive Valley by Gonzalo Percaztegi in 1523, the same year that corn first made its appearance there. At first it was thought to be related to black pepper and was even called "long black American pepper," and it wasn't until the seventeenth century that it was placed in its own genus.

Much like ristras in the American Southwest, the red pods of the Espelette peppers are threaded on cords and are hung on the sides of buildings and from racks. The strings of peppers—translated variously as "braids" or "tresses"—are allowed to dry in the sun. They are then ground into powder or made into commercial pastes. Interestingly, the earliest use of the ground Espelettes is connected to yet another uniquely American crop: cacao, or chocolate.

In the seventeenth century, chocolate became very popular in Europe both in candies and in drinks. Chocolatiers in Bayonne, perhaps influenced by tales of Montezuma's favorite drink, combined Espelette powder and chocolate. A century later, hams from the Basque area were covered with Espelette pepper to redden the ham before curing. The powder was also used in the making of Bayonne hams and some pâtés, sausages, blood sausages, rolls, and pies. From this point on, Basque cooks began using the Espelette pepper in place of black pepper in seafood dishes.

About the same heat scale as hot paprika, the Espelette pepper is regarded by the French as a four on the scale of one to ten. In fact, hot paprika powder can be substituted for Espelette, as can New Mexico red chile powder.

The Celebration of Peppers and Controlled-Name Status

Up until 1940, the Espelette peppers were not made into strings because the harvest was not big enough; the peppers were merely ground into powder. But as more of the peppers were grown, farmers started selling them as strings for decorative as well as culinary purposes. By the 1960s, the Espelette peppers had become so popular that the village of Espelette, population 1700, established the Celebration of Peppers, a festival much like the Hatch Chile Festival in New Mexico. The first festival was in 1967, and it is held annually the last Sunday in October. It now attracts more than 10,000 people and features food, music, dance, and games.

As the popularity of the peppers grew in France, the farmers realized that they had a very unique product, one that deserved recognition and protection. They did not want farmers in other regions to grow, for example, paprika and call it Espelette. At first they formed cooperative enterprises to protect their interests, and eventually they applied to the National Institute for Trade Name Origins for an *appellation d'origine contrôlée* (AOC). On December 1, 1999, an AOC was granted to Espelette peppers and products, giving them the same protection as more famous names, such as Champagne sparkling wine. Only 10 communities are allowed to use the name Espelette: Espelette, Ainhoa, Cambo-les-Bains, Halsou, Itxassou, Jatxou, Larressore, Saint-Pée-sur-Nivelle, Souraïde, and Ustaritz. The total growing area is about 3,000 acres.

Paprika vendor in Budapest. Photograph by Istvan Takacs. Wikimedia. Creative Commons Attribution-ShareAlike 3.0 Unported License.

HOW PAPRIKA CONQUERED HUNGARY

Paprika, of course, is a New World chile pepper that was spread around the world by way of agriculture. But paprika, in the words of Zoltán Halász, author of *Hungarian Paprika through the Ages* (1963), "found its second and, at the same time, true home in Hungary." He adds: "It was in this country that such a high level and veritable cult of the growing, the processing and the use of paprika has been achieved, the like of which cannot be found anywhere else."

Since Columbus was working for the Spanish royalty and brought back chile peppers to Spain on his second voyage in 1493, there is little doubt that Spain was the first point of their entry into Europe. But their spread throughout Europe was not only the result of the international trading of the empire of Charles V, but also resulted from the expansion of the Ottoman Empire in the eastern Mediterranean. In the sixteenth century, the empire included Bulgaria, a country called the "gardens of Europe," according to Hungarian food expert George Lang. The Turks were in possession of chile peppers, or paprika in the parlance, and they taught the Bulgarians to grow the plants. Many Bulgarians emigrated to Hungary, fleeing the Turks but also looking for better land and climate. They found it and began growing paprika, but the common belief that the Turks introduced paprika directly into Hungary is not true. "There is ample evidence that the Bulgarians brought paprika to Hungary and started its cultivation," writes Lang in *Cuisine of Hungary* (1971).

"It was at this point that paprika appeared in the history of spices," writes Halász. "Almost unnoticed, it made a modest, but, it could be added, a cheerful and charming entrance. No countries were subjugated for its sake; no brave Indians put to forced labour." But why were chile peppers immediately accepted in Hungary when it took tomatoes 300 years to enter mainstream Italian cuisine?

I think it's because paprika was originally thought to be "red pepper," just a variant of familiar but expensive black pepper, while tomatoes had no reference fruit or vegetable in the Old World and thus remained strange and suspicious to most cooks. The word "paprika" derives from the Hungarian *paparka*, which is a variation on the Bulgarian *piperka*, which in turn was derived from the Latin *piper*, for "pepper."

Tomatoes, however, made an early appearance in Hungarian cuisine. The Turks occupied parts of Hungary for 150 years, and they also appeared to have transferred both tomatoes and maize to the Hungarians via the Bulgarians. The tomato, writes Lang, "became very popular during this time and remained an essential part of the past three centuries of Hungarian cuisine." This is mostly because tomatoes and paprika were immediate paired together in *lecsó*, an essential condiment that can stand on its own as an appetizer or be used as the main flavoring ingredient of soups and stews. It is made by cooking onions in lard and then adding slices of Italian frying or banana peppers, followed by fresh tomatoes, sugar, salt, and paprika.

The most likely scenario for the introduction of paprika into Bulgaria and Hungary holds that the Turks first became aware of chile peppers when they besieged the Portuguese colony of Diu, near Calicut, India, in 1538. This theory suggests that the Turks learned of chile peppers during that battle and then transported them along the trade routes of their vast empire, which stretched from India to Central Europe. According to Leonhard Fuchs, an early German professor of medicine, chiles were cultivated in Germany by 1542, in England by 1548, and in the Balkans by 1569. Fuchs knew that the European chiles had been imported from India, so he called them "Calicut peppers." However, he wrongly assumed that chiles were native to India.

So, sometime between 1538 and 1548, chiles were introduced into Hungary, and the first citizens to accept the fiery pods were the servants and shepherds who had more contact with the Turkish invaders. Zoltán Halász tells the tale: "Hungarian herdsmen started to sprinkle tasty slices of bacon with Paprika and season the savory stews they cooked in cauldrons over an open fire with the red spice. They were followed by the fishermen of the Danube . . . who would render their fish-dishes more palatable with the red spice, and at last the Hungarian peasantry, consuming with great gusto the meat of fattened oxen and pigs or tender poultry which were prepared in paprika-gravy, professed their irrevocable addiction to paprika, which by then had become a characteristically Hungarian condiment."

In 1569, an aristocrat named Margit Széchy listed the foreign seeds she was planting in her garden in Hungary. On the list was "Turkisch rot Pfeffer" (Turkish red pepper) seeds, the first recorded instance of chiles in Hungary. Upon Mrs. Széchy's death and the subsequent division of her estate, her paprika plots were so valuable that they were fought over bitterly by her daughters, and the litigation went on for 25 years before the supreme court awarded title to Mrs. Széchy's youngest daughter.

After the settlement of this dispute, there was no mention of paprika in Hungarian writings for many years, and Halász speculates that the century between the turn of the sixteenth and seventeenth centuries was when "the silent revolution in Hungarian cooking" developed, "with paprika conquering the common people first of all." In 1604, a Hungarian dictionary listed the spice for the first time as "Turkish pepper, *piper indicum*," and the word "paprika" didn't make an appearance until 1775, when J. Csapó called it "paprika garden pepper" in his *Herbarium*.

During this time, "townspeople sprinkled their bacon with paprika, made of crudely crushed 'cherry paprika' and added it to a variety of dishes, mixing it with sour cream," notes Lang, who adds that the "landed gentry" were slower to adopt the spice but eventually "recognized that not only was paprika cheaper than black pepper, but it stimulated the appetite and had a most delightful character of its own." Also during this time, Hungarian growers developed the hundreds of paprika varieties ranging from "very hot to sugar sweet," with a wide range of colors and textures. "Somewhere along the line, the Hungarians hit on the holy trinity of lard, onion, and pure ground paprika," and "this simple combination became the base of virtually unlimited taste combinations."

Capsaicin, the chemical that makes chile peppers hot, became a major focal point of the paprika debate that soon ensued. At the end of the eighteenth century, a visiting nobleman named Count Hoffmanseg tasted paprika for the first time in a cabbage stuffing and wrote to his sister, "It stings terribly, but not for long, and then pleasantly warms the stomach!" On the other side of the debate was, of course,

Roasted pepper goulash. Photograph by Ralf Roletschek. Wikimedia. GNU Free Documentation License, Version 1.2.

the Catholic Church, with the ultraconservative Capuchin priest Ubaldis writing around the same time about Hungarian sins: "The spice of their food is some sort of red beast called paprika," he railed. "It certainly bites like the devil."

Lang notes that the nobility was the very last part of Hungarian citizenry to adopt paprika, "probably because it did not stem from aristocratic tradition." But even that refined segment of the population would eventually succumb to the conquering spice. The first time paprika turned up in a cookbook recipe was 1817, when F. G. Zenker, chef of Prince Schwarzenberg, published his *Theoretical and Practical Compendium of Culinary Arts*, which was printed in Vienna. He listed paprika as an ingredient in Chicken Fricassee in Indian Style. This was followed in 1829 with the appearance of two classic Hungarian dishes in István Czifrai's (or Czifray's) cookbook, apparently titled, simply, *The Cookbook of the Master Chef István Czifray*. The first was *halász-hal*, or fisherman's soup, mentioned above, and the second marked the first appearance in print of *paprikás csirke*, or chicken *paprikash*, perhaps the most famous Hungarian dish in the world.

It wasn't until 1844 that this dish appeared on the menu of the National Casino, the rather exclusive club of the House of Lords, but it soon became the favorite dish of Queen Elizabeth, the consort of Franz Josef I. "A queen couldn't be wrong!" proclaims Lang. "Paprika's victory was now complete." This triumph was followed by another in 1879, when the famous French chef Escoffier bought paprika during his visit to Szeged and, on his return to France, introduced it into the *grande cuisine* in the form of *gulyás hongrois* (Hungarian goulash) and *poulet au paprika* (paprika chicken), two of the most typical paprika-laden Hungarian dishes.

Around this same time, chile peppers, known as *peperoncini*, and tomatoes, known as *pomodori*, were just becoming accepted into Italian cuisine, an adoption that would forever change that country's cuisine. In 1881, bowls of chiles were often described in Giovanni Verga's realistic novel, *I Malavoglia* (rough translation: Me, Reluctantly); in 1889, Pizza Margherita with tomatoes was named for King Umberto's wife, Queen Margherita; and in 1891 the first all-Italian cookbook, *La scienza in cucina e l'arte di mangiar bene* (The Science of Cooking and the Art of Eating Well) by Pellegrino Artusi, included many tomato recipes.

Today, the great pepper-growing areas around Kalocsa and Szeged have just the right combination of soil characteristics, temperature, rainfall, and sunshine required to cultivate the numerous varieties of paprika successfully. In March, the pepper seeds are put in water to germinate, then transferred to greenhouse beds. Seven weeks later, in May, the small pepper shrubs are replanted in the open fields. Harvesting starts at the end of the first week in September and lasts for about a month, depending on weather conditions. By harvest time, the mature plants will have grown to a height of 16 to 24 inches. And the pepper pods—3 to 5 inches long and about 1 to 1 ½ inches wide—will have ripened from green or yellow to bright red.

In Kalocsa, the annual harvest is celebrated with a paprika festival in September. Known as the Kalocsa Paprika Days, it features an exhibition of food products and agricultural machinery, a professional conference on the topic of paprika, various sports events, a "Paprika Cup" international chess tournament, and a fish-soup cooking contest. But the highlight of all this is the Paprika Harvest Parade, complete with local bands and colorful folk-dancing groups, followed that same night by a Paprika Harvest Ball.

With regards to paprika, the Catholic Church seems to have reversed its original opinion of the "devilish" aspects of this pepper. "It isn't surprising how many religious festivals are connected with phases of its cultivation," Lang notes; "man sore felt the need for divine help." For example, the seeds are placed in water for germination precisely on St. Gregory's Day in early March, and the harvest begins on September 8, the feast day of the Nativity of the Holy Virgin, which in reality is a combination of a medieval festival and a "vast block party."

Types of Hungarian Paprikas

note In Hungary, paprika has a great variation and depth of flavor, having not only distinct pod types but also specific grades of the powders made from these pod types. The hottest paprikas are not the bright red ones but rather the palest red and light brown ones.

Special Quality (*különleges*): The mildest and brightest red of all Hungarian paprikas, with excellent aroma.

Delicate (*csípmentes csemege*): Ranging from light to dark red, a mild paprika with a rich flavor.

Exquisite Delicate (*csemegepaprika*): Similar to Delicate, but more pungent.

Pungent Exquisite Delicate (*csípös csemege, pikant*): A yet more pungent Delicate.

Rose (*rózsa*): Pale red in color with strong aroma and mild pungency.

Noble Sweet (*édesnemes*): The most commonly exported paprika; bright red and slightly pungent.

Half-Sweet (*félédes*): A blend of mild and pungent paprikas; medium pungency.

Hot (*erös*): Light brown in color, this is the hottest of all the paprikas.

So how do those tons of newly picked peppers get turned into the condiment known as paprika, in all of its many forms? Before the Industrial Revolution, farmers used to string all their ripe peppers by hand and hang them up in a protected place to dry. After a certain period of time, the drying process was completed in large earthenware ovens. The peppers were then crushed underfoot, and finally, pounded into a powder by means of a *kulu*, a huge mortar with a large pestle driven by human power. Water mills later replaced the kulu for grinding paprika, and by the late 1800s steam engines were being used for this task.

But until the mid-1800s it was difficult to control the pungency of the paprika produced. The capsaicin that gives paprika its spicy flavor is found in the pod's veins and seeds, which were removed by hand before the crushed dried peppers were ground into a powder. This was a time-consuming and inexact process, which yielded paprikas in taste from rather mild to fairly hot. The results were unpredictable. In 1859, the Pálfy brothers of Szeged invented a machine for removing the veins and seeds, then grinding the dried pods into a quality-controlled powder. The mill master could now determine exactly how much capsaicin was to be removed and how much should be retained. The Pálfys' technique continued to be used in Hungarian factories for almost a century—until the fairly recent introduction of modern automatic machines that wash, dry, crush, sort, and grind the peppers in a continuous process.

The Pálfys' invention made possible the large-scale commercial production of very mild (Noble Sweet) paprika, which had a much bigger export market than the hotter-tasting varieties. As the industry expanded to meet both local and foreign demand for this mild (but still richly flavored) paprika, the growers saw the advantage of cultivating a spice pepper that did not need to have its veins and seeds removed.

Ferenc Horváth of Kalocsa developed the first cultivar of Hungarian pepper that was "sweet" throughout—meaning that its veins and seeds contained very little capsaicin indeed. This kind of pepper is now favored by growers in the regions of Kalocsa and Szeged. It can be used alone, ground to produce a mild but flavorful paprika powder—or used in combination with other, hotter peppers to produce some of the standard varieties of paprika marketed by the Hungarians. But with all this emphasis on the demand and supply of *mild* paprika during the past 100 years, one is tempted to speculate that Hungarian food *before* Horvath and the Pálfys must have been much hotter than it is today.

Other countries also grow and consume paprika, including Spain, Serbia, Romania, Slovakia, Croatia, and the United States, but in only one does it reign supreme: Hungary.

In the Hungarian countryside, paprika peppers are threaded onto strings and are hung from the walls, porches, and eaves of farmhouses, much like the chile ristras in the American Southwest. As mentioned previously, today Hungary produces both pungent and sweet paprikas, but originally all Hungarian paprika was aromatic and quite hot. It was evidently too hot for some tastes, for by the turn of this century other countries were requesting that Hungary develop a nonpungent variety. By accident, farmers produced a sweet variety in their fields when they planted milder "eating" paprika with hotter "seasoning" paprika in proximity and insects cross-pollinated the two. The resulting hybrid reduced the pungency of the paprika pods and probably led to the nonpungent varieties now grown in Spain.

Food authority Craig Claiborne notes, "The innocuous powder which most merchants pass on to their customers as paprika has slightly more character than crayon or chalk. Any paprika worthy of its name has an exquisite taste and varies in strength from decidedly hot to pleasantly mild but with a pronounced flavor."

This is why, for cooking, Hungarian paprika should be favored over that produced in the United States or Spain.

Paprika has exerted a great influence on the culture of the people of central Europe. Hungarians believe that the passion of a woman is reflected in her capacity to consume the fiery, paprika-spiced food, and bad moods are often blamed on paprika considered too pungent. Paprika also has its own very popular folkloric figure, Jancsi Paprika. Often represented as a puppet, Jancsi has the shape of a red chile, complete with a large chile hat and a pod-shaped nose. Jancsi Paprika is the prototype of the folk hero, being at once valiant, generous, knowledgeable, humorous, and ingenious. He is often called the Hungarian Sancho Panza—an appropriate personification of the pungent paprika pod so beloved by the people of the region of the Danube.

For a country of just 10 million people, Hungary has some impressive agricultural production. Although it does not rank in the top 20 countries for tomatoes or potatoes, it is the number 12 country in the world for maize production, number 20 for green chile peppers—producing about 18 percent of what the US grows—and it's 19th in the world for dry chile-pepper production, which is a result of all that growing, drying, and grinding of paprika.

THEY CALL ME IL PAPA DEL PEPERONCINO

When we arrived in northern Italy, we were not expecting torrential rains and flooding, so we were relieved when the rains ended and we were greeted with a rainbow of color, which symbolized a new direction for our travel: dry and warm.

Our trip to spicy Italy was organized by Marco Del Freo, a food lover and chile-head who came out to our National Fiery Foods and Barbecue Show and invited us to visit his haunts and witness how Italians were learning to love everything hot and spicy. First we visited the wine country of Lombardy, where we stayed in an *agriturismo* B&B and nearly got flooded out when the rains hit the area hard. The first night, we and 60 other foodies attended a launch party for two new products developed by Marco that help create spiced-up dishes, including seafood, risotto, and even dessert.

With Marco translating, I gave a brief address to the diners at the restaurant associated with the Il Montù winery and *grapperia*. Based on their applause, I could tell that not only were they impressed with the food but with the products themselves. Nettare di Habanero, or Habanero Nectar, is a first pressing of olive oil and habaneros to create an aromatic and medium-hot olive oil that is used to dress foods such as salads, breads, and even grilled meats. Spirit of Habanero is an

Lombardy vineyards. Photograph by Dave DeWitt.

award-winning grappa infused with habaneros until a medium heat level is achieved to make a delicious—and spicy—cordial or liqueur.

Of course, while in this area, we were surrounded by vineyards. Lombardy has the highest concentration of vineyards in the entire country, and although it was too wet to walk through them, they were truly beautiful right after the rain. I particularly enjoyed the fruits of these vineyards in the form of an Il Montu Bonarda, a tasty and dry red wine. After two nights at the B&B, we moved on to Marco's house and the rainbow. Marco and his wife, Maggie, live on top of a small mountain near Parma in the agricultural village known as Salsomaggiore, and their view is the valley called Bellacavalle, known for its incredibly tasty Parmesan cheese.

On Sunday, May 9, Marco and I worked the chile plant sale and food fair at the Azienda Agraria Sperimentale Stuard (Stuard Agricultural Experiment Station) in Parma with his new products, Spirit of Habanero grappa and Habanero Nectar olive oil. Mario Dadomo, the station director and the "Paul Bosland of Italy," had 442 different varieties of chiles to choose from, which was like having ChilePlants. com in one convenient greenhouse. The public was there in good numbers to buy the plants and sample products both spicy and nonspicy. A group of about 30 Italian chileheads showed up, and I had my picture taken with them. On one side of us was a honey producer, and on the other side our friend Mauritzio was selling his 'Jolokia' products, including Big Bang Powder, so Marco joked that the public could choose from Paradiso (Heaven), Purgatorio (Purgatory), or Inferno (Hell).

This was an allusion to Dante's *Divine Comedy* but I'm not sure that the Italians got the literary joke. As a show producer, it was interesting for me to watch the flow of the crowd: in the morning there was a strong crowd, then it dropped off to nothing during lunch and "siesta time," and then was strong again after about 3 p.m. Marco's sales were good, which bodes well for the new products. We closed down about 6 p.m., then drove to a winery with nearly vertical vineyards atop Monte Roma (Mount Rome), 350 meters above sea level. Then, in typical Italian fashion, another 30-mile drive to dinner at an agriturismo (agricultural tourism) restaurant atop another "mountain." I loved the grilled sirloin steak served on top of a solid block of salt. We got back to Marco's house at midnight—16 hours of hustle—but fun!

THE PEPERONCINI OF ITALY

Note: This section was compiled and illustrated by Harald Zoschke, the German chile-pepper expert who now lives with his wife, Renate, in Bardolino, Italy.

Just like corn and tomatoes, chile peppers were unknown in Italy before Columbus's discovery of the New World in 1492. Imagine Italian cuisine without tomato sauce, polenta, risotto, and peperoncini. This all changed in the sixteenth century, when trade ships distributed the New World goodies across the globe. At first hot peppers were considered poisonous because they are Nightshades, but soon they became the spice of choice, especially in the Calabria, Puglia, and Basilicata regions, as well as in Sicily. Why particularly in the South? One reason could be the antibacterial properties of the fiery fruit, quite helpful in a hot climate with no refrigeration back then. For example, there's a lot of *peperoncino piccante* in *'nduja*, the traditional Calabrian spreadable sausage. Despite the fire that came with the hot pods, peperoncini are mostly used with moderation in traditional Italian cuisine—flavor is considered more important than heat.

As in Mexico and New Mexico, chiles mild and hot are tied to *trecce* (ristras) and air-dried. The mild dried *peperoni* are often fried crispy in olive oil (*peperoni cruschi*, pronounced "kruushki"), a tasty appetizer. The hot ones are used for pepper flakes and for powder (*peperoncino macinato*).

Today there are endless varieties of peperoncini in Italy, as well as the mild relatives derived from them, the peperoni. Numerous are also the names given to them, and these vary from region to region. They're all of the *Capsicum annuum* species. But with the many chileheads also in Italy these days, "international" chiles like jalapeño, habanero, or even 'Carolina Reaper' can also be found here. In fact, many Italian interest groups, on Facebook as well as in real life, enjoy growing and consuming peppers from all over the world.

SHORT DESCRIPTIONS OF THE ITALIAN PEPERONCINI/PEPERONI

1 *cornetto* Horn-shaped, cayenne-like chile with pleasant heat. 7/10. With the same appearance, there is also a 'Diavolicchio Diamante' cultivar that's being used for the annual Peperoncino Eating Championship in Diamante, Calabria. With 40,000–50,000 SHU, it is even hotter— HEAT 8/10.   SUBSTITUTE cayenne.

2 *bacio di Satana* The "Satan's kiss" peppers from the Italian region of Abruzzo are often filled with capers or tuna and packed in oil as an appetizer (antipasto). Shape sometimes round, sometimes slightly longish. HEAT 6/10.   SUBSTITUTE 'Cherry Hot.'

3 *naso di cane* Named for its dog-nose shape, great for filling and drying. The latter often done in southern Italy, threaded as trecce (ristras). HEAT 6–7/10.   SUBSTITUTE 'Cherry Hot.'

4 *ciliegino* A small cherry-pepper type that's often packed in olive oil, used for antipasti or as a tasty snack. HEAT 0–1/10.   SUBSTITUTE 'Cherry Mild,' cascabel.

5 *dolce calabrese* Heatless thin-fleshed pepper that's widely used in this region. Used fresh green or red-seared in oil, as a side dish, or dried after frying in olive oil (peperoni cruschi). Many Calabrians dry their peperoni dolce tied as trecce (ristras) on their balconies in late summer. Also used ground as a paprika powder. HEAT 0–1/10.   SUBSTITUTE milder New Mexican green chile varieties.

6 *sigaretta di Bergamo* With the slim shape slightly suggestive of a cigarette, this thin-walled pepper from the northern Italian Lombardy region can be pickled green or used fresh in salads, but the red mature pods also dry well. HEAT 1–3/10. (Other regions also have sigaretta peppers with different shapes.) SUBSTITUTE cayenne with larger pods.

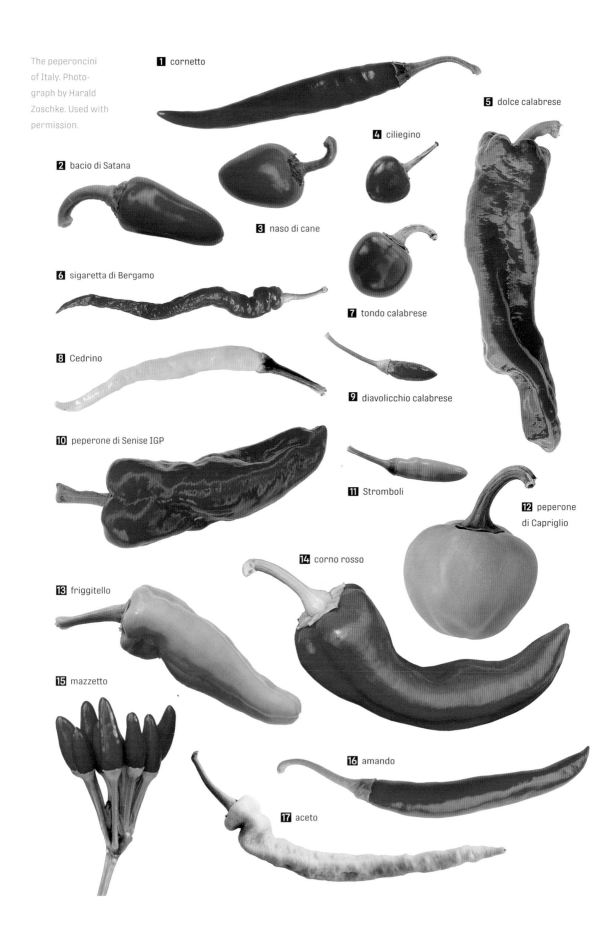

The peperoncini of Italy. Photograph by Harald Zoschke. Used with permission.

1 cornetto

2 bacio di Satana

3 naso di cane

4 ciliegino

5 dolce calabrese

6 sigaretta di Bergamo

7 tondo calabrese

8 Cedrino

9 diavolicchio calabrese

10 peperone di Senise IGP

11 Stromboli

12 peperone di Capriglio

13 friggitello

14 corno rosso

15 mazzetto

16 amando

17 aceto

7 *tondo calabrese* The ball-shaped pepper from Calabria, served stuffed with tuna or porcini mushrooms as an antipasto.
HEAT 6/10.   SUBSTITUTE 'Cherry Hot,' 'Cherry Bomb.'

8 *Cedrino* Originally from Panama, now common in Italy. Bright yellow pods with a slight citrus note, surprisingly hot.
HEAT 7–8/10.   SUBSTITUTE yellow cayenne.

9 *diavolicchio calabrese* Most likely the hottest Calabrian chile, "little devils" indeed. Prolific, dries well.
HEAT 9/10.   SUBSTITUTE *pequin* (piquin), chiltepín.

10 *peperone di Senise IGP* Red and horn-shaped, used since the sixteenth century crisped in olive oil (peperoni cruschi) and dried/ground for a flavorful paprika powder.
HEAT 0/10. Pods vary in actual shape, even on the same plant.
SUBSTITUTE milder New Mexican green chile varieties.

11 *Stromboli* Named after the famous Sicilian volcano, this attractive pepper grows in clusters. Great ornamental, also in containers.
HEAT 6–7/10.   SUBSTITUTE pequin (piquin), chiltepín.

12 *peperone di Capriglio* Grown in the area around Capriglio in the province of Asti, located in the Piedmont region of northwestern Italy, not far from Turin. Recognized since 2010 by the Presidio Slow Food, this more than 100-year-old cultivar resembles a small bell pepper, maturing to a nice yellow color. The fruits have a mild, sweet flavor and crisp, juicy flesh, ideal to just slice and munch, to fill, to put in salads, or to put on the grill.
HEAT 0/10 (Harald's mild-pepper favorite.)   SUBSTITUTE yellow bell peppers.

13 *friggitello* The Italian frying pepper. Originally from Campania, now available all over Italy, even in supermarkets. Various cultivars go by this name. Matures to red but is usually sold and consumed green.
HEAT 0/10.   SUBSTITUTE pimientos de padrón, *shishito*, mild New Mexican green chiles.

14 *corno rosso* A tasty bell pepper alternative from Piedmont (Northern Italy).
HEAT 0/10.   SUBSTITUTE *corno di toro*, Carmen (named after the opera), *cubanelle*, gypsy, bell pepper.

15 *mazzetto*   A hot beauty from Sicily that grows in clusters that look like bouquets, hence the name. Widely used in the Italian kitchen.
HEAT 7/10.   SUBSTITUTE 'NuMex Mirasol,' thin-fleshed cayenne (milder), *santaka* (hotter).

16 *amando*   From Calabria, similar to cayenne but meatier.
HEAT 6/10. SUBSTITUTE meaty cayenne (Louisiana or 'NuMex Las Cruces Cayenne').

17 *aceto*   Named "vinegar" because that's how these pale green peppers are canned; used on pizza or for antipasti.
HEAT 1/10.   SUBSTITUTE green (immature) cayenne of a larger pod type.

THE PEPERONCINO-EATING CONTEST: A BURNED-OUT THEATER OF THE ABSURD

It took a long time for chile peppers to have any impact on Italian cuisine, despite the fact that they first appeared there in 1526, which indicates that they were transferred about the same time as tomatoes were, which makes sense because of Spain's control over Naples at the time. Antonio Latini briefly mentioned them as an ingredient in some sauces, and a century later Vincenzo Corrado called peppers a "vulgar, rustic food." It wasn't until the nineteenth century that pickled peppers were mentioned; however, in the twentieth century chile peppers called peperoncini were grown extensively in the regions of Calabria and Senise, where they have gradually dominated the local cuisine.

Since Columbus was responsible for the introduction of chile peppers into Europe, it was only fitting that the first Peperoncino Festival was held in 1992, 500 years after he found them in the New World. Organized by the Accademia Italiana del Peperoncino, or the Italian Pepper Academy, and its leader, Enzo Monaco, the festival started out small but in recent years has drawn tens of thousands of visitors to the small town of Diamante in Calabria, the "toe" of the "boot" that is Italy. The festival is held for four days surrounding the first weekend in September, on the Lungomare, the promenade on Diamante's seaside. The Italian and other European chileheads are drawn by a unique blend of a chile-vendor market, music, movies, satire, art, folklore, and samplings from local restaurants. More than a hundred vendors have booths offering up everything imaginable related to the beloved peperoncini, including these items:

Peperoncino stand, Diamante. Photograph by Dave DeWitt.

- *salsiccia*, a lean pork sausage with fennel seeds and peperoncini

- *la bomba*, a sort of spiced-up sangria

- a Calabrian peperoncino chocolate liquor called *crema di cacao al peperoncino*

- pungent peperoncino pasta products

- Grappa al Peperoncino di Calabria, the famous Italian grape brandy in a kicked-up version with chiles floating in the bottle

- Olio Santo (holy oil), bright red chile-infused olive oil in decorative bottles

- *alici al peperoncino*, a Calabrian specialty, freshly hatched sardines densely packed with peperoncini and some salt

- a plethora of sweet-heat products, including *baci di Casanova*, dark chocolates with a creamy-smooth chile-spiced center; *confettura di peperoncino al cioccolato*, a spicy chile-chocolate spread; *crostata piccante*, a short pastry tart with a spicy-sweet icing; *cannoli al peperoncino*, crunchy pastry pipes filled with vanilla creme, spiced up with plenty of peperoncino bits; and *dolce della nonna al peperoncino*, grandma's sponge cake with a kick

- *vinagra*, a red wine infused with chiles

The Accademia del Peperoncino was predicting an attendance of 150,000 for the five days of the Peperoncino Festival the year I visited it as the guest of honor, in 2010. Being a show producer, I was skeptical of the estimate, but after witnessing the crowds myself, I was convinced that the projection was not exaggerated. Of course, peperoncini were just an excuse for the Italians to party, and there were many different foods being served, but that said, the festival focused on chiles to the point of madness usually found only at the National Fiery Foods and Barbecue Show held annually in Albuquerque. So of course they had to have a chile-eating contest, and I had to be a judge of it. I had thought that my nickname, the Pope of Peppers, might offend the Catholic Italians, but not so. I saw newspaper headlines that called me "Il Papa del Peperoncino."

The idea that 10 victims would attempt the torture of eating nearly the weight of a chihuahua of hot chiles at one sitting in front of a cheering crowd of 2,000 peperoncinoheads may seem strange to Americans, but just consider the extreme eating contests we have in the US. Stuffing down dozens and dozens of hot dogs or funnel cakes while attempting to avoid vomiting is great fun for everyone, right?

Well, I had been drafted, protesting, into serving as one of the head judges, and my job was to first avoid laughing while judging, and second to make sure the contestants were not stuffing the chopped chiles into their pockets and shoes. Third, I had to count the number of each contestant's finished plastic plates and multiply it by 50 grams to determine total weight—all while Queen's "We Are the Champions" blared from the speakers at top volume. And without even a *birra* to help me through it.

The champion from 2009, Anna Greco, was in the number-one position and was determined, it seemed, to surpass her own record of 750 grams. She got off to a great start, wolfing down with a spoon what seemed to be finely chopped serranos while her fans chanted "Anna, Anna, Anna" to the beat of the Queen song. Her competition was not much, and they began to drop like burned-out flies. One ate 50 grams and then ran from the stage, the wimp. Two more soon gave up with embarrassed looks as if they had farted during confession. Anna hung in there, plowing through the peperoncini, but hey—she outweighed most of the men. Finally, after 15 minutes or so, everyone gave up except for Anna, who was now holding her stomach—11 ½ plates of hot stuff devoured—and slowing way down, her face red and contorted with pain. Was that froth on her mouth?

All eyes were on Anna, and all the TV cameras too. Would she break the record? Would she get a medal from the Italian prime minister? But then, in a shocking turnaround, Anna clutched a napkin to her lips, staggered to her feet, and left the table bending over. Anna, it seemed, had lost her peperoncini. Would she be disqualified? Would she return to the table, now having more room in her stomach? To the "Anna, Anna, Anna" chants, she *did* return, and could not continue, but was crowned the champion with a lousy 640 grams, about 1.4 pounds. I wanted my money back.

Suddenly, I remembered the Italian Party Principle: The length of time it takes for a party to break up is directly proportional to the number of Italians there. Once my friend Marco took me to a dinner party where it took the 20 guests about an hour to devour the five courses but just to say all the good-byes took another 45 minutes! I looked around and calculated 35 people on stage and 2,000 in the audience. We would be there until the Christmas presents were opened! In the confusion, I snuck to the back of the stage, down the small steps, and out to the street—ciao, baby, bye-bye! I found the nearest bar and to hell with the birra, I was soon sipping a whiskey—that's Italian for Scotch. A reliable witness told me, the next day, that a half hour later, the on-stage host, Gianni Pellegrino, was still asking into the mike, "Mr. DeVitt, Mr. DeVitt, where are you?"

Chile peppers had conquered yet another European country.

Chicken tikka masala. Photograph by bhofack2. iStock.

INDONESIA IN AMSTERDAM

The first thing we did after our train arrived in Amsterdam was to check into the appropriately named Eden Hotel. Our room was much larger than we expected and nicely furnished. However, we weren't going to spend much time in it. The second order of business was to find some fiery food, so we asked the concierge to suggest a good Indonesian restaurant, and he pulled a card for the Indrapura and gave directions. It was just a few blocks away on Rembrandtplein (*plein* means "plaza").

Along our walk to Rembrandtplein, we passed several coffee shops where the patrons, sitting outside, were sipping either coffee or beer and casually smoking joints or puffing on hashish pipes. Amsterdam is a very liberal city, we discovered, but we had other spices on our minds. The Indrapura turned out to be a beautifully furnished medium-size restaurant with teak-lined walls and attractive Indonesian Dutch waitresses dressed in batik sarongs. We were asked if we had reservations, which, of course, we did not. But fortunately, we were there early, so we promised them we would be finished before the crowd arrived.

We ordered some wine for Mary Jane, a dark beer for me, and some Indonesian-style egg rolls with a spicy chile sauce to dip them in. For our main courses, Mary Jane tried the Beef Rendang, and I feasted on the Udang Rica (Spicy Prawns). Both were excellent, with medium heat, and Peter ten Cate, one of the owners of Indrapura, provided recipes—see the end of the article. Mary Jane can never resist dessert, but at least she ordered one with spice in it—Indonesian Cinnamon Cake, topped with Cinnamon Ice Cream. I took a little taste and it was superb. By the time we finished dessert, the restaurant was full, with people waiting, so we took our leave of the charming establishment and walked off the dinner by wandering through the neighborhood.

The following day we had a lesson on why Indonesian restaurants are so popular in the Netherlands. We visited the Scheepvaartmuseum (Netherlands Maritime Museum) and went on board the *Amsterdam*, a replica of a Dutch spice-trading ship that was built from 1985 to 1990. The original was launched in 1749. It was an interesting experience for me because I had been on board a replica of the *Batavia*—an earlier spice ship that dated from 1628—when we had visited Australia. The improvements in 121 years of shipbuilding were remarkable. Not only was the *Amsterdam* considerably larger and more luxuriant, I could actually stand up in its cargo holds, which was impossible inside the *Batavia*. The originals of both vessels carried vast quantities of spices and other precious cargo from the Spice Islands, now Indonesia, back to the Netherlands.

Indonesia was, of course, a Dutch colony, but the Dutch interest in the area dated back to 1595, when they began colonization. In 1602, they established the Dutch East India Company to exploit the riches of the region: nutmeg, cloves, mace, and later, black pepper. The Dutch domination of the archipelago lasted until 1949 when Indonesia achieved independence. During that long period of time, there was an enormous amount of interaction and trade, and quite a bit of Indonesian immigration into the Netherlands, which accounts for the popularity of Indonesian food. Chile peppers, introduced by early Portuguese traders, quickly became popular in Indonesian cooking and became a valuable spice commodity in themselves. Indonesia is the third largest grower of chiles in the world. Many Dutch greenhouses grow Indonesian varieties to supply the restaurant trade in the Netherlands.

So the Netherlands is yet another country where the people have fallen in love with chile peppers due their colonial history.

ENRAGED PASTA (*PENNE ALL'ARRABIATA*)

yield 4 servings   *heat scale* hot

Of all the spicy Calabrian dishes, this one is probably the best known. Feel free to increase the heat scale by adding more peperoncini. This recipe is from Harald Zoschke, who lives with his wife, Renate, in their house overlooking Lake Garda. The name arrabiata means "angry" in Italian.

2   tablespoons olive oil

2 to 3 medium onions, chopped

2 to 3 cloves garlic, finely chopped

2   small chile pods, red, hot (Thai, serrano, or bird's eye), seeds and stems removed, finely chopped

2   fourteen-ounce cans chopped tomatoes; for example, Progresso

1   pound *penne rigate* pasta

3 ½   ounces Parmesan cheese, grated

    Pinch of sugar, salt

In a pan, heat the olive oil over low heat. Add the onions, garlic, and chiles, and cook until the onions are golden brown. Add the tomatoes and cook, uncovered, for about 15 minutes over low to medium heat.

Meanwhile cook the pasta al dente in lightly salted water, according to the instructions on the package.

Grate the Parmesan cheese and stir half of it into the sauce. Season with salt and sugar to taste.

Drain the pasta well, mix thoroughly with the sauce, and sprinkle with the remaining Parmesan cheese. Serve piping hot.

CHORIZO SAUSAGE

yield about 2 pounds   *heat scale* medium

This is the classic Spanish sausage, which was later transplanted to Mexico and flavored with different chiles. Traditionally, the links are air-dried in a cool place before being refrigerated. For a great breakfast treat, remove the sausage from the casings, crumble, and fry it in a pan. Add eggs that have been whisked, and scramble them with the sausage. Serve with a chile sauce made from pimentón. You will need a sausage-stuffer attachment for your grinder for this recipe. In some versions of this recipe, other seasonings, such as cinnamon and coriander, are added.

2	pounds lean pork, coarsely ground	1	teaspoon freshly ground black pepper
3	cloves garlic, mashed in a press	2	teaspoons salt
¼	cup vinegar	¼	teaspoon ground cumin
1	teaspoon oregano	1	teaspoon oregano
¼	cup hot pimentón	1	yard of sausage casing

In a large bowl, combine all ingredients. Using the sausage stuffer, force the mixture into the casings and twist off links and tie them.

CHICKEN TIKKA MASALA

yield 6 to 8 servings   *heat scale* medium-hot

British foreign secretary Robin Cook once commented: "Chicken Tikka Masala is now a true British national dish, not only because it is the most popular, but because it is a perfect illustration of the way Britain absorbs and adapts external influences. Chicken Tikka is an Indian dish. The masala sauce was added to satisfy the desire of British people to have their meat served in gravy." There are dozens and dozens of recipes for this dish, but this one is typical. Note: This recipe requires advance preparation.

THE CHICKEN

¼	cup yogurt
3	teaspoons minced ginger
3	teaspoons crushed garlic
¼	teaspoon white pepper
¼	teaspoon cumin powder
¼	teaspoon ground mace
¼	teaspoon ground nutmeg
¼	teaspoon green cardamom powder
½	teaspoon hot red chile powder
¼	teaspoon turmeric
3	tablespoons freshly squeezed lemon juice
¼	cup vegetable oil
2	pounds boneless chicken breast, cut into 1-inch cubes
	Melted butter for basting

THE TIKKA SAUCE

¾	cup tomato paste
1	cup tomato sauce
2	large tomatoes, chopped
2	teaspoons minced ginger
2	teaspoons minced garlic
2	green chilies, such as serranos, seeds and stems removed, minced
1	tablespoon red chile powder
2	teaspoons ground cloves
8	green cardamoms
	Salt to taste
3	tablespoons butter
⅔	cup cream
1	teaspoon ground fenugreek
2	teaspoons minced ginger
	Honey to taste, if needed

In a large bowl, combine all the ingredients for the chicken, except the chicken and melted butter, and mix well. Add the chicken and marinate overnight in the refrigerator.

The next day, allow the chicken to come to room temperature and preheat the oven to 350 degrees F. Bake the chicken for 8 minutes, basting with the butter twice. Drain the excess marinade and bake for another 2 minutes. Turn off the oven but don't remove the chicken.

To make the sauce, heat 4 cups of water in a pot and add the tomato paste, tomato sauce, chopped tomatoes, ginger, garlic, green chiles, chile powder, cloves, and cardamoms, and cook over medium heat until reduced to a thick sauce. Strain the sauce, adjust the salt, and return it to the heat. Bring to a boil, then turn off the heat. Add the butter, cream, fenugreek, and ginger, and stir. If the sauce tastes too sour, add honey to taste.

On each plate, serve the chicken and spoon the sauce over it.

MOLHO DE PIRI-PIRI

yield 1 ¼ cups   *heat scale* medium

Thanks to Blaise Lawrence for contributing this recipe. This is the traditional sauce or marinade that is offered throughout Portugal in restaurants, cafés, and bars. The recipe can vary a little from place to place, but this is the basic one. Note: This recipe requires advance preparation.

1 cup olive oil	Combine the ingredients in a jar and shake vigorously. Then store in a refrigerator for a few weeks to blend the flavors.
1 ½ tablespoons ground piri-piris, or substitute piquin or Thai chiles	
½ tablespoon paprika	
1 clove garlic, minced, or more to taste	
2 teaspoons sea salt	
½ teaspoon dried oregano	

CHICKEN *BASQUAISE* WITH ESPELETTE *PIPERADE*

yield 4 to 6 servings   *heat scale* mild to medium

Piperade is a colorful pepper sauce that is only spicy when made in the Basque region. This simple but delicious dish is often served at the Celebration of the Peppers. Serve it boiled with potatoes and green beans.

½	cup olive oil
4	medium onions, chopped
3	cloves garlic
4	green bell peppers, seeds and stems removed, chopped
2	red bell peppers, seeds and stems removed, chopped
4	large tomatoes, peeled and chopped
3	tablespoons Espelette powder, or more to taste (substitute hot paprika or New Mexico red chile powder)
	Pinch of thyme
1	chicken, cut up
	Salt and pepper to taste

Heat ¼ cup olive oil in a large sauté pan and sauté the onions and garlic for 5 minutes, stirring occasionally. Add the bell peppers and cook over medium heat for 10 minutes. Add the tomatoes and Espelette powder and cook for 20 minutes, stirring occasionally. Add the thyme, salt, and pepper, and transfer to a bowl. Wipe out the pan and heat the remaining ¼ cup of oil. Brown the chicken in the oil until golden, turning often. Pour the piperade over the chicken, reduce the heat, cover, and simmer until tender, about 30–40 minutes. Add salt and pepper to taste.

SPICED COCONUT BEEF (RENDANG)

yield 4 to 6 servings   *heat scale* medium

In Indonesia, this is the preferred method of cooking water buffalo, a fairly tough meat. Since these animals are scarce in Amsterdam, this recipe from Indrapura Restaurant features beef. It is served over rice. The chef at Indrapura notes: "Use mature coconuts. Taste before you add salt during the cooking." To make coconut milk from scratch, grate the coconut and soak the flesh in hot water.

SPICE PASTE

20   shallots, peeled and chopped

5   cloves garlic, peeled

½   teaspoon turmeric powder

1   small fresh piece of ginger, peeled

½   teaspoon salt

7   fresh red chiles, such as jalapeño, seeds and stems removed, chopped

Small amount of water, if needed

THE RENDANG

1   3-pound chuck steak, cut into 1-inch cubes

8   cups coconut milk (unsweetened)

2   lemongrass stalks, bruised

1   whole tamarind pod

In a blender or food processor, combine the ingredients for the spice paste and puree until smooth.

Place the beef and spice paste in a wok over high heat and sauté for 5 minutes. Add the remaining ingredients. Stirring continuously, bring the mixture to a boil and cook until the coconut milk has thickened.

Turn the heat down to low and cook until the oil comes out of what is left of the gravy, and stir continuously. Let the meat and spices fry in the oil until the color is deep dark brown, still stirring. The length of the cooking process should be around 4 hours. Remove the lemongrass stalks and the tamarind pod before serving.

Chile peppers are ubiquitous in Africa. We saw in chapter 5 how they took over the entire country of Hungary, but here they conquered a continent. They are produced commercially by every country on the continent and have entered every possible niche in the complex cuisines in Africa countries, which not only have their own culinary creations but also have those of the colonizing countries of England, France, Portugal, Spain, Belgium, Italy, the Netherlands, and Germany. Out of the 54 African countries and 2 disputed territories (Western Sahara and Somaliland), only 2 were never colonized: Ethiopia and Liberia.

According to the 2009 statistics provided by the Food and Agriculture Organization of the United Nations, 7 African countries are among the world's top 20 producers of fresh chiles and peppers: Egypt (#7), Nigeria (#8), Algeria (#11), Tunisia (#12), Morocco (#14), Ethiopia (#16), and Ghana (#18). Hungary finished at number 20. In the production of dried chiles and peppers, Hungary did a little better, finishing 19th to Morocco's number-20 position, but it was still beaten by 6 African countries: Ethiopia (#6), Ghana (#10), Nigeria (#12), Egypt (#13), Benin (#16), and Côte d'Ivoire (#18).

Because the subject of chile peppers and cooking with them in Africa is so complex, the standard region-by-region examination will not suffice here. To show the depth of the chile pepper's adoption by the Africans, I'm going to use a cuisine-based model rather than the regional model simply because there are too many countries to cover for the geographical approach. From the pods themselves, I'm going to move on to spice mixtures and curries, hot sauces and pastes, and finally the most common types of other chile foods, from snacks to main dishes. Hopefully, this will be a better way to demonstrate the use of chiles with both native African ingredients and the imported New World foods.

PILI-PILI AND THE PODS THEMSELVES

Since the Arabic countries north of the Sahara are linked culturally, economically, and gastronomically more closely with the Mediterranean region than with the rest of Africa, there is little doubt that chiles first appeared in North Africa. In the first place, the Strait of Gibraltar separates the Iberian Peninsula and North Africa by only a few miles, so it is a logical assumption that chiles would filter

Kirstenbosch National Botanical Garden near Cape Town. Photograph by Dave DeWitt.

southward from Cadiz to Tangier by at least the early 1500s. In the second place, the Turks completed their conquest of North Africa in 1556, and since they had already introduced chiles into Hungary, it makes sense that they also carried them to Tunisia, Algeria, and Libya.

Although chiles probably appeared first in North Africa, they did not spread into the rest of Africa from that region but rather were brought by Portuguese explorers and traders. Even before Columbus, Portuguese exploration of Africa had proceeded down the west coast of the continent between 1460 and 1488. When Vasco de Gama rounded the Cape of Good Hope, crossed the Indian Ocean, and landed in India in 1498, he established the trade route for spices and other goods that the Portuguese controlled for more than a century.

By 1482 the Portuguese had settled the western "Gold Coast" of Africa, and by 1505 they had colonized Mozambique on the east coast. By 1510 they had seized Goa in India and had established a colony there. During this time, it is suspected that chile peppers were introduced by way of trade routes between Lisbon and the New World. By 1508 Portuguese colonization of the Pernambuco region of Brazil meant that both the *annuum* and *chinense* chiles prevalent there were made available for importation into Africa. The introduction of sugarcane into Brazil in the 1530s and the need for cheap labor was a cause of the trade in slaves, and an active passage of trade goods between Brazil and Africa sprang up.

The most likely scenario for the introduction and spread of chile peppers into Africa south of the Sahara is as follows. Varieties of *Capsicum annuum* and *chinense* were introduced into all West and East African Portuguese ports during the 40 years between 1493 and 1533, with the introduction into West Africa logically preceding that into East Africa. The chiles were first grown in small garden plots in coastal towns by the Portuguese settlers and later by the Africans. Although it has been suggested that chiles were spread throughout Africa by Europeans during their search for new slaves, the simplest answer is the best. The Portuguese may have been responsible for the introduction of chiles into Africa, but spreading them was for the birds. History—and evolution—repeated themselves. Precisely in the same manner that prehistoric chiles spread north from South to Central America, chiles conquered Africa.

African birds fell in love with chile peppers. Attracted to the brightly colored pods, many species of African birds raided the small garden plots and then flew further inland, spreading the seeds and returning the chiles to the wild. Chiles thus became what botanists call a subspontaneous crop—newly established outside of their usual habitat, and only involuntarily spread by man. From West Africa, birds moved the peppers steadily east, and at some time chiles either reached the coast of East Africa or met the advance of bird-spread chiles from Mozambique and Mombasa. They also spread chiles south to the Cape of Good Hope. We must remember that these chiles were being spread by birds centuries before the interior of Africa was explored by Europeans. So when the early explorers encountered chiles, it was only natural for them to consider the pods to be native to Africa.

A nineteenth-century traveler to Angola, Joachim Monteiro, commented on the wild chiles he saw there.

> It grows everywhere in the greatest luxuriance as a fine bush loaded with bunches of the pretty bright green and red berries. It seems to come up spontaneously around the huts and villages, and is not otherwise planted or cultivated. . . . It has a most violent hot taste, but the natives consume it in incredible quantities; their stews are generally of a bright-red colour from the quantity of this pepper added, previously ground on a hollow stone with another smaller round one. Their cookery is mostly a vehicle for conveying this chili pepper.

This bird-planting cultivation was still evident in 1956 when Pierre de Schlippe, a senior research officer at the Yambio Experimental Station in the Congo, reported that chiles had become the most important cash crop after cotton in the Zande District with, as he put it, "very little encouragement and no supervision whatsoever." When he asked a Zande tribesman whether he preferred chiles to cotton as a cash crop, the farmer replied, "Do the birds sow my cotton?" De Schlippe noted in his book on the Zande system of agriculture that the tribesman was suggesting that one should never do for oneself what others will do. "It is safe to assume that chiles as a cash crop had no influence on agricultural practice whatever," wrote de Schlippe.

The famous and notorious African bird's eye chile is both wild and domesticated and is also known in English as African devil chile, in Swahili as pili-pili, and in Kamba (a Bantu language) as *ndul*. It should be pointed out that pili-pili (also spelled *piri-piri* and *peri-peri*) simply means "pepper-pepper" and is a generic term for any African chile. Most sources state that the bird's eye is *Capsicum frutescens*, making it a relative of the Tabasco chile. It has grown wild in Africa for centuries but has been under commercial cultivation for many years in Uganda, Malawi, and Zimbabwe. Growing African bird's eye chiles is very labor-intensive and they require handpicking. Pungency can vary according to precise variety of bird's eye, where it is grown, and environmental conditions. The bird's eye, particularly the Ugandan variety, is thought to be the most pungent chile that is not of the *chinense*

species (hence its notoriety), measuring up to 175,000 SHU. In a test of a variety provided by German chile gardener Harald Zoschke, the Malawi bird's eye variety from Africa was measured at 112,226 SHU, and the same variety grown in Harald's garden was measured at 99,579 SHU.

Reputedly, the hottest African chiles are those called "Mombasa" and "Uganda," which are *Capsicum chinense*, probably introduced by the Portuguese from Brazil. In some parts of Africa, these habanero-type chiles are called "crazy-mad" peppers, and "in Manyuema and Urua [in the Congo] there grows a pepper so excessively hot that Arabs who would eat bird's eye chilies by handfuls were unable to touch it," writes Verney Lovett Cameron in his book *Across Africa* (1877). "It is a small, round, red fruit about the size of a marble." One of the most notorious, the ominously named *fatalii* of the Central African Republic is a superhot *chinense* that analytical chemist Marlin Bensinger has measured in his laboratory at 350,000 SHU.

Pili-pili (and its variant spellings) has become the de facto common term for the chile pepper in Africa. There are hundreds of other names for the chile peppers of Africa because of the sheer number of languages spoken on the continent. The Portuguese there call the chile *pimento*, the English refer to it as *chilli* and *capsicum*, the Arabic words for it are *shatta* and *felfel*, and the French word for chile is *piment*. Tribal names vary greatly: chile is *mano* in Liberia, *barkono* in northern Nigeria, *ata* in southern Nigeria, *sakaipilo* in Madagascar, *pujei* in Sierra Leone, and *foronto* in Senegal. All of these names can be confusing, as well as the hot sauces and spice mixtures made with them, but I will try to sort them out.

FROM HARISSA TO BERBERE: THE HOT SAUCES

A complex and powerful spice compound is the chile-based *harissa*, of Tunisian origin but found all over North Africa. Harissa sauce is a classic North African condiment, which combines cayenne or other dried hot red chiles with cumin, cinnamon, coriander, and caraway. It is extremely hot and is used as a condiment, a marinade, a basting sauce, and as a salad dressing. Harissa is often served on the side as a dipping sauce for grilled meats such as kebabs and is also served with couscous.

A similar spice paste, essential in Ethiopian cooking, is called *berbere*, which is made with the hottest chiles available, plus up to eleven spices. It is served as a side dish with meat, or used as a coating for drying meats, and is an indispensable ingredient in the dishes known as *wat*, or *wet* (depending on the transliteration), which are spicy, curry-like stews of lamb, beef, chicken, beans, or vegetables (never pork).

Identical to berbere in terms of ingredients, *awaze* takes the paste concept into a new dimension by creating a thinner hot sauce from it. The paste is spread thin and dried in the sun, combined with more cinnamon, salt, cardamom, and cloves, and then ground to a fine powder. This powder is mixed with water and mashed

Olives and harissa sauce, Tangier, Morocco. Photograph by Dave DeWitt.

with cooked garlic and onion to a thin consistency. As is typical with Ethiopian hot sauces, it is generally served over raw meats. Sometimes green chiles are used with basil to make a much milder version of awaze, but it's still used over raw meats.

Captain Theophilus Conneau mentioned West African "palavra sauce," which is the same as the *palaver* sauce. The name is borrowed from the Spanish *palabra* meaning "word" or "discussion," and in English it specifically means a discussion with or among African tribes. "Its hot, pungent ingredients mingle in the pot as heated voices mingle in the excitement of a palaver," writes Carol MacCormack, an anthropologist who studied the sauce-making techniques of the Sherbro tribe of southern Sierra Leone, where this sauce is called *pla'sas*. Red palm oil is a key ingredient in this sauce, as are chopped greens such as cassava leaves (called "callaloo" in the West Indies) or spinach. Locally grown leaves such as *platto*, *bologi*, and *bitterleaf* are often utilized.

Among the Yoruba of West Africa, "meat is always cut fine to be cooked," according to T. J. Bowen, author of *Central Africa* (1857). "Sometimes it is stewed, but it is usually made into *palaver* sauce which the Yorubas called *obbeh*, by stewing up a small quantity of flesh or fish, with a large proportion of vegetables, highly seasoned with onions and red pepper. *Obbeh*, with *ekkaw* or boiled yam, pounded or unpounded, is the customary diet of all classes, from king to slave."

In Ghana, "for a quick sauce, onions, peppers, tomatoes, and salt are ground together raw," writes Lynn Bryden, an anthropologist, "mixed with a tin of mackerel or sardines in oil, and served with other 'slices' (slices of boiled vegetables—yam, plantain, *cocoyam* [taro], cassava) or *kenkey* (steamed fermented maize dough)." Bryden also writes about the importance of these kinds of stews at a nubility [coming of age] ceremony of the Avatimes, a tribe living in the Togo hills. The girl sits on a low stool while her aunt from her father's side places porridge and stew in front of her. Eager children are then called and they "wolf down the food." Water is poured over their hands and falls into the empty food dish. The children are sent away and the father's sister gives the girl this water "three times to drink." I'm no anthropologist, but it seems to me that this ritual is the symbolic passing on—to the girl who is now ready for marriage and having children of her own—of the essence of feeding children.

A famous African food based on a hot sauce is piri-piri, Mozambique's "national dish." The same word describes small hot dried red chiles; a sauce or marinade made with those chiles; and the recipes combining shrimp, chicken, or fish with the piri-piri sauces. Such fiery combinations are so popular in Beira and Maputo that piri-piri parties are organized. The dish has even been introduced into Lisbon, where it is served with considerably less chile heat. Laurens van der Post, the famed South African historian, describes the process of making the sauce:

> Of course, every cook in Mozambique had his own particular way of preparing *piri-piri*. I have chosen one provided by a Portuguese housewife of Mozambique. According to her instructions, one begins by squeezing out some lemons, passing the juice through a sieve, warming it in a pan, inserting peppers and chillies that must be red (and freshly picked, she emphasized). They are simmered on low heat for just five minutes. The mixture is then taken from the stove, drained of its juice and the peppers are pressed into a fine paste. A pinch of salt is added and the pounding continues until there are no lumps left in the pulp. The pulp is returned to the pan with the original lemon juice and further simmered while being constantly stirred. This then is the *piri-piri* sauce which can be eaten with steak, mutton, fowl, fish, and crustacean and always best I should say with rice of some kind to provide the exact civilising corrective to the pagan excitement of the sauce.

As we've seen, some distinctive sauces sprang up from numerous collisions of cultures, but there were some hot sauce duplications and amalgamations. A perfect example is South Africa. With its culinary influences from England, the Netherlands, India, and Malaysia, it's a place where sambals are not quite sambals and chutneys are *blatjangs*. South African food authority Renata Coetzee observes: "The Cape Malays are past masters at combining a variety of spices in one dish or at serving 'hot' dishes with a cool 'sambal' or, alternatively, hot chutney or pickles to add piquancy to bland foods."

Hot sauces take three forms in South Africa: sambals, blatjangs, and *atjars*. Because of the influence of the Cape Malays, the immigrants who first arrived as "indentured servants" from what is now Malaysia and Indonesia, there are the sambals. But these are not the original Malaysian and Indonesian sambals—they are more of a hot-chile paste, while according to South African food expert Hilda Gerber, "Cape Malays today [1949] understand the term *sambal* to be a grated vegetable or fruit, notably quince, apple, carrot, or cucumber, salted and seasoned with vinegar and chillies. The same vegetables are called *slaai* or salad when then are not grated

but shredded, although the dressing may be the same." Van der Post states that "no Malay feast is complete without a *sambal* of some kind."

Other sources reveal how sambals have come from far afield: "*Sambal* is a mixture of gherkins cut small, onions, anchovies, cayenne pepper, and vinegar," explains a South African traveler known only as Lichtenstein. He adds: "The natives, the South-African-born colonists, commonly season these dishes with the green pods of cayenne pepper, some of which they have lying by during winter." Hilda Gerber, author of *Traditional Cookery of the Cape Malays* (1949), comments: "This condiment might colloquially be described as a hot favourite. Some make it thin enough to pour, others make it rather thick, but whatever its consistency, it must be 'hot.'"

The other two South African hot sauces are blatjangs and atjars, both of which are also served with curries and other main dishes. As with sambals, they had their origin in Java and were taken to South Africa by the Cape Malays. Blatjangs, though originally from Indonesia, are a South African version of Indian chutneys, and some of the same spices appear in them. Blatjang "acquired its name from a prawn and shrimp mixture that was sun-dried, pounded in a wooden mortar, and shaped into masses resembling large cheeses," writes Van der Post. "In this form it was imported to the Cape." Blatjangs eventually evolved and were combined with European fruits and vegetables grown in South Africa. Van der Post notes: "But the importance of blatjang is not in its modern complexities but in the fact that it became for South Africa what Worcestershire sauce became for the English." The South African poet and chef C. Louis Leipoldt describes it as "bitingly spicy, pungently aromatic, moderately smooth and a very intimately mixed association of ingredients." The hot sauce is traditionally served with bobotie (see page 191).

Curiously, blatjangs contain vinegar but are not thought of as pickles, while atjars have no vinegar but are referred to as a type of pickle. Atjars consist of vegetables and/or fruits that are pickled in oil with chiles and certain curry spices. "The Cape colonists of the eighteenth and nineteenth centuries used a variety of *atjars*, as inventories show," writes Hilda Gerber, who laments the loss of knowledge of local recipes. "Although a number of Malay women know how to make several kinds of *atjar*, only very few bother to do so. Most of them are satisfied to use the two varieties they can get without difficulty from the Indian shops, viz. green mango *atjar* and lemon *atjar*, and quite a large percentage of Malay women do not even know that other varieties can be made."

Van der Post describes his family's atjar as "a wildly miscellaneous affair." The Van der Post family combined as many as 20 miniature or immature vegetables from the garden, from "tiny cobs of corn" to "the youngest of cucumbers" and beans

sliced thinly, cauliflower, carrots, apricots, peaches, and more. They were simmered together with many spices and garlic until the vegetables were tender. They were then sorted to remove any inferior pieces, and the remainder was pickled in the usual oil and spice mixture with some curry powder added. Is this a pickle? A hot sauce? A condiment? All three—as the liquid was often used as a dressing after the fruits and vegetables were eaten. The old-style, homemade atjars were a thing of the past as recently as 1945, going the way of homemade chutneys as housewives just bought the jarred kind. "We do not find it anymore," laments C. Louis Leipoldt. "And, my goodness, do not come and tell me it is still made; that in every Afrikaans cookbook and in some English ones you will find recipes for its preparation . . . that kind of atjar has disappeared completely. It has melted away like snow on the Cederberg mountains in August."

PUNGENT NORTH AFRICAN SPICE MIXTURES AND CURRIES

"The North African housewife can choose from up to 200 different spices and herbs when she stops to replenish her supplies at a spice stall in the souks of the medinas," observes African cookbook author Harva Hachten. This diversity is reflected in the unique spice mixture *ras el hanout*, which is prepared with 20 to 30 spices ranging from the familiar to the downright weird. Paula Wolfert, in her book *Couscous and Other Good Food from Morocco*, states that "it is incorrect to think of *ras el hanout* as curry powder by another name" because it lacks sufficient amounts (or any, in some cases) of cumin, coriander, fenugreek, and mustard. However, most versions of ras el hanout contain other major curry spices, such as turmeric, ginger, cinnamon, nutmeg, black pepper, and chiles, so let's compromise and say that the mixture is a variation on curry powders. Some recipes for it call for using shiny green cantharides beetles called "Spanish fly," which are reputed to have an aphrodisiac quality, and other recipes call for additional iffy ingredients like belladonna berries (don't try this at home!), nigella (aka "black cumin" or "black onion seed"; it is neither) and orris root (a rhizome of an iris flower).

Less controversial curry mixtures found in North Africa include the basic Tunisian *tabil* mixture of coriander, caraway, garlic, and crushed red chile; *la kama*, a Moroccan blend of black pepper, turmeric, ginger, cumin, and nutmeg; *zahtar*, a combination of sesame seeds, ground sumac, and powdered thyme; and *qalat daqqa*, or Tunisian five-spice powder, which is another simple mixture—similar to a basic masala—of five curry spices, with cloves, black peppercorns, and nutmeg providing the dominant flavors.

The most famous North African curries, or curry-like dishes if you prefer, served from Morocco to Egypt, are called tajines, and they are named after the earthenware tajine pot in which they are cooked. Just about any meat—chicken, pigeon, mutton, beef, goat, and even camel—can be made into a tajine with the exception of pork. The meat is usually cubed, and, according to Harva Hachten, writing in *Kitchen Safari: A Gourmet's Tour of Africa*, "The cooking liquid is the secret of a

tajine's tastiness. This is usually a combination of water and butter or oil (characteristically, olive oil) and seasonings to suit what's being cooked." The long cooking time allows the ingredients to become very tender, and the cooking liquid to reduce to a thick, savory sauce.

Chicken Tagine is what my wife and I were served in a restaurant near the Kasbah in Tangier, Morocco, and I remember it as being mildly spicy. Unfortunately, we were on a group-tour day trip from Spain and lunch had been preordered for everyone, so there was no opportunity to order from the menu. The visit to the Kasbah had been extremely unpleasant as we were constantly hounded by hawkers trying to sell us trinkets. Then at lunch the restaurant servers confiscated our water bottles and gave us new ones, from which I contracted giardia. Fortunately my wife did not. If readers wish to visit Tangier, I advise skipping the Kasbah and drinking beer instead of water.

In 1902, Budgett Meakin, a traveler in North Africa, described a recipe for the preparation of couscous made with maize that involved mutton curried with ginger, pepper, nutmeg, allspice, turmeric, and saffron. The mutton was sautéed in a tajine with butter and onions, the spices were added along with freshly chopped parsley, marjoram, and cilantro, and to the mixture water was added for stewing. When the meat was nearly done, a steamer filled with couscous was placed on top of the tajine and the rising steam finished the cooking. Meakin, writing in *The Moors*, notes that "a specialty of their kitchens is . . . the use made of raisins, dates, etc. in their meat stews, with most excellent results. After *keksoo* [couscous], their stews are their strong point, and right tasty and tender they are, whatever the age of the creature supplying the meat, as they needs must be, when they have to be carved with the fingers and thumb of one hand." He also comments that the Moors use some red pepper in their dishes but don't like their curry meals really hot. Not so the Nigerians and other West Africans.

WEST TO EAST: CURRIES GET HOTTER

Over in West Africa, particularly the former British colony of Nigeria, the curries are distinguished by an extra infusion of hot chiles. As Ellen Wilson, author of *A West African Cookbook*, observes: "Learning to eat West African food means learning to enjoy [chile] pepper." She adds: "West African dishes can be searing or simply warm, but it is noticeable that the [chile] pepper never conceals the other ingredients; in fact, it seems to enhance them."

Another distinguishing characteristic of Nigerian curries is that they are served

Packaging sundried tomatoes and peppers in Hunkuyi, Kaduna State, Nigeria. After the rainy season, fresh tomatoes, bell peppers, and Scotch bonnet peppers are preserved by spreading them on the ground to dry under the sun. Photograph by Fatima Bukar. Wikimedia. Creative Commons Attribution-ShareAlike 4.0 International License.

with an inordinate number of accompaniments. In addition to the usual chutneys and raisins and shredded coconuts, the Nigerians offer as many as 25 condiments, including chopped dates, diced cucumber, diced citrus fruits, ground dried shrimp, diced mangoes and papayas, peanuts, grapes, fried onions, chopped fresh red chiles, and bananas. "Nigerians and old African hands," notes Harva Hachten, "spoon out a portion of everything so their plates become a mound of curry and rice completely hidden by a patchwork of color and tastes."

The famous African traveler and adventurer, Sir Richard Burton, writing in *Wanderings in West Africa from Liverpool to Ferdinand Po*, volume 2 (1863), maintains that "'Palm-oil chop' is the curry of the Western coast, but it lacks the delicate flavour which turmeric gives, and suggests coarseness of taste." Thus the "chop" is another African "almost curry." Burton continues: "After some time Europeans begin to like it, and there are many who take home the materials to Europe. Besides palm-oil, it is composed of meat or fowl, boiled yam, pepper, and other minor ingredients. I always prefer it with rice; pepper, however, is the general fashion." In the book, Burton uses the generic term "pepper" to mean both chile peppers and malagueta peppers, so he probably means here that both peppers were used in the chop.

Here's what Sir Richard Burton was eating in Uganda in 1858:

> Dinner was an alternation of fish and fowl, game and butchers' meat being rarely procurable and the fish were in two extremes, either insipid and soft, or so fat and coarse that a few mouthfuls sufficed; most of them resembled the species seen in the seas of Western India, and the eels and small shrimps recalled memories of Europe. The poultry, though inferior to that of Unyanyembe, was incomparably better than the lean stringy Indian chicken. The vegetables were various and plentiful, tomatoes, Jerusalem artichokes, sweet potatoes, yams, and several kinds of beans, especially a white haricot, which afforded many a puree; the only fruit procurable was the plantain, and the only drink—the toddy [liquor] being a bad imitation of vinegar—was water.

East African foods are as heavily spiced with chiles as are the West African dishes. Kenyans serve a stew called *kima*, which combines chopped beef with red chile powder and curry spices. It is obviously derived from the *keema*, or mincemeat curries of India. East African cooking has been greatly influenced by Indian curries, which are usually not prepared from powders but rather from combinations of chiles and curry spices that are custom mixed for each particular dish. Tanzanians are fond of combining goat or chicken with curried stews, or simply charcoal-broiling the meats after they have been marinated in a mixture of curry spices and chiles.

Curries are also important in the cookery of Mozambique, despite its history as a Portuguese colony. Its proximity to Natal in South Africa is probably the reason for that. Sometimes cashew nuts, a major crop in Mozambique, are added to their curries, much as candlenuts are added to Malaysian curries. Mozambique cooks are known for a chile paste that's almost a curry paste. Piri-piri, made not with bird's eye chiles but with the long, thin fiery African chiles that are probably cayennes, contains garlic, herbs, and oil too—but no curry spices. It is, however, analogous to curries in the native cuisines of East Africa that were not influenced by Arabs, Indians, or the British.

Ethiopia is one of those East African countries least influenced by British and Indian versions of curry—instead, they evolved their own unique curry tradition.

Daniel J. Mesfin, author of *Exotic Ethiopian Cooking*, asserts: "Marco Polo did not visit our country. And Ethiopia was never conquered. It came under brief Italian rule during Mussolini's time, but for the most part, we did not have direct and intimate dealings with foreign powers." Ethiopia was isolated from Europe but not from the spice routes. "Since Ethiopia was located at the crossroads of the spice trade," observes Michael Winn, owner of New York's Blue Nile restaurant, "its people began to pay keen attention to blending spices. Fenugreek, cumin, red chiles, and varieties of herbs are used lovingly in creating meat, fish, and vegetable dishes."

Even the butter is curried in Ethiopia, with ginger, garlic, turmeric, basil, cardamom, and other spices combined to make a ghee-like concoction known as *nit'ir qibe*, or Ethiopian curried butter. But the most important spice mixture is a condiment called berbere, which is made with the hottest chiles available, plus other spices, and served as a side dish with meat, used as a coating for drying meats, or used as a major ingredient of curried meats.

Tribal custom dictated that berbere be served with *kitfo*, a warm, minced, raw meat dish. According to legend, the more delicious a woman's berbere was, the better chance she had to win a husband. Recipes for berbere were closely guarded since the marriageability of women was at stake.

Laurens van der Post philosophized on berbere in 1970: "Berbere gave me my first inkling of the essential role played by spices in the more complex forms of Ethiopian cooking. . . . It seemed to me related to that of India and of Indonesia, particularly Java; I suspect that there may have been far more contact between Ethiopia and the Far East than the history books indicate." Most berbere recipes contains about 11 curry spices in addition to garlic; notable for its absence is turmeric, a popular ingredient in Indian-influenced curries but not in Ethiopian ones. Some berbere recipes call for up to a cup or more of powdered hot chiles, so they are extremely important to berbere. And they have even inspired a derogatory expression, *ye wend alich'a*, meaning a man who has no pepper in him. The average daily consumption of chiles in Ethiopia is a little more than half an ounce per person, so they are as much a food as a spice. Berbere is an indispensable ingredient in the "national dishes" known as wat or w'et (depending on the transliteration), which are spicy, curry-like stews of lamb, beef, chicken, beans, or vegetables (but never pork).

AMBROSIA FROM THE CAPE

The curries of the Cape of Good Hope, often called "ambrosia," came from two sources: the early Malayan slaves who served their Dutch masters as farm workers, and the Indian indentured servants who came first to work in the sugar fields of Natal around 1860 and later to work on South African railroads. The Dutch had colonized South Africa because of its ideal position halfway between the Netherlands and their possessions in the Spice Islands. It was a perfect outpost for raising the vegetables and livestock necessary to replenish their ships. In 1652, the Dutch East India Company dispatched a party of officials to the Cape to establish a "revictualing station." Renata Coetzee, in *The South African Culinary Tradition*, observes: "Within fourteen days of their arrival these early settlers had laid out a vegetable garden." Their plantings included New World crops like chile peppers, sweet potatoes, pumpkins, and pineapples, plus Old World foods such as watermelons, cucumbers, radishes, and lemon and orange trees.

Late in the seventeenth century, with the revictualing station in operation, commerce between the Dutch East India Company and the new Dutch colony of South Africa picked up considerably because of an important commodity: Malay slaves, referred to in South African literature as "the king of slaves." The men were utilized as farmers, carpenters, musicians, tailors, and fishermen, while the women were expert cooks who not only introduced exotic Spice Islands dishes but also imported the spices necessary to prepare them. Among the Malaysian spices transferred by the slaves to South Africa were anise seed, fennel, turmeric, ginger, cardamom, cumin, coriander, mustard seed, tamarind, and garlic.

The Cape Malays, as the slaves' descendants were called, developed a unique cuisine called, by some, "Old Cape cookery." It evolved into a mixture of Dutch, English, and Malay styles and ingredients—with an emphasis on the Malay. Predominant among the numerous cooking styles were curries and their accompaniments. As early as 1740, "kerrie-kerrie" dishes were mentioned in South African literature. That terminology had changed by 1797, when Johanna Duminy of the Riviersonderend Valley, wrote in her diary: "When the evening fell I had the candles lit, the children were given their supper and put to bed. At nine o'clock we are going to have a delicious curry."

Johanna's curry probably was milder than that of today in South Africa because for a time chiles and green ginger were greatly reduced for the Dutch palate. But the Cape Malays relished the heat, and Harva Hachten, author of *Kitchen Safari*, points out: "Curries are as much a part of Malay cooking as they are of Indian."

But they also became English too, for the British had seized the Cape in 1795 to prevent it from falling into French hands, then lost it for a few years to the Dutch, starting in 1803, before finally conquering it in 1806. British sovereignty of the area was recognized at the Congress of Vienna in 1815. As in India, the British settlers fell in love with curries.

Sylvester Stein, the former editor of *Drum* magazine, describes his childhood in 1920s Durban, South Africa: "In the Indian area you could get a really hot chilli curry and rice, as opposed to the insipid Raj-English curry elsewhere in white cafes." In nearby Rhodesia there was a similar situation, as Zimbabwe-born artist Trevor Southey observes: "Curries were perhaps the most distinctive food we ate. Indeed, strange though it may seem, I tend to think of curry as the closest to a national Rhodesian dish there is."

AT LAST, A PROFESSIONAL AFRICAN FOOD HISTORIAN

C. Louis Leipoldt was the inspiration for the name of Leipoldt's Restaurant in Brooklyn, Pretoria. The restaurant describes him on their website as a "poet, playwright, pediatrician, botanist, journalist, novelist, cook and connoisseur of food and wine." The son of a preacher with a mother so strict she forbade her children from "mingling with the town folk," Leipoldt was confined to his house and began to hang around the kitchen, where he helped Maria, the Malay cook, prepare all the family meals. She was his first culinary inspiration, and he writes about her in *Leipoldt's Cape Cookery*: "She presided over a kitchen whose cleanliness could have served as model for an operating theatre of a modern hospital." Maria taught him the basic principles of Malay slow-cooked food "accompanied by a good-natured but nevertheless painful prodding of [his] juvenile person with the large wooden spoon that was her sceptre." She helped him "to realise how any infringement of the [principles] impairs the excellence of all cookery." Maria also told him the secret of using curry spices and chiles: "Get the soul out of the spice and into the meat."

Leipoldt left South Africa to pursue his medical career, and while studying medicine at Guy's Hospital in Chelsea in London in 1907, when he had had enough of dissecting bodies, he went across to the Strand to wash dishes in the kitchen of one of the greatest of all chefs, Auguste Escoffier, at the Savoy. "Quite remarkably," writes Paul Murray in his online article, "The C. Louis Leipoldt Trail," "it was not long before he sat for his exams in cookery under the maestro and returned successful, with an international qualification in cuisine." Now a chef as well as a doctor, he returned to South Africa to pursue his many careers simultaneously.

Brian Lello, who wrote the preface to the 1976 edition of *Leipoldt's Cape Cookery*, describes the author as "an anti-pedant" who "eschews finicking precision about quantities. Let others write medical prescriptions for food instead of cultivating their flair." For one recipe, Leipoldt writes: "Collect as many limpets of the rocks as your backache will allow." Once, when an editor questioned the meaning of one of his passages, he cried out testily: "How should I know what I meant; that is your job."

Leipoldt's cookbook, *Kos vir die Kenner* (Food for the Connoisseur), first published in 1933, was republished in June 2011 by Human and Rousseau in Cape Town. It has 2,000 South African and international recipes. In *Leipoldt's Cape Cookery*, written in the 1940s but not published until after his death

in 1947, Leipoldt gives his philosophy about chiles in cookery: "Whatever it is that imparts this extraordinarily sharp, stimulating quality of chillies [capsaicin], also imbues then with distinctively individual merits that have long been appreciated by South African cooks. . . . It is also so stimulating, so valuable as a contrasting flavour, and so delicious when properly used, that other dishes, without it, are insipid and altogether lack distinction."

Laurens van der Post, who says that "the person who has once acquired a taste in the tropics for Indian curries, Oriental spices or African chillies becomes an addict," knew Leipoldt so well that they often discussed their philosophies about spicy South African specialties. And both of them agreed that curry manages to find its way into very unusual dishes. Take bobotie, for example, which Van der Post says "is to South Africa what *moussaka* is to Greece"—except for the fact that it contains both turmeric and curry powder. And those are only two of the variations of a dish about which Van der Post observes: "There are as many *boboties* as there are homes in South Africa." Leipoldt points out that bobotie "was known in Europe in the middle ages when the Crusaders brought turmeric from the East." This of course was bobotie without chile peppers, which arrived centuries later. Essentially, boboties are spiced-up meat pies. Leipoldt explains the process of making a dish that is quite similar to moussaka but one spiced up with fresh ginger, chiles, and curry powder. It is one of what Van der Post calls the "the three great Cape Malay main dishes." The other two are bredie and *sosatie*.

Bredie is a spiced-up stew of meat, a starch such as potatoes, and various vegetables—a dish Leipoldt describes as "intimately stewed so that the flesh is thoroughly

impregnated with vegetable flavour." Van der Post adds that "the chosen vegetables, sliced or cubed, are placed on top of the meat with various seasonings, but always with chilies." Sosaties, or "curried kebabs," as Leipoldt calls them, are derived from two Malay words, *saté* (satay), a spiced sauce, and *sésate*, which means meat skewered on a stick. Sosaties have "endless variations," according to Van der Post; and Leipoldt, in his typical lyrical manner, writes that "there is perhaps no other single dish that can be regarded as more genuine Africans than *sosaties*. . . . *Sosaties*, when properly made, should be tender and tasty, yet with a crispness that rivals a grilled chop, and bitingly spicy yet with a suavity that rivals the best made curry." In South Africa, it's all about getting back to curry.

A PERI-PERI GOOD TIME: SPICED UP SOUTH AFRICA

Chile peppers lured us to South Africa. One was a popular pickled pepper that was the focus of a plant patent matter that I was consulting on, the Peppadew®. The other was the peri-peri, the principal pepper used in the hot sauces of Nando's, a large chain of spicy chicken restaurants based in South Africa.

The adventure began with an e-mail from Derek Harms, a barrister who was handling a legal action challenging a plant patent. Would I consult on the case as an expert? Yes, I replied. Would I travel to South Africa as the client's guest expert and testify at the hearing in front of the Registrar of Plant Patents of the South Africa Department of Agriculture? You bet!

By a weird coincidence, I also had an e-mail from another South African deeply involved with peppers, Chris Thorpe, the general manager of the international grocery division of Nando's. Chris offered me a tour of South Africa and the Nando's operations there if I were ever in the country. I replied yes, of course, and told him about legal case I was consulting on, and a deal was struck. The first week I'd be in Pretoria for the hearing, but after that Chris would show us around his country.

Pretoria and Johannesburg

To get to South Africa, we first flew from Albuquerque to Minneapolis, where we caught a flight to Schiphol Airport in Amsterdam. That remarkable airport has both a casino and a museum! We were able to change our dollars for rand, the currency of South Africa. Then we boarded the nonstop flight to Johannesburg that went nearly the entire length of the African continent. At the airport, we were picked up by a polite but reticent driver who drove us to the Holiday Inn in Pretoria, the capital of the country. Our room overlooked a lovely garden of tropical plants surrounding the swimming pool.

For the first few days I was constantly in meetings with Derek as we planned out the testimony for the hearing. During the downtime, we did touristy things like visiting the National Zoo and the impressive Voortrekker Monument that was a tribute to the Dutch settlers. I also watched several rugby matches that I enjoyed enormously. We ate hotel food that was pretty good, including bobotie, a curry mince pie, fiery mutton chops, chicken that tasted like chicken in the old days, and spicy masala chickpeas. However, the South African beer was very disappointing. All the brands are owned by South African Breweries, which also owns Miller Beer in the US, and although there is a great wine tradition in South Africa, the beers are very ordinary.

The hearing in the plant patent case went very well, but I had to fight off an aggressive attorney for the other side who kept trying to put words in my mouth. But I had previous experience in court, kept my cool, and some of my sarcastic replies to questions made the registrar laugh. I can't really go into the details of the case, but

although we won the first round, that ruling was overturned on appeal. With the work over, it was time for some fun. Big-game fun.

A bowl of Peppa-dew® peppers. Photograph by Duplass. Bigstock Photo.

Kruger National Park

Chris picked us up at the hotel in a van that held numerous other people, including his girlfriend, Valerie; Selwyn Bron, the personal assistant to the owner of Nando's, Robbie Brozin; and Rochelle Schaetzl, director of new product development. John Paidoussi, the CEO of the grocery division of Nando's, and his wife, Dawn, met with us later that evening.

We were headed to Robbie's lodge at Leopard Creek, the exclusive golf estate just across the Crocodile River from Kruger National Park. The three-hour drive on excellent highways took us through rolling grassland, patches of forests, lakes with trout in them, and mountain passes—but no jungles. Forget jungles, because South Africa doesn't have them.

Apparently Robbie does a lot of entertaining at his lodge, because the five guest rooms were beautifully decorated and each had its own luxurious bath. There was cable TV for watching the rugby matches, or you could go out on the verandah and watch the hippos in the Crocodile River or the vervet monkeys in the trees. I'm no expert, but the golf course was amazingly beautiful, with ponds and perfectly manicured greens. There were birds like fish eagles and little antelopes called bushbucks everywhere. That night, Rochelle, who's the de facto Nando's Official Corporate Chef, prepared an amazing dinner with nearly every course spiced up with various Nando's products, especially their peri-peri sauces.

The next day we took an eight-hour tour of Kruger National Park with hopes of seeing the Big Five: elephant, rhino, Cape buffalo, lion, and leopard. Paved roads loaded with elephant and other animals' droppings took us through the park, and only at official tourist stops with buildings were we allowed to get out of the van. Our hosts were extremely knowledgeable about the wildlife. The scenery was pure savannah, with open spaces, brush, acacia trees, and the occasional watering hole. Finally, we were in what looked like the African plains of the movies.

We had mammal and bird identification books, and I kept a list of what we

saw—in all, 16 species of animals and 23 species of birds. We didn't see any lions, leopards, or Cape buffaloes, but we did see elephants, rhinos, hippos, baboons, impalas, kudus, giraffes, wildebeests, zebras, crocodiles, monitor lizards, and a warthog. The most impressive bird was a gigantic martial eagle, and we also spotted hornbills, ox pickers, herons, plovers, vultures, shrikes, kingfishers, and a black-breasted snake eagle. It was the most amazing nature tour I've ever taken. Rochelle, Selwyn, and Chris even prepared a bush breakfast for us at one of the camps, fired up with Nando's sauces, of course.

Back in Johannesburg, we were given a tour of Nando's manufacturing and bottling operation, including their beautifully decorated Brand Room where they give seminars to their restaurant and grocery managers. Nando's now has 1,186 restaurants in more than 32 countries, and they expanded into the US in late 2007 with a restaurant in Washington, DC. As of 2019, Nando's has 42 restaurants in the US: 12 in Illinois, 6 in Washington, DC, 14 in Maryland, and 10 in Virginia.

They also have dozens of products on the market, including hot sauces and other condiments. Their products are available at www.nandosperiperi.com. Mary Jane fell in love with their PERinaise, a mayo with hot sauce added, but it's not yet available in the US. (Fudge it by adding your favorite peri-peri sauce to a good mayonnaise, to taste.)

Chris took us to a Nando's location in Parktown North in J-Burg, and I ordered the ¼ chicken meal, with spicy rice. When asked if I wanted it mild, medium, or hot, I said "hot." After biting into a chicken thigh, I knew immediately that this was not just hot—it was very hot. The chicken was extremely tasty, much more so than US poultry. The chicken is marinated in hot sauce, then basted with more hot sauce as it is grilled over open flames.

Our next diversion was a flight to Cape Town, probably the most beautiful city I've ever seen. Within a few miles, the landscape rises thousands of feet, from the sea-level beaches to the flat top of Table Mountain, which is reached via a tram. The views are nothing but spectacular. Cape Town spreads from the front of Table Mountain to the back, and the outlying areas, including Stellenbosch, boast the best vineyards and wineries in South Africa. We stayed at the five-star Lanzerac Manor and Winery in the heart of wine country. Our room was 720 square feet plus the bath and walk-in closet. The grounds were beautiful, and every morning a flock of guinea fowl would assemble for breakfast outside in a courtyard visible from one of our windows. It was here that I started drinking wine instead of beer!

Chris then took us to his prototype peri-peri chile field, where we met Riaan Breet and Marianna Smith, who were consulting on the breeding program. I examined the small plants and concluded that the sandy soil needed more organic material to hold the moisture. Nando's has several experimental fields, and they are hoping to develop their own variety of peri-peri.

One of the glories of Cape Town is the Kirstenbosch National Botanical Garden, which is one of eight gardens of the South African National Biodiversity Institute in the country. I have visited botanical gardens all over the world, and this one is the most dramatic and beautiful that I've ever seen. Their succulent collection is outstanding and they have many theme gardens and a nature reserve. Kirstenbosch stretches over about 1200 acres with the magnificent Table Mountain as a backdrop.

Another fascinating nature display is Boulders, the part of Table Mountain National Park that is host to hundreds of African penguins (formerly called "jackass penguins" for their braying-like mating call). Lots of animals want to eat these penguins, including sharks, Cape fur seals, killer whales, mongooses, cats, dogs, and kelp gulls, but somehow they manage to survive. Maybe it's their charm, as they are very cute.

FEATURED CHILE PEPPER: AFRICAN BIRD'S EYE

The African bird's eye pepper, called peri-peri in South Africa, most resembles the 'NuMex Bailey Piquin' pod in the bird-peppers photograph on page 170. Since many wild chiles have the word "bird" in their names, distinguishing among them can be difficult. Most bird peppers are undomesticated varieties of four species: *annuum*,

baccatum, *chinense*, *and frutescens*. The most familiar bird peppers are the Mexican chiltepín and the Texan chilipiquin. The African bird's eye chile is both wild and domesticated and is also known in English as African devil chile, in Swahili as pili-pili, and in Kamba as ndul. Some sources state that this chile is also *prik kee nu*, the Thai "mouse dropping pepper," but that is a different, much thinner chile. It should be pointed out that pili-pili simply means "pepper-pepper" and is a generic term for any African chile.

Most sources state that the bird's eye is *Capsicum frutescens*, making it a relative of the Tabasco chile. Depending on growing conditions, the plants range in height from 1 ½ to 4 feet tall and are usually very bushy. The leaves vary in length from 1 ½ to 3 inches, and in width from ½ inch to 1 inch. The fruits generally measure between ½ and 1 inch long and taper to a blunt point. Immature pod color is green; mature color is bright red.

Pungency can vary according to precise variety of bird's eye, where it is grown, and environmental conditions. The bird's eye, particularly the Ugandan variety, is thought to be the most pungent chile that is not of the *chinense* species, measuring up to 175,000 SHU. In a test of a variety provided by chile gardener Harald Zoschke, the Malawi bird's eye variety from Africa was measured at 112,226 SHU, and the same variety grown in Harald's garden was measured at 99,579 SHU.

The bird's eye chile has grown wild in Africa for centuries but has been under commercial cultivation for many years in Uganda, Malawi, and Zimbabwe; and now South Africa is looking to catch up. Other countries where it is cultivated include Papua New Guinea, China, Mexico, Chile, and India. The plants are perennial and sometimes produce for three years before they are plowed under. Growing African bird's eye chiles is very labor-intensive and they require handpicking. The pods are picked when they are bright red and 2 or less centimeters (¾ inch) long. A single plant yields about 300 grams (⅔ pound) of fresh pods. Yields of about 1.8 metric tons per hectare are typical (a hectare is 2.47 acres).

Because of the extremely high heat levels, most African bird's eye chiles are processed into oleoresin capsicum (pepper extract) for use in commercial food processing and the pharmaceutical industry. The ground powder is often sold as extremely hot cayenne powder and is packaged in capsules. These are the prices paid for bird's eye pods in July 2001: Zimbabwe, US$2,750 per metric ton; and Malawi, US$2,800 per metric ton.

Take care in using African bird's eye chiles in the kitchen because of the extreme pungency of the pods. You would not, for example, want to make a hot sauce out of a cup of the pods and some vinegar.

recipes

Bobotie. Photograph by Elizabeth Hoffmann. iStock

BOBOTIE

yield 4 to 6 servings   *heat scale* medium

Rich golden curry powder is at the heart of Cape Malay cooking. The lemon juice, the fruit, and the spiciness of the chile add a real flavor dimension to this South African ground-meat dish. Serve this dish with rice and a fruit salad.

3	tablespoons vegetable oil	1	tablespoon minced jalapeño chile
1	pound lean ground lamb	½	teaspoon salt
1	onion, finely chopped	⅔	cup half-and-half cream
1 ½	tablespoons commercial curry paste	½	cup fine dry white breadcrumbs
4	large garlic cloves, minced	1	cup milk
½	cup raisins	2	eggs
¼	cup fresh lemon juice, strained	¼	teaspoon salt
1	tablespoon apricot preserves		Freshly cooked rice
¾	cup dried apricots, coarsely chopped		

191

Heat the oil in large skillet over medium-high heat. Add the ground lamb and cook until no longer pink, breaking up with a fork, about 5 minutes. Add the onions and stir until lightly browned, about 3 minutes. Drain off all fat. Add the curry paste and garlic, and stir for 2 minutes. Add the raisins, lemon juice, preserves, apricots, chile, and salt, and stir until the mixture thickens and most of the lemon juice evaporates, about 5 minutes. Mix in the half-and-half and breadcrumbs. Cool completely.

Preheat the oven to 350 degrees F. Transfer the mixture to a 7 by 12–inch ovenproof glass baking dish. Whisk the milk with the eggs in a small bowl until thick and add the salt. Pour this over the meat mixture. Bake until custard topping is set, 35 to 45 minutes.

Serve immediately with the rice.

HARISSA SAUCE

yield 1 ½ cups   *heat scale* hot

This classic sauce is thought to be of Tunisian origin but is found throughout all of North Africa. It is used to flavor couscous and grilled dishes such as kebabs. Harissa sauce reflects the region's love of spicy combinations, all with a definite cumin and coriander flavor. Cover this sauce with a thin film of olive oil and it will keep up to a couple of months in the refrigerator.

10	dried whole red New Mexican chiles, stems and seeds removed
	Hot water
2	tablespoons olive oil
5	cloves garlic
1	teaspoon ground cumin
1	teaspoon ground cinnamon
1	teaspoon ground coriander
1	teaspoon ground caraway

Cover the chiles with hot water and let them sit for 30 minutes until they soften. Place the chiles and remaining ingredients in a blender and puree until smooth, using the chile water to thin it. The sauce should have the consistency of a thick paste.

yield 1 ½ cups   *heat scale* extremely hot

Berbere is the famous—or should I say infamous?—scorching Ethiopian hot sauce. One recipe I ran across called for over a cup of powdered cayenne! It is used as an ingredient in a number of dishes, a coating when drying meats, and as a side dish or condiment. Tribal custom dictated that it be served with kitfo, raw-meat dishes that are served warm. This sauce will keep for a couple of months under refrigeration. Serve sparingly as a condiment with grilled meats and poultry or add to soups and stews.

4	whole cardamom pods
2	teaspoons cumin seeds
½	teaspoon black peppercorns
½	teaspoon fenugreek seeds
1	small onion, coarsely chopped
4	cloves garlic
1	cup water
15	dried piquin chiles, stems removed
1	tablespoon ground cayenne
2	tablespoons ground paprika
½	teaspoon ground ginger
¼	teaspoon ground allspice
¼	teaspoon ground nutmeg
¼	teaspoon ground cloves
3	tablespoons vegetable oil

Toast the cardamom pods, cumin seeds, peppercorns, and fenugreek seeds in a hot skillet, shaking constantly for a couple of minutes, until they start to crackle and pop. In a spice mill, grind these spices to form a powder.

Combine the onions, garlic, and ½ cup water in a blender, and puree until smooth. Add the chiles, cayenne, paprika, ground spices, ginger, allspice, nutmeg, and cloves, and continue to blend, slowly adding the remaining water and oil, and blend until smooth. Remove to a saucepan and simmer the sauce for 15 minutes to blend the flavors and thicken.

CAPE MALAY FRESH CURRY PASTE

yield makes approximately 1 ½ cups of curry paste   *heat scale* medium

Diana G. Armstrong provided this recipe, adapted from C. Louis Leipoldt's Cape Cookery, written in the 1940s. It is especially good for making bobotie.

2	small red bell peppers		2	cloves garlic
2	jalapeño peppers, seeds and stems removed		1	teaspoon finely diced fresh ginger
1	tablespoon cumin seeds		½	teaspoon salt
2	tablespoons coriander seeds		¼	stick cinnamon, crushed a little
2	tablespoons turmeric		½	teaspoon finely grated lemon rind
1	teaspoon fenugreek		4	ounces butter

Crush all ingredients together with a mortar and pestle, or pulse in a blender. Store in the refrigerator.

PERI-PERI NUTTY CHICKEN

yield 4 to 6 servings   *heat scale* varies according to the amount of Nando's sauce used

This will give you an idea of how Nando's works with chicken!

8	chicken portions, drumsticks or thighs
3	tablespoons Nando's Peri-Peri Sauce, more if you like it hot
¼	cup vegetable oil, peanut preferred, to oil the baking dish
2	tablespoons soy sauce
2	tablespoons creamy peanut butter
1	clove garlic, crushed
⅓	cup finely chopped peanuts or cashews
2	tablespoons finely chopped cilantro
	Salt and freshly ground black pepper

Preheat the oven to 400 degrees F.

Season the chicken pieces with salt and pepper, and place in a single layer in a well-greased baking dish. Bake in the oven for 30 minutes or until they become brown and crisp.

Place the Nando's Peri-Peri Sauce, soy sauce, peanut butter, and garlic in a saucepan, and stir to combine. Heat the sauce over a low heat, stirring frequently until smooth. Stir in the nuts.

Brush the chicken generously with the sauce and continue to bake for an additional 15 to 20 minutes.

The word "curry" refers to both a spice mixture and a style of cooking. The spice mixture usually contains chile peppers in the form of a hot powder along with up to thirty other spices and herbs. The cooking style is essential for stewing meats, seafood, poultry, or vegetables in the spice mixture.

A BRIEF ETYMOLOGY OF CURRY

One of the most intriguing theories about the ancestry of curry was advanced by Captain Basil Hall, a traveler in India, Ceylon, and Borneo. "It will surprise most people," he writes in 1930, "to learn that the dish we call curry is not of India, nor, indeed, of Asiatic origin at all. There is reason to believe that curries were first introduced into India by the Portuguese." Hall reasoned that since the Portuguese had introduced chile peppers into India, and since hot peppers are a primary ingredient of curry, ergo, they must have introduced curries as well.

Hall was dead wrong, of course. Curry-like spice mixtures date back to at least 4000 BC. In excavations of the ancient cities of Harpatta and Mohenjo-Daro in the Indus Valley in what is now Pakistan, grinding stones were found that contained traces of mustard seed, cumin, saffron, fennel, and tamarind. Since all of these spices appear in curries, it is not unreasonable to assume that the ancient Indus Valley people were cooking with curry spices 6,000 years ago—although no recipes survive.

"Many people consider them [inhabitants of Mohenjo-Daro, called the Harappa culture] the world's first gourmets and creative cooks," writes William Laas in *Cuisines of the Eastern World.* "Their achievements may be measured by the fact that their seasonings were adopted by all who came after them."

One of the first written mentions of curry-style cookery is attributed to Athenaeus, a Greek miscellanist who lived about AD 200. In his *Deipnosophistae* (The Gastronomers), a fascinating survey of classical food and dining habits, he quotes Megasthenes, the third century BC author of *Indica*: "Among the Indians at a banquet a table is set before each individual . . . and on the table is placed a golden dish, in which they first throw boiled rice . . . and then they add many sorts of meat dressed after the Indian fashion."

"The Indian fashion," as mentioned by Athenaeus, has sparked most of the curry controversies because some writers and cooks believe that the "Indian fashion" of curry has been stolen and ruined by the rest of the world, especially by the English. Other writers think that notion is nonsense, and they believe that cookery continues to evolve as the world shrinks. In fact, there are multitudinous definitions and beliefs about curry, and rarely do two writers agree on precisely what curry is.

"Curry in its twentieth century manifestation—a meat or occasionally vegetable stew flavoured with commercial curry powder—is essentially a British dish," writes John Ayto, author of *The Glutton's Glossary*. He is taking the oversimplified stance that all curries are made with commercial curry powder, which simply is not true, despite a plethora of commercial curry powders and other products.

M. F. K. Fisher, the famous gastronome, disagrees with the curry-powder-stew concept, believing the preparation of curries to be a high art: "Books about curries," she writes, "are published continually, with the success of a well-ticking clock. Special restaurants all over the world serve nothing but curries. Spice merchants grow rich on making their regional and private blends of curry powder. In other words, reputations can and do depend upon the authenticity of the recipe first and then of the powder that goes with the sauce, the skill with which the sauce is made, and in many cases the atmosphere in which the whole is served."

Some curry lovers carry things too far. "The word curry is magic," gushes William Kaufman in his book *The Art of India's Cookery*. "Its mention conjures up for us the romance and mystery of the far-off land of the Taj Mahal. The best way to create the Indian atmosphere is to perfume your house with curries."

His comment may have some truth, but the worship of curry irritates famed

Curry powder ingredients. Photo by miansari66. Wikimedia. Creative Commons Attribution-ShareAlike License.

Indian chef and author Madhur Jaffrey, who writes in her book *An Invitation to Indian Cooking*: "To me the word 'curry' is as degrading to India's great cuisine as the term 'chop suey' was to China's. If 'curry' is an oversimplified name for an ancient cuisine, then 'curry powder' attempts to oversimplify (and destroy) the cuisine itself."

Jaffrey may call the word "curry" "degrading," but actually, it is not meant to be insulting. The term "curry" reflects the evolution of language and the need to designate, in English, dishes that were based on various spice mixtures. Indeed, curry has come to mean, in English, different spice mixtures that are used in a similar manner in countries throughout the world. "Curry," explains Yohanni Johns, author of *Dishes from Indonesia*, "is a word frequently used by foreigners to describe Indonesian dishes cooked with coconut milk." Santha Rama Rau, author of the Time-Life book on Indian cooking, says that the "proper sense" of the word "curry" is "a highly seasoned stew with plenty of sauce." There is even controversy over the etymology of the word "curry." Most sources attribute it to a British colonial corruption of the Tamil (South Indian) word *kari*, meaning sauce. Indian food expert Julie Sahni notes that the word *kari* is also a shortened version of *kari pulia*, or kari leaves, meaning the leaves of the curry plant, *Murraya koenigii*, a common ingredient in Indian curry blends.

But other writers disagree with the kari origin of curry. Dharam Jit Singh, author of *Classic Cooking from India*, writes that "curry is a word that comes from the Hindustani: *turcarri*. In the colloquial it is shortened to 'turri,' which in Anglo-Saxon usage is called 'curry.'" William Laas, author of *Cuisines of the Eastern World*, agrees with this etymology. Other writers believe that the word is derived from *karhai*, a wok-like metal implement made of silvered brass in which curried dishes are cooked, or *khari* (sometimes *khadi*), a soup made with buttermilk and chickpea flour.

Julie Sahni claims that curry is derived from *curryup*, an ancient Tamil word for "blackened" or "crisp-fried." She also notes that *curry* is Tamil for uncooked vegetables. She concludes: "Curry powder was thus originally the seasoning blend used for flavoring fried vegetables."

Perhaps the most unusual theory of the origin of the word "curry" comes from Selat Elbis Sopmi of London's Punjab restaurant, who writes in *The Curry Club Magazine* that some centuries ago an Irish sea captain married into a wealthy family. The captain's gambling led to the demise of the family, which kept a large stable of racehorses. They were forced to sell the best of the horses and eat the rest. The Irishman used the word *cuirreach*, Irish for racetrack, and told everyone he had been reduced to eating *cuirreach gosht*, or racetrack meat. "Over the ages, this has become, through usage," claims Sopmi, "the word as we know it, curry."

The *Oxford English Dictionary* prefers the Tamil *kari* as the word of origin and defines "curry" as "a preparation of meat, fish, fruit, or vegetables, cooked with a quantity of bruised spices and turmeric, and used as a relish or flavouring, especially for dishes composed of or served with rice." A secondary definition says that curry powder may be used in the cooking process.

Interestingly enough, the English were already predisposed to accept the word "curry," regardless of its precise Indian ancestry. First, there was the influence all over Europe of Marco Polo, who, in the late thirteen century, reported on the Asian origin of "ginger, galingal, spikenard, and many other kinds of spices" that were just starting to be used in the English kitchen.

Second, the word *cury*, with an Old French word *keuerie* as its root, first appeared in English as *kewery*, meaning cookery and also the "concoction" of substances in alchemy. As early as 1390, a manuscript of the first English cookbook appeared, entitled *Forme of Cury* (Art of Cookery), and it was supposedly written by the master cook of King Richard II. *Forme of Cury* was not actually printed as a book until 1780, about 30 years after Robert Clive of the East India Company captured the fort of Arcot, west of Madras, and began the British Empire in India. Thus the first printed English cookbook was contemporaneous with the early rise of the British Raj—but that is not the only curry coincidence.

In *Forme of Cury*, hot spices were considered to be, according to culinary historian L. Patrick Coyle, an "essential luxury" because of the medieval belief in their digestive qualities and their ability to mask the tastes and odors of food spoilage. "Pepper was the most highly prized," writes Coyle, "followed by ginger and a related root called galingal, then cubeb, a berry whose taste suggests allspice and peppercorn, and clove, cinnamon, cardamom, cumin, and coriander." Given the fact that all of these spices appear in curries, it was inevitable that the English would warmly embrace Indian curries.

As for the word "curry," it soon had its own variants throughout the British Empire, including *currie*, *carrye*, *curree*, *kerry*, and *kerrie*. It was transferred to other languages, appearing as *poudre de cari* in French and *indisches Currypulver* in German, but remaining simply as *curry* in Italian and Spanish. The word has even crept into slang, as in the American and British phrase "currying favor" (which originally meant "to please with cookery") and the Australian "to give curry" (which means to abuse or rebuke someone).

Julie Sahni takes a liberal view of the most basic ingredients required to make a curry: "For a spice blend to be called a curry powder, the mixture must contain three core spices: coriander, turmeric, and pepper." Others will disagree, asking "Where's the cumin?"—or any other of their favorite spices. The point here is that many spice blends not originally defined as curry powders, such as those from North Africa and the Middle East, can fit into the broad category of curries.

The Portuguese forever changed curries by introducing chile peppers, which became the principal hot spice

During the research for this book, four main curry myths were evident:

curry myth number 1 Curry is a spice. This fiction continues to spread despite numerous books on spices and Indian cooking. Curry leaf is a single herb used in some curries, but in reality there are dozens and dozens of herbs, spices, fruits, rhizomes, bulbs, pulses, nuts, and other ingredients that are combined to make curries.

curry myth number 2 All curries are the same. Nothing could be further from the truth. "Contrary to popular belief," notes Sri Lankan food importer Anura Saparamadu, "there are about as many types of curries as there are spices." And given the total number of curry ingredients, the combinations and permutations of those ingredients provide a nearly infinite variety of flavors in curries. "Even the best Indian cooks will argue endlessly over the inclusion and exclusion of particular spices and herbs," adds Santha Rama Rau.

curry myth number 3 Authentic curries cannot be made outside their countries of origin. Purists often say that to enjoy genuine curries, one must travel to all the regions where curry dishes are popular. Can authentic curries be made in America? The answer is a resounding yes. Virtually every exotic curry ingredient (and every one in this book) is available in the United States in Asian markets or by mail order. Besides, across the Indian subcontinent, as well as in other curry countries, cooks boldly experiment, and it is possible to get five or six variations for the same recipe. In all cases, even with a few substitutions, the recipes will be authentic—meaning, as in the dictionary, reliable and genuine.

curry myth number 4 No self-respecting Indian cook would ever use commercial curry powder. Virtually every writer on the subject of curry or Indian food falls for this falsehood, or some variation on the theme, as if to say that all commercial curry products are bogus. Expatriate Indians in other parts of the world, such as the United States and Canada, commonly use commercial powders, pastes, oils, and sauces. And in India, as Tom Stobart, author of *The Cook's Encyclopedia*, observes, "books commonly say that Indians do not use curry powder. This may have been true in the days when even the servants had servants and the masala of fresh ginger, garlic, onion, coconut, green chile, and spices was ground on the stone freshly for each dish. But today [1980], a First World cost of servants has caught up with Third World households, and ready-ground spice mixtures are no longer beyond the pale." This is not to say that Indian cooks now use commercial preparations to the exclusion of homemade curries, but rather that they now have the option because of the vast number of commercial products on the market.

in curries from then on. Christopher Columbus brought chile peppers and their seeds back from the New World in 1493, and they were grown mostly by monks in monasteries. Portuguese explorers carried the chiles to their ports in Africa and Goa, India shortly thereafter. Although the exact date of their introduction into India is not known, most experts believe that it was in the early 1500s.

Garcia de Orta, a Portuguese chronicler, writes in 1593: "This Capsicum or Indian pepper is diligently cultivated in castles by gardeners and also by women in their kitchens and house gardens." Chiles became an integral part of Indian cooking and religious lore. They are believed to ward off the "evil eye," and in many houses and offices, chiles are hung for just such a purpose. In the home, chiles are burned in the kitchen to intimidate the evil eye and protect children.

Most curry cooks recommend using only freshly ground spices; however, there are many convenient commercial curry preparations. Masalas are spice blends that usually lack turmeric. Curry powders contain turmeric (the yellower the powder, the more turmeric it contains) and a large percentage of coriander. Imported powders are generally superior to domestic ones. Curry pastes are sealed, moist blends of herbs, spices, and other ingredients such as coconut, onions, fresh chiles, and ginger. They are imported from India, Thailand, Indonesia, and Sri Lanka. Curry sauces are available either in bottles or in mixes, and are used as marinades or to make an "instant" curry gravy for meats. Curry oils are vegetable oils steeped in curry spices, and they are generally used as a condiment to add a curry flavor to prepared foods.

RELIGION AND SUPERSTITION IN CURRY COOKING

It is a Hindu belief that food was created for humans by the gods. Because of this conviction, cookery on the Indian subcontinent over the centuries became not only an art but a sacred ceremony. Certain prayers were said before preparation began and ritual methods were observed during the cooking. For example, Indians ate two meals a day and believed that each meal should consist of precisely 32 mouthfuls. Under the doctrine of karma, with its successive states of existence, and in an adherence to the caste systems, various foods were considered either clean or unclean. For example, one could not eat food prepared by a murderer or one might become one in the next life. Likewise, to eat food prepared by someone of a lower caste would cause the diner to be reduced to that caste.

Religion and superstition pervade Indian cookery even today, and many early customs, rituals, and food prohibitions are still observed. Hindus, who compose 80 percent of the population, will not eat beef because the cow is sacred to them;

Muslims eat beef and lamb but abhor pork; and Buddhists and Jainists will not take any animal life and so will not even crack an egg. Considering such attitudes, it is no wonder that highly spiced vegetarian cooking is so popular all over India.

In the fifth century AD, all of the references to food found in the Vedas and Upanishads, the holy books of the Hindus, were collected by the Brahmin Khema Sharmin. He determined that the three classical elements of food were nutrition, flavor, and aesthetic appeal. The belief that food should consist of these three qualities has persisted throughout the centuries as cooking became an honored and skilled art.

It was this world of cookery that chile peppers invaded, latecomers to the development of Indian cuisines. Yet despite the complicated customs and rituals of cookery in India, chiles eventually dominated the cuisines and even became the principal spice of the region.

THE 400-YEAR-LONG INVASION

When the Portuguese arrived in India, the west coast of the subcontinent, known as the Malabar Coast, was one of the most important trading centers of the Old World. Huge camel caravans and shipping fleets were drawn to the Malabar Coast by an abundance of spices that were eagerly sought after in Europe. Vasco da Gama was the first European to visit the Malabar Coast, landing in Calicut in 1498. He brought back to Portugal an offer from the ruler of Calicut to trade spices and gems for gold, silver, and scarlet cloth.

Such temptations were more than the Portuguese could resist. They were eager to wrest the spice trade from Arab sailors, while at the same time outmaneuvering the Spaniards to the lucrative business; so they did what most powerful European countries did to less powerful nations: they took what they wanted.

Under the leadership of Afonso de Albuquerque, the Portuguese conquered the city of Goa on the Malabar Coast in 1510 and gained control of the spice trade. Goa was rich in spices—cloves, cinnamon, cardamom, ginger, and black pepper— which were shipped to Lisbon in return for silver

The Portuguese arrive in Goa, India. Image from *A Century of Discovery: Biographical Sketches of the Portuguese and Spanish Navigators from Prince Henry to Pizarro* (1877). Wikimedia. Public domain.

and copper. These spices were essential to Indian kari cooking. *Kari* is a Tamil, or South Indian, word for sauce—or, more correctly, the combination of spices that are added to meat, fish, or vegetables to produce a stew. It was the word *kari* that was Anglicized to become the famous "curry." Before chiles, Indian cooks used white pepper and mustard seeds to "heat up" their kari mixtures.

It is suspected that shortly after the fall of Goa to the Portuguese, chile peppers were introduced there by way of trade routes with Lisbon. Because of their familiarity with all kinds of pungent spices, the Indians of the Malabar Coast were undoubtedly quite taken with the fiery pods, and they planted seeds that had been imported from monks' gardens on the Iberian Peninsula.

By 1542, three varieties of chiles were recognized in India, according to Dutch botanist Carolus Clusius, and by the middle of the century chiles were extensively cultivated and exported. One variety of Indian chile was called Pernambuco, after a town in Portuguese Brazil, giving rise to speculation that the chiles had passed from Brazil to Lisbon and then round the Cape to Goa. The difficulty with such a theory is the fact that the principal chile of Brazil was *Capsicum chinense*, yet that species is rare today in India with the exception of 'Bhut Jolokia' in Nagaland, which was transferred from Trinidad in 1854. A more likely scenario is that the chiles introduced into India were of the *annuum* species and from the West Indies, the first chiles grown in Spain and Portugal. This theory is supported by the fact that *Capsicum annuum* became the most extensively cultivated chile in India and its main *Capsicum* of commerce.

Unlike Africa, where chiles were dispersed primarily by birds, in India they were spread by more deliberate cultivation. The capsicums became known as *achar*, a term probably derived from the Native American name *ají*, and as *mirch* in northern India, and *mulagay* in the southern regions of the country and in Sri Lanka. Incidentally, achar is also the name of a spicy pickle.

No matter what they were called, chiles eventually appeared in such a variety of ways in Indian cookery that the diversity and intensity of their use rivals that of Mexico, the Southwestern United States, and some parts of Asia. Four hundred years after chiles first entered India, the degree of their penetration into the various Indian cuisines was vividly illustrated by the cooking experiences of Robert H. Christie.

Christie, a British Army officer, collected recipes from India and used them to prepare elaborate banquets for his fellow members of the Edinburgh Cap and Gown Club in Scotland. In 1911, he published his landmark book on Indian cookery, *Twenty-Two Authentic Banquets from India*, which contains recipes for dishes from all parts of India and from neighboring regions that are today separate countries.

An examination of the ingredients of these recipes reveals that fully two thirds of the nondessert and nonbread recipes contain some form of hot chiles!

In some regions, chiles totally dominated the food. In Christie's chapter on Bengal, for example, 22 of 23 entrées contain chile peppers. In the Madras chapter, the count is 11 of 13, and in the Kashmir chapter, 7 of 8 recipes call for hot chiles in various forms, including fresh green and red plus dried red pods and powders.

Christie's recipes from some regions, such as Punjab, are not nearly so hot, but still it is evident that in 400 years chiles had completely conquered the cuisines of India, a land already rich in spices. They became an essential ingredient in both vegetarian and nonvegetarian cooking—imparting color, flavor, heat, and nutrients.

CHILES CONQUER A SUBCONTINENT

Today in India, the chile is even more prevalent than it was in Christie's time, primarily because of increased agricultural acreage devoted to growing the crop. The most recent figures I could find for Indian chile production were for the year 2013, when India was the top producer of dry peppers in the world, producing 1.4 million metric tons. Their cultivation is widely scattered throughout the country and the amount of consumption varies from state to state. The central and southern states of Andhra Pradesh, Maharashtra, and Tamil Nadu grow and consume the most chiles. India exports nearly a thousand metric tons of red chile pods and 35 metric tons of ground red chile to the United States each year.

The most commonly grown chile is *Capsicum annuum*, of which the New Mexican and cayenne types are most common. Farmers in some locales plant and harvest the chiltepín-like *C. annuum* var. *glabriusculum*, known locally as bird's eye chile. The Tabasco-like *frutescens* species is grown primarily to be a green chile in India. Some chiles are harvested in their green stage and taken directly to produce markets, but most are allowed to dry to their red stage, harvested, and then spread out over sand to dry. Near Madurai in southern India, red chiles in the process of drying can be seen covering a vast area of dozens of acres. After they are sun-dried, the chiles are tossed into the air to allow the wind to blow away sand and straw. Then they are bagged and taken to spice markets where they are sold as whole pods or as various grinds of chile powder.

Spices in general and chiles in particular are so important to the Indian kitchen that they are purchased in *maunds*, a unit of 90 pounds. Once in the kitchen, they are stored until the cook is ready to use them in freshly ground spice mixtures called masalas, which vary greatly from region to region and are designed for

Chilli bajji food stand. The banana peppers advertising the food stand are called chilli bajji and when battered and deep-fried are a popular street-food snack with the same name. Photograph by Shijan Kaakkara. Wikimedia. Creative Commons Attribution-ShareAlike 3.0 Unported License.

specific applications. The masalas generally combine red chiles with cardamom, cinnamon, cloves, cumin, coriander, and black pepper. However, ginger, mustard seeds, fennel, mace, poppy seeds, nutmeg, and saffron also make an appearance in various incarnations of masala.

Whichever spices are chosen to blend with the chiles, they are first roasted separately and then ground together in a *chakki*, a stone mill, or in a *kootani*, an iron mortar and pestle. The dry masala can then be stored in airtight containers or used immediately in cooking. When the dry masala is mixed with water, garlic, and fresh ginger, it becomes a "wet" masala. This paste is generally cooked by itself before adding the vegetables, meat, or fish to the pan.

If the masalas and their culinary use seem familiar, it is because Western cooks often use such spices but substitute commercial curry powder for the freshly made masala. However, such commercial curry powders are not recommended. According to Indian-food expert Dharam Jit Singh, "Curry powders are anathema to Indian cookery, prepared for imaginary palates, having neither the delicacy nor the perfume of flowers and sweet smelling herbs, nor the savour and taste of genuine aromatics."

In India, homemade masala preparations vary from region to region, cook to cook, and dish to dish. They usually contain chiles but occasionally do not. Variations may be thick or watery, or colored white, yellow, green, or red. Whatever kind the cook prepares, it will always be made from freshly ground and mixed spices. I believe that commercially prepared blends of curry spices mask the natural taste of the dishes and make all "Indian" dishes taste the same.

Chile peppers not only transformed the masalas of India but also the chutneys, the primary condiments of the country. "Chutney" is an Anglicized version of the Hindi *chatni*, a word that refers to licking the fingertips, which were the utensils originally used to eat this mixture of chiles, fruits, various vegetables, and spices. Originally, the making of chatni was a method of preserving ripe fruits in the tropical climate. Today, Indian cooks prepare fresh chutney just hours before each meal by mixing fresh ingredients and then chilling them before serving.

Indian cooks are not impressed with Major Grey, the famed brand of bottled relish. They say that this commercial mango preserve bears no resemblance to homemade chutneys because it is too sweet and not hot enough. Also, the prepared chutneys contain too much vinegar and ginger but not enough of the other ingredients that make homemade chutneys superior: mixtures of different chiles

Tomato chutney. Photograph by Shashimangu. Wikimedia. Creative Commons Attribution-ShareAlike 4.0 International License.

and "exotic" ingredients (for bottled chutneys) such as tamarind, bananas, chopped green tomatoes, fresh coriander, coconut, and freshly ground spices.

Despite these complaints, the British and now the Americans are quite fond of the commercial chutneys and serve them with dishes prepared with commercial curry powders. Such a practice is mystifying, especially considering how easy it is to prepare much better-tasting chutneys from scratch.

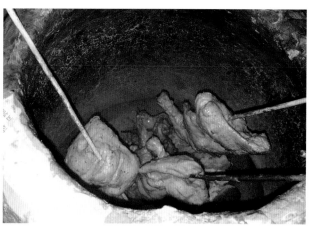

Tandoori chicken with oven. Photograph by Nitin-maul. Wikimedia. Creative Commons Attribution-ShareAlike 4.0 International License.

In addition to their use in masalas and chutneys, chiles also appear as part of various styles of cooking such as vindaloo and tandoori. In vindaloo cooking, meats such as pork, goat, lamb, shrimp, or chicken are marinated for hours or even days in a mixture of vinegar, fiery chiles, fruit pulp, and spices. Then the meat is simmered in the same marinade, a process that melds the marinade with the meat juices and the chiles and reduces the entire mixture to an extremely powerful sauce.

The other style of cooking, tandoori, is very popular in Punjab and also uses chiles as a marinade ingredient; however, the method of cooking the meat is quite different. Instead of being stewed, it is baked in the intense heat generated in a tandoor, a clay oven that is sunk vertically into the ground. The chicken is first scored and then slathered with a yogurt-chile-lime paste. Then the bird is marinated for at least 12 hours in the mixture before it is skewered and inserted into the tandoor.

Cooking the chicken in the intense heat of the tandoor causes two delicious things to happen. The marinade dripping onto the coals below produces an aromatic and pungent smoke, and the dry heat of the oven causes the skin of the chicken to become very crisp while the meat beneath becomes succulent. Combining chiles with yogurt tempers the heat of the chiles while improving the taste of the yogurt. Cooking a whole skewered chicken in a tandoor takes only 20 minutes.

During festival times in India, chiles take center stage—virtually every important dish from every region contains them in great numbers. In Bengal, a whole fish is covered with a paste of chiles, turmeric, and mustard, and then baked. By the way, seafood-chile combinations also figure prominently in festival foods of the state of Kerala; *meen vevichathu*, fish in a hot red chile sauce, is a favorite there, as is *meen*

molee, fish in a creamy green chile–coconut sauce. A leg of lamb roasted with chiles and coriander is a popular festival dish in Rajasthan.

IS GUNTUR THE HOTTEST CITY IN THE WORLD?

The fact that chiles occur in the majority of Indian entrées, side dishes, snacks, and festival specialties is not really surprising. In India it is said, "The climate is hot, the dishes are hotter, and the condiments are the hottest." This saying supports the legendary Indian tolerance for hot chiles. In southern India, a typical meal for four persons can include the following amounts and types of chiles: a handful of soaked and drained whole red chiles, two tablespoons of cayenne powder, two tablespoons of freshly chopped green chiles, and a bowl of whole green chiles on the table for snacking. These chiles are, of course, in addition to the masalas and chutneys that are also used.

In fiery south India, there is another saying, "Heat plus heat equals cool," an allusion to the gustatory sweating caused by hot chiles. The southern state of Andhra Pradesh is the chile capital of the entire country, and, according to the *Wall Street Journal,* the city of Guntur is the hottest city of that state and is another location competing for the title of the hottest city in the world. In 1988, the *Journal* sent reporter Anthony Spaeth to India to investigate rumors that chile peppers had completely conquered the local cuisine. His report was shocking, to say the least.

"In Guntur," he wrote, "salted chiles are eaten for breakfast. Snacks are batter-fried chiles with chile sauce. The town's culinary pride are fruits and vegetables preserved in oil and chile, particularly its karapo pickles: red chiles pickled in chile." Another popular snack is deep-fried chiles dipped in chile powder.

Hot and spicy food is so predominant in Guntur that the agricultural market in town sells a single commodity: chile in its myriad forms. Legend and lore about chiles figures prominently in the culture of Guntur. The people often dream about them, and they believe that hot tempers arise from heavy chile eating and that chiles increase sexual desire. Children begin to eat chiles at age five and quickly build up an incredible tolerance. In addition, the burning of red chile pods is said to ward off evil spells.

In Guntur, as in other worldwide hotbeds of chile consumption, those who do not eat chiles are viewed with concern, if not suspicion. The people of Guntur attribute the abnormal avoidance of chiles to several causes: the offenders have lived abroad, are from out of town, or have married someone from a less fiery state.

THE MIGRATION OF HEAT

Southern India was the starting point for the dissemination of chile peppers north to Nepal, Tibet, and western China; northwest to Pakistan and Afghanistan; west to the Middle East and Central Europe; and east to the Spice Islands and Asia. There is little doubt that the spread of chiles throughout the Indian subcontinent and beyond was along established spice-trade routes. However, chiles were unique among the spices traded—they could grow virtually anywhere. Other spices such as black pepper, ginger, cardamom, nutmeg, and cloves were restricted to certain climactic and geographic zones.

The adaptability of the capsicums led to their quick adoption into the cuisines of the other regions surrounding India. To the north, mountainous Nepal and Tibet adopted not only chiles but another important Andean-mountain food crop combined with them from ancient times: potatoes.

Nepalese food tends to be spicy as well; a popular breakfast chile dish is *khuras ko anda*, eggs scrambled with green chile, onions, tomato, cilantro, and ginger. In another example of parallel cookery, khuras ko anda is virtually identical to the Mexican scrambled-egg dish *huevos revueltos*. In Nepal and northern India, dozens of different kinds of lentils are grown and other popular sources of starch are rice and wheat, which are usually served with a fiery dish such as *masma*, a mixed vegetable curry, or *sungor ko tarkari*, curried pork with chiles.

The Pakistanis' love affair with chiles would seem to be never ending. There is no vegetarian tradition in that Muslim country, so chiles are most often served with the meat, fowl, and fish of choice, which is grilled, roasted, curried, or steamed; lamb, chicken, and beef are the main meats served. The cooking of Pakistan is as closely related to the Middle East as it is to India, so grilled kebab dishes are very popular.

In the Middle East, chiles appear only occasionally in the main dish itself but often in condiments. In Yemen, a powerful sauce called *zhoug* is considered to be not only a condiment; it is said to ward off disease, warm the people in the winter, and burn off calories. Zhoug is made with small green chiles, garlic, fresh parsley and coriander, cumin, and olive oil.

Since chile heat on the Indian subcontinent is greater in the South than in the North, perhaps it is not surprising that Sri Lanka has gained the reputation for the hottest cuisine of the region, although the people of Guntur would surely protest this claim. In this island nation south of India, it is not uncommon for cooks to use as many as 30 large dried red chiles to heat up a dish that serves between six and eight people!

Sri Lanka's reputation for heat rests with its red, white, and black curries. The color of the red curry is derived, not surprisingly, from a preponderance of red chile pods of varying shades. White curries are considerably milder because the chiles are tempered with coconut meat and milk. But it is the "black curries," with dark-roasted curry spices, that give, according to Sri Lankan cooks, better aroma and flavor.

Typically, a Sri Lankan black curry is made as follows: coriander, cumin, fennel, and fenugreek seeds are roasted separately, then combined with whole cinnamon sticks, cloves, cardamom seeds, and leaves from the curry tree. This mixture is then finely ground with mortar and pestle. The finishing touch is the addition of no fewer than three types of chiles. Medium-hot yellow wax chiles are ground together with bush-ripened, dried red chiles called *valieche miris* plus the tiny but deadly hot bird's eye chiles, a form of chiltepín.

From India, chiles also spread east to Bangladesh and Burma, where they are often combined with seafood and poultry. In Bangladesh, whole fish are coated with a hot red-chile masala, then fried in hot mustard oil. In Burma, a dish known as *naga pi* has both Indian and Chinese influences. The spices and the curry cooking style are Indian; the addition of the soy sauce is an adaptation from Asia.

In addition to their culinary usage, chile peppers have worked their way into the customs and traditions of the region to an unusual degree. Many people on the Indian subcontinent believe that the smoke of roasting or even burning chile peppers protects the house and gives a feeling of warmth and security. On the other hand, chiles can be an instrument of terrorism. In 1988, a gang of hoodlums boarded a train in India and began robbing the passengers. Anyone who dared to resist got a handful of chile powder thrown in the face and eyes.

On a lighter note, as our final example of how ingrained chiles are in the cuisines of India, I offer the kitchen of the Taj Mahal Palace Hotel in Mumbai, which now serves Mexican food! Because this famous hostelry must cater to tastes of international guests, it now experiments with a cross-cultural cuisine known as Indian-Mexican food.

In this cross-cultural cuisine, corn masa is replaced with yellow corn flour for making tortillas and tacos. In the tacos, lamb meat is spiced with ginger and turmeric, laced with a paneer salsa made with serrano-like chiles, and sprinkled with distinctive Indian cheeses. Nachos, the familiar snack of the American Southwest, are transformed with the addition of spiced garbanzo beans covered with a red chile sauce made with a combination of New Mexican–type chiles and the far hotter Japanese santaka variety.

Such a collision of cultures recalls that of Latin America, where totally dissimilar foodstuffs were combined with spectacular results to produce coherent cuisines. At the Taj Mahal Palace Hotel, 500 years after chiles were first introduced into India, history repeats itself. However, this time it is two completely different chile-based cuisines that have collided.

Cross-cultural cuisines are inevitable as the world becomes more cosmopolitan, but that fact does not prevent a feeling of disappointment when we travel to an exotic city halfway around the world and are confronted by a Kentucky Fried Chicken franchise. We can only hope that the adoption of foreign foods, such as tacos in India and hamburgers in Pakistan, does not cause the ethnic cuisines to be spoiled or completely lost.

AT THE HUNTING LODGE IN UDAIPUR

Mary Jane and I were about to leave for the cooking demonstration when the roof of our room caved in—or sounded like it was about to. The noise was like a combination of thunder and a herd of water buffaloes, and room 15 at the Shikarbadi Hunting Lodge seemed to shake as if we were suddenly in the epicenter of an aerial earthquake.

"Get the gun," I yelled, imagining an invasion by scimitar-wielding bandits.

"We didn't rent one," Mary Jane reminded me. Amazingly enough, back in 1996, rifles were available for rent at the front desk. That place really *was* a hunting lodge then.

There was only one thing to do—confront the situation directly. My heart was pounding as I wrenched open the door and ran down the steps of the porch and into the trees. The noise was still deafening. I turned around, looked up to the roof, and saw them staring back at me: a troop of sacred langur monkeys jumping up and down on the tile roof and having one hell of a good time.

As Mary Jane and I watched, laughing, one of the security guards came over and attempted to drive the troop away by throwing rocks at them. He finally managed to get them off the roof and into the trees, so, still laughing, we crossed the lawn beside the small lake and joined Pat and Dominique Chapman and the rest of our culinary tour group.

We were nearing the end of our two-week culinary tour of India, a 900-mile bus journey that had taken us from New Delhi to Agra, Jaipur, Jodhpur, and finally to Udaipur. After today, we would fly on to Mumbai and from there back to London. Pat, our tour leader and England's King of Curries, had booked us into the Shikarbadi because of its rustic beauty and its setting in the bush country outside of Udaipur. While walking to the cooking demo, we saw a wild boar drinking at the edge of the lake.

A troop of langur monkeys. Photograph by Alverdissen. Bigstock Photo.

San Jay Anand
(right) and chef
Singh at the cook-
ing demo. Pho-
tograph by Dave
DeWitt.

Chef Chattar Singh led a spirited demonstration of Indian snacks, including *poori*, *pakoras*, *samosas*, *boondi*, and *paneer*. Boondi is a simple fried bread made with chickpea flour and ground lovage seeds (lovage is also known as Italian parsley—substitute celery seeds) while pakoras are deep-fried vegetables that are first coated in a batter of chickpea flour, red chile powder, and turmeric. My favorite pakoras were made of green chile strips, onion, and eggplant. The samosas were the familiar fried triangular turnovers, while the boondi looked a bit like vermicelli but was really from a batter passed through a colander and into hot oil for deep frying. The Indian cottage cheese known as paneer is an acquired taste, but it's a fascinating process to make it.

Water buffalo or whole cow's milk is boiled, then vinegar or lemon juice is added, instantly curdling it. The heat is turned off and the curdled milk is transferred to a fine cloth, which is hung outdoors to drip. After only 30 minutes, the cheese is ready to eat.

Next up for the demo was one of our fellow members of the tour, Sanjay Anand, who owns Madhu's Brilliant Restaurant in Middlesex, England. He gave a spirited demonstration of the incredibly simple—and amazingly tasty—*jeera* chicken, which contains only chicken, salt, black pepper, cumin, and butter. He told us it was his father's favorite recipe.

Another simple yet wonderful fast food was prepared for us at the Rajasthan Painting Development School, where we were buying some fine paintings on camel bone. Pat and one of the directors there fixed *jungli maas*, one of the most basic chile-pepper dishes in the world. All it took was a pot and a small gas burner to make it. They served it to us with no accompaniment except for a bottle of Super Strong Beer, with 8.7 percent alcohol. "Strong chiles call for strong beer," the director told us.

Later that night we sat by the lake sipping nightcaps and listening to the sounds of the countryside. We had learned at dinner that the monkeys were part of the show at the Shikarbadi, as the chefs fed them leftovers and turned them into Indian-food aficionados. But they were asleep now, as we soon were with the full moonlight streaming over the lake and into room 15.

Cows were ubiquitous in India, but not all Hindus love them. At the New Delhi airport, we saw a cabbie whose vehicle was blocked by cows. He got out of his cab and started kicking the cows on their butts, and people were cheering him on. In another part of New Delhi we saw a scene that was so typically Indian that I imagined I was a filmmaker. Our bus was parked near a roundabout. There were four cows milling about in the traffic circle, and every vehicle imaginable was trying to avoid running into them—cars, bicycles, motorcycles, buses, and lorries. I imagined a locked-down shot of that chaos that lasted about 30 seconds, and then a camera tilt up to reveal a billboard advertising computers for sale. India is the weirdest country I visited on my chile pepper quest but also one of the most charming and endearing ones.

As with Stonehenge in England, the Taj Mahal was a bit of a disappointment. It was a sterile monument to love in a dirty, gray, polluted city called Agra. The food was great, however, at a nearby restaurant, despite the fact that it catered to tourists, not locals.

We also stayed at the five-star Taj Lake Palace Hotel in Udaipur, where parts of the James Bond movie *Octopussy* were filmed. The hotel was built as a summer palace in the middle of Lake Pichola between 1743 and 1746 under the direction of the Maharana Jagat Singh II, and it seems as if it is floating on the water. The Internet Movie Database comments, "Permission to shoot in the region of Udaipur had to be sought and granted from the reigning Royal Maharana Bagwat Singh. He would frequently entertain the A-list of the cast and crew at dinners during production, where they would be served specially made Rose Wine."

The most romantic dinner of the entire India trip was set aboard a small replica of the Royal Barge of the Maharaja of Udaipur, which launched after sunset from the Lake Palace, accompanied by a motorboat tender to ferry people back to the hotel to use the restrooms. A nearly full moon reflected off the lake as we ordered drinks from the full bar aboard the boat. The food was mostly seekh kababs, spiced with a green chile paste, that were grilled on small charcoal units resembling Japanese hibachi grills, and the kababs were served over premade rice. But they were spicy and delicious.

After Udaipur, we were done with the bus and took a jet to Mumbai, where we stayed at the Taj Mahal Palace Hotel near the Gateway of India, an arch monument erected to commemorate the landing of King George V and Queen Mary on their visit to India in 1911. I remember walking along the beach near the location of the

immersion of the Ganesh Statues during the 10-day Ganesh Chaturthi festival. Ganesh, of course is the beloved elephant god who is the lord of arts and sciences and the deva of wisdom. Mary Jane and I bought so much stuff on the India trip that we had to buy an additional suitcase, and the walk to the luggage store required us to step over many people sleeping on the sidewalks. We tried not to disturb them.

The highlight of our stay in Mumbai was the extensive set of cooking demonstrations given by the chefs of the Taj Mahal Palace Hotel. Just 12 years after our visit, Pakistani terrorists attacked the hotel, killing 166 people and wounding some of the chefs. When Mary Jane and I, safe in our home in Albuquerque, heard about the horrible attack, we were having "there but for the grace of God" thoughts.

FEATURED CHILE PEPPER: CAYENNE

Most of the chiles grown on Indian farms are varieties of the cayenne pod type. This *annuum* pod type was named after either the city of Cayenne or the Cayenne River, both in French Guiana. However, the chile is not grown commercially there—or anywhere in South America.

The plant is treelike with multiple stems and an erect habit, often reaching 3 feet in height with foliage 2 feet in width. The leaves are ovate, smooth, and medium green in color, measuring 3 ½ inches long and 2 inches wide. The flowers have white corollas with no spots. The pods are elongate and sharply pointed, pendant to curving erect, measuring 6 to 10 inches long by 1 inch wide, and turn red at maturity. A good-sized plant can easily produce 40 or more pods during a season.

There is good reason for Cayenne's reputation as one of the hottest of the chiles. This type consistently measures between 30,000 and 50,000 SHU, making them 10 times hotter than a jalapeño.

A mystery surrounds the origin of cayenne. Possibly this chile was transferred to Europe by the Portuguese, who later introduced it into Africa and India. Cayenne is grown commercially in New Mexico, Louisiana, Africa, India, Japan, and Mexico. The growing period is 90 days or more. In 1988, 15,087 metric tons of dried red chiles—mostly cayenne—were imported into the United States. Dried cayenne pods are known as "Ginnie peppers" in world commerce. Popular cultivars of the cayenne type are 'Hot Portugal,' 'Ring of Fire,' and 'Hades Hot.' They are grown only for their heat, not for color or flavor.

Legend holds that cayenne is the hottest chile pepper of them all, but it is not—the 'Carolina Reaper' holds that honor. The cayenne chile has long been thought to have therapeutic properties. In 1832, herbalist Samuel Thompson writes, "It is no doubt the most powerful stimulant known; its power is entirely congenial to nature, being powerful in raising and maintaining heat, on which life depends. . . . I consider it essentially a benefit, for its effects on the glands causes the saliva to flow freely and leaves the mouth clean and moist."

Primarily this chile is ground into cayenne powder (also called red pepper) or processed into hot sauces. It is quite important in spicing up Cajun dishes such as gumbos and seafood, and the dried pods can be used—carefully—in Asian stir-fry dishes. The fresh green or red pods can be chopped for use in salsas or salads.

recipes

Mango chutney. Photograph by Solnuha, iStock.

CLASSIC MANGO CHUTNEY

yield 1 ½ cups   *heat scale* hot

The word "chutney" comes from the Hindi word chatni, and this fruit version is a fa-vorite during the summer months in northern India. It is not unusual to find multiple chile heat sources in one recipe. This chutney is served with curries or can be used as a glaze for grilled chicken or lamb chops.

2	teaspoons ground cayenne	2	teaspoons ground coriander
5	small green chiles such as serranos, stems and seeds removed, chopped	1	teaspoon ground cumin
		1	teaspoon ground ginger
1	large ripe mango, peeled and chopped	¼	teaspoon ground cloves
3	dried apricots, soaked in water until soft, chopped	¼	teaspoon ground nutmeg
		2	teaspoons honey or sugar
2	tablespoons orange or lime juice		

Place all ingredients in a blender and puree until smooth. Allow the chutney to sit for a couple of hours to blend all the flavors.

JUNGLI MAAS

yield 4 to 6 servings   *heat scale* hot

In the Mewari language of Rajasthan, jungli maas refers to a dish that would be prepared by a stranded hunter who only has the basics with him. It is amazingly tasty considering the limited ingredients. It is also quite hot, so serve it with some plain white rice.

2 cups ghee (clarified butter), or substitute vegetable oil

2 pounds lamb, cut into 1-inch cubes

10 *lal mirch* chiles, or substitute dried cayennes or 'Mirasol' peppers, stems removed, left whole

2 teaspoons salt

Water as needed

In a pot, heat the ghee or oil and add the meat, stirring constantly for 10 minutes. Add the whole chiles and salt, and continue cooking. Add water as necessary to make sure that the meat neither fries nor boils but is essentially braised. Continue cooking until the meat is tender, about an hour more, stirring occasionally. Remove the chiles before serving.

MADRAS CURRY POWDER

yield about 1 cup   *heat scale* hot

The British took the name "curry powder" from the Indian kari podi, which refers to a turmeric-based powder used in the South of India. There is no single recipe for curry, as each dish requires its own spice mixture to produce its own unique taste. However, there are many recipes that call for curry powder, and the following all-purpose mix is a welcome change from commercial products.

5 tablespoons dried, ground red New Mexican chile

2 teaspoons ground cayenne

4 tablespoons ground coriander seeds

4 tablespoons ground cumin seeds

½ teaspoon ground ginger

1 teaspoon ground fenugreek seeds

1 teaspoon freshly ground black pepper

1 tablespoon ground cardamom

1 teaspoon ground cloves

Mix all the ingredients together and grind in a blender or mortar and pestle until fine. Store in a tight-fitting jar.

LAMB VINDALOO

yield 4 servings   *heat scale* very hot

Vindaloo, one of many types of curry, originated in the western region of India. It is derived from the Portuguese dish carne de vinha d'alhos, pork marinated in wine and garlic. It can be prepared with beef, chicken, lamb, or seafood; although not traditional, potatoes sometimes are added. Almost universal on Indian-restaurant menus, vindaloo is one of the hottest curry dishes. Traditionally, it is extremely hot, so adjust the amount of chile to your tolerance level. This recipe has three steps: preparing the marinade, making the curry paste, and cooking the curry. The curry paste and marinade may be made one day ahead.

CURRY PASTE

¼ cup whole grain mustard

2 to 4 tablespoons crushed red pepper flakes (or 4 to 6 dried chiles)

1½ tablespoons ground cumin

1 tablespoon coarse kosher salt

1 tablespoon red wine vinegar

2 teaspoons ground turmeric

MARINADE

1 yellow onion

3 tablespoons coriander seeds

4 to 6 dried Kashmiri or Thai (hotter) chiles

1 tablespoon cumin seeds

8 cloves garlic (about 2½ tablespoons)

1 (1-inch) stick cinnamon

1 teaspoon black peppercorns

2 teaspoons fenugreek seeds

1 teaspoon fennel seeds

1 (1-inch) piece fresh ginger, peeled and chopped

¼ cup white vinegar

2 pounds lamb shoulder, trimmed and cut into 1-inch cubes

¼ cup vegetable oil

2 yellow onions, halved and sliced thinly

8 garlic cloves, minced (about 2½ tablespoons)

1 (13½-ounce) can coconut milk

Prepare the curry paste by combining all of the ingredients in a glass bowl.

Prepare the marinade by grinding the coriander, cumin, cloves, cinnamon, peppercorns, fenugreek, and fennel in a spice grinder or with a mortar and pestle. Process the chiles with the garlic, onion, and ginger to form a paste. Place the meat into a container. Pour the marinade over the meat and marinate, refrigerated, for at least 3 hours or overnight. Remove the lamb from the marinade and drain. Combine the curry paste with the vinegar. Rub the paste onto the meat.

Put oil in a large pot over medium-high heat. Add the onion and fry until it is dark brown but not burnt. Add the garlic and fry for 30 seconds. Add the meat, and stir and brown for about 5 minutes. Pour in the coconut milk. Add more water, if necessary, to just cover the meat. Bring to a boil, cover the pot, reduce to a simmer, and cook for about an hour or until the lamb is tender. Stir occasionally and add more liquid if necessary.

Garnish with chopped cilantro and serve over hot basmati rice with mango chutney and naan bread.

TANDOORI *MURGH* (CHICKEN TANDOORI-STYLE)

yield 4 servings   *heat scale* medium

Tandoori chicken, a famous Indian dish, is also one of the tastiest. The word tandoori refers to any food cooked in a tandoor, which is a giant unglazed clay oven. The chicken in this recipe is marinated twice, first with the lemon juice, then with the yogurt mixture. You can approximate a tandoor by using a charcoal grill or gas broiler, but the food won't achieve the exact flavor. The texture is difficult to duplicate since the tandoor reaches such high temperatures, up to 800 degrees F., but even if the chicken is not strictly traditional, it's still flavorful. Those who are watching their fat intake will like cooking chicken in the tandoori style since the skin is removed from the chicken before it is cooked. And, by using a low-fat yogurt in the marinade, the fat is reduced even further. This chicken is traditionally served with cooling mint chutney. Note: This recipe requires advance preparation.

THE CHICKEN

4	chicken breasts, skin removed
2 to 3 teaspoons ground cayenne chile
1	tablespoon ground paprika
½	teaspoon freshly ground black pepper
½	cup lemon juice
3	tablespoons melted butter
	Garnish: lemon slices, mint raita

THE MARINADE

1	cup plain yogurt
¼	teaspoon crushed saffron threads dissolved in ¼ cup hot water
1	tablespoon grated ginger
1	tablespoon chopped garlic
3	teaspoons ground red chile, such as New Mexican or piquin
2	teaspoons garam masala
1	teaspoon ground coriander
½	teaspoon ground turmeric
½	teaspoon freshly ground black pepper
½	teaspoon ground nutmeg
½	teaspoon ground cinnamon
¼	teaspoon ground cumin
¼	teaspoon ground cloves
½	teaspoon salt

Line a strainer with a dampened cheesecloth, add the yogurt, and place over a bowl. Put the bowl and strainer in the refrigerator, and let the yogurt drain for 4 hours to thicken.

Make slashes in the chicken about 2 inches deep. Combine the cayenne, paprika, and black pepper, and rub the mixture into slashes. Add the lemon juice and coat the chicken. Marinate the chicken for 30 minutes at room temperature, then drain.

Put the drained yogurt and all the rest of the ingredients for the marinade in a blender or food processor and puree until smooth. Pour the marinade over the chicken and, using your fingers, rub it into the meat. Cover the chicken and refrigerate for 24 hours, turning at least once.

Start a charcoal or hardwood fire in your barbecue. Place the grill 2 inches over the coals and grill the chicken for 10 minutes, turning once. Use the marinade to baste the chicken as it cooks. Raise the grill to 5 inches and continue cooking for another 5 minutes, turning once.

Remove the chicken and brush with the melted butter. Return the chicken to the grill and continue to cook for another 5 minutes, turning once, until the chicken is done and the juices run clear.

Serve the chicken garnished with lemon slices and with the mint raita on the side.

PAKORAS SHIKARBADI-STYLE

yield 6 servings   *heat scale* mild

These are some of the easiest Indian snacks to make. You can use any vegetable you like, but we recommend the softer vegetables such as pepper, eggplant, onion, and thinly sliced potato.

2	cups gram (chickpea) flour
1	teaspoon red chile powder
1 t	easpoon salt
1	teaspoon turmeric
1	teaspoon baking powder
	Water
	Peanut oil for frying
	Thinly sliced green chiles, onions, eggplant, and potatoes

In a bowl, combine the gram flour, chile powder, salt, turmeric, and baking powder, and mix well. Add water and mix well until the batter has a creamy consistency. Heat the oil in a deep pan until water splatters when sprinkled on it. Dip the vegetables in the batter, drop them in the oil a few at a time, and cook them until they are golden brown.

SANJAY'S JEERA CHICKEN

yield 8 servings   *heat scale* varies

A high-heat source is essential for this dish. It was cooked for us outdoors over a large gas flame and consequently took only a few minutes to prepare. It is usually served over plain white rice. Sanjay says this chicken tastes better if the bones are left in. He also says that chileheads are permitted to add red chile powder.

1	cup water	3	tablespoons ground jeera (cumin)
1	pound butter	1	teaspoon cumin seeds
2	chickens, skin removed, chopped into 3-inch pieces	3	tablespoons ground black pepper
1	tablespoon salt	1	tablespoon red chile powder (optional)

In a large pot, heat the water to boiling, then add the butter. When the butter is melted and well mixed with the water, add the chicken and salt. Stir for 2 to 3 minutes over high heat. Then add the ground cumin, whole cumin seeds, black pepper, and red chile, if using, and continue stirring and cooking for about 20 to 25 minutes over high heat. The sauce needs to be almost a paste, and the chicken is usually done when the butter returns to the top of the paste. Cut a piece of chicken open to make sure that all the pink is gone from the meat.

Oh soul, come back! Why should you go so far away?
All your household have come to do you honor:
All kinds of good food are ready:
Bitter, salt, sour, hot, and sweet:
There are dishes of all flavors.
Chao Hun, ca. 200 BC

This ancient poem predicts the use of chile peppers in China 20 centuries before they arrived there. It is a fragment from "The Summons of the Soul," written in the third century BC by the Chinese poet Chao Hun, which illustrates an ideal of Asian cookery that persists to this day: the merging of all possible taste sensations into a single dish, or over the course of the meal. Although the poem establishes the necessity of hot spices in Asian cooking, there was one slight problem: chile peppers did not exist in Asia at that time, so the "hot" flavors of good food could not be fully accomplished.

What spice fired up Asian cooking before chiles arrived on the scene? Most probably, the fruit of a thorny shrub called *Fagara*, also known as prickly ash. The berries of this bush are called brown pepper or Sichuan pepper and are pungent in a manner similar to peppercorns, ginger, or horseradish but are not truly hot like chiles. They tend to numb the mouth. Yes, they assault the senses momentarily, but then quickly fade away because they lack the real burn of capsaicin. Alas *Fagara* was a modest flame compared to what was on the way.

Fagara, or Sichuan pepper. Photograph by Dave DeWitt.

Asians waited 2,000 years for a truly hot ingredient to complement their other classic flavors and to fulfill the prophecy of Chao Hun's poem. They were finally rewarded in the sixteenth century, when the real heat arrived: chile peppers. Asian cuisines would never lack for heat again.

Fire in the wok: cooking in a Singapore hawker center. Photograph by Rick Browne. Used with permission.

As often happens during the transfer of foods around the world, the New World origin of chile peppers is unknown or forgotten. European explorers and colonists assumed the plants were native to Africa or India because the natives they encountered so loved the hot fruits. In effect, chiles spread across the globe faster than history could keep track of them. The reason for this quick dissemination of chiles was simple: supply and demand. The traders and their customers simply loved the new hot spice.

Portuguese traders introduced the capsicums into Thailand as early as 1511, probably from their trading base in Malacca, between the Malay Peninsula and Sumatra. Although hard evidence is lacking, ethnobotanists theorize that Arab and Hindu traders carried the Indian chile peppers to Indonesia around the late 1520s, and from there to New Guinea. In 1529, a treaty between Spain and Portugal gave the Spanish control of the Philippines and the Portuguese control of Malaysia. By 1550, chiles had become well established in the East Indies, probably spread both by birds as well as by human trade and cultivation.

Some theories hold that either Malay, Chinese, or Portuguese traders first introduced chiles to China through the ports of Macao and Singapore, although other scenarios suggest that the chiles in western China were imported from India. The expansion of chile agriculture into Asia was assisted by the Spanish, who had colonies in the Philippines by 1571, and had established trade routes to Canton, China, and Nagasaki, Japan.

From Manila in the Philippines, the Spanish established a galleon route to Acapulco, Mexico, by way of Micronesia and Melanesia, thus spreading chile peppers into the Pacific Islands. So by 1593, just a century after Columbus "discovered" them and brought them back across the Atlantic, chile peppers had encircled the globe. It is an ironic culinary fact that the imported chiles became more important than many traditional spices in Asian cuisines, thus illustrating how the pungency of chiles has combined with other flavors to win a fanatic following of devotees.

Although chile peppers are present to some extent in all Asian countries, they are particularly beloved in the cuisines of three distinct regions: Thailand and nearby Laos and Vietnam; Indonesia and Malaysia; and China and Korea. Chile peppers do appear as condiments and occasionally in recipes from the Philippines and Japan, but they are less of a factor in those cuisines.

THE FIERY TRIANGLE: THAILAND AND ITS NEIGHBORS

The San Francisco Bay Area, with a total Thai population of about 1,000, has more than 100 Thai restaurants. The Los Angeles area, with fewer citizens of Thai heritage, has more than 200 Thai restaurants! It is for good reason that Thai cuisine has become a favorite of American fiery-food aficionados—it is one of the hottest cuisines in the world, and also one of the most diverse in terms of the different varieties of chiles that are used. As Thai-food expert Jennifer Brennan describes the process, chile peppers were "adopted by the Thai with a fervor normally associated with the return of a long-lost child."

Perhaps, then, it is no surprise that Bangkok is also in the running for the title of hottest city in the world. This city is populated not only by the chile-loving Thais and Chinese but also by other ethnic groups that use them heavily in their cuisines: East Indians, Pakistanis, and Malays. Bangkok markets rival those of Mexico for the varieties of chiles (called *prik*) that are offered for sale. One of the most common chiles, *prik chee fa*, is fat and about four inches long and closely resembles a small version of the New Mexican pods. According to one source, the favorite chile of Thailand is *prik kee nu luang*, a small orange variety. Other chiles include a wax-type chile; the long, thin "Thai" chiles; cayenne or piquin varieties such as Thai bird pepper and the Japanese santaka; and Kashmiri chiles, which are close relatives of the jalapeños and serranos.

Chiles in the wholesale market, Bangkok. Photograph by Dave DeWitt.

The Kashmiri chiles are also called sriracha chiles. They are so named because a sauce made from these chiles originated in the Thai seaside town of Sriracha as an accompaniment to fish, and it became so popular that it has been bottled and sold around the world.

Another popular Thai sauce is *nam prik*, which consists of a bewildering number of possible ingredients including fish sauce, chiles, garlic, sugar, lime juice, and even egg yolks. The same traders who brought the chile pepper to Thailand also spread the use of curries from India to all parts of the globe. Consequently, Thailand is a perfect example of a culinary collision of cultures; Indian curry spices were combined with the latest exotic import—chile peppers—to create some of the hottest curries on earth. In fact, hot curries are staples in Thai cooking and take several forms. One form is curry pastes, which consist of onions, garlic, chiles, and curry spices such as coriander and cardamom all pounded together with mortar and pestle until smooth. Commercially prepared curry pastes can be purchased in Asian markets or made at home by utilizing a food processor or blender.

Another type of curry, *kaeng*, is a term for a bewildering variety of Thai curries. Some kaengs resemble liquid Indian curry sauces and are abundant with traditional curry spices such as turmeric, coriander, and cardamom. Another type of kaeng curry omits these curry spices and substitutes herbs like cilantro, but the chiles are still there. This second group of kaeng curries is said to be the original Thai curries, invented long before they were influenced by Indian spices. As with the curries of Sri Lanka, these kaeng curries are multicolored; depending on the color of the chiles and other spices, and the amount of coconut milk added, they range from light yellow to green to pale red.

Kaeng kari is yellow colored because it contains most of the curry spices, including turmeric, and is fairly mild. One of the more pungent of these kaeng curries, *kaeng phet*, is made with tiny red chiles, coconut milk, and basil leaves, and it is served with seafood.

Such a culinary practice illustrates yet another aspect of Thai cuisine: the presentation of the meal. "The Thais are as interested in beautiful presentation as the Japanese are," writes Jennifer Brennan. "The contrasts of color and texture, of hot and cold, of spicy and mild, are as important here as in any cuisine in the world."

Considering the emphasis on both heat and presentation in their cuisine, it is not surprising that the Thais love to garnish their hot meals with—what else?—hot chiles. Their adoration for the chile pepper extends to elaborately carved chile-pod flowers. They use multicolored small chiles for the best flower effect, with colors ranging from green to yellow to red to purple. The procedure for creating chile pepper–pod flowers is quite simple. Hold the chile by the stem on a cutting board and use a sharp knife to slice the chile in half, lengthwise, starting an eighth of an inch from the stem and moving down to the point (or apex, for the botanically minded). Rotate the chile 180 degrees and repeat the procedure until the chile is divided into sixteenths or more.

The thinner the "petals," the more convincing the chiles will be as flowers when the chiles are soaked in water containing ice cubes, which is the next step. Immerse the chiles in ice water until the slices curl—a few hours—and then remove the seeds with the tip of a knife. The chile flowers are then arranged artistically on the platter and later devoured as a spicy salad condiment that accompanies the traditional Thai curries.

The influence of such curries, with all their multiple spices, did not extend into Laos, which borders Thailand to the northeast. Rather, fresh small red and green chiles are used extensively in a number of chile pastes there. Jalapeño- and serrano-type chiles are beaten with pestles in huge mortars, and locally available spices are added. My favorite Laotian creation is a dish called *mawk mak phet*, which is a delicious example of a fresh-chile recipe from that country.

It features poblano or New Mexican chiles that are stuffed with vegetables, spices, and white fish, and then steamed.

Fish combined with chiles also provides the essential flavor of the third country of our "fiery triangle." In Vietnam, where the heart of the chile cuisine coincides with the center of the country, principally in the city of Hue, a fish and chile sauce called *nuac cham* reigns supreme. It consists of fish sauce, lime, sugar, garlic, and fresh small red serrano-type chiles.

THE SPICIEST ISLANDS: INDONESIA, MALAYSIA, AND SINGAPORE

The spice trade was one of the primary motivating factors in European exploration of the rest of the world, so it is not surprising that many countries sought to control the output of the "Spice Islands." These islands, which now comprise parts of the countries of Indonesia and Malaysia, produced cinnamon, cloves, nutmeg, black pepper, and many other spices. What is surprising about the Spice Islands is that they were infiltrated and "conquered" by a New World spice—chile peppers.

After the Portuguese won control of the Strait of Malacca in 1511, it is probable that chile peppers were imported soon afterward by traders sailing to and from the Portuguese colony of Goa, India. Asian food authority Copeland Marks observes that the cuisine of the region would be "unthinkable without them. . . . When the chile arrived in Indonesia it was welcomed enthusiastically and now may be considered an addiction."

In Indonesia, where chiles are variously called *cabe* or *lombok*, they are added to many dishes and often combined with coconut cream or milk. On the island of Java, sugar is added, making that cuisine a mixture of sweet, sour, and fiery hot. Some cooks there believe that the addition of sugar keeps the power of the chiles and other spices under control.

Perhaps the principal use of chiles in this part of Asia is in sauces that are spread over rice or are used as a dip for satay, barbecued small chunks of meat. Chiles are often combined with peanuts for the satay dips. Other favorite hot-chile sauces are the *sambals*, which are relishes made from lime

Indonesian *sambal terasi* that is served with raw vegetables (*labab*). Photograph by Gunawan Kartapranata. Wikimedia. Creative Commons Attribution-ShareAlike 3.0 Unported License.

juice, shallots or onions, garlic, and fresh chiles, and are usually served over plain white rice. An Indonesian legend holds that even a plain-looking girl will find a husband if she can create a great sambal. On the island of Sumatra, cooks make *lado*—a sambal consisting of chiles, salt, tamarind, and shallots—which is stir-fried with seafood, hardboiled eggs, or vegetables.

One of the most interesting chile cuisines of Asia is the Nonya cooking of Singapore, which illustrates the collision of Chinese dishes with Malay spices such as curries and chiles. The Nonyas are descendants of mixed marriages of Malay women and Chinese men, who insisted that their wives cook in the Chinese style. The necessity of using Malaysian rather than Chinese produce resulted in the addition of chile peppers to the recipes.

A Singapore Fling

In 1992, people laughed in disbelief when we told them we were going to Singapore on business. "Yeah, right," said one skeptic, "you foodies will use any excuse for a gourmet holiday." But we were telling the truth. In fact, we took along our bathing suits on the trip but were so busy we never got to wear them.

Of course, we did dine out a bit—after all, it was our job. We were in Singapore to plan a culinary tour for the following year. Besides myself, along for the feast were my wife, Mary Jane Wilan, Ellie Leavitt of Rio Grande Travel, and her daughter, Laura Brancato.

We flew into Singapore from Bangkok aboard Cathay Pacific Airlines—certainly one of the best carriers in the world. The efficient folks from Franco-Asian Travel picked us up at the airport, checked us into the Regent hotel, and wasted no time introducing us to the wonders of Singapore's great food.

"We're off to the Newton Circus Hawker Centre," announced Jeanne Seah, our culinary guide for the evening. Within minutes, we were sampling barbecued stingray—and other strange but delicious foods.

The Hawker Centre—so named because in the past the cooks would "hawk" their food to customers—consisted of perhaps 50 open-air stalls and 100 tables, and was jam-packed with hungry diners. Intense and exotic aromas wafted from the food stalls, which sported an intriguing array of signs, such as "Juriah Nasi Padang" and "Rojak Tow Kua Pow Cuttlefish." The hawkers specialized in a bewildering selection of quick and inexpensive foods from many cuisines. Among the delicacies we tasted on our first night in Singapore were Chinese 1,000-year-old eggs, the famous Singapore chilli crab, Indonesian satays, Indian curried dishes, and the Malayan stingray.

I was intensely curious about how and why so many cuisines were represented in one place. Later, back at the Regent, I bought a copy of *Singapore: 101 Meals* (published by the Singapore Tourist Promotion Board), which explains the history behind the foods we had just tried.

Flashback: Singapore's Culinary Heritage

Singapore is the melting pot (or maybe the tossed salad) of Southeast Asia, so it's not surprising that many ethnic influences are present. Originally, this tiny island nation—smaller than New York City—was part of what is now Malaysia, which means that its original cuisine was Malay. Fresh spices are the key to Malay cookery, and they include lemongrass, turmeric, kaffir lime, galangal (a rhizome similar to ginger), and, of course, the ubiquitous chiles—spelled "chillis" over there.

Since Singapore is so close to Indonesia (Sumatra is just across the Strait of Malacca), the influences from that huge archipelago-nation are significant. In fact, since the words for rice (*nasi*), chicken (*ayam*), hot sauce (*sambal*), and many other food terms are identical, it is difficult if not impossible to separate the Malaysian and Indonesian influences on Singaporean food. The famous satays, barbecued meats and seafood, occur in both countries and are very popular in Singapore. Interestingly enough, the satays are thought to have originated with early Arab spice traders who introduced the concept of kebabs to the region.

In 1819, Sir Stamford Raffles colonized Singapore for the British, and soon the small fishing village became the leading port east of the Suez Canal. The British influence accounts for the fact that the principal language of Singapore is English (other official languages are Tamil, Malay, and Cantonese), but the impact of the Brits on food was not so great. Nowadays, about the only surviving British culinary heritages involve drink; the hotels and restaurants serve high tea in the afternoon, excellent Singapore-brewed beers and stouts, and plenty of gin drinks.

The expansion of Singapore as a major trading center led to settlement by other ethnic groups. By 1821, the population was over 5,000, and besides Malays and Europeans, there were numerous Chinese and Indian settlers. Under British control, the settlers were kept in their own ethnic enclaves so they could not easily unite and rebel. These enclaves—such as Chinatown, Arab Street, and Little India—though unofficial now, still exist to this day. Singapore was a British colony until 1959, when it became autonomous within the Commonwealth. In 1963, Singapore joined with Malaya and neighboring straits states to form the Federation of Malaysia, but that union did not last and Singapore became an independent nation in 1965.

The influence of the Chinese—who now make up about three-quarters of the population—has been vast. The major Chinese immigrants were Hokkiens (from Fujian Province), Teochews, Cantonese, and Hainanese. All brought their own regional cultures and food traditions to Singapore and settled in their own enclaves. Many of earliest Chinese settlers were men, and because of the lack of Chinese women in Singapore, they married Malay women. Thus a distinct subculture was born, known in Malay as Peranakan (meaning "to be born here"). The women of that subculture were known as Nonyas, Malay for "ladies." The intermarriage of Chinese and Malays ended once the population of Singapore grew large enough to include Chinese women, and Nonyas soon became part of the mainstream of Singapore culture. But one Nonya tradition—cooking—lives on. Nonya cuisine is an excellent example of a collision of cultures as it combines the subtlety and relative blandness of Chinese cooking with the spiciness of Malay food. It has been said that "in one meal, you get a perfect balance of opposing flavors, textures, and colors." Some notable Nonya dishes include *assam gulai*, fish in spicy tamarind sauce; *buah paya masak titek*, papaya soup with chillis; *sayor nanka masak lemak*, jackfruit and chicken in spicy coconut gravy; and the notable Nonya *kuehs*, elegant dessert cakes fashioned from glutinous rice, coconut milk, palm sugar, and fruits.

After boning up—so to speak—on the history of the Singaporean cuisines, I felt ready to eat my way across the city. Of course, there was the usual problem: so much food, so little time.

Off to the Markets

With Anthony as our driver and Vincent as our guide, we continued our tour the following day with a trip to the dry and wet markets of Little India and Chinatown. In Little India, we first visited the "dry" markets selling the various spices that comprise the curries: chillis, cloves, turmeric, star anise, peppercorns, cinnamon, coriander—and more. It was a vivid sensory assault on the eyes and nose. As Mary Jane put it, "I've never been any place that smelled so wonderful and exotic." We watched Indian cooks prepare the chapati flatbread, and we tasted a wide variety of "chips" made from various flours.

The "wet" market, so named because there was water on the floor from the cleaning of seafood and meats, was a huge warehouse-like affair with the sides open to the air. It was neatly divided into sections: fruits, vegetables, meats, seafood, groceries, and food vendors. Despite the noise and crowded conditions, I was surprised by how clean everything was. All vendors touching meats or seafood wore plastic gloves, and everyone was low-key and very friendly—even urging me on occasion to photograph them in action cleaving the heads off of fishes. We found out later what the fish heads were used for.

There was a profusion of food in the wet market. Lamb and mutton were hanging to age, every type of tropical fruit was available for sale—except the notorious durian, which was out of season—and there were tiger prawns seven to eight inches long. The fresh chiles for sale looked just like the ones we had seen the week before in Bangkok, and I soon found out why: they were imported from Thailand because Singapore does not have much of an agriculture industry. Typical of chile nomenclature around the world, the kinds available were "bird peppers," green or red piquin-like, fiery little devils less than an inch long; "yellow chillis," about three inches long; and "red chillis," which looked like a cross between cayenne and New Mexican varieties and were also sold in the green form.

We took a break to sample Indian rose milk and tea, and then pushed on to the Chinatown wet market, where I was surprised by the number of live animals for sale. There were large fish swimming in aquariums—the freshest imaginable—and huge crabs crawling around in cages. I recall one memorable transaction where the vendor removed several frogs from a cage to show a customer how fresh they were. The woman shopper chose the one that jumped the farthest and the vendor quickly killed and skinned it on the spot. I was relieved to note that there were no live pigs for sale in the market.

But there were some black chickens—described by our guide, Vincent, as "another race" of fowl. The plucked flesh is naturally black, not dyed, and is used by Chinese cooks for medicinal purposes—like helping people regain their strength after illness. Chicken soup must be a worldwide cure.

Alimentary Adventures

The next couple of days were a blur. We took a trip across the causeway to Johore Bahru, Malaysia, where we toured the Sultan's palace, now a museum, and then stopped at a very modern supermarket where we found a wealth of Malaysian hot sauces filling the shelves of three aisles. On the way back, we toured the excellent Singapore zoo and an orchid farm, and finally stopped for a late lunch at a neighborhood Chinese coffee shop. It was unlike any coffee shop in the States because we feasted on "rib tea," *bak kut teh*, a pork-rib soup with spices. The dining technique called for removing the pork, dipping it in two different chilli sauces, and then drinking the soup later. Since it was about 90 degrees with no air conditioning in the restaurant, I opted for a Tiger Beer instead of coffee.

The following day, it was time to split up. The women in the group wanted to shop along Orchard Road, Singapore's fabulous row with designer shop after shop. I, as the lone male, opted for the Singapore Botanic Gardens and its great collection of tropical plants and trees.

After shopping, Mary Jane, Ellie, and Laura visited the famous Raffles Hotel, where they took Rudyard Kipling's 1888 advice, "Feed at Raffles when visiting Singapore." Fortified with Singapore Slings and gin and tonics, they snacked on tiger prawns with a spicy herbal dip and curried mutton samosas (turnovers) with a yogurt-dill dip. Then they discovered that Raffles has a "Provisions" shop, where locally-produced food products can be purchased, so more shopping was in order.

Hungry after wandering for miles through the Botanic Gardens, I ate at an Indonesian restaurant on upper Orchard Road (I confess I forgot to write down the name). It must be a local favorite, because no tourists were in sight. The mutton soup, flavored with coconut milk and highly spiced with chiles, was fabulous. I spooned it over a side dish of *nasi kunyit*, yellow festive rice, and had no idea if

Raffles Hotel.
Photograph by
James Mason-
Hudson. Wikimedia.
Creative Commons
Attribution-
ShareAlike 3.0
Unported License.

that technique was proper or not. But since no one yelled at me or even gave me that "funny foreigner" look, I guess I did okay.

After playing tourist for a day, it was time to get back to the business of planning the culinary tour, so we arranged to interview two of Singapore's noted cooking authorities. Our first visit was to the Thomson Cooking Studio, where Mrs. Devagi Shanmugam was preparing dishes that were being photographed for a brochure for McCormick Spice Company. Mrs. Shanmugam is of Indian heritage but has mastered all of Singapore's numerous cuisines. We tasted her green beans with spicy prawn paste, which was excellent, and some stir-fried sea cucumbers, which are definitely an acquired taste. Sea cucumbers, for the biologists in the crowd, are echinoderms related to starfish and sea urchins, and their flesh is gummy and bland. They were the only food on the entire trip I didn't love—but they are considered to be quite a delicacy in Singapore.

Mrs. Shanmugam showed us her huge recipe collection, and I decided to take a chance.

"Do you happen to have recipes for mutton soup and nasi kunyit?" I asked. She smiled, quickly produced recipes for the very dishes I had tried the day before, and urged me to share them with our readers.

Our next culinary advisor was Violet Oon, the foodie star of Singapore. Violet is one of those people who have so many enterprises going at the same time that she probably has a fax machine in her Mercedes. Along with her assistant, Diana Lynn, she operates a cooking school, publishes *The Food Paper* (one of the most interesting food publications I've ever read), and manufactures her own line of food products, which are sold by the Raffles Hotel.

For our last evening in Singapore, Violet decided that since we had already sampled Chinese, Indonesian, Malay, and Nonya foods, it was time for some Indian treats. She and Diana drove us to Little India where we dined at the Madras New Woodlands Restaurant and the Banana Leaf Apolo.

We sampled every curry imaginable, using banana leaves for plates, and I was particularly impressed with the fish-roe curry cakes (I ate shad roe for breakfast when I lived in Virginia). And, although it doesn't sound very appetizing, the fish-head curry was nothing short of spectacular—once I got used to the fish staring at me. The curries were a fitting end to a whirlwind week in Singapore.

Planning an overseas tour may be hard work, but when it involves food, it's fun too.

PS. I gained 15 pounds in Singapore.

Fish head curry on a banana leaf. Photograph by Pelican. Wikimedia. Creative Commons Attribution-ShareAlike 2.0 Generic License.

CHINA AND BEYOND

Despite the recent popularity of Thai cooking in the United States, there is little doubt that the Asian reputation for hot-chile cooking began with China, particularly the regions of Sichuan and Hunan. However, we should not ignore other parts of China. Although most current Chinese cookbooks are devoid of chile pepper recipes from Canton and other areas of south China, two members of the family Solanaceae eventually were adopted there. According to Chinese food expert E. N. Anderson, "Tomatoes and chiles not only transformed the taste of southern Chinese cooking, they also provided new and very rich sources of vitamins A and C and certain minerals, thus improving the diet of the south Chinese considerably. Easy to grow, highly productive, and bearing virtually year-round in the subtropical climate, these plants eliminated the seasonal bottlenecks on vitamin availability."

But it was in the West where chiles really triumphed in Chinese cuisine, and there are at least two mysteries about the use of chiles in western China. The first question is, how did they get there? The second, why did the Chinese love them so much?

Some experts speculate that chiles were imported from Singapore, or carried inland from Macao, where hot dishes are more popular today than in neighboring Canton. More likely is the theory that chiles were introduced into Sichuan by sixteenth-century Indian Buddhist missionaries traveling the Silk Route between India and China. After all, western Sichuan is closer to India than to either Macao or Singapore.

According to Jeremiah Jenne, writing in *The Beijinger*, the first record of chiles in China is from a 1671 gazetteer in Zhejiang Province: "It is red and can be used for seasoning." He also cites a reference in 1682 from Liaoning, giving credence to the theory that chiles arrived in China by sea. The first reference to chiles in Hunan was in 1684, but surprisingly, the first mention of them in Sichuan Province was much later, in 1749. China has "pockets of heat" like we've seen in Central and South America. Some provinces, like Guangdong and Zhejiang, where chiles first appeared, did not develop chile cuisines, while other provinces, namely Sichuan, Hunan, Guizhou, Yunnan, and Xinjiang, adopted chile peppers with great enthusiasm. Another *Beijinger* writer, Robynne

'Facing Heaven' chiles. Photograph by Richard Elzey. Wikimedia. Creative Commons Attribution 2.0 Generic License.

Tindall, observes: "Chiles have conquered the palates of most of China in one way or another but each province has its own way of applying them and other spices based on the local climate and produce."

Tom Arnstein, also writing in *The Beijinger*, notes that "it was Mao Zedong who famously said, 'no chiles, no revolution.' A native of Hunan, Mao was no stranger to the fiery effect that chiles could have on a person and although we can't be sure whether it was the power of spice that fueled his fighting spirit, we can only assume that it provided a helping hand." Then he went on to write that there are 2,000 types of chiles in China, but 5 of the most notable cultivars are 'Facing Heaven' (40,000 SHU), 'Yunnan Wrinkled Skin' (55,000 SHU), 'Sichuan Seven-Star' (60,000 SHU), 'Hainan Yellow Lantern' (170,000 SHU), and the hottest of them all, 'Yunnan Shuan Shuan' (1,000,000 SHU).

No matter how they arrived in western China, chiles soon became enormously important to the food of the people. E. N. Anderson, who has studied the chile situation in China extensively, describes the effect of chiles on the cuisines of East Asia as "epochal." The use of the large varieties of *Capsicum annuum*, called *la chiao*, was important because of the addition of vitamins A and C to low-vitamin grains such as rice. In western China, chiles were easy to grow and simple to preserve, and soon became vital to life there.

The second mystery is why chiles were embraced with such fervor in western China. As usual, many theories have been advanced by ethnobotanists, anthropologists, and Asian-studies experts. The three most likely theories are the Perennial Cool-Down Principle, the Food Preservation Scenario, and the Poetic Proposition.

The Perennial Cool-Down Principle holds that since New World cultures utilized chiles to cool down in hot climates, it makes sense that they would be put to the same use when introduced into other regions. In China, there are hot tropical inlands similar to regions in South America and Mexico, where chiles were first adopted into the human diet. In such regions where it doesn't freeze, chiles grow as perennials, so they are available all year long.

Another possible reason for the popularity of chiles in western China is the Food Preservation Scenario. Before salt was mined in the region, the Sichuanese utilized hot spices as a substitute. Later, chile peppers came into use as a food preservative in the form of chile pastes and chile oils.

Perhaps the most persuasive theory for the popularity of chiles is the Poetic Proposition, which recalls Chao Hun's poem. According to author-chef Karen Lee, "The hot peppers stimulate the palate, causing a sensitivity that brings an awareness of the spectrum of flavors to follow: after the hot and spicy, the mild, mellow, sour,

Demonstration Chilli Field. Photograph by Dave DeWitt.

salty, sweet, aromatic, bland, bitter, and pungent flavors linger in the aftertaste." This theory echoes Chao Hun's "Summons of the Soul" because it utilizes the combination of multiple flavors in a single meal.

In addition to fresh and dried chiles, Sichuan and Hunan cooks depend upon chile pastes and oils to provide the heat in their meals. Fresh peppers are more commonly used in Hunan than Sichuan, where small dried santaka-type chiles are commonly added whole, seeds and all, to stir-fry dishes. Other commonly used seasonings in the cooking of Sichuan and Hunan are sesame-seed paste, chile paste with garlic, and an aromatic chile vinegar.

Chile in such forms is often combined with ground rice, sesame seeds, and peanuts as a snack or a coating for grilled meats. The combination of chiles with nutty products like sesame seeds and peanuts is called *ma la* and is one of the essential flavors of western Chinese cooking.

Contrary to popular belief, chefs cooking in the Sichuan or Hunan style are not trying to incinerate the people who eat their creations. Howard Hillman, an expert on world cuisines, writes of the way heat is applied in western China: "Even on the peasant level, the people prefer the dishes on the table to have degrees of hotness varying from mild to fiery. This is in contrast to the monotonous everything-as-hot-as-possible approach favored by many non-Chinese Sichuan restaurant-goers. Making one Sichuan dish hotter than another is not a measure of a chef's talent; all it takes is the addition of extra chile, a feat that could be performed by a trained monkey. Epicures judge a Sichuan chef by the subtly complex overtones of his sauces and whether they complement the other ingredients in his dishes."

Robynne Tindall, writing in *The Beijinger*, comments on the differences between Hunan and Sichuan food: "Hunan food is close to Sichuan food in terms of spice level but there are a few key differences. Firstly, most dishes eschew Sichuan pepper [*Fagara*], allowing the flavor of the chilies (used liberally, both fresh and dried) to shine through. Secondly, Hunan cuisine makes much greater use of dried, preserved meats, giving many dishes a smoky, savory edge."

She thinks the food of Guizou is the hottest of all the provinces. "To give you an idea of just how spicy the food is, turn to the popular saying, 'Sichuan people don't fear spicy; Hunan people can eat anything no matter how spicy; Guizhou people fear their food won't be spicy enough.'" As far as Yunnan is concerned, she writes: "Traveling further south into the region on the border with Laos and Myanmar, dried chilies are replaced with fresh and lime juice makes an appearance in cold dishes and salads—think Thai cuisine without the sweet-sour-salty balance."

Perhaps the most obscure fiery cuisine of Asia is that of Xinjiang, China's largest province. Located in the northwest part of the country, surrounded by Tibet, Russia, Mongolia, Afghanistan, and Pakistan, Xinjiang is the land of the Uygurs, the

Chile decorations in a store in Haikou, the capital of Hainan. Photograph by Gerald Zhang-Schmidt. Used with permission.

Mongols, and other peoples related to Turkic central Asians. The capital of Xinjiang is Urumchi, the most inland city in the world. Here, where most of the population is Muslim, pork is replaced by lamb, which is commonly combined with chile peppers.

My favorite lamb and chile dish from Xinjiang is *kao yang ruo chuan*, Xinjiang lamb and chile barbecue, in which lamb kebabs are marinated in garlic, lemon, and an extremely hot chile-oil sauce, and then barbecued with jalapeño-type chiles. Other lamb and chile dishes from the region include a sliced-lamb meal with onions and jalapeño-type chiles; *la tiao zi*, which combines noodles and lamb with a garlic and chile pepper sauce; and lamb-filled pot stickers with hot chile-vinegar-soy sauce.

Tindall's observation about Xinjiang is that "for many, the defining flavor of this region is the chili-cumin mix that gets sprinkled on grilled lamb kebabs. In an area that mostly cooks with lamb and beef, cumin is the perfect complementary spice.

Xinjiang isn't the only cuisine to use cumin, however; it crops up in Hunan cuisine, too, and other areas with a largely Hui Muslim population."

What does the future hold for China's ever-growing fascination with chile peppers? At first, the New World furnished chiles to China, which returned the favor by inventing great recipes for their use. But now Asia is selling us their chiles and thus starting a chile trade war that may eventually lead to a serious balance-of-chiles deficit.

In 1988, China was the second largest exporter of whole chile pods into the United States, shipping 2,400 metric tons that year. Ground red chiles transported from Hong Kong contributed another 254 metric tons to the total. It seems that these days the Chinese are as interested in chile money as chile poetry, and although precise figures are not available, there is little doubt that the People's Republic of China is now the greatest producer and consumer of chile peppers in the world, surpassing even India, Mexico, and the United States. In 2018, China produced 16.1 million metric tons of fresh chile peppers and is by far the largest grower of chiles in the world.

At the Chinese Capsicum Expo

In August of 2018, I accepted the invitation of the Organizing Committee of the Zunyi International Capsicum Expo and DeZhuang International Limited to attend the third annual International Capsicum Expo in Zunyi, China, in Guizhou Province. It was an incredible experience.

As Wang Xiaobing, director general of the information center of the Ministry of Agriculture and Rural Affairs said in his opening address at the expo, "Zunyi City, in particular, thanks to years of hard work, has made itself a nationally renowned advantageous area of its specialty produce Facing Heaven Chilli, built China's largest chilli wholesale market network" and become "the most important chilli trading hub." Zunyi is the true Chile Pepper Capital of China.

A requirement of the trip was that I, too, had to deliver a speech at the opening ceremony, and I chose to speak about New Mexican chiles. Fortunately, there was simultaneous translation of English to Chinese and vice versa. And I was provided a personal assistant and translator. Her name was Jo and she was 50 years younger than I. Many Chinese women adopt English names for professional reasons. She spoke excellent English and was funny and charming, not to mention beautiful.

After the opening ceremony, we were taken on tours of Xiazi Town's ultramodern China Pepper Quality Testing Center and the Global Chilli Processing and Trading Center, where companies can process their chiles and manufacture chile products. Also in Xiazi Town was the five-acre Demonstration Chilli Field where we could examine a thousand different varieties of Chinese chiles. A large red banner about 200 feet long above the field advertised the Capsicum Expo. Finally we explored the Expo Center where the wholesaling and retailing of chile products occurred in a complex of warehouses divided into booths for the exhibitors.

DeZhuang International, one of my sponsors, exhibited there, selling their numerous products. In their company brochure is a description of their operation: "DeZhuang owns 17 subsidiaries so far and has expanded into a business of 900 Huo Guo [hot pot] restaurants over China and internationally. With over 30 product lines, 120 products, and around 300 distributors, DeZhuang has already become a highly recognized brand."

After Zunyi, our group took the high-speed train to Chongquin, the largest city in the world with 30 million inhabitants. I stayed at the Radisson Hotel overlooking the Yangtze River, visited restaurants and the Three Gorges Museum, and had meetings with the management of DeZhuang International. It was a spice-laden trip I will never forget.

JAPAN'S SPICY SNACKS

Even the Japanese, who are not known for fiery cuisines, are becoming more interested in and devoted to the chile pepper. Soon after the Portuguese arrived, the Japanese began cultivating a cayenne-type variety called santaka, which is one of the hottest chiles grown today. Japan even exports about 14 metric tons per year of ground red chiles into the United States! Although it has taken centuries, chiles have finally invaded Japanese food, although not the classic cuisine. The fastest-growing

fast-food chain in Japan during the late 1980s was Taco Time, which did not cater to traditional Japanese tastes but boldly advertised its food as the hottest around—and foreign as well.

So, a spicy sun is rising over Japan. Long believed to be the land of only sushi, tempura, and yakitori, Japanese taste buds are now aflame with habaneros, curries, and spicy snacks.

It all began with Tohato, the Japanese snack-food company, entering their habanero-spiced snacks into the American Scovie Awards Competition in 2005, 2006, and 2007. (The Scovie Awards Competition is produced by our company, Sunbelt Shows, Inc.) They consistently won Scovies every year, which must have inspired the company to encourage Mr. Sakiyama, owner of Kadokawa X Media, publisher of the *Walker* magazines, to sponsor the 2006 Scovie Awards Japan. Thus, sponsorship went to *Tokyo Walker* and the seven other regional *Walker* publications. They are thick, glossy popular-culture magazines that feature food prominently.

Because I had given permission for them to use the Scovie name and logo, they invited Mary Jane and I to be their honored guests and judges for their awards ceremony. Our whirlwind Japanese adventure lasted a mere six days—and two of them were travel days. Our hosts—who, in addition to Mr. Sakiyama, included Jun Ikeda of Plus J. Inc., and Mr. Kokubo and Anna Berry of Sunny Side Up, Inc.—put us up at the elegant Takanawa Prince Hotel in Tokyo and fed us a welcoming dinner of sushi and tempura specialties.

The Japanese Scovie Awards are different from the contest that we produce. Because there are not hundreds of companies that produce hot and spicy products in Japan, there are only four categories: restaurant specialties voted on by the general public, spicy recipes submitted by the general public, commercial curries, and commercial snacks. The producers decided to produce a lavish multimedia production at a hotel near the one where we were staying. So, with the Doors' "Light My Fire" blasting and strobe lights flashing, I took the stage with Anna Berry translating and gave my report on the 2007 American Scovie Awards while the media cameras were rolling.

Mary Jane and I were placed in the same position as our own Scovie judges as we judged the finalists in the curries and snacks categories. Tohato won the award for Best Snack, which did not surprise us. Once again, I took the stage with Mr. Sakiyama to present the award to a representative of Tohato.

On our one day off, Mary Jane and I visited the Institute for Nature Study, a gigantic nature reserve in the middle of Tokyo that has preserved the native forest, ponds, and streams in a pristine environment since 1917. We also visited the Tokyo Metropolitan Teien Art Museum with their excellent exhibit on art-deco jewelry. The museum also has a classic koi pond.

Our hosts splurged on a celebratory dinner at a Korean restaurant. Spicy kimchi led off the feast, and then came marinated raw beef liver, which Mary Jane refused to eat, but of course I did indulge. It was very flavorful and the texture was perfect. Someone at the table said, "The Japanese are into raw." I lifted up a chopsticks-filled portion of the liver and said, "No fish here." There was a gas grill on each table and we grilled beef tongue, heart, and liver, which all were excellent.

We also discovered that the Japanese media had covered the Scovie Awards, and that Mary Jane and I were stars for a day in the newspapers. Finally, I got to see my own name in Japanese script.

SPEAKING OF KOREA

It is said that Koreans have the highest per capita chile consumption in the world. In 2017, the typical adult Korean ate 6.6 pounds of chiles. Of course, I am discussing the Republic of Korea, known in the West as South Korea. Total chile production there is about 200,000 tons on 326,000 acres, making South Korea the fifth largest producer of chile peppers in the world. Chile peppers utilize 35 percent of the

Kimchi jars in a home in South Korea. Photograph by Joriola. Wikimedia. GNU Free Documentation License, Version 1.2.

agricultural area for vegetables, far ahead of two other crops, Chinese cabbage and garlic. The main production areas are Chungcheongbuk-do and Kyungsangbok-do Provinces, which are located in the central part of the country. The production technique calls for transplanting seedlings rather than direct seeding.

Before the mid-1970s, virtually all of the chile varieties grown in Korea were open-pollinated landraces. But following extensive research by their Horticultural Experiment Station, now F1 hybrids constitute 80 percent of Korean production. There are 10 major Korean cultivars of these hybrids: *hongilpoom*, *bulamput*, *hanpyul*, *Cheongyang*, *Cheonghong*, *jinpoom*, *sinhong*, *hongsil*, *Koreagon gochu*, and *ilwolgon gochu*. They were all introduced between 1979 and 1985. These cultivars resemble the cayenne pod type in North America.

It is not a coincidence that chiles, cabbages, and garlic are South Korea's primary crops, because they are all ingredients in what might be called the Korean National Dish, kimchi. Food expert Sharon Hudgins writes that there are more than 100 distinct varieties of Korean kimchis, and many of them do not include cabbage. Of course, the most famous kimchis are the cabbage salads with chiles that are fermented in large ceramic jars. Another important culinary use of chiles in Korea is in the manufacture of *kochujang* chile paste, the country's most popular condiment. Tall jars of homemade kochujang, condiments fermenting and mellowing in the sun, line terraces all across Korea. It is a salty hot pepper paste with a touch of sweetness. This is one of the most important ingredients in Korean cooking, and it is as common in South Korea as ketchup is in the United States.

Homemade kochujang requires months of work by Korean housewives, who must grow and dry the ingredients, grind them by hand, cook them, and cure the resulting mixture in the sun. Although some traditional households still prepare their seasonings in this way, the making of kochujang is now a dying art. Traditionally, kochujang contains glutinous rice, fermented soybean cake, hot red chile, salt, and malt syrup from barley and water. This mixture was placed in jars on March 3 of each year and allowed to ferment for a minimum of three months. Today, Korean grocery stores carry small jars of kochujang made from furnace-dried peppers and filled with preservatives and MSG. However, these mass-produced pastes are fairly good, especially when cooks add other spices to them. Commercial kochujang is available in Asian markets.

Other fiery dishes from Korea include green chile–pepper pickles and green chile–pepper pancakes; *buldak* is a savory barbecue chicken dish swimming in chile sauce; *ddeokbokki* consists of soft rice and fish cakes cooked in a sweet red chile sauce; *nakji bokkeum* is stir-fried octopus slathered in a generous amount of red pepper sauce; *jjambbong* is a ridiculously spicy seafood noodle dish; and *maeundae galbijjim* consists of sweet and savory short ribs. Maeundae (meaning spicy) restaurant has made it into one of Seoul's hottest dishes, both in terms of spiciness and popularity.

In 1988, South Korea exported 88 metric tons of ground red chiles and about 4 metric tons of New Mexican–type chiles into the United States; however, precise production figures for the country are difficult to obtain because they are not regularly reported.

PACIFIC ISLAND PODS

From eastern Asia, chiles were transferred to the Pacific Islands. How and when this dispersal occurred is the subject of much debate. Some experts theorize that after chiles were introduced into New Guinea, they were carried by native traders to Melanesia and then to Polynesia. Once there, the fiery fruits were adopted into the island cuisines and combined with both indigenous and imported foodstuffs such as fish, coconuts, and bananas.

Other theorists believe that chiles were carried on Spanish galleons, leaving from Acapulco and bound for the Philippines. However, the main galleon route ran south of the Hawaiian Islands and north of the rest of Polynesia, and a landing at either island group would have been extremely unlikely considering the galleon captains were under orders not to change the route. In fact, the Pacific both north and south of the galleon route remained unexplored until Cook's voyages between 1768 and 1780.

A third theory, proposed by Pacific explorer Thor Heyerdahl, holds that chiles were introduced into Polynesia by pre-Columbian Indians such as the Incas. In 1964, Heyerdahl published an article in which he alleges that chiles were growing on Easter Island at the time of the arrival of Europeans, approximately 1768. Botanists, however, dispute Heyerdahl and point out that chiles are conspicuously absent from the plant lists of the Polynesian Islands compiled by the botanists aboard Cook's ships. Although it is exciting to think that the Incas were sailing the Pacific, or that pre-Columbian visits to the Americas were made by Polynesians and others, there is simply not enough scientific evidence to support such a theory.

So although we do not know precisely when or how they accomplished it, chile peppers crossed the Pacific and eventually appeared on the Galapagos Islands, which are only about 600 miles from the South American coast. In fact, those islands have their own species of chile, *Capsicum galapagoense*, a wild variety. However the final leg of the journey occurred, chiles in fact circumnavigated the globe and ended up very close to the nuclear region where they originated millennia before. In doing so, they forever fired up most of the important world cuisines.

TASTING THE HEAT IN OZ

We completely lost Friday on our trip to Sydney in 2000. Mary Jane and I took off from Los Angeles at 10 o'clock Thursday night and, after crossing the International Date Line, arrived at the Sydney airport at 6:00 a.m. Saturday morning. Since we had been flying for nearly 15 hours, I didn't mourn the loss of Friday—I just wanted off the plane. Fortunately, Robynne Millward and her friend Wayne were waiting to pick us up, so within 45 minutes we had checked into our apartment at the Radisson Kestrel Hotel on the beach in Manly (north of Sydney) and were having our second jet-lagged breakfast of the morning at a beachfront café. The weather? Think summer in San Francisco.

"So how goes the show?" I asked Robynne, the editor and publisher of *The Chilli Press* and producer of the third annual Australian National Fiery Food Festival. It was the final event in the three-week-long Feast of Sydney promotion.

Robynne shrugged. "Things could be better in Oz" (Oz being the Aussie nickname for their country).

Customs House, Circular Quay, Sydney, location of the Australian National Fiery Foods Festival. Photograph by Greg O'Beirne. Wikimedia, GNU Free Documentation License, Version 1.2.

Uh-oh, I thought, the show-production instincts in my brain on alert, "What's wrong?"

It turned out that the problems had to do with the venue itself. The show was being held in the ground-floor lobby at the old Customs House. It is located at the Circular Quay (pronounced "key," the traditional British pronunciation), which is the main wharf for the commuter ferries and a major train station as well. In a city of nearly four million people, it was about as central a location as one could find. But it wasn't designed for shows. And the city government, which owned the building, was not cooperating.

"They won't let me do cooking demonstrations in the building," Robynne said, "and I've got the biggest star of Mexican cooking performing—Diana Kennedy."

"Why not?"

"Against their policy—that's all they'll say."

"What are you going to do?"

"Erect a tent outside on the plaza for the cooking demos—that's all I can do."

"But what about crowd control?" I asked. "They'll have to present ticket stubs to get into the tent."

"Not to worry," Robynne replied. "We're not allowed to sell tickets."

"What?"

Robynne explained that since it was a public building, with three restaurants and numerous galleries, she was not allowed to charge admission to the show in the lobby. She could, however, asked for a "gold coin donation" (a $1 or $2 gold coin, worth about US 60 cents or $1.20, respectively) and charge admission to the cooking tent and to my slide-show lectures.

"At least they're not charging me rent," she said. "And I'm not spending much on advertising because you're here to get me all this free publicity, starting this afternoon."

The Media Blitz

Jet-lagged or not, I was scheduled for a book signing and lecture at Collins Book-sellers, the equivalent of a Barnes & Noble store in the States. Robynne showed me an article promoting the signing from the Sydney events magazine *Where*. The blurb described me as a "famous American chef" and an "acclaimed author" in the same sentence.

"But I'm not a chef at all, much less a famous one," I protested.

"Don't tell anyone," Robynne ordered.

The book signing went surprisingly well. About 25 people showed up, and while Robynne made three or four salsas, I gave my talk on chiles and fiery foods and soon learned from the responses that there was a strong chilehead contingent in Australia—and that my books were as popular among those as they were among their American counterparts. Not only did these fans buy books at Collins, they also brought their dog-eared copies of *The Pepper Garden* for me to sign. I had a great time and by 4:30 p.m. it was time to go. As we left the mall, the sky had darkened significantly. There were no clouds. I checked my watch again. What was going on? Then I realized that we had traveled from the longest day of the year in the Northern Hemisphere to the shortest one in the Southern Hemisphere.

The week of the show was a blur of activities—press conferences, radio and television appearances, and newspaper interviews—as I worked hard to earn my keep and promote the festival. In between these events, we managed to do touristy things like buy superb aboriginal art in shops at the Rocks, stroll through the enormous—and beautiful—Botanical Gardens, visit the Taronga Zoo, tour the famous Sydney Opera House, and shudder when totally surrounded by those Great Barrier Reef predators in the shark tunnel at the aquarium.

Apparently the festival publicity was working, because there were more media messages every evening at the Radisson Kestrel, after we returned by ferry from the Circular Quay. The buzz was building.

The Australian Scovies

The heat was building as well, for I was one of the judges of the Australian Fiery Food Challenge, held at the Customs House before the show. It was a blind tasting with the labels of the products obscured as with our Scovie Awards in the US. The judges were mostly media people who cover food. More than a hundred products were entered, and they were generally of good quality, with a notable sweetness as compared to the US products—apparently the Aussies have quite a sweet tooth. There were two excellent salsas and a number of tasty chutneys. I made a noble attempt to taste every one of the products, but I made a crucial error: I tasted the habanero hot sauces before the group of "regular" hot sauces. I was so burned out that not only could I not finish the tasting but I felt dizzy and flushed—definitely a victim of an endorphin rush.

The grand-prize winner was the Byron Bay Chilli Company, and they won, among other prizes, a booth in the 13th annual National Fiery Foods Show in Albuquerque, March 2–4, 2001, and they promised me they'd be there. And they were.

A SPICY DIVERSION

At the tasting, we were delighted to meet Carol Selva Rajah, a noted Australian food writer and cookbook author. She promptly adopted us and gave us a copy of her latest book, *Makan-lah!: The True Taste of Malaysia*. One of her projects during the Taste of Sydney was to produce the Batavia Rijsttafel Banquet, a 14-course spice dinner held at the National Maritime Museum. Because of our intense interest in spices of all kinds, she really wanted us to attend this exclusive dinner. The main problem was that the museum had sold all the tickets in a matter of hours and there were no seats left. So Carol gave me her seat at the banquet! Unfortunately, there was no room for Mary Jane, so she was on her own back in Manly while I hobnobbed with the museum elite.

Cocktails and starters were served aboard the *Batavia*, a full-size reproduction of the original Dutch spice ship that wrecked off the coast of Western Australia in 1629. It was moored at the museum, and I was fascinated to go aboard the remarkable replica. The ship was built by the Dutch government (it took 10 years) and was transported to Sydney for the Olympic celebrations aboard a floating-dock ship, and then was released to cruise into Sydney Harbor under sail, accompanied by fireworks and the booming of its own cannons. Sipping on a Heineken (what else?), I went down the ladders to the spice-storage deck and was amazed how cramped it

was, with ceilings only about five feet off the deck. Here, the sacks of spices were stored—black pepper, long pepper, nutmeg, mace, cloves, and cinnamon. The sailors—all 300 of them—slept among the spice sacks because of the lack of room on the 193-foot-long ship.

Carol did a superb job with the banquet and my seating. On my left was Christine Salins, the food editor of the *Canberra Times*, and on my right was a retired radio-comedy writer. The wines, from Rosemount Estate, were great and readily consumed as course after course of spicy food arrived. The feast was a bit overwhelming, and I had to pace myself when trying something particularly tasty and spicy, like the *rendang bambu sapi*, her beef and chile dish loaded with spices, and the *sambal goreng udang kering*, a delicious prawn sambal. In between courses, I discussed the spicy-food movement in Australia with Christine, and the comedy writer explained the finer points of rugby and Australian-rules football. I hadn't been in Australia a week yet, but I felt right at home. It didn't hurt that, in addition to socializing, I was reading Australian newspapers and magazines and watching TV.

A day later, Carol took us to Cabramatta, a town outside Sydney where many of the Asian immigrants live. It was rather like being in Singapore, with Vietnamese soup shops, Cambodian discos, Chinese grocery stores, and Thai herb shops. We all ate the Vietnamese beef soup called pho with chilli-garlic sauce, and it was unforgettably good. Carol also took us to one of the largest distributors of Indian food, herbs, and spices in Australia, and she referred us to Herbie's Spices in nearby Rozelle. Herbie—or rather Ian Hemphill—recognized me because he sells dried chiles in addition to literally dozens of varieties of spices. It was there that I bought the wild spicy mountain pepper that is gaining in popularity in Australian gourmet circles.

Replica of the spice ship *Batavia*. Photograph by Malis. Wikimedia. I, the copyright holder, release this work into the public domain.

Show Time

The immigration of Asians has helped spread fiery foods across the country. One of the biggest influences on fiery food in Australia has been the introduction and spread of habaneros. They are now second in popularity to the Asian varieties. Exhibitor Geoff Love likes to tell the story that he got into the fiery foods business because he couldn't find a good Thai garlic-chilli-ginger sauce, so he had to make his own.

It's always fun greeting the exhibitors at a show, and this one was particularly interesting because I'd never actually met any of these chile lovers, although I had exchanged e-mails with some of them. Geoff Love, of Love's Pantry, manufactures a line of 40 different products, of which 28 are chilli-oriented. The spicy products are his BHM brand, which stands for "Bloody Hot, Mate!" Formerly in advertising and marketing, jovial Geoff told me that his products are selling well because they are distributed to both supermarkets and specialty food shops. Business is good, he said, because Australians are becoming more aware of chillis and the food that goes best with them.

Carol Selva Rajah and the author eat pho in Cabramatta. Photograph by Mary Jane Wilan. Used with permission.

An aerial view of the festival. Photograph by Mary Jane Wilan. Used with permission.

John Boland, the owner of Byron Bay Chilli Company and the winner of the grand prize in the Australian Fiery Food Challenge, is a transplanted American who emigrated from southern California in the 1980s and started making salsa in 1993. He was previously a caterer, so it was easy to transfer his experience to the manufacturing sector. He has about a dozen products, including a Black Bean Salsa, which is one of the ones I preferred at the tasting. John told me that the fiery foods industry in Australia is expanding rapidly, and that during the last three or four years his business has grown dramatically. John and I have stayed in touch for nearly 20 years, and I helped him find distribution in the US. He exhibited again in our 2019 National Fiery Foods and Barbecue Show.

A REAL CHILLI WINE

One of the most interesting and unusual chilli products we found was a chilli wine from the ominously named but fully flavorful Disaster Bay Chilli Company. Every chile wine I've tasted in the US simply had some chile—green, red, or jalapeno—added to grape wine. But Stuart Meagher and his partner, John Wentworth, have developed a technique for making wine from fermented chillis. They got the initial recipe from an Aboriginal tribesman named Old Didler and experimented with it by using jalapeños, 'Big Jim' New Mexican chiles, fresh cayennes, and a few habaneros thrown in. They used a French yeast and added a little sugar since chillis don't have the high sugar content of grapes. The resulting chilli wine tasted like a good dessert wine, with a noticeable bite, and I thought it was rather good. So did the public who tasted it during a talk I gave on chilli beverages.

They make the wine in a temperature-controlled cellar, and it takes about 660 pounds of chillis to make 2000 liters of wine, which is aged for one year in barrels. The wine was entered in a wine festival in the town of Bega, where it was judged according to Australian wine-making criteria, and it won a Bronze Medal. They use the chilli byproducts of wine making to create their other products, which are hot sauces and chutneys.

The third annual Australian National Fiery Food Festival was a rousing success and the crowds were so large on Sunday that it was difficult to move around in the hall. The exhibitors were happy with the attendance, and as often happens during a show, the initial problems faded away. The cooking demonstrations went well, with many of the national magazines sending their food writers to watch Diana Kennedy and Carol Selva Rajah cook on stage. Attendance at my slide shows increased steadily throughout the show, and I was happy to discuss chillis with the attendees, sign books, and help them identify the pods they brought with them.

ASHIF'S CHILLI EXPERIENCE

Our final evening in Australia was spent with Robynne and Wayne at Red Gum, a restaurant in Manly that served what might be called gourmet bush food. We did a post-show analysis and all were convinced that fiery foods are not only here to stay in Oz but probably will become a major food movement. Robynne asked if we would be interested in returning for the show the following year, and we enthusiastically said yes. After all, we didn't even get to go crocodile hunting!

On the flight back, we landed before we left and recovered the Friday we had lost on the way to Oz. That's right—we took off from Sydney Airport at 9:30 a.m. on Thursday and landed at LAX at 6:30 a.m. the same day. Now that's a fast plane!

An exhibitor shows off his hot sauce. Photograph by Mary Jane Wilan. Used with permission.

FEATURED CHILE PEPPER: 'FACING HEAVEN'

The Chinese name of this variety of chile pepper (*C. annuum* var. *chao tian jiao*) literally means "skyward-pointing chile pepper" because the pods are erect rather than pendant. The plant's upright growing habit is typical of ornamental peppers, yet this pepper is grown for culinary use. The plants grow bushy and are high yielding. The pods are cone shaped, between three and six centimeters in length, and one to two centimeters in diameter at the base, and they have a very thin skin. They have a slight lemon flavor, and the heat averages 40,000 SHU. They are a staple in Sichuan cooking.

The pods are used both fresh and dried, and often entire pods will be added to various Sichuan dishes such as kung pao chicken. There are often used in conjunction with *Fagara*, the Sichuan peppercorn that has a numbing effect on the mouth. Both the seeds and the pods are available from online sources.

recipes

CHICKEN AND BEEF SATAY WITH SPICY PEANUT SAUCE

yield 8 servings   *heat scale* hot

This recipe, by Chef Abdul Wahab of the Equatorial Penang Hotel in Penang, Malaysia, is a classic Malay dish that combines the heat of chiles with the nutty taste of peanuts and the exotic fragrances of the Spice Islands. Note: This recipe requires advance preparation.

THE MARINADE

4	large pieces of ginger, peeled	1	teaspoon anise seeds
5	cloves garlic, peeled	1	tablespoon ground turmeric
3	shallots, peeled	3	pieces lemongrass
1	teaspoon cumin seeds	2	teaspoons sugar
		1	pound boneless chicken, cut into strips

Combine the first 8 ingredients in a food processor and puree, adding a little water if necessary. Marinate the chicken and beef strips in this mixture for 12 hours.

THE PEANUT SAUCE

½   cup red chile paste (or red chiles pureed with water)

¼   cup peanut oil

5   cloves garlic, peeled and minced

3   shallots, peeled and minced

3   pieces lemongrass, minced

3   large pieces ginger, peeled and minced

2   tablespoons poppy seeds

4   tablespoons minced cashews

¼   cup minced peanuts

1   teaspoon tamarind paste (optional)

2   teaspoons sugar

Diced cucumbers and onions for garnish

Heat the peanut oil in a pan and add the chile paste and the next 6 ingredients. Simmer for about 30 minutes, stirring occasionally. Add the remaining ingredients and simmer for an additional 5 minutes.

TO ASSEMBLE

Thread the chicken and beef strips on separate satay sticks that have been soaked in water. Grill the satay sticks over coals until the meats are done, about 10 minutes, turning often.

Serve the satays with the sauce on the side and garnished with diced cucumbers and onions.

ROYAL THAI BEEF CURRY

yield 4 to 6 servings   *heat scale* hot

This recipe was a favorite of King Rama V, who reigned in Thailand from 1869 to 1910. It is tasty, rich, and very spicy, and should be served over hot cooked rice or cooked Thai noodles.

½	cup thick coconut milk
1	tablespoon fish sauce
1	tablespoon brown sugar
2 ½	cups coconut milk
1 ½	pounds beef, sliced thinly across grain into 1-inch pieces
1	cup eggplant, cubed
⅓	cup fresh sweet-basil leaves, chopped
4	fresh red serrano or jalapeño chiles, stems and seeds removed, finely chopped
	Red curry paste, to taste

In a small, heavy skillet, boil the coconut cream until it reaches the oily stage, then stir in the red curry paste. Add the fish sauce and the sugar. Set aside.

Pour the coconut milk into a saucepan and add the beef. Simmer for 8 to 10 minutes. Add the seasoned curry paste to the simmering beef, bring to a boil, and add the eggplant, basil, and chiles. Reduce the heat and simmer for 3 minutes.

INDONESIAN MUTTON SOUP

yield 6 to 8 servings *heat scale* medium

Indonesia grows goats rather than sheep, yet "mutton" was the meat of choice in the wet market of Little India in Singapore, so I can only assume that this delicious curry-like soup can be made from either lamb or goat meat. The recipe is courtesy of Mrs. Devagi Shanmugam of the Thomson Cooking Studio.

2	pounds lamb or goat meat, cubed		3	tablespoons coriander seeds
3	quarts water		1	stick cinnamon
5	small green chiles, stems and seeds removed, chopped		5	bay leaves
			1	cup fresh mint leaves
5	small red chiles, stems and seeds removed, chopped		4	pieces lemongrass, crushed
	2-inch piece of ginger, peeled and chopped		1	teaspoon ground turmeric
			4	curry leaves (optional)
2	teaspoons black peppercorns		1	cup water
2	teaspoons anise seeds		4	tomatoes, diced
2	teaspoons cumin seeds		5	tablespoons vegetable oil
5	cardamoms (or 2 tablespoons cardamom powder)			Chopped spring (green) onions for garnish
3	cloves		3	teaspoons rice flour for thickening (optional)

Put the mutton and the water in a pot. In a food processor, coarsely grind together the next 16 ingredients along with the cup of water. Using a strainer, strain this mixture into the pot with the mutton. Save the residue, tie it up securely in a muslin or cotton cloth, and add it to the pot.

Fry the tomatoes, cinnamon, cardamoms, and cloves in the oil until the tomatoes are soft, and add the mixture to the pot.

Boil the soup until the mutton is tender and nearly falls apart. Remove the spice bundle, thicken the soup with rice flour if necessary, and garnish with the spring onions. Serve the soup over, or on the side with, Nasi Kunyit (see page 262).

NASI KUNYIT (YELLOW FESTIVE RICE) WITH PRAWNS

yield 4 to 6 servings   *heat scale* mild

Also from Mrs. Devagi Shanmugam, this rice recipe makes a very colorful, fragrant dish that goes well with the mutton soup. Remember to use coconut milk, not canned coconut cream, which is too sweet. If you're not serving the rice with soup, add chile powder to taste.

4	teaspoons ground coriander	6	tablespoons vegetable oil
2	teaspoons ground cumin	6	cups coconut milk
1	teaspoon ground turmeric	3	cups rice, washed and drained
	5-inch piece ginger, peeled and chopped	4	pieces lemongrass
			Salt to taste
3	garlic cloves, peeled		
20	shallots, peeled		Fried spring (green) onion rings, sliced into rings for garnish
1	cup water		

Puree the first 7 ingredients in a blender. In a pan, fry the pureed ingredients in the oil until fragrant. Add the coconut milk and bring to a boil. Reduce the heat to a simmer, add the rice and lemongrass, cover, and cook until the rice is done, about 40 minutes. Add salt to taste and garnish with green onion rings.

RED CHILE OIL

yield Makes approximately 2 cups chile oil   *heat scale* hot

This recipe is from Dr. Gerald Schmidt, who has traveled extensively in China. He writes, "Here is a quick and easy way to make a versatile chile oil that can be used in stir-fry, as a salad dressing, or as a spicy topping for all grilled meats. Sichuan pepper (fagara) are the spicy seeds from a native bush. Omit the Sichuan pepper if you can't find it. This oil can be stored in a glass bottle in the refrigerator and used as an all-purpose seasoning."

⅔	cup dried red-chile pepper pods, coarsely chopped	2	tablespoons Sichuan pepper, crushed
2	cups cooking oil, peanut preferred		

In a saucepan, warm the oil over medium heat, then add the chile pieces. Simmer for 20 minutes, stirring occasionally. Add the Sichuan pepper and allow to cook for an additional 15 minutes. Do not let the oil get too hot or it will scorch the chiles. When the oil turns red, remove it from the heat and allow to cool. Filter out the solid material using a sieve and cheesecloth, and reserve the red oil.

TANGY CHICKEN AND PEANUTS (*GONG BAO* CHICKEN)

yield 2 servings, or 4 with side dishes and/or rice   *heat scale* hot

This recipe is by Kimberly Dukes, who writes: "This is an immensely popular dish that you can find in nearly every restaurant or home." I like the crunch of crisp American celery with the chicken and peanuts. Play with the recipe by replacing the chicken with shrimp or tofu, or by replacing the peanuts with cashews to dress it up a bit more. If you use peanuts, look for "Spanish" peanuts, which still have their reddish skins. In Sichuan, "Facing-Heaven" chiles are used in spicy dishes. They add visual appeal as well as flavor, but if you can't find these, substitute other peppers that are medium-hot and richly flavorful. Here I use small Japanese chiles easily available in most supermarkets. Note: Because this is a stir-fry and must be cooked quickly, do all your chopping and measuring before starting to cook.

MARINADE INGREDIENTS

3	teaspoons sherry
1 ½	teaspoons light soy sauce
2	teaspoons dark soy sauce
½	teaspoon salt
2	teaspoons cornstarch
1	teaspoon water

SAUCE INGREDIENTS

4	teaspoons sugar
1 ½	teaspoons cornstarch
2	teaspoons dark soy sauce
2	teaspoons light soy sauce
4	teaspoons vinegar
2	teaspoons sesame oil
2	teaspoons water

1 to 2 boneless chicken breasts, cubed
(about ½ pound)

3 tablespoons peanut oil

24 small Japanese chiles, halved,
most seeds discarded

2 teaspoons Sichuan peppercorns

Chunk of ginger about the same size
as the garlic, minced

4 medium cloves of garlic, minced

1 cup chopped celery (cut on a slant)

1 bunch green onions or scallions,
chopped in 1-inch sections
(about ½ cup)

½ cup peanuts

Cilantro or parsley, chopped, to
garnish (optional)

In a medium bowl, combine the marinade ingredients and stir well. Add the chicken and let it sit while you chop, measure, and combine the other ingredients.

In a small bowl, combine the sauce ingredients.

In a wok, heat the oil over high heat. When it is quite hot, add the chiles and the Sichuan peppercorns, and stir continually for about half a minute, until the oil smells spicy. Be careful not to let the spices burn—you might want to take the wok off the heat for a moment or two.

Add the chicken and whatever is left of the marinade, stirring continually for a few minutes, until the chicken is cooked through. Add the ginger and garlic, stir-frying until it smells fragrant, 15–30 seconds. Be careful not to burn them.

Stir the sauce again and add it to the wok, stirring for about 30 seconds. Add the celery and stir for about 15 seconds. Add the spring onions and stir for about 15 seconds. Add the peanuts and stir for about 15 seconds.

Serve on a flat oval plate in a single layer so that the sauce is distributed evenly. Garnish with cilantro or parsley if desired. Eat with chopsticks if you can!

KIMCHI

yield 4 to 6 servings   *heat scale* medium

This recipe is by Richard Sterling, who collected it in South Korea. Note: This recipe requires advance preparation.

1	head white cabbage
½	gallon fresh water
1	cup salt
1	pint vinegar
1	quart water
1	cup salt
6	cloves of garlic, chopped (optional)
1	tablespoon ground red chile

Dissolve the salt in the water. Cut the cabbage into chunks about the size of an egg, and soak them overnight in the salted water. Drain the cabbage and squeeze it dry. In a pot, combine the water, vinegar, and salt, and bring the mixture to a boil, then let cool to room temperature. Combine the cabbage, garlic, and chile in a glass container, pour the vinegar mixture in, and cover. Store the jar in a cool, dark place for 1 week. Drain off the liquid and bring it to a boil in another pot. Place the cabbage in a clean container, pour the hot liquid over it, let it cool, then cover it. It will keep for several weeks in the refrigerator.

The active principle that causes the heat in chile peppers is a crystalline alkaloid generically called *capsaicin*. It is produced by glands at the junction of the placenta and the pod wall. The capsaicin spreads unevenly throughout the inside of the pod and is concentrated mostly in the placental tissue, except for the superhot chiles in the *chinense* species.

THE NATURE OF CAPSAICIN

Capsaicin is an incredibly powerful and stable alkaloid that retains its original potency despite time, cooking, or freezing. Because it has no flavor, color, or odor, the precise amount of capsaicin present in chiles can only be measured by a specialized laboratory procedure known as high-performance liquid chromatography (HPLC). Although it has no odor or flavor, capsaicin is one of the most pungent compounds known, detectable to the palate in dilutions of 1 to 17 million. It is slightly soluble in water but very soluble in alcohols, fats, and oils.

P. A. Bucholtz in 1816 first discovered that the pungent principle of peppers could be extracted from the macerated pods with organic solvents. In 1846, L. T. Thresh reported in *Pharmacy Journal* that the pungent principle could be extracted in a crystalline state. It was Thresh who named the substance *capsaicin*. In 1878, the Hungarian medical scientist Endre Hogyes extracted capsaicin, which he called *capsicol*, and discovered that it stimulated the mucous membranes of the mouth and stomach and increased the secretion of gastric juices. Capsaicin was first synthesized in 1930 by E. Spath and F. S. Darling.

The word *capsaicin* actually describes a complex of related components named *capsaicinoids* by Japanese chemists S. Kosuge and Y. Inagaki in 1964. Capsaicinoids are the chemical compounds that give chile peppers their bite. Scientists have identified and isolated six naturally occurring members of this fiery family and one synthetic cousin, which is used as a reference gauge for determining the relative pungency of the others.

The major capsaicinoids that are contained in the crystalline extract are capsaicin (69%), dihydrocapsaicin (22%), and three minor related components: nordihydrocapsaicin (7%), homocapsaicin (1%), and homodihydrocapsaicin (1%). The synthetic capsaicinoid vanillylamide of n-nonanoic acid (VNA) was administered to 16 trained

Rezolex extraction plant, Radium Springs, New Mexico. Photograph by Dave DeWitt.

tasters by researchers Anna Krajewska and John Powers at the University of Georgia. The tasters compared the heat of VNA to the four natural capsaicinoids and the results were as follows.

The mildest capsaicinoid was nordihydrocapsaicin (NDHC), which was described as the "least irritating" and "fruity, sweet, and spicy." Next was homodihydrocapsaicin (HDHC), a compound described as "very irritating," and one that produced a "numbing burn" in the throat, which also was the most prolonged and difficult to rinse out.

The two most fiery capsaicinoid compounds were capsaicin (C) and dihydrocapsaicin (DHC), which produced burning everywhere from the midtongue and palate down into the throat. Evidently, all of the capsaicinoids work together to produce the pungency of peppers, but capsaicin itself is still rated the strongest. The chemical formula for capsaicin is $C_{18}H_{27}NO_3$ and its structure is shown below.

A 1980 study by P. Rozin and P. Schiller concluded that people love chiles because they are receiving pleasure from a "constrained risk," or a thrill. Such people are risk takers and eat chiles for the same reason that they may climb mountains or skydive. "These benignly masochistic activities are uniquely human," Rozin and Schiller point out.

Dr. Andrew Weil believes that the chile eater experiences a "rush" similar to that produced by psychotropic drugs. "He knows that pain can be transformed into a friendly sensation whose strength can go into making him high," Weil writes. He theorizes that familiarity with eating hot chiles enables the chile eater to "glide along on the strong stimulation, experiencing it as something between pleasure and pain that enforces concentration and brings about a high state of consciousness. This technique might be called 'mouth surfing.'"

Pure capsaicin is so powerful that chemists who handle the crystalline powder must work in a filtered "tox room" in full body protection. The suit has a closed hood to prevent inhaling the powder. Says pharmaceutical chemist Lloyd Matheson of the University of Iowa, who once inhaled some capsaicin accidentally: "It's not toxic, but you wish you were dead if you inhale it." Another capsaicin expert, the late

Chemical structure of capsaicin. Wikimedia. GNU Free Documentation License, Version 1.2.

analytical chemist Marlin Bensinger, adds, "One milligram of pure capsaicin placed on your hand would feel like a red-hot poker and would surely blister the skin."

Did capsaicin evolve to protect chile peppers from mammalian predators? That's the theory of Dr. Michael Nee, emeritus associate curator of the New York Botanical Garden. Scientists have long speculated that plants produce secondary metabolites, chemicals that are not required for the primary life support of the plant. These metabolites fight off animal predators and perhaps even competing plant species.

Nee speculates that the capsaicin in chiles may be such a metabolite. It prevents animals from eating the chiles so that they can be consumed by fruit-eating birds who specialize in red fruits with small seeds. Mammals perceive a burning sensation from capsaicin but birds do not. The seeds pass through a bird's digestive tract intact and encased in a perfect natural fertilizer. Many experts believe that the wild chiltepín (*C. annuum* var. *glabriusculum*) was spread by this method from South America to what is now the US-Mexico border.

It has long been believed that capsaicin was present only in the pods of the *Capsicum* genus and in no other plant or animal material. However, during my research I uncovered a quote from W. Tang and G. Eisenbrand in *Chinese Drugs of Plant Origin*: "Capsaicin, the pungent principle of Capsicum species, was isolated from ginger rhizome." Marlin Bensinger strongly believes this finding to be in error. He says the proper chemical precursors are simply not found in ginger.

TOXICITY OF CAPSAICINOIDS

To determine the lethal toxic level of capsaicinoids in animals, and to extrapolate that level for humans, researchers in 1980 performed a rather gruesome experiment with mice, rats, guinea pigs, and rabbits. Pure capsaicin was administered intravenously, subcutaneously, in the stomach and applied topically until the animals died. The lethal toxic doses of capsaicin, measured in milligrams per kilogram of animal weight, ranged from a mere 0.56 milligrams when administered intravenously, to 190 milligrams when consumed, to 512 milligrams when applied topically—which means that the poor animals were drowned in it. Indeed, the probable cause of death in all cases was presumed to be respiratory paralysis. Guinea pigs were the most sensitive to capsaicin, while rabbits were less susceptible. The author of the study, T. Glinsukon, concluded that the acute toxicity of capsaicinoids as a food additive for humankind was negligible. If humans are about as sensitive as mice, the acute fatal toxicity dose for a 150-pound person would be about 13 grams of pure crystalline capsaicinoids, which, frankly, sounds high to me. I think that less than that would be lethal.

There have been investigations focused on dangerous doses for humans of the various substances that have capsaicin as an ingredient. For example, C. L. Winek conducted a study, published in *Drug and Chemical Toxicology*, that examined the overdose potential of Tabasco Sauce. He concluded that a person of average weight would have to consume nearly a half gallon of the sauce to overdose and become unconscious.

In a related study, rats were fed large amounts of Tabasco Sauce and suffered "no gross or microscopic pathological changes or any significant biochemical changes." Their growth rate also remained normal. In a similar study, rats were fed crude extracts of chile pods and crystalline capsaicinoids by stomach tube while allowed access to normal food and water. None of the rats died and they all appeared normal throughout the study. Of course, the rats were killed and then autopsied, but no gross pathological changes were detected.

Humans have also acted as guinea pigs with oleoresin capsicum. It is an ingredient in superhot sauces with words in the name like insanity, death, and suicide. These sauces are tasted at food shows by people who have no idea of how hot they are. Some people, with few capsaicin receptors (see page 273) in their mouths, are not bothered by the extreme heat. But most people react very negatively to the superhot sauces, experiencing severe burning and sometimes blistering of the mouth and tongue. Other immediate responses have included shortness of breath, fainting, nausea, and spontaneous vomiting. People should be very careful of commercial hot sauces that list oleoresin capsicum as an ingredient.

Aside from the above adverse effects, the superhot sauce will not hurt you. "Comprehensive nutritional studies have not shown any adverse effects of chile or capsaicinoids even at ten times the maximum use levels," writes one of the world's experts on capsaicin, V. S. Govindarajan, author of the mammoth study, *Capsicum—Production, Technology, Chemistry, and Quality*. But even if you do overindulge in capsaicinoids, do not worry, for they are quickly metabolized in the liver and excreted in urine within a few hours.

The chemical that makes chile peppers hot is becoming more popular every day in applications that range from the strange to the ingenious. In 1995, Jack Challem wrote in *The Nutrition Reporter* that more than 1,300 studies on capsaicin had been published in medical journals since 1990, and that number surely is much larger now. But medicine is far from the only use of capsaicin.

Around 1990, reports were all over the media about an inventor who was adding capsaicin to the paint used on boat hulls and intake valves on municipal water systems, to prevent the growth of barnacles and zebra mussels. That story just faded away, but now it's back as scientists from Burlington Bio-Medical and Scientific Corporation of Farmingdale, New York, have announced the development of a method of making large quantities of denatonium capsaicinate. The compound, which includes capsaicin and the anesthetic lidocaine, is both painfully spicy and intensely bitter. Denatonium capsaicinate is being proposed for a paint additive because it is nontoxic to marine life and will effectively repel barnacles. Other uses for the compound include applying it to veterinary sutures to prevent pets from pulling them out with their teeth. Also, coating fiber-optic cables with the chemical could prevent rodents from gnawing on them.

Capsaicin has a well-documented history as an animal repellent. Chile powder is added to birdseed to prevent squirrels from eating it; there is no effect on birds, and the vitamin A in the powder brightens the birds' plumage.

One company, IntAgra, manufactures Get Away Repellent spray in two formulations: Dog and Cat, and Squirrel and Raccoon. The Dog and Cat repellent is used to keep those animals out of garbage, gardens, lawns, and landscaped areas. The Squirrel and Raccoon spray is used on bird feeders and gardens.

One of the more interesting uses of capsaicin as an animal repellent involves insects. My wife, Mary Jane Wilan, applies superhot sauces with oleoresin capsicum in them on the threshold of our front door to deter the large outdoor cockroaches from crawling in under the door. Now we learn that she was ahead of her time. NTI International has released NouGuard, a biorepellent for ants that is made mostly from capsaicin. It is sprayed around the perimeter of structures to keep the ants outside.

Harald Zoschke of Suncoast Peppers reported that two of his customers in Arizona order his extremely hot Liquid Ax hot sauce to prevent woodpeckers from pecking holes in their wooden garages. Birds enjoy eating pepper pods, but they have an aversion to the highly concentrated oleoresins. He also says his neighbor puts Liquid Ax on his phone cords to deter their cats from chewing on them.

But, depending upon the concentration of capsaicin, chiles or chile sauces are not always an effective deterrent for mammals. My wife and I had a cat named Attila the Hungry who would dip his paw in red chile sauce cooking on the stove and lick it off. One year in southern New Mexico, the Department of Game and Fish issued special out-of-season hunting licenses to farmers so they could legally remove deer that were raiding green chile fields and eating the plants and pods all the way down to the ground. And the skins, stems, and seeds of processed chiles are often fed to cattle.

By now everyone probably knows that there are dozens of brands of capsaicin creams on the market to combat the pain of arthritis, as well as shingles, psoriasis, and other skin disorders. Researchers are putting new twists on these medications almost weekly. One complaint about creams is that, when applied, they burn the fingers and the user has a good chance of getting some of the cream in his or her eyes. Therefore, it was only natural to find new application techniques. Penecine Topical Pain Reliever is sold in three-fluid-ounce plastic containers that feature a hands-free roller-ball applicator. Zostrix, one of the first creams on the market, is now available as Zostrix Topical Analgesic in stick form. It is advertised as portable, convenient, and drip-free. A single stick comes in a 0.7-ounce rack-displayable blister pack. Another application format is the patch. Capsaicin patches, like mustard plasters, have been around for a while, but now they are making a comeback as TheraPatch Penetrating Pain Relief Patches.

Other medical developments include the introduction of capsaicin gels and the addition of other medicines or herbs to make the capsaicin products more efficacious. Heritage Consumer Products has released Eucalyptamint 2000 Arthritis Pain-Relieving Gel that contains capsaicin and menthol. Another analgesic gel is Arthogesic, which claims to give temporary relief from minor muscle aches, joint arthritis, backache, bruises, strains, and sprains.

Some manufacturers believe that the addition of herbal remedies assists the capsaicin. JUSTIA Patents observes: "Sports Med and Arth DR utilize capsaicin plus glucosamine, raspberry leaf, valerian, and white willow bar." Nature's Sunshine Product's Capsaicin Gel has twice as much capsaicin as usual (0.05 rather than 0.025 percent), plus yucca, horsetail, chamomile, elder flower, peppermint oil, spearmint oil, aloe vera, and allantoin, a component of comfrey herb. NatureWorks manufactures Swedish Bitters Capsaicin Cream, which contains capsaicin and Swedish bitters extract for use in treating arthritis, backache, and pains in the muscles and joints.

One company, Thione International, has been granted a US patent for its compositions for relief of the symptoms of arthritis. The patent protects Thione's healthcare preparations that are based on L-glutathione, "the body's key protector and most important anti-oxidant," according to company spokesman Dr. Theodore Hersh. The first Thione product based upon the patent is Pain Relief Rx, which combines the company's antioxidant complex with capsaicin.

CAPSAICIN RECEPTORS

I admit it, I was completely wrong in past articles. But I have an excuse: I was misled by published articles. For years I have written that the sensitivity in the mouth for capsaicin was controlled by the number of taste buds, and that supertasters, people with a higher concentration of taste buds, couldn't take the hot stuff as well as the nontasters, who had a genetically-linked fewer number of them in their mouths. Sometime in 2002, I received an e-mail from a reader telling me I was wrong and that taste buds could only detect sour, sweet, bitter, salty, and umami flavors. (Umami is the flavor of monosodium glutamate, or MSG.) He wrote that capsaicin is not detected by the taste buds because it does not fall into any of those five categories. This person promised to forward links to prove me wrong, but he never did, so I forgot about it.

But in May 2003, the proof was, well, in the spicy pudding. Scientists David Julius and Elizabeth D. Prescott Julius of the University of California, San Francisco, announced they had identified a lipid molecule called PIP2 that plays a crucial role in controlling the strength of the burning sensation caused by capsaicin. A lipid molecule is a fatty molecule, insoluble in water but soluble in fat solvents and alcohol—just like capsaicin. In the mouth, there is a capsaicin receptor called TRPVI, and the lipid molecule PIP2 is bound to it. In the presence of capsaicin, the PIP2 molecule separates from the receptor, causing a painful sensation. Here's the scientific description: "In this process, the capsaicin receptor (TRPVI) is sensitized by phosphatidylinositol-4,5-bisphosphate (PIP2) hydrolysis following phospholipase C activation." That's quite a mouthful.

Now, what governs the degree of pain? The strength of the binding of the molecule to the receptor, say the scientists—the stronger the binding, the more powerful the pain sensation when the capsaicin causes the separation. And what determines the strength of the binding? To quote the researchers: "Thus, modification of this PIP2 regulatory domain by genetic, biochemical, or pharmacological mechanisms may have profound effects on sensitivity of primary afferent nerve fibers to chemical and thermal stimuli under normal or pathological conditions."

Now I'm no scientist, but it seems to me that they are saying the sensitivity to capsaicin is determined by genetics—some people's lipid molecules have a stronger bond with the capsaicin receptors than do others. But the fact that biochemical and pharmacological mechanisms can also play a role could explain why some people become desensitized to capsaicin and can take more and more heat.

I'm certain that further study will reveal even more information regarding this process, so stay tuned. And by the way, if you are worried about capsaicin destroying your five to ten thousand taste buds, you should know that all of them are replaced every two weeks anyway. So forget about your taste buds and concentrate on the binding of your lipid molecules!

OLEORESIN CAPSICUM AND THE SUPERHOT CHILES AND PRODUCTS

Oleoresins are extracts from the dried pods of both hot and nonpungent capsicums. There are three types, from most to least pungent: oleoresin capsicum, oleoresin red pepper, and oleoresin paprika.

Oleoresin capsicum is made from the hottest chiles available, usually from African, Indian, or Asian chiles, although any hot chile can be used. The heat rating is generally between 500,000 and 1,800,000 SHU, or about 4–14 percent capsaicin. A single pound of 500,000 SHU oleoresin will replace 20 pounds of cayenne pods.

This extremely hot oleoresin is used in personal-defense pepper sprays, in superhot sauces such as Dave's Insanity Sauce, in pharmaceuticals such as topical analgesic creams, and in some manufactured foods. Since its heat can be precisely measured, manufacturers can make foods consistently of the same heat level.

A milder extract is oleoresin red pepper, produced from larger, milder red-chile pods grown in Mexico, the US, India, and Turkey. It ranges from 80,000 to 500,000 SHU, and a pound of 200,000 SHU–oleoresin red pepper will replace 10 pounds of good quality red chiles. It is mainly used in food processing.

Oleoresin paprika is extracted from a large number of paprika varieties and is nonpungent. However, the milder the chiles, the higher their color content, so oleoresin paprika is used primarily as a red dye in food manufacturing.

Oleoresin manufacture is a relatively simple process that takes a large, expensive plant with a lot of machinery. The chiles are ground to a coarse powder and then treated with a solvent. To produce a fat-soluble oleoresin, dichloroethane, hexane, or benzene is used. For a water-soluble oleoresin, acetone or ethanol is the usual solvent.

The solvent, sometimes heated, is percolated through a bed of the powdered chiles. Then the solvent must be removed from the crude oleoresin by distillation, a tricky process because if the mixture is overheated there is a loss of flavor and solubility. After distillation, the oleoresin is sometimes purged of fats with ethanol, a process that keeps it from turning rancid and further concentrates the capsaicin. The result is a very thick dark reddish-brown liquid concentrate. The percentage of capsaicin varies according to the chiles used and the methods used to extract the oleoresin.

The Rezolex plant in Radium Springs, New Mexico (see the photograph at the beginning of this chapter), has great access to the raw product because operator Lou Biad owns extensive farming operations and three pepper-dehydrating plants. They process mostly nonpungent American paprika types.

The Rezolex process begins with dehydrating the pods to 3 percent moisture. The pods are then ground into a powder and pelletized. The pellets are washed with hexane continuously until they release their natural oils. The solids that are left over are turned into feed for sheep and goats, and they are so tasty that longhorn cattle used to break down the fences around Rezolex to feed on spilled spent pellets.

The oil and hexane mixture is called *miscella*, and this must be carefully heated to remove the hexane, which constitutes 90 percent of the miscella. The heating reduces the hexane to 2 percent, and then to get it below the federal regulations of 25 parts per million, the miscella is treated in a thin-film evaporator under a heavy vacuum. It takes 15 pounds of pods to make one pound of oleoresin paprika.

If Lou Biad were processing pungent pods for oleoresin capsicum, the oleoresin would be recovered by further treating with methanol, which binds with the capsaicin. The mixture settles and can be drained off, and then the methanol is distilled off and the result is concentrated oleoresin capsicum.

The oleoresin paprika produced by Rezolex is used primarily by food processors to add color to their products. It is an ingredient in chicken feed because it enriches the color of egg yolks and gives gray chicken meat a pinkish hue. It is sprayed on potato chips to give them a golden color when baked. One of the oleoresin's principal uses is by the meat industry, particularly by the manufacturers of pepperoni, bologna, and wieners. It gives meat the appearance of being leaner than it really is, and is used in spice blends such as black pepper and garlic oil that are used to treat processed meats. It also shows up in ketchup and margarine, and in frozen-food batters for fish and chicken.

Oleoresin capsicum is used in food processing to provide a precise heat level to various foods. For example, it could be added to tortilla chips to add color and a measured level of pungency. Besides its use in food processing and pharmacology, other uses of oleoresin capsicum include mixing it with paint to make an antifouling coating for the hulls of boats. The coating prevents the accumulation of barnacles. In 1995, a US patent was issued for the coating, which is also used to prevent zebra mussels from fouling water-intake valves along the Great Lakes. Other uses include spraying it on lambs to repel coyotes in Wyoming and Colorado, and on fence posts to prevent "cribbing"—excessive chewing by cattle and horses.

Oleoresin capsicum is also sold in a concentrated "hot sauce" form as a repellent for deer, rabbits, and mice, and is applied to fruit and nut trees, vegetables, and shrubs. Hot-pepper wax, a concentrate that is also mixed with water and sprayed on foliage, is a repellent for aphids, spider mites, thrips, and whiteflies.

The hotter the chile, the fewer that have to be used to make the oleoresin capsicum, so that's where superhot chiles come into the picture. In fact, because oleoresin capsicum has an unpleasant flavor, many product manufacturers are foregoing oleoresin and are just using the superhot pods or the mash—made of ground chiles, salt, and/or vinegar—which ferments.

To make the mash from the Rica red habaneros described in chapter 3, the pods are picked, destemmed, sorted, bagged, and moved to the plant from the field by pickup truck. A flowing water wash cleans the chiles, which are further sorted, and then they are treated with an organic grapefruit extract for disinfection. The chiles are moved from the wash by conveyor belt into a revolving cylinder that spin-dries the chiles. From the dryer, the chiles move to the grinder, where they are ground into one-half- or one-quarter-inch pieces. Salt is added at this stage to 15 percent of the weight of the chiles. The rough mash is pumped into sealed tanks and ferments for 10 to 12 days. The fermented mash is pumped into nylon bags with polyethylene liners, which are supported by heavy wooden frames. The package is called a "tote" and weighs 2,200 pounds. The totes are sealed with nylon ties and are transported by truck to Limón, where they are sent in containers to Louisiana. The mash continues to ferment about 5 percent more during shipping.

Rica-red chile mash before fermentation. Photograph by Dave DeWitt.

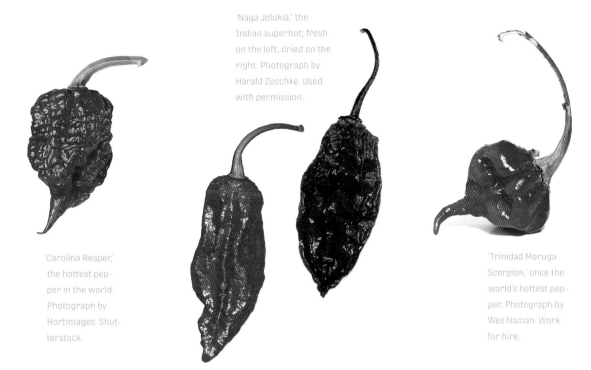

'Naga Jolokia,' the Indian superhot; fresh on the left, dried on the right. Photograph by Harald Zoschke. Used with permission.

'Carolina Reaper,' the hottest pepper in the world. Photograph by Hortimages. Shutterstock.

'Trinidad Moruga Scorpion,' once the world's hottest pepper. Photograph by Wes Naman. Work for hire.

After further aging in Louisiana, the mash is used by hot sauce manufacturers to add heat to cayenne sauces. At the plant, a pulper removes seeds and skin particles before it is blended. Dilution with water or vinegar reduces the salt concentration to less than 10 percent.

Above is a gallery of the most popular superhot chile peppers:

WILBUR SCOVILLE AND THE ORGANOLEPTIC TEST CENTENNIAL

The year 2012 marked the centennial anniversary of the Scoville Organoleptic Test, so I decided to apply all my food-history online-research skills that I've honed over the past five years to create what is the first definitive—however brief—biographical essay on Wilbur Scoville. Fortunately, the combination of Google Books, Google Scholar, and other online resources proved successful, and at least now we know quite a bit more about Professor Scoville's professional life. His personal life remains shrouded in mystery.

I seriously doubt that Wilbur Scoville ever imagined he would be most remem-

bered for his Scoville Organoleptic Test, which, in 1912, was the first attempt ever to quantify the heat of chile peppers. He probably had convinced himself that he would be most famous for authoring *The Art of Compounding* in 1895, which is now in its ninth edition, a facsimile, published in 2010. Although he was interested in chile peppers, he didn't write much about them, preferring to focus on even more bizarre chemicals like the cantharides in Spanish fly.

A pharmaceutical chemist, college professor, magazine editor, laboratory director, and author, Wilbur Lincoln Scoville was born in Bridgeport, Connecticut, in 1865. We know little about his early life except that his involvement with pharmacy began in 1881 when, at the age of 14, he worked at a drugstore owned by E. Toucey in Bridgeport. This apparently influenced him greatly, for in 1887 he moved to Boston to attend the Massachusetts College of Pharmacy. He graduated in 1889 with a PhG (Graduate of Pharmacy) and married Cora B. Upham in Wollaston, Massachusetts, in 1891. They had two daughters together, Amy Augusta, born August 21, 1892, and Ruth Upham, born October 21, 1897. In 1892 he accepted the position of professor of pharmacy and applied pharmacy at his alma mater, where he taught until 1904. He also took on specialized journalism, becoming editor of the *New England Druggist* in 1894.

In 1895, after just three years on the college faculty, when he was just 30 years old, his best-known work was published: *The Art of Compounding*. The book was used as a standard pharmacological reference up until the 1960s. The subtitle of the book, *A Text Book for Students and a Reference Book for Pharmacists at the Prescription Counter*, gives us a clue as to why the book was so popular—there were two markets for it. I found a copy of this book in Google Books, and here are two notable quotes that I discovered. Scoville was one of the first, if not the first, to suggest in print that milk is an antidote for the heat of chiles. "Milk, as ordinarily obtained," he writes, "is seldom used except as a diluent [diluting agent]. In this capacity it serves well for covering the taste of sharp or acrid bodies as tinctures of capsicum, ginger, etc., and for many salts, chloral, etc."

And he was insightful into the process of drug addiction as well as the addicts themselves. "The renewal of prescriptions is also a question for individual judgment," he writes. "In the majority of cases renewals are expected and granted, on demand, but occasions sometimes arise where a single vial-full is all that is needed or advisable. The notion that a medicine 'can do no harm, if it does no good,' is in most cases erroneous, sometimes very decidedly so." Then Scoville gets down to the real nitty-gritty: "Moreover, the pharmacist should remember that such conditions as are found in opium or cocaine habitués (not to say drunkards), often originate in the use of a prescription containing one of these drugs in some form, originally prescribed for a legitimate purpose, but renewed from time to time until the habit is established." Early OxyContin, anyone?

In 1897, he resigned as editor of the *New England Druggist* and the following year accepted the position of pharmacy editor of *The Spatula*, the journal-cum-magazine of the Massachusetts College of Pharmacy. It was called "The Illustrated Monthly Publication for Druggists" and carried ads for Clifford's Moustache Wax; Parke, Davis & Company's Pure, Uncolored Insect Powder; and the Clean Font Modern Nursing Bottle; among others for industry products such as drug bottles. The magazine was a chatty, informative publication featuring articles about new products, notable druggists, drug laws, and a bit of gossip. During his time there and beyond, from 1900 to 1910, Scoville was on the committee to revise the US Pharmacopoeia and he chaired that committee during his final year on it. He also worked on revising the National Formulary and was a staunch advocate of pharmacy standards.

Scoville had a lively, inquisitive mind and did studies on the extracts of witch hazel and cinchona, and he wrote an article entitled "Some Observations on Glycerin Suppositories." In 1903, his article "Standards for Flavor Extracts" was published in the *American Journal of Pharmacy*, and it proves that Scoville was part of the same debates we have today over natural versus artificial flavors. A review of his article appeared in the *Journal of the American Chemical Society*, and the reviewer had this to say about it: "Professor Scoville points out that flavoring extracts are not all used for the same purposes, that, of those who use them, few are good judges of quality. He who 'lives to eat,' the epicure, demands the very best of flavoring, not in the so-called 'extracts' only, but in the flavoring and seasoning of all of his dishes. He who 'eats to live,' the non-epicure, he whose sense of taste has not been carefully educated, and is not infallible, will allow to pass unnoticed a heavy or even a coarse flavor, or an inharmonious flavoring of the various dishes composing his meal."

In 1904, Scoville resigned from the college, and Benjamin Lillard, editor of *The Practical Druggist*, had this to say about it: "Professor Wilbur L. Scoville, who has been known for many years as a prominent professor in the Massachusetts College of Pharmacy, has resigned his position and accepted a berth with a large firm of Boston retailers owning four stores. It is unfortunate that the independent colleges are not in position to pay larger salaries and keep men of Professor Scoville's ability." Scoville was director of the Jaynes Analytical Laboratory, just purchased by the Riker Drug Stores, where for $2.50 per patient, his staff performed urine analyses. And he continued to publish articles in the *American Journal of Pharmacy*, such as "Aromatic Elixir" in the April 1904 issue.

But commercial laboratory work didn't last long. Scoville was recruited in 1907 by one of *The Spatula*'s advertisers, Parke, Davis & Company, and moved his family from Boston to Detroit. *The Bulletin of Pharmacy*, published in Detroit, had this to say about Scoville's hire: "In a great house like Parke, Davis & Company, Professor Scoville will have ample opportunity to utilize his varied abilities to the utmost." And one of those abilities—his work with Heet, a muscle salve manufactured by the company he had just joined—would make him famous.

Heet was made with chile peppers, and the problem was standardizing the type and the amount of chile that needed to be added to the other ingredients of Heet to standardize the formulation and avoid burning the skin of the person using it. Scoville was assigned to solve this problem, which took a few years due to his other duties. In the earliest reference to his work on chiles, the *American Journal of Pharmacy* notes in 1911: "Wilbur L. Scoville presented a Note on Capsicum, showing the great variation in the strength of capsicum, and suggesting the possibility of the pungency of this drug being used as a simple test for quality. This paper elicited some discussion in the course of which it was pointed out that the physiological test for capsicum was infinitely more delicate and more reliable than the similar test that has been proposed for use in connection with aconite."

At the American Pharmaceutical Association annual meeting in Denver in 1912, Scoville presented a paper on his solution to the Heet problem: the Scoville Organoleptic Test. Albert Brown Lyons, writing in *Practical Standardization by Chemical Assay of Organic Drugs and Galenicals* (1920), explains:

It is quite possible to form a reasonably "exact judgment" of the "strength" of a sample of the drug [capsaicin] by the simple expedient of testing its pungency. W. L. Scoville proposes the following practical method. Macerate 0.1 gm. of ground capsicum overnight in 100 mils of alcohol; shake well and filter. Add this tincture to sweetened water (10% sugar) in such proportion that a distinct but weak pungency is perceptible to the tongue or throat. According to Scoville official capsicum will respond to this test in a dilution of 1:50,000. He found the Mombassa chillies to test from 1:50,000 to 1:100,000; Zanzibar chillies, 1:40,000 to 1:45,000; Japan chillies 1:20,000 to 1:30,000. Nelson found that a single drop of a solution of capsaicin in alcohol 1:1,000,000, applied to the tip of the tongue produced a distinct impression of warmth.

"Organoleptic" means using the sense organs for taste, color, aroma, and feel to evaluate a food or drug, and Scoville's test worked because the flavor was not important, just the perceived pungency. Scoville used a panel of tasters who kept sampling the mixture of chiles and sugar water until the pungency was gone. At that point the amount of dilution, such as 1 to 50,000, gave the chile a heat level of 50,000 SHU. Of course today, this tedious, expensive, and subjective test has been replaced by chromatography, but in 1912 this was breakthrough technology. As a result, Scoville's career blossomed.

In 1913, Scoville was elected second vice-chairman of the American Pharmaceutical Association and read his paper "Tincture of Cantharides and Its Assay" at the annual meeting. Years later, he would be nominated as president of the association, but he withdrew his name because he was too busy working on revising the National Formulary. In 1918, his book *Extracts and Perfumes* was published. It was a pharmacology study containing hundreds of formulations. The book, published in hardcover, sold for one dollar. In 1922, Scoville won the Ebert Prize from the American Pharmaceutical Association; the prize, established in 1873, is the oldest pharmacy award in existence in the United States and is awarded to the best essay or written communication—appearing in the *Journal of Pharmaceutical Sciences*—that contains an original investigation of a medicinal substance. In 1929 he received the Remington Honor Medal, the American Pharmaceutical Association's top award "to recognize distinguished service on behalf of American pharmacy during the preceding years, culminating in the past year, or during a long period of outstanding activity or fruitful achievement." Scoville also received an honorary doctor of science from Columbia University the same year.

In 1934, at the age of 69, Scoville retired from Parke, Davis. The company had this to say about him, probably written by Frank G. Ryan, the president, writing in *Modern Pharmacy* but covered in the *Journal of the South Carolina Medical Association*:

Three or four years ago, in the gradual development of our scientific staff, we secured the services of Professor Wilbur L. Scoville, a pharmacist well known to the country and a man preeminent in the field of what has been termed pharmaceutical elegance. Professor Scoville may well be considered an artist in questions concerning odor, flavor and appearance of galenicals.

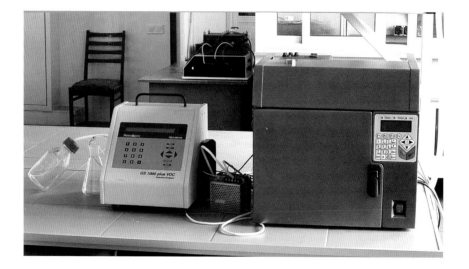

The first task assigned to Professor Scoville was to go systematically and patiently through our entire line of elixirs—regardless of what other workers had done before him, and regardless of what changes were under consideration at the time. He was given carte blanche to go ahead and suggest any modification and improvements which seemed to him necessary.

Wilbur Lincoln Scoville died in Detroit in 1942 at the age of 77.

MEASURING THE HEAT

In the past, when human taste tests were used to determine the pungency of chile peppers and products, wide variations in the capsaicin levels occurred even in the same variety of chile, accounting for the wildly differing Scoville Heat Scales appearing in various publications. The technique for determining *Capsicum* pungency by high-pressure (now, "high-performance") liquid chromatography (HPLC) was developed by James Woodbury of Cal-Compack Foods in 1980. This process dissolves the powdered chile sample in ethanol saturated with sodium acetate. The sample is then analyzed with a spectrofluorometer that measures the capsaicin levels in parts per million, which is then converted to Scoville Heat Units, the standard industry measurement.

The test is sensitive to two parts per million—about 30 Scoville Heat Units—which means that testing individual chiles is now much more accurate. Home cooks wishing to test their chiles will need to buy an Altex Model 322 Liquid Chromatograph equipped with a solvent programmer and dual pumps.

Chile Heat Scale in Scoville Heat Units of Chile Varieties and Commercial Products

1,000,000+ 'Carolina Reaper,' 'Trinidad Moruga Scorpion,' 'Bhut Jolokia,' 'Bih Jolokia,' 'Naga Morich'

100,000–500,000 habanero, congo pepper, Scotch bonnet, South American *chinense*, African bird's eye

50,000–100,000 santaka, chiltepín, rocoto, Chinese kwangsi

30,000–50,000 piquin, 'Cayenne Long,' Tabasco, Thai prik khee nu, Pakistan dundicut

15,000–30,000 de árbol, crushed red pepper, habanero hot sauce

5,000–15,000 'Early Jalapeño,' ají amarillo, serrano, Tabasco Sauce

2,500–5,000 'TAM Mild Jalapeño I,' 'Mirasol,' 'Cayenne Large Red Thick,' Louisiana hot sauce

1,500–2,500 'NuMex Sandia,' cascabel, 'Yellow Wax Hot'

1,000–1,500 ancho, pasilla, 'Española Improved,' Old Bay Seasoning

500–1000 'NuMex Heritage Big Jim,' 'NuMex Heritage 6-4,' chili powder

100–500 'NuMex R Naky,' 'Mexi-Bell,' cherry, canned green chiles, Hungarian hot paprika

10–100 pickled pepperoncini

0 'Mild Bell,' pimiento, 'Sweet Banana,' US paprika

Incidentally, pure capsaicin equals 16 million Scoville Heat Units. Included here are ratings based on various tests on chiles with HPLC as reported by the Texas Agricultural Experiment Station, New Mexico State University, and several chile-processing companies. Because of the variability in heat levels caused by mis-identification, hybridization, local variation, and growing conditions, these ratings should only be considered a general guide. Cooks are advised to pretest chiles by tasting a minute amount to determine approximate pungency.

Despite the accuracy of HPLC testing, we should remember, as Dr. Ben Villalon of the Texas Agricultural Experiment Station points out, "Capsaicin can and is quantitatively measured by high performance liquid chromatography, to exactness for that particular pod only, that particular plant, that particular location, and that particular season only." Thus, chiles will sometimes deviate from the heat scale because of local conditions.

Results of Riley's Heat-Remedy Test

REMEDY	TOTAL MINUTES
Rinse the mouth with water only	11
Rinse the mouth with one tablespoon olive oil	10
Drink one half cup heavy fruit syrup	10
Rinse mouth with one tablespoon glycerol	8
Drink one half cup milk, rinsing well	7

PUTTING OUT THE FIRE

It is senseless to serve or consume dishes that are too hot to eat with comfort. If the discernible flavors of both the meal and the chiles are unidentifiable, the pleasure of dining is gone. But sometimes accidents happen, and inexperienced diners get burned out.

In 1989, John Riley, editor-publisher of the quarterly journal *Solanaceae*, tested various remedies reputed to remove the heat of the capsaicin in chile peppers. In each test, a slice of serrano chile was chewed for one minute, and then one of the remedies was applied. The amount of time until the burning sensation eased was measured and the results were recorded. As we always suspected, ordinary milk was the clear winner.

If a prepared recipe is too blistering, here are some ways to cool it down:

- Always wear gloves or you'll be sorry on your next trip to the restroom.
- Reduce the amount of chile in the recipe to begin with. More heat can always be added later.
- Remove the seeds and membranes (placental tissue) from the chile pods.
- Increase the amount of tomato products (if any) used in the recipe, such as tomato sauce, puree, or whole tomatoes.
- In appropriate recipes, such as enchiladas, add a side of sour cream or yogurt.
- If using canned chiles, rinse them well to remove the canning liquid.
- Soak the chiles in salted ice water.
- If making a sauce calling for green chiles, add pureed bell peppers to dilute the heat.

- When buying crushed red chiles, avoid products with yellow flakes, which indicate the presence of seeds and membrane.

Now, if anyone is literally burned out, here are some suggestions to cool down the mouth, tongue, and throat:

- Casein is the protein found in dairy products that strips the capsaicin from the receptors in the mouth and on the tongue. The thicker the dairy product, the greater the presence of casein. So eat yogurt, sour cream, or ice cream.
- Starchy foods such as bread and potatoes tend to absorb or dilute capsaicin. In New Mexico, we use sopaipillas with honey.
- Various cultures have their own cures. The Chinese use white rice, the Vietnamese suggest hot liquids such as tea, and East Indians utilize yogurt-based drinks and sauces.
- A Mexican cure says that if enough beer is consumed, no one will care how hot the chiles are!

Regarding cooking with the superhot chiles, Harald Zoschke, author of *Das Chili Pepper Buch*, grows superhot chiles in his garden in Bardolino, Italy. Here are his suggestions:

- To tame the heat, remove the veins and seeds by scraping the inside of the pods with a spoon. Rinse superhot pickled chiles with water.
- When cooking with superhot chiles and expecting guests, take it easy on the number of chiles. Not everyone might have the tolerance for heat that you have developed yourself.
- It is easier to kick up a dish at the table (chopped chiles or hot sauce) than toning down the heat of a finished one!
- Be particularly careful with the superhots—one pod, fresh or dried, goes a very long way.

But if a dish turns out to be too hot, here are a few tips on how to lower the heat:

- Chili con carne: add more beans or tomatoes (or tomato sauce).
- Soups: thin with broth or—if recipe allows—stir in sour cream or cream.
- Serve sour cream or shredded cheese on the side.
- Fruity salsas: add more fruit (mango, peach, pineapple, banana).

- Water does not lower the capsaicin heat although it will momentarily relieve some of the pain.

AN UNDESERVEDLY BAD REPUTATION

Because they are so hot, legend has held for centuries that chiles must be dangerous. Interestingly enough, they are reputed to aggravate some of the very conditions they are supposed to relieve, such as acid indigestion, cancer, dysentery, ulcers, and wounds.

We have demonstrated that capsaicin can cause burning of the skin and hands, a malady now known as "Hunan hand." Yet a topically applied, capsaicin-based cream is used to treat phantom-limb pain, a painful condition experienced by amputees. Another example of chiles as cause and cure is *jaloproctitis*, a burning sensation that occurs during and after the elimination of jalapeños. Yet red chiles are reputed to be a cure for hemorrhoids.

A 1988 study at the Veterans Administration Medical Center in Houston backs up the contention that chiles are safe to eat. As reported by the *Journal of the American Medical Association*, a team of doctors at Baylor College of Medicine in Houston conducted a unique experiment utilizing *videoendoscopy*, the high-tech procedure of inserting a fiber-optic tube and a miniature video camera into the stomach to inspect it visually.

The object of the experiment was to test the generally held theory that capsaicin, the active heat chemical in chile peppers, damages the lining of the stomach. The research team, led by Dr. David Graham, subjected 12 volunteers (none were chile lovers) to a series of test items—bland food, plain aspirin, "Mexican" food, and pizza. After each meal, the endoscope was inserted to determine if "gastric erosions" of the lining had occurred. By far, the most damaging meal was the bland one combined with aspirin.

Not believing their results, the research team then sprayed Tabasco Sauce directly on the stomach lining. There was mucosal damage this time, but it was linked to the vinegar in the sauce. To further test capsaicin alone, the good doctors then injected 30 grams of freshly ground jalapeños directly into the stomach. There was no visible mucosal damage.

Dr. Graham concludes in his study: "We found that ingestion of highly spiced meals by normal individuals did not cause endoscopically demonstrable gastric or duodenal mucosal damage." However, in an interview published in the *Los Angeles Times*, Dr. Graham admits that chiles increase gastric acid secretion, but "they add to the flavor and enjoyment of eating and do not appear to cause stomach lining damage." In fact, some gastroenterologists suggest that capsaicin may actually protect the lining of the stomach from damage due to aspirin or alcohol.

Some medical researchers have suggested that capsaicin is both a cause and potential cure of some forms of cancer. According to one report, capsaicin has been linked to colon cancer through studies conducted among chile pepper eaters in India and Korea. In 1984, researchers at the Eppley Institute at the University of Nebraska reported that capsaicin had flunked the Ames test—a quick bacterial assay used to screen possible carcinogens.

But additional research has indicated that the reputed carcinogenic properties of chile peppers have been highly exaggerated. During the same study, the Eppley research team also discovered that the antioxidant properties of the capsaicin may be capable of neutralizing harmful chemicals in the body that are responsible for some types of cancer. Investigator Peter Gannett states that capsaicin prevents the formation of dimethylnitrosamine (DMN)—a known animal carcinogen—by binding to and inactivating the enzymes that produce the chemical. In the liver, capsaicin is apparently transformed into a compound that soaks up chemicals called free radicals, which are thought to cause cancer.

"Some of the chemicals in hot peppers appear to be cancer-causing, but the same ones can protect against cancer," says Peter Gannett of the University of Nebraska Medical Center. "The overall effect depends upon how much you eat." Skeptics insist that the researchers are trying to scare us again with another potential carcinogen, just as they have in the past with the highly exaggerated dangers of coffee, sugar, and cranberries.

One critic calculates that a person would have to consume two pounds of capsaicin to see the effects the Nebraska research suggested. Since we can taste capsaicin in solutions as diluted as one part per million, there may only be a few pounds of capsaicin in the entire annual world crop of chiles!

PEPPERS AS PANACEA

It is now evident that the value of chile peppers as a nutritional food and a medicine far outweighs any supposed risk. A 1982 study of chile consumption in Thai people, conducted at the Siriraj Hospital in Bangkok, concludes: "Capsicum, a hot appetizer and seasoning, has been found to induce increased fibrinolytic activity and simultaneously cause hypocoagulability of the blood when ingested." Translated, the statement means that Thais have a lower risk of blood clots because they eat chiles!

Recently, capsaicin has been used in yet another medical application—to treat the intense pain caused by shingles. Shingles is an eruption of unpleasant skin blisters caused by herpes zoster, the chicken-pox virus. Topically applied capsaicin depletes substance P, which carries pain impulses to the brain from nerves in the skin, thus effectively short-circuiting the agony. It is basically the same process that allows the chile lover to adapt to greater and greater amounts of hot chiles. The treatment for shingles is now available in an over-the-counter cream called Zostrix™, which is also being tested for the relief of mastectomy pain, diabetic neuropathy, and phantom-limb pain.

Undoubtedly, further medical uses of chile peppers and capsaicin will be found. I believe, however, that their greatest benefit to mankind is their addition to the foods we eat.

Wholesome Heat

Pity the poor maligned pods! Ever since their first usage in prehistoric South America, chile peppers have gained a reputation for being both a remedy for some ailments and an aggravation of others. The first warning was issued in 1590, when the Jesuit priest and historian José de Acosta warned of the reputed aphrodisiac qualities of chiles, saying the fruit of the pepper plant was "prejudicial to the health of young folks, chiefly to the soul, for it provokes to lust." Unfortunately, this assertion was never proven to be true.

Today, chiles are sometimes cited as being both the cure and the cause of the same ailment! For example, chiles have a reputation in the United States for irritating the digestive tract, yet a popular Mexican stomachache cure is to chew up and swallow a whole serrano chile. Such a contradiction begs for resolution, and the only way to proceed is to examine the historical record and compare it to modern experiments—a tedious and frustrating task, since all the research has not been completed.

Since I began researching chile peppers in 1977, I have maintained a list of the maladies supposedly treated or cured by the use of chile peppers, both topically applied and eaten. The efficacy of chile as a treatment for most of these conditions has not been scientifically verified and thus remains on the level of a folk remedy. However, as we shall see, some of the following conditions have been successfully treated with capsaicin, the chemical that gives chiles their heat: acid indigestion, acne, ague, alcoholism, anorexia, apoplexy, arteriosclerosis, arthritis, asthma, blood clots, boils, bronchitis, cancer, catarrh, cholera, colic, colds, congestion, conjunctivitis, coughs, cramps, croup, dropsy, dysentery, ear infections, epilepsy, fever, gout, headache, hemorrhoids, herpes, liver congestion, malaria, migraine, night blindness, phantom-limb pain, low blood pressure, rheumatism, seasickness, scurvy, sore throats, stomachaches, tonsillitis, toothaches, tumors, ulcers, vascular problems, venereal disease, vertigo, and wounds.

One of the first real breakthroughs to prove the efficacy of chile peppers occurred when vitamin C was determined to be a link between chiles and scurvy prevention.

Wholesome Heat: Vitamins C and A

Chile peppers were responsible for the awarding of a Nobel Prize. In 1928, Albert Szent-Györgyi, a professor at the University of Szeged in Hungary, was experimenting with a then- mysterious chemical he called "God-knows" because no one knew what its uses were. At first he produced small quantities of the chemical from the adrenal glands of cattle, and eventually he named it ascorbic acid.

Since Szent-Györgyi lived in the heart of paprika country, it was only natural that his wife would prepare a dish made from those chiles, but the professor did not care for her meal and joked that if he could not eat it, he could at least experiment with it! He took the paprika to his laboratory and made history by discovering that the pods were an excellent source of ascorbic acid, which we now call vitamin C.

In 1937, Szent-Györgyi was awarded the Nobel Prize in physiology and medicine for his work with vitamin C. In 1978, he wrote, "I strongly believe that a proper use of ascorbic acid can profoundly change our vital statistics, including those for cancer. For this, ascorbic acid would have to cease to be looked upon as a medicine, sold in milligram pills by the druggist. It would have to become a household article, like sugar and salt and flour." Of course, today vitamin C is both a medicine and a household article!

One of the earliest uses of the vitamin C in chile peppers was, as with citrus fruits, in preventing that scourge of the high seas, scurvy. The historian and naturalist Bernabé Cobo wrote in 1653 that after the Spanish sailors discovered chiles in Mexico, they took *ají en escabeche* with them on voyages. Today, chile peppers are used as an excellent source of both vitamins C and A.

Vitamin C promotes growth and tissue repair and is important for healthy blood vessels, bones, and teeth. Undoubtedly, vitamin C is essential in resisting diseases, but the way it functions is not clear despite claims by some promoters that large doses will prevent colds and other maladies.

Green chiles are quite high in vitamin C, with twice the amount as citrus, while dried red chiles contain more vitamin A than carrots. In this way the two chile pepper vitamins are complete opposites. Vitamin C is one of the least stable of all the vitamins; it will break down chemically through heat, exposure to air, solubility in water, and dehydration. Vitamin A, however, is one of the most stable vitamins and is not affected by canning, cooking, or time.

Despite its tendency to break down, a high percentage of vitamin C in fresh green chiles is retained in canned and frozen products; however, the vitamin C content drops dramatically in the dried red pods and powder. Each 100 grams of fresh, ripe chile pods contains 369 milligrams of vitamin C, which diminishes by more than half to 154 milligrams in the dried red pods. Red chile powder contains less than 3 percent of the vitamin C of ripe pods, a sorry 10 milligrams.

However, in an incredible turnabout, vitamin A dramatically increases as the pod turns red and dries, from 770 units per 100 grams of green pods to 77,000 in freshly processed dried red pods. This hundredfold rise in vitamin A content is the result of increasing carotene, the chemical that produces the orange and red colors of ripe peppers. Vitamin A helps maintain normal vision in dim light, is important for skeletal growth and tooth structure, and is necessary for proper birth and lactation. The recommended daily allowances for these vitamins are 5000 international units for A, and 60 milligrams for C. These allowances can be satisfied daily by eating about a teaspoonful of red chile sauce for vitamin A, and about one ounce of fresh green chile for vitamin C.

Chiles as Calorie Conquerors

Stated in simple terms, the weight of any animal is a matter of balance: the intake of food versus the expenditure of energy. If we consume more calories than our bodies need for daily activity, the excess energy is stored as fat; if we consume fewer calories than we need, our bodies burn the stored fat.

The most efficient way to lose weight is to cut down on caloric intake while burning off excess calories through exercise. To lose one pound a week, we must decrease our daily food intake by 500 calories or burn 500 additional calories by exercise. But moderation is important; severe dieting or excessive exercise is not recommended. Since caloric and exercise levels vary dramatically from person to person depending on age, height, weight, gender, metabolic rate, and body frame, I suggest that persons who are severely overweight or need a special diet should consult with their physician or dietitian.

Because chiles are naturally low in calories, there is little worry about gaining weight while eating peppers. However, dieters should be careful about the foods they combine with hot peppers. And believe it or not, evidence has come to light indicating that chiles may indeed assist in burning calories. In 1986, researchers at Oxford Polytechnic Institute in England conducted an experiment in TEF, an acronym for "thermic effects of food." Twelve volunteers ate identical 766-calorie meals. On one day, three grams each of chile powder and mustard were added to the meals; on the next day, nothing was added. On the days chile and mustard were added, the volunteers burned from 4 to 76 additional calories, with an average of 45.

A possible explanation for the process is the fact that certain hot spices—especially chiles—temporarily speed up the body's metabolic rate. After eating, the metabolic rate increases anyway, a phenomenon known as "diet-induced thermic effect." But chiles boost that effect by a factor of 25 percent, which seems to indicate that increasing the amount of chile in a recipe could reduce the effective caloric content—provided, of course, that one does not drink more beer to counter the added heat.

Another intriguing possibility has been suggested by T. George Harris, who writes in *American Health* magazine that chiles stimulate the taste buds but not the sense of smell. Thus they "perk up food without adding fat." Harris adds that he formerly made jokes about the hot pepper diet; but now, "over the last couple of years, chile peppers have begun to emerge as the nutritional heroes of the future."

Chiles as Cholesterol Conquerors

Although cholesterol is necessary for the formation of hormones and cell membranes, the substance has been associated with coronary artery disease and other circulatory disorders, primarily because the human body manufactures its own cholesterol and consequently does not need the excess supplied by meats, poultry, seafood, and dairy products. Cholesterol is totally absent from plant tissue, and that is where hot peppers enter the picture.

In some cuisines, chiles have long been associated with high-cholesterol ingredients such as lard, dairy products, and fatty meats such as pork and beef. Eating chile pepper–laden food will help reverse this trend by utilizing low-cholesterol substitutions. Perhaps the most important substitution is the replacement of solid fats with nonsaturated oils, such as the use of margarine for butter—or, better still, vegetable oil for either. Soups and stews should be chilled so that solid fat can be skimmed off before serving. Another important low-cholesterol substitution in Mexican cooking calls for the replacement of hard cheeses (such as cheddar and Jack) with cottage, pot, feta, or skim-milk ricotta cheeses. Low-fat or skim milk should replace whole milk and cream; egg yolks should be used sparingly, if at all. As protein sources, choose lean meat, fish, poultry, beans, and peas.

Here are some hints for reducing the cholesterol levels in the recipes:

- Limit the use of fats and oils by substituting unsaturated oils such as corn or safflower for lard, butter, and palm oil– and coconut oil–based shortenings.

- Remove fat from meat, and fatty skin from poultry and fish, before cooking.

- Avoid frying or deep frying foods; broil, bake, steam, or poach instead.

- Substitute chile pepper–based dressings (such as salsas) for fatty (mayonnaise-based) dressings.

Fiery Fiber and Starch

I recommend the combination of chiles with starchy foods to provide needed fiber and starch without increasing the calories consumed. Fiber is the part of the plant cell wall that cannot be totally digested by humans. The benefits of fiber in the diet, and in the treatment of colon cancer, heart disease, and diabetes, are still under investigation, but most dietitians recommend consumption of a wide variety of vegetables, fruits, and whole grains.

Starch is a complex carbohydrate occurring naturally in foods such as beans, peas, corn, breads, cereals, and pasta. It is widely thought to be fattening, but starch provides a mere four calories per gram; what are fattening are the additional ingredients we add to starchy foods, such as butter on potatoes. The best chiles for high-fiber cookery are those that are used whole, with seeds and skins intact. In this category are pickled peppers and small hot chiles such as serranos and jalapeños used in salsas. Remember that fresh green chiles do not have to be peeled and seeded in all cases; for use in salsas and salads, they can simply be chopped up. For extra fiber, add chopped bell peppers to recipes, mixed, of course, with the proper balance of hot chiles.

Low-Sodium Spiciness

One of the diets people have the most trouble following is one that is sodium-restricted. As the level of sodium is lowered, the meals become less tasty to the dieter accustomed to a high salt level. Also, the recipes become more difficult to prepare because of the varying sodium levels of the ingredients themselves. I suggest that chile peppers are very useful for the low-sodium dieter.

The substitution of hot peppers for salt makes gustatory sense because the pungency of the peppers counteracts the blandness of the meal resulting from salt restrictions. In other words, the heat masks the absence of salt. Fortunately, fresh or frozen chile peppers have an extremely low sodium content.

According to a study at New Mexico State University, "Even in a severely restricted diet, the sodium content of 3.7 to 5.7 milligrams per 100 grams found in fresh chile peppers is reasonable to include as a food choice." However, the study warns that canned green-chile peppers should be avoided because of the salt used in the canning process, which can be over a hundred times the amount in fresh or frozen chile peppers.

recipes

The recipes in this chapter were developed by Nancy Gerlach, who is my coauthor of 10 books. Nancy, in addition to her work on those books, and the decade she spent as the food editor of *Chile Pepper* magazine, is a registered dietitian.

HERB SHAKER

yield ¼ cup   *heat scale* medium-hot

This recipe for a salt substitute is based on one from the American Heart Association. Reach for the chile instead of the sodium!

3 teaspoons ground cayenne	1 teaspoon ground mace
1 tablespoon garlic powder	1 teaspoon onion powder
1 teaspoon ground basil	1 teaspoon ground black pepper
1 teaspoon ground thyme	1 teaspoon ground sage
1 teaspoon ground parsley flakes	1 teaspoon marjoram
1 teaspoon ground savory	

Combine all the ingredients in a salt shaker, label it "Herb Shaker," and use it to flavor meats, vegetables, starches, or anything that would usually need salt.

HIGH "C" SALSA

yield 2 cups   *heat scale* medium

This all-purpose "chunky" salsa is a good source of vitamin C, as well as being low in sodium. There are four sources of "C" in this recipe: the chiles, the tomato, the parsley, and the lime juice. Although vitamin C is affected by contact with the air, this salsa contains such a large amount that a single serving still meets the daily requirement.

This salsa can be served as a dip with chips, as a salsa over foods such as burritos or steaks, or over shredded lettuce as a salad dressing.

4 to 6 green New Mexican chiles, roasted, peeled, stems and seeds removed, chopped

3 jalapeño chiles, stems and seeds removed, chopped

4 tomatoes, chopped

1 medium red onion, chopped

1 clove garlic, minced

2 tablespoons chopped fresh cilantro or parsley

2 tablespoons vegetable oil

1 tablespoon fresh lime juice

½ teaspoon ground cumin

¼ teaspoon ground cloves

Combine all ingredients in a bowl and allow them to sit for at least an hour before serving.

MONKFISH WITH CHILE ORANGE OIL

yield 4 servings   *heat scale* medium

The dried red chile used in this recipe provides an ample amount of vitamin A even when used as a marinade. Note: This recipe requires advance preparation.

¼ cup dried, crushed red New Mexican chiles, seeds included

2 cups peanut oil

1 teaspoon sesame oil

Zest of 3 oranges, finely minced

2 cloves garlic, finely minced

1 ½ pounds monkfish fillets

Heat the peanut oil to about 325 degrees F. Remove from the heat and stir in the sesame oil, orange zest, garlic, and chile. Allow the oil to cool, add the fish, and marinate overnight in the refrigerator.

Grill the fish until done, basting frequently with the marinade.

LOW-CALORIE HOT SALAD DRESSING

yield 1 ⅓ cups   *heat scale* medium

Try this recipe in place of commercial low-calorie dressings, which may have up to 90 calories per tablespoon; this one has only 15 calories per tablespoon, and much less sodium.

1 teaspoon ground cayenne	1 teaspoon sugar
2 green New Mexican chiles, roasted, peeled, stems and seeds removed, chopped	½ teaspoon dry mustard
	2 cloves garlic, finely chopped
½ cup ketchup	1 tablespoon chopped fresh parsley
¾ cup cider vinegar	Freshly ground black pepper
1 tablespoon vegetable oil	

Combine all the ingredients and refrigerate for at least an hour before serving.

POTATOES WITH CHILE COLORADO

yield 4 servings   *heat scale* mild

This easy, flavorful recipe is high in complex carbohydrates and low in sodium while providing an outstanding source of vitamin A. One serving of these potatoes more than exceeds the daily requirement for this vitamin, supplied here by the dried red chile. These potatoes go well with broiled meats or baked chicken.

2 tablespoons dried, crushed red chiles, seeds included	Sauté the onion and the chiles in the margarine.
¼ cup chopped onion	Toss the potatoes in the mixture and bake in a 350-degree F. oven until heated through.
1 tablespoon margarine	
2 medium potatoes, baked with the skins on, cubed	

LOW-SODIUM CHILE SAUCE

yield 2 cups   *heat scale* mild

Use this low-sodium sauce in place of bottled "chili sauce," ketchup, or commercial bar-becue sauce that can contain up to 130 milligrams of sodium per tablespoon. This recipe has less than 5 milligrams of sodium per tablespoon. Experiment with the levels of spic-es to suit individual tastes. Use in place of ketchup in any recipe, on sandwiches, or as a basting sauce when grilling. Note: This recipe requires advance preparation.

5	teaspoons dried, ground pasilla chiles, or substitute red New Mexican chiles
8	tomatoes, peeled, seeds removed, or 1 three-pound can of low-sodium canned tomatoes
1	cup low-sodium tomato juice
1	large onion, chopped
1	cup cider vinegar
¼	cup brown sugar
1	teaspoon dried mustard
¼	teaspoon ground cinnamon
¼	teaspoon ground cloves
¼	teaspoon ground nutmeg
¼	teaspoon ground ginger

Combine the chiles, tomatoes, tomato juice, and onion in a nonaluminum pan, and simmer for 15 minutes or until the tomatoes break down.

Add the remaining ingredients and sim-mer for 3 to 4 hours until the sauce is the consistency of thick ketchup. Store in the refrigerator for at least 24 hours before serving.

LOW-SODIUM *CALDILLO*

yield 6 servings   *heat scale* medium

Caldillo (light broth) is the Southwest's answer to beef and vegetable soup. The heat and taste of the chiles masks the lack of salt in the following soup. This recipe is low in calories, with each serving having fewer than 200. Serve with a crisp salad with Low-Calorie Hot Salad Dressing (see recipe this chapter) and a fruited yogurt for a complete, flavorful meal.

6	green New Mexican chiles, roasted, peeled, stems and seeds removed, chopped
¾	pound round steak, cut in ¾-inch cubes
2	tablespoons vegetable oil
2	large potatoes, diced
1	small onion, chopped fine
2	stalks celery, chopped fine
4	cups low-sodium beef broth
1	teaspoon powdered cumin
1	teaspoon freshly ground black pepper
1	teaspoon chopped fresh cilantro

In a soup pot, brown the meat in the oil, remove, and drain.

Add the potatoes, onions, and celery, and sauté until the potatoes are browned.

Add the broth, chiles, cumin, and black pepper. Bring to a boil, reduce the heat, and simmer until the potatoes are done, about 35 minutes. Five minutes before serving, add the meat.

Top with the cilantro and serve.

ten

According to Google, there are about 30 synonyms for the adjective "legendary," so I'd like to start this chapter by informing readers about those that are particularly applicable to chile peppers. They are *traditional* in many world cuisines; *famous* for their spicy history; *celebrated* with festivals; *acclaimed* for their healing powers; *esteemed* for their colors; *honored* in festivals; *notable* for their long history; *popular* in recipes; *lauded* for their flavors; *prominent* in their pungency; *great* in cooking; *outstanding* in their flavor; *revered* in cookoffs; *glorious* in gardens; and *unforgettable* as superhots.

CHILE PEPPERS IN EARLY LEGEND AND LORE

The ritual uses of the genus *Capsicum* range from the innocuous to the murderous, but the fiery pods are always powerful. In astrology, capsicums fall under the dominion of Mars, ancient god of war, so that should be some indication of respect. Fuentes y Guzmán wrote in 1682 that those who frequently ate red pepper were protected against poison, while the Incas prohibited the use of chiles at initiation and funeral rites. We do not know why the pods were precluded by the Incas, but we console ourselves with the knowledge that capsicums were associated with lightning bolts in Incan mythology—that we can easily understand.

One of the commonest household uses of chile peppers in cultures all over the world is burning them as a fumigant for vermin ranging from bedbugs to rats. Since fumigation in ancient times was also believed to be protection against vampires and werewolves, we have a good introduction to the concept of the magical powers of peppers.

"Chile is used as an amulet, probably because of its well-known protective pharmacological properties, and in religious ceremonies, witchcraft, and conjuring; its fiery potency is considered a powerful means to any end," observes Beatrice Roeder, author of *Chicano Folk Medicine from Los Angeles, California.*

In a ritual from Coahuila, Mexico, chiles are instrumental in countering the effects of "salting," which is casting a spell on a person to cause them harm, particularly mental problems. Such witchcraft is called *maleficio* in Mexico. To cast the spell, the evildoer gathers dirt from the grave of a person who died a violent death. Then he or she gathers salt from the homes of three widows, or from the homes of three women named Jane (Juana). The salt is mixed with the soil and is sprinkled in front of the door of the victim.

If the victim finds the salt and soil, he or she burns it immediately and then must counter whatever evil effects are left by smoking them out. To accomplish this *sahumerio* ritual, on the first Friday of the month hot coals are placed in a bucket, and myrrh, storax, the peeling of a clove of garlic, rosemary, rue, star anise, and chiltepín chiles are added. The victim carries the smoldering bucket throughout the house, adding extra smoke to the corners where evil may hide, while reciting a prayer that evil depart and good arrive through the sahumerio.

Further, the salting victim must perform another chile ritual. He or she stands outside on the patio, holds twelve ancho chiles in the left hand—plus three pinches of coarse salt—and rubs them over his or her body in the form of a cross. Then the salt and the chiles are thrown into a fire. The victim believes that burning chiles and salt will cause the malefactor to burn in the same manner. Then the victim recites the following three times: "Ghost of the cemetery, may those who have salted me receive this salt."

Chiles are considered to be a cleanser for evil eye (*mal de ojo*), bad luck, and bewitchment among Hispanics in the United States, a practice imported from Mexico. This parallels usage among Native Americans in Guatemala. When a child is thought to have the evil eye, the parents spray the child's face with a mixture of rue, and then a little aguardiente (liquor, usually brandy), mixed with a crushed hot pepper, is rubbed on the child's feet. Another cure for the evil eye calls for mixing a little annatto seed with chile peppers in a cloth bag and passing it over the child's body while making the sign of the cross. Then the bag is thrown into a fire.

A cure for the evil eye from Coahuila, Mexico, calls for the child to be wiped with the inside of an ancho chile. The child is patted on the head, crosses are made over the eyelids and forehead, and the child is laid on a bed with the arms outstretched in the form of a cross. The chile is wiped over the body to absorb the occult power, and then it is burned. *Curanderas* (female healers) often treat the hexing of adults by rubbing the inflamed areas (such as the feet) with whole eggs, a lime, and an ancho chile, which are then thrown into a fire. Perhaps because of their fiery nature, chiles are thought to absorb evil influences, which are then destroyed by fire.

In a remarkable parallel usage between totally different cultures, the East Indian population of Trinidad wraps seven red-pepper pods with salt, onion skins, and garlic skins in paper and passes the bundle seven times around a baby to remove najar, the evil eye, which is believed to cause unnecessary crying. Also, green chiles are dropped around the doorway to keep away evil spirits.

Interestingly, however, some cultures believe that the chiles themselves can bring on trouble. African Hispanics from islands like Cuba and Hispañola believe that

top Red chiles on
a doorstep.
Photograph by
Dave DeWitt.

bottom Chiles
and salt on a nail
cross. Photograph
by Dave DeWitt.

red pepper pods on a doorstep are the sign of a malignant influence and may give a man the "hot foot." Likewise, chiles are associated with the *luban oko*, or "red demon," of the Tsachila or Colorados Indians of the Amazon. This demon is said to suck the blood out of its victims, leaving them "as white as a boiled yuca." The chiles are burned in a fire while being served in food, and the demon is foiled in two ways: he is asphyxiated by the fumes, and he cannot eat any of the food because it is too spicy. Again there is the recurrent image of burning, and this time it is specifically related to the heat of the chiles.

Now some negativity starts to creep into the lore. "A case of death has been reported due to eating of excessive quantity of chillies," warns R. N. Chopra in his classic book, *Poisonous Plants of India*. I doubted that Indians indulged in pepper-eating contests, but when I read that chiles are one of the ingredients in the arrow poison of indigenous Dayak tribesmen of Borneo, I began to wonder how far chile powers extended—even to cause death? Again I checked with R. N. Chopra and learned: "In the past, chillies were frequently used in the Orient for the purpose of torture, some of the common methods being by introducing them into the nostrils, eyes, vagina or urethra, and burning under the nose."

There is no doubt that chiles indeed do have a darker side. In northern Mexico, chiles are still used as part of spells to make people ill or even to kill them. One "potion" consists of a rag that contains chile seeds, scorpions, sow bugs, mustard, and a strand of red silk. In a scenario recorded by Isabel Kelly in her book *Folk Practices in North Mexico*, another spell proved to be deadly. "Another time they threw chiles through the door of the butcher shop. They were two large chiles anchotes [probably anchos], wrapped in a newspaper. The chiles were 'prepared.' They stuck the package in, through a hole in the door. May God receive him, because he fell ill and died."

Needless to say, I am sobered by these wholly (and holistically) impure uses of chiles. I am heartened, however, by a report from one of my peripatetic friends, Lorenzo Fritz, who travels regularly to South America to live with the Indians, trade for crafts, and collect chile information for me. He told me that the Aymara Indians of Bolivia conduct a spiritual cleansing ritual in which a mixture of various herbs, flowers, and *locoto* chiles (*Capsicum pubescens*) are placed in a pail of boiling water. The subject sits on a stool nearby, and a blanket is placed over him and the pail to form a minisauna. Lorenzo, who observed the ceremony, noted: "This exercise is said to be an exorcism for *malas energías*, or bad energies."

And my friend Gary Nabhan, who is an ethnobotanist, revealed that the Tarahumara Indians of Sonora, Mexico, use the tiny chiltepíns in curing ceremonies—not to rid someone of a current affliction but to prevent maladies as a result of future witchcraft. According to Gary,

> Such witchcraft is caused by a sukurame sorcerer who uses a special bird called a disagiki as a pathogenic agent to transmit illness. He is the only one who can see the bird, which is no bigger than a finger tip but lives on meat and tortillas. It flies into houses crying 'Shit! Shit!' and then eats your food or defecates on you. The only way to prevent its coming is to throw some chiltepíns into the air and eat some yourself. The bird is like no other birds. More like evil people than its feathered kind, it cannot stand chiles.

Neither can sharks, if the Indians of the Cuna Islands off Panama can be believed; they tow chiles behind their boats to ward them off.

In the American Southwest there is a fascinating witchcraft cure. Two nails are tied together in the shape of a cross with a piece of wire. The cross is placed in a fire, and when it is red hot, it is removed from the fire and placed on a rock. A trinity of small chiles is placed on it, and then some rock salt. The resulting vapors are said to banish any witchcraft in the area.

In the Ozarks and deep South of the United States, an African American legend holds that for peppers to grow out and be hot, you have to be very angry when you plant them. The best peppers are said to be planted by a lunatic!

Perhaps the oddest legend I encountered came from Jethro Kloss's herbal bestseller, *Back to Eden*. He quotes the *Standard Guide to Non-Poisonous Herbal Medicine*: "A peculiar effect of capsicum is worth mentioning. In Mexico the people are very fond of it; and their bodies get thoroughly saturated with it,

Stained glass window in the vestibule of the Sanctuary of the Transcendental Capsaicinophilic Society in Santa Fe. Photograph by Dave DeWitt. Note: This is a joke.

and if one of them happens to die on the prairie the vultures will not touch the body on account of its being so impregnated with the *Capsicum*."

But apparently folklore and the ancient mystical remedies are not enough for devoted chile aficionados. There is an online cult that has its own website on the Internet: the Transcendental Capsaicinophilic Society. According to the tongue-in-cheek site, the cult is devoted to the worship of chiles, the life-long dedication to chile consumption, and making fun of people who "just can't take that spicy food." In the "Chants and Rituals" portion of the site, there is the "Litany Against Pain," "to be repeated silently when tempted to complain of burning":

Teach me, Chile, and I shall Learn.
Take me, Chile, and I shall Escape.
Focus my eyes, Chile, and I shall See.
Consume more Chiles.
I feel no pain, for the Chile is my teacher.
I feel no pain, for the Chile takes me beyond myself.
I feel no pain, for the Chile gives me sight.

OF CONTESTS, COOKOFFS, AND FESTIVALS

During the second half of the twentieth century, the legend of the chile pepper exploded as enthusiasts began to glorify its fiery nature with celebrations in various parts of the country. Some of the earliest celebrations were pepper-eating contests, which apparently originated in Louisiana. In 1956, *Newsweek* magazine reported such a contest in the Bayou Teche country near New Iberia. The contestants were required to munch their way through progressively hotter chiles and were penalized if they winced, shuddered, or flinched. It is interesting to note that the magazine stated that jalapeños were "the hottest pepper known," which we know is not true. The winner of that contest, Ed "Hot Mouth" Taylor, "munched his way right through the jalapeño as nonchalantly as if he had been eating turnip greens," reported the magazine.

Chile-eating contests are now commonplace throughout the US, with jalapeños often the chile of choice. In 1988, John Espinosa of San Antonio, Texas, gulped his way into the *Guinness Book of World Records* by consuming an amazing 29 jalapeños in two minutes flat! It should be noted that I neither endorse nor encourage hot pepper–eating contests because of the danger of capsaicin burns and other medical complications.

Plates of 50-gram portions of chopped pepperoncini for the Peperoncino Eating Contest. 'Diavolicchio Diamante' is the official championship cultivar of the contest. It roughly translates as "most devilish diamond." Contest winners these days force down about two pounds of these quite hot peppers. Photograph by Harald Zoschke. Used with permission.

In the late summer of 2006, I gave writer Gwyneth Doland an assignment to cover such an event, and here is her abbreviated report:

On the Saturday before Labor Day I drove out to Sky City Casino at Acoma Pueblo for the 2006 World Championship Jalapeño Competition, an event attended by about 100 people, but nevertheless officially sanctioned by the International Federation of Competitive Eating (IFOCE). It was the most awe-inspiring, uvula-tickling, gut-churning spectacle I have ever witnessed in what I must say is a long personal history of watching people eat. There were moments when I could only peek through cracks in the fingers I had clenched over my eyes, and there were moments when my lunch only stayed down because of the fingers clenched over my mouth. . . .

When time was up, it was too close to call between Bertoletti and Le-Fevre. The contestants all lingered, looking pained and ill as they wiped their faces and awaited the results. When "Jalapeño" Jed Donahue darted away from the table, we weren't sure where he was going—until we all heard a really, really loud splash hitting asphalt. The crowd collectively groaned, and when Donahue returned to the table there was some confusion about whether or not he would be disqualified for what the IFOCE affectionately terms a "reversal of fortune." As the 15 minute mark drew near, several contestants came dangerously close to reversal.

In the end it was determined that Pat Bertoletti had put down 177 pickled jalapeños, a feat rewarded with the $1,000 grand prize.

The 1950s also witnessed the beginning of chili con carne cookoffs, which are now some of the largest celebrations in the country involving chile peppers. The Chili Appreciation Society was formed in 1951 by George Haddaway and Jim Fuller to "improve the quality of chili in restaurants and broadcast Texas-style recipes all over the earth." The organization was headquartered in Dallas, and when chapters began to form in other countries, the "International" was added to the name.

The Chili Appreciation Society International (CASI), was a non-dues-paying organization, and members did their own secretarial work. Their bible was *With or Without Beans* by Joe Cooper of Dallas, which is still in print at Amazon.com. The society slogan was "The aroma of good chili should generate rapture akin to a lover's kiss."

The society's chapters had luncheon or dinner meetings about once a month over steaming "bowls of red." Their "missionary endeavors" were debated and members spent a lot of time answering letters from all over the world and sending out "approved" recipes to those who requested them. Vats of chili were even packed in dry ice and shipped to chili-starved members in Europe. By 1964, Haddaway and his buddies headed for Los Angeles to establish a California chapter, which was duly installed at the Airport Marina Hotel. The Californians liked the chili and the society but warned the inexperienced: "Real chili con carne is not for sissies. Fowler's Four-Alarm Chili is reputed to open 18 sinus cavities unknown to the medical profession."

The first Terlingua, Texas, cookoff, held in 1967, was a promotion for Frank X. Tolbert's book *A Bowl of Red* (also still in print) and featured a cookoff between Wick Fowler, inventor of Four-Alarm Chili Mix, and humorist H. Allen Smith, author of the article "Nobody Knows More About Chili Than I Do," which appears

in a 1967 issue of *Holiday* magazine. Because of the remoteness of the Terlingua cookoff, no one thought very many chili fans would show up, but 209 chapters of CASI were represented and over a thousand spectators attended. The contest ended in a draw between Fowler and Smith. In 1968, the second cookoff at Terlingua was also declared a draw by Tolbert. But, of course, he had no choice since the ballot box was stolen by masked men with guns. These desperadoes threw it into an outhouse located over a mine shaft!

By 1970, over 5,000 spectators trekked to Terlingua, and it was evident that a major event had been created. CASI started to get organized, and local "Pods" were formed to hold preliminary cookoffs. The number of contests grew, and eventually "chili-heads," as they were called, developed such a listing of cookoffs that competition cooking is now similar to a professional sports circuit. Most members of CASI belong to Pods, and cooks are given points for placing at sanctioned cookoffs throughout the year: four points for winning, three for second, two for third, and one for fourth. At the end of the year, all cooks having enough points to qualify are invited to cook at Terlingua, always the first Saturday in November.

The Terlingua cookoff can no longer legally be called the "World Championship" because that phrase has been trademarked by the International Chili Society (ICS). The International Chili Society was booted out of Texas in 1974 and was reborn in California. During the 1974 Terlingua cookoff, CASI celebrities C. V. Wood and Carroll Shelby flew a network television crew in to cover the festivities. Of course, it was only natural that the media people would interview the people who had provided the transportation, but Frank Tolbert did not appreciate the promotion. After standing around on the sidelines and not receiving any attention from the TV crew, he became angry. In a letter to Wood and Shelby, he "invited" them to promote their own chili cookoff in California and "save the freight." So they did.

They formed the International Chili Society and made plans for a major cookoff. After searching for a suitable location for the ICS cookoff in California, the Tropico Gold Mine, located three miles west of Rosamond in the Mohave Desert, was selected. The International Chili Society also thumbed its nose at CASI by trademarking the phrase "World Championship Chili Cookoff."

The ubiquitous pot of chili con carne is seen at every major cookoff. Photograph by Derek Ramsey. Wikimedia. GNU Free Documentation License, Version 1.2.

The first Championship Chili Cookoff held in California was twice as big as expected—about 20,000 people attended. Perhaps some of them were star-struck by the celebrity judges: William Conrad, Robert Mitchum, Ernest Borgnine, Peter Marshall, Dale Robertson, and John Derek. The Miss Chili Pepper was Diana House, who went on to spice up *Playboy* magazine.

Meanwhile, back in Texas, Frank Tolbert was busy organizing CASI and promoting the Terlingua cookoff. Although relations between the two societies seemed to be "heated," they were in constant communication with each other. Early in 1976, ICS began to get organized by finding corporate sponsors. Pepsi, Budweiser, Hunt-Wesson, Tabasco, the American Spice Trade Association, and Tequila Sauza came on board to help raise money for various charities. By 1977 the turnout at Tropico Gold Mine for the championship exceeded 35,000. That year Tommy Lasorda, Leslie Uggams, Andy Granatelli, and Bobby Unser were added to the celebrity judging staff, and by the end of the fourth championship, over $50,000 had been raised for charity.

Cash prizes were growing as well. In 1978, the World's Champion Chili Cook, LaVerne "Nevada Annie" Harris, picked up $14,000—which was great pay for three hours of cooking. Ten years later, the 1988 championship was held on October 30 in Tropico with over $35,000 in cash prizes and awards. Since 1975, ICS has raised over $10 million for charities and nonprofit organizations. There are nearly 15,000 members worldwide, who sanction about 350 cookoffs every year with nearly 10,000 contestants and 5,000 judges. Obviously, chili cookoffs today are no longer off-the-wall events but, rather, viable fund-raising efforts.

In addition to raising money, ICS has a lot of fun, which is demonstrated by some of the events at the Tropico Gold Mine cookoff. In 1988, the Tulsa, Oklahoma, Jaycees built the World's Largest Pot of Competition-Style Chili. The 750 gallons of chili was made with 75 pounds of bacon, 3,000 pounds of chili-grind meat, 1,500 pounds of onions, 1,200 cloves of garlic, nearly 30 pounds of spices—and, of course, more than 50 pounds of fresh chiles. The concoction, based on a recipe called Chili from Hell, was served to more than 20,000 chiliheads at Tropico in a benefit for the St. Jude's Children's Hospital in Memphis.

Chili lovers are never satisfied. Despite the fact that the bowl o' red is the Texas State dish, a movement has begun to have Congress declare chili con carne America's Official Food. Led by self-proclaimed World Chili Ambassador Ormly Gumfudgin, and supported by the International Chili Society and Maximum Strength Pepto-Bismol, the movement hopes to obtain the signatures of one million chiliheads on a petition to support passage of the bill, which has been before Congress

Cookoff contestants love to dress up in weird costumes, but this is the real deal. Here, Staff Sergeant Carlos Morales prepares his own recipe for chili as he participates in the Last Battle Over Baghdad Chili Cookoff. The cookoff took place at the Sather Air Base pavilion, Baghdad. It was a Chili Appreciation Society International–sanctioned event with all proceeds benefiting the Boy and Girl Scouts of Iraq. Photograph by Staff Sergeant Daniel Yarnall. Wikimedia. This image is a work of a US Army soldier or employee, taken or made as part of that person's official duties. As a work of the US federal government, the image is in the public domain.

but never acted upon. Considering the fact that the ICS sanctions more than 150 chili cookoffs each year, and CASI sanctions more than 450—meaning that more than 750,000 people attend chili cookoffs each year—perhaps this goal is reachable.

There seems to be no end to the ever-growing number of other festivals celebrating the chile pepper. Laredo, Texas, holds a Jalapeño Fiesta each year, while tiny Hatch, New Mexico, draws more than 10,000 people to its Hatch Chile Festival, held every year over the Labor Day weekend. Tucson, Arizona, holds its Fiesta de los Chiles in mid-October at the Tucson Botanical Gardens, complete with a chile rap song performed by a puppeteer. Las Cruces, New Mexico, produced an annual Enchilada Fiesta for 34 years, at which they created the World's Largest Enchilada, nearly eight feet in diameter. But in 2015, Robert Estrada, who made the Guinness World Record–holding enchilada, said he was retiring and could not make the enchilada anymore.

According to the Clifton Chilli Club, whose leaders visited our 2019 Fiery Foods and Barbecue Show, there are about six chilli festivals in the UK, one in the Netherlands, and four in Australia. There are hundreds of chile festivals and chili con carne events in the US. In 2017, through online searching, I found about 300 retail-store locations that have "Hatch Green Chile Roasting" events.

The latest US chile-contest craze has Southwestern cities competing for the title of "Mexican Food Capital" by way of a cookoff challenge. In 1987, Tucson mayor Lew Murphy proclaimed his city to be the "Mexican Food Capital of the World and Elsewhere." In a blistering letter to the mayors of San Antonio, El Paso, Los Angeles, Dallas, San Diego, Phoenix, Santa Fe, and Albuquerque, Murphy challenged those cities to a chile-cooking contest in Tucson. "It's time to put your Mexican menu where our mouth is," Murphy dared them.

Such a cavalier attitude produced fumes from Santa Fe's mayor, Sam Pick, who retorted: "We've been eating chile here in Santa Fe before Tucson was even thought of." Pick was alluding to the fact that Santa Fe was founded 165 years before Tucson, and he added: "Everyone knows that Santa Feans are bred on red and weaned on green." Eventually, the cities of Phoenix, El Paso, Albuquerque, and Santa Fe collided with Tucson in early December 1987, to give a heated response to the chile challenge. The event was called, improbably enough, the Great American Mexican Food Cook-Off. The judges of the contest were all Mexicans—not Hispanics, mind you, but real Mexican chile aficionados imported from Tijuana. One of them was the president of the Tijuana restaurant owners' association.

The results of the contest proved that Tucson's claim to be the capital of Mexican food was invalid. Overall winners were, in order, Santa Fe, Phoenix, and Albuquerque. The following year, Santa Fe chefs and cooks again seized control of the title of "Mexican Food Capital of the World and Elsewhere" at the 1988 Mayor's Chile Challenge held in Santa Fe.

Such contests inevitably bring up questions. What city is America's spiciest? Which state offers the greatest wealth of fiery food? In 1988, the *Whole Chile Pepper* magazine (with me as the editor) conducted a study based upon a compilation of nationwide Yellow Page classifications. The listings of over 2,800 Mexican-food restaurants and Mexican-food retail-product producers were analyzed. Since Mexican food contains one of the highest percentages of chile peppers of any cuisine, it was regarded as a prime indicator for the popularity of fiery foods in general.

The data were examined on a state-by-state and city-by-city basis, then compared to the population of each area to determine the number of people per Mexican-food retailer, thus giving a good indication of the demand for fiery foods in each region. The study of the states indicated—not unexpectedly—that New Mexico and Texas ranked at the top of per capita consumption of Mexican food. New Mexico was the hottest state with one retailer per 11,900 residents. Texas was close behind with one outlet for every 13,700 Texans. California, despite its proximity to Mexico, ranked a weak eleventh, with only one retailer for every 53,000 residents. The southern area of that state was stronger than the northern part, as might be expected. Surprisingly, Kansas ranked third, with one retailer for every 17,200 people.

In the city-by-city study, two New Mexico cities took the top spots. Santa Fe ranked as the top fiery-food city in the country, with one retailer for every 4,890 residents. Las Cruces was close behind, with one outlet per 5,000 people. Austin, Texas, came in third with one hot retailer per 6,700 residents.

It should be pointed out that the data are not complete. To compile a truly comprehensive study of the geography of fiery food markets, it would be necessary to go beyond Mexican-food retailers and include Thai restaurants, East Indian restaurants and products, Hunan and Sichuan restaurants and markets, Caribbean and Cajun food, and New Southwestern restaurants and products. Although Mexican food currently constitutes the largest share of the chile pepper market, the other spicy cuisines are becoming quite popular as well.

A BRIEF HISTORY OF THE NATIONAL FIERY FOODS AND BARBECUE SHOW

In 1987, two things happened that would change my life forever. That was the year that Robert Spiegel, Nancy Gerlach, and I launched *Chile Pepper* magazine as a quarterly publication. Robert was the publisher and owned all the stock in the company. Nancy was the food editor and I was the editor in chief. Being editor of a growing and successful magazine enabled me to have a platform and sell book after book about chiles and spicy foods. One of our greatest accomplishments with the magazine, though, was how we popularized the habanero chile, then thought to be the hottest pepper in the world. We constantly published news items, articles, and recipes about the habanero, and a lot of other media outlets followed our lead. In 1995, Ten Speed Press published *The Habanero Cookbook*, by Nancy Gerlach and me, and it sold well. About a year later, I noticed that Albertson's supermarket was

carrying fresh habaneros in the produce section, right next to the jalapeños. I felt proud. I know that sounds weird, but I couldn't help but think I was at least partially responsible for the habaneros going mainstream.

The other thing that happened in 1987 was that I saw a tabletop display of Old El Paso products at the New Mexico Chile Conference, and that got me thinking. I had been a show producer for years, doing mostly custom-car shows, and as I drove back to Albuquerque, I thought, "This is a multibillion-dollar industry without a trade show. We ought to produce one."

I told my wife, Mary Jane, about the idea when I got back. She was teaching at Manzano High School but had the summer free, and as it turned out, she was a remarkably good phone salesperson. We decided to launch the show in a hotel venue because we had no idea how it would go, and the Convention Center was too big and expensive for us. The show was held in the fall of 1988, and we had 47 exhibitors and attendance of only about 500 people, but everyone loved the show and considered it a success. We made a net profit of about a hundred dollars. Hey, it was a start.

We stayed in hotel venues for another couple of years as we grew the show. After we doubled exhibitors in our third year, we moved it to a small venue of about 15,000 square feet at the Albuquerque Convention Center, and attendance doubled. The following year, we took a 30,000-square-foot hall and nearly filled it. Time went by, attendance grew, and the Convention Center built the east complex and we moved to a 60,000-square-foot hall in it. Attendance at this time was about 10,000 people, and Budweiser, through its New Mexico distributor, became a major sponsor and remains one today. We stayed in the Southeast Hall for more than a decade and attendance grew to 12,000.

Soon, a new opportunity presented itself. The biggest casino in New Mexico, Sandia Resort and Casino, expanded and had an exhibit hall plus meeting rooms and two large lobbies. I contacted them and they offered us a deal: free rent for three years if we would relocate the show. Who wouldn't take an offer like that? We moved, and because the venue was a better destination than a building downtown next to the railroad tracks, our attendance increased 38 percent the first year we produced it there.

We're still there, looking forward to the exhibit hall's expansion sometime in the near future. During Saturday morning's opening, about 3,000 people lined up to come in; we filled up the entire parking lot for 2,000 cars, and the gamblers complained about not finding a parking space. So what did the casino do, kick us back to the Convention Center? No, they built a 2,500-car parking deck that opened in time for our 2015 show.

The appeal of the show is so broad that it's difficult to pinpoint demographics. We used to have more men than women attend the show, but now it's 50-50—and

Our exhibitors love to wear costumes at the show. At left is the drumstick guy, Sean of Sean's booYah!; on the right is Anna Shawver of Apple Canyon Gourmet. Photographs by Mark Masker. Work for hire.

that's true for exhibitors too. And I would estimate that a third of exhibitors sell out of all the products they bring to the show.

These days we have about 170 exhibitors and excellent attendance over the three days of the show. In 2019 we enjoyed our largest attendance ever—17,500 people.

We have exhibitors and attendees from all over the world and get massive national publicity. We use a top-notch advertising agency and PR company to get the publicity and attendance, and we produce cooking demonstrations to entertain the public. I do probably 12–15 TV and radio interviews during the show, where I'm like a mayor of a small city for three days. It sure is fun. In 2019, a vote on USA *Today* online made us one of the top 10 specialty food festivals in North America, despite the fact that we're a trade/consumer show, not a festival.

WHY CHILES CONQUERED AMERICA

I am constantly asked to explain the exponential growth of interest in chile peppers and the boom in fiery foods products in the US over the past few decades. How did a meat-and-potatoes America become enamored of hot sauces, salsas, spicy snack food, chili con carne, and hundreds and hundreds of other fiery foods? First, we must look at the historical trends for why cooks add spices to their foods in the first place.

There are a number of explanations for why we have added spices such as chile peppers to our foods over the tens or hundreds of thousands of years that we have been cooking:

- Spices make foods taste better.
- The "eat-to-sweat" hypothesis: eating spicy foods makes us cool down during hot weather.
- Spices disguise the taste of spoiled food.
- Spices add nutritional value to food.
- The antimicrobial hypothesis: spices kill harmful bacteria in food and aid in food preservation.

Which of these explanations are correct?

THE FIRST CORNELL UNIVERSITY STUDY

In 1998, Jennifer Billing and Paul W. Sherman published a study in *The Quarterly Review of Biology* entitled "Antimicrobial Functions of Spices: Why Some Like It Hot." The study examined the reasons why humans might use spices. They studied 4,578 recipes from 93 cookbooks on traditional, meat-based cuisines of 36 countries; the temperature and precipitation levels of each country; the horticultural ranges of 43 spice plants; and the antibacterial properties of each spice.

The first thing they discovered was that many spices were incredibly antibacterial. For example, garlic, onion, allspice, and oregano were the best all-around microbe killers, killing almost everything. Next were thyme, cinnamon, tarragon, and cumin, which kill about 80 percent of all bacteria. Chile peppers were in the next group, with about a 75 percent kill rate. In the lower ranges of 25 percent were black pepper, ginger, and lime juice.

Next, they learned that "countries with hotter climates used spices more frequently than countries with cooler climates. Indeed, in hot countries nearly every meat-based recipe calls for at least one spice, and most include many spices, especially the potent spices, whereas in cooler countries substantial fractions of dishes are prepared without spices, or with just a few." Thus the estimated fraction of food-spoilage bacteria inhibited by the spices in each recipe is greater in hot than in cold climates, which makes sense since bacteria grow faster and better in warmer areas.

The researchers addressed the various theories. First, obviously spices make food taste better, "but why do spices taste good? Traits that are beneficial are transmitted both culturally and genetically, and that includes taste receptors in our mouths and our taste for certain flavors. People who enjoyed food with antibacterial spices probably were healthier, especially in hot climates. They lived longer and left more offspring."

Billing and Sherman discounted the "eat-to-sweat" theory, noting that not all spices make people sweat and that there are easier ways to cool down, like moving into the shade. Regarding the theory that spices mask the odor of spoiled food, they noted that it "ignores the health dangers of ingesting spoiled food." And since spices, except for chiles and citrus, add minimal nutritional value to food, that theory goes nowhere.

That leaves just two theories: that spices make foods taste good, and that they kill harmful bacteria—and those two theories are inseparable. "I believe that recipes are a record of the history of the co-evolutionary race between us and our parasites. The microbes are competing with us for the same food," Sherman says. "Everything we do with food—drying, cooking, smoking, salting or adding spices—is an attempt to keep from being poisoned by our microscopic competitors. They're constantly mutating and evolving to stay ahead of us. One way we reduce food-borne illnesses is to add another spice to the recipe. Of course that makes the food taste different, and the people who learn to like the new taste are healthier for it. We believe the ultimate reason for using spices is to kill food-borne bacteria and fungi."

THE SECOND CORNELL UNIVERSITY STUDY

In 2001, Paul W. Sherman and Geoffrey A. Hash continued the examination of spices in human diet with a study entitled "Why Vegetable Recipes Are Not Very Spicy," published in *Evolution and Human Behavior*. They compiled information from 2,129 vegetable-only recipes from 107 traditional cookbooks of 36 countries. Then they examined the history of the spice trade and discovered that for thousands of years spices have been traded all over the world, resulting in their availability in most world cuisines. The most traded spices are black pepper and chile peppers, in that order.

Many studies have proven that spices have antibacterial properties, that spices are more prevalent in warm climates than cool climates, and that the concentrations of spices in recipes are sufficient to kill bacteria. It is true that cooking eliminates the antimicrobial properties of some spices, such as cumin, but has no effect on others, such as chiles.

The researchers compared the vegetable-only recipes to the previously studied meat recipes, according to the spices found in the recipes, and discovered that the vegetable recipes used far fewer spices than the meat recipes. They attributed this to the fact that bacteria "do not survive or proliferate as well in vegetables, so adding spices is not as necessary." Interestingly, the four most common spices in both the meat and vegetable recipes were onion, black pepper, garlic, and chile peppers. Onion appeared in more than 60 percent of both types of recipes; black pepper in about 60 percent of the meat recipes and 48 percent of the vegetable recipes; garlic in 35 percent of the meat recipes and 20 percent of the vegetable recipes; and chile peppers in 22 percent of the meat recipes and 18 percent of the vegetable recipes.

Within each of the 36 countries, vegetable-based recipes called for fewer spices than did meat recipes. The countries using the most spices in both vegetable and meat recipes were—in order from the most used—India, Vietnam, Kenya, Morocco, Mexico, Korea, and the Philippines. Following were France, Israel, and South Africa.

In their second study, the researchers concluded: "By every measure, vegetable-based recipes were significantly less spicy than meat-based recipes. Results thus strongly support the antimicrobial hypothesis."

CHILE PEPPERS TAKE OVER

But in the United States, with refrigerators and freezers in almost every home, the antimicrobial hypothesis simply does not explain the rush to embrace chiles and spicy foods over the past two decades. After answering questions verbally for literally dozens of media interviews, I finally decided to keep track of my reasons for why chile peppers have conquered the United States.

- Ethnic diversity. Immigration patterns have changed and now feature new citizens with hot and spicy ingredients and cuisines imported from Asia, Latin America, and the Caribbean. They immigrate and open restaurants and markets, making ethnic chiles and spicy foods commonplace.

- Greater chile knowledge among Americans. They now realize that most chiles and spicy foods won't hurt them.

- Increasing interest in the hobbies of cooking, gardening, and traveling.
- The large number of ethnic and hot and spicy cookbooks published since 1978—literally hundreds of them.
- The increasing availability of chiles and fiery foods products in mainstream locations such as supermarkets and fast-food outlets.
- The publicity generated by the constant media attention. The recent National Fiery Foods and Barbecue Show in Albuquerque generated more than 5,000 column inches of coverage in US newspapers. Do a web search for terms like "chile peppers," "spicy," "hot sauce," or "habanero" and stand back—you will get thousands and thousands of solid citations.
- Trade and consumer shows and festivals featuring chiles and fiery foods.
- The enormous increase in manufacturing, with thousands of fiery foods products now on the market.
- The hobby of gardening. According to the National Gardening Association (NGA), 35 percent of households in the US grow food either at home or in a community garden. This means that two million more families are involved in gardening now, up 200 percent since 2008. All of these statistics were calculated by a special five-year report by the NGA, *Garden to Table: A 5-Year Look at Food Gardening in America*. The study tells us that many things have changed over the past five years—which age groups are most likely to garden, the types of food that are most popular to grow, why people garden, and garden location and size. Bonnie Plants, the largest US national grower and supplier of vegetable and herb plants for consumers, offers 53 different pepper varieties. That's nothing compared to my friend and coauthor Janie Lamson. Her website, ChilePlants.com, offers 500 different varieties of chile-pepper bedding plants. Now, in addition to taking over the cuisines of countries and continents, they're taking over our gardens.
- The "addiction syndrome." Chiles are not physically addicting—you don't have withdrawal symptoms when you stop eating them. But they are psychologically addicting because chileheads miss the burn if they don't have any spicy food for a while. I never hear anyone say, "Oh, I used to eat spicy food, but now I'm back to bland." Once someone starts liking hot and spicy foods, he or she is likely to be a chilehead for life.

THE ROZIN THEORY

But perhaps the most fundamental reason for the boom in fiery foods is a major shift in the way many Americans are eating. My revelation began in Philadelphia while dining with Liz Rozin, who hosted an incredibly diverse dinner at Serrano Restaurant during the Book and the Cook Festival. She is a food historian with fascinating insights into the origins of spicy cuisines. "When we look at the broad spectrum of human flavoring practices, we see one curious correlation," she writes in *The Primal Cheeseburger*. "The heavier the dependence on plant or vegetable foods, the more pronounced the seasonings; the heavier the consumption of animal foods, the less pronounced the seasonings. Those cuisines that clearly demonstrate a highly spiced or complex seasoning profile—Southeast Asia, India, Africa, Mexico—all have long relied on high-plant, low-meat diets." Her theory, interestingly enough, directly contradicts the Cornell University studies just discussed!

Of course, the US was just the opposite: a culture that in its early days relied on beef, pork, and chicken, as well as dairy foods. Vegetable foods in the US were eaten primarily in the same regions where the cuisine was also the spiciest: the South and the Southwest.

When Rozin turns her attention to chile peppers in high-vegetable, low-meat cultures, she notes: "The pattern of acceptance, the level of enthusiasm with which the pungent chiles were enfolded into certain existing traditions, seems to indicate that the unique stimulation they provide is an important compensation for foods that are somehow less satisfying, less perfect when eaten unseasoned. And on the other hand, the chiles were largely ignored or rejected by cuisines and areas of the world where meat and other animal foods were a significant focus of the diet."

At least three other major food trends have paralleled the move to spicy foods over the past two decades: natural foods, vegetarian foods, and low-fat foods. Meat consumption has declined as well, setting the scene for the modern return of Liz Rozin's theory of why ancient "less satisfying" foods were highly spiced: we need the heat and flavor of chiles and other spices to make up for the flavors of meat and fat lacking in more spartan cuisines. The new

The cover of *The Primal Cheeseburger*. Scan by Sunbelt Archives.

Chile pepper windsocks. Photograph by Chel Beeson. Work for hire.

corollary of eating in the twenty-first century might be: "The healthier you eat, the more you need to spice it up with chile-laden condiments."

The Primal Cheeseburger was published in 1994. Liz will be happy to know that since then the green chile cheeseburger has become a cultural icon in New Mexico. The state fair has a Green Chile Cheeseburger Challenge, in which restaurant chefs compete to see who makes the best one. The year I was a judge, the winning restaurant was Fuddruckers, proving that even a fast-food restaurant chain with 223 locations can step up and make a great green chile cheeseburger. The tourism campaign for the state, "New Mexico True," has an interactive New Mexico Green Chile Cheeseburger Trail that features restaurants specializing in that signature dish. And the Albuquerque Isotopes, a Minor League Baseball team in the Pacific Coast League, have joined the spicy promotion too. Their website reads, "With respect to one of the iconic culinary customs of New Mexico, on June 16, for one night only, the Albuquerque Isotopes will become the Albuquerque Green Chile Cheeseburgers. Isotopes Park will be decked out in a Green Chile Cheeseburger theme that night, with green chile cheeseburger sliders being served throughout the ballpark's concession stands. Green chiles will be roasted on the concourse, as 'The Lab' will also be transformed into 'The Grill.'"

To sum up, Paul Sherman thinks we added chiles to meat-based recipes to prevent the growth of bacteria, while Liz Rozin believes we used to chiles to spice up bland food. Perhaps they are both correct. But we do know one thing: chile peppers have conquered America, and they are not going away.

CHILES AS A TREND, NOT A FAD

It is now possible to wake up in the morning, put on a pair of chile pepper underpants, dress in a chile pepper T-shirt or skirt, drink coffee from a chile pepper–emblazoned mug, eat breakfast from plates decorated with red chiles, check a chile-pepper wind sock for wind direction, address a chile-pepper greeting card to a friend, and then drive into town to visit a chile-pepper specialty shop to buy even more chile pepper food and nonfood items.

Since there are now dozens—if not hundreds—of nonfood products based on chile peppers, speculation has arisen that we are experiencing a fad that will soon fade away. People still remember Hula-Hoops, coonskin caps, and Nehru jackets, and some skeptics think that chile peppers fall into the same category. I believe that the confusion about chile peppers (and, by extension, fiery foods) being a fad arises from the fact that chile peppers have the trappings of a fad.

Within just a few decades, chiles became enormously popular in the United States. The phenomenon was sparked by media attention and was driven by vehicles such as *Chile Pepper* magazine and then the Internet. Suddenly, it seemed, everyone was talking about, writing about, cooking with, and eating chile peppers. But such media attention came after the fact, not before it, for chile peppers were already firmly established in the cuisines of the Sunbelt states from Louisiana west to California. The media attention did not create the popularity of chile peppers as it did that of the Hula-Hoop; it merely reported what was already happening.

The other trapping that makes chile peppers appear to be a fad is the "warm fuzzy" concept. "Warm fuzzy" is a marketing expression for a "cute" product that is popular because it stimulates several senses simultaneously. An example of a warm fuzzy is the cartoon cat Garfield, which is embraced by sight in comic strips and television, and by touch when a stuffed toy is cuddled. Chile peppers—because of their shape, color, heat, and fragrance—embrace the sensations of sight, taste, and smell simultaneously, and thus have become warm fuzzies in the perception of consumers.

The shape and color of chile pods are visually pleasing, and they are easy to caricature. Red chile ristras, which originated as a preservation method, are now a home decoration. They are not only symbolic of the Southwest but also are now popular all over the country. In New Mexico, the aroma of roasting green chiles is associated with the changing of the seasons from summer to fall and is so traditional that it conjures up nostalgic emotions in those who inhale the fragrant fumes. The beloved heat of chiles—and the near addiction it causes in those people who consume them regularly—has been detailed in chapter 9.

The "warm fuzzy" concept has caused chile peppers to be plastered over every product imaginable because the public loves everything about the chile pepper. Chiles appear to be a fad, but they are not. First, they have been around a long time in the human diet—since about 7500 BC. Second, they have penetrated into most of the world's regions and cuisines, and it is estimated that three-fourths of the world's population use chile peppers as a regular part of their diet.

Third, for additional evidence supporting my contention that chile peppers—and fiery foods in particular—are a trend, not a fad, I have collected some interesting statistics. Sales of Mexican food in grocery stores rose 230 percent between 1980 and 1987, and well over a hundred new gourmet brands of fiery foods now enter the marketplace each year. Sales of Texas picante sauces and salsas have increased at the rate of 25 percent a year, and Mexican sauces in general now are the biggest sellers of all sauce and gravy products, with a 16 percent share.

In 1988, Mexican food became the most popular ethnic cuisine in the United States, with total restaurant sales surpassing those of Italian food (excepting pizza), according to the research firm of SAMI-Burke. Even McDonald's, that bastion of bland burgers and fries, is test marketing breakfast burritos with green chiles and quarter pounders ranchero-style!

One of the most impressive statistics comes from the fiery foods industry—consisting of those whose products contain chile peppers. In 1989, I researched extensively to find a value of the entire fiery foods industry, from agricultural production to retail sales of fiery foods products like hot sauce and salsas. I made a few estimates and did some guessing too. I attempted to be as conservative as possible and came up with a value of $1.7 billion for 1989. No other person or company has ever offered any other estimated value. I wondered how much the industry had grown in the 30 years since I valued it at that figure, so I turned to our company's accountant, Michael Tamasi, MBA, and he asked me what the possible growth rate might be. I knew that, in some decades, hot sauce sales had grown 10 percent or more each year, but for the past few years the figure for hot sauce sales had averaged 4.5 percent per year; so to be conservative, we used that figure, and Michael came up with a table that calculated the estimated value of the fiery foods industry at $6.6 billion, nearly quadrupling the 1989 estimate.

But there are some important qualifications to the 2019 estimate. First, it assumes that the original 1989 valuation was accurate to some degree. But it does *not* take into account the immigration patterns over the last 30 years of people arriving from areas or countries that have a predilection for fiery foods—like Mexico, the Caribbean, and many African and Asian countries. Also, the new estimate does not take into account the ever-growing love of chile peppers and fiery foods in the US. Also not considered, and probably not counted, are the sales of fiery foods products in 60 different categories produced by hundreds of small companies that have sprung up and survived over those 30 years.

So I suggest that the figure of $6.6 billion is a minimum, and that a rigorous audit of the industry would show that it is worth more than that, maybe as much at $10 billion. This figure leads to the inescapable conclusion that chile pepper–based food and nonfood products comprise a large, rapidly growing industry. The forces driving this growth are an ever-increasing demand from the American public for more hot and spicy foods, and a growing love affair with chile peppers themselves. Chile peppers are now firmly entrenched in the diet of tens of millions of Americans through their enjoyment of fiery cuisines such as Mexican, New Mexican, Tex-Mex, Cajun, Thai, Sichuan, East Indian, and Caribbean.

With chile peppers and fiery foods becoming solidly in the mainstream American diet, what developments can we expect to see? I believe that fiery foods—and especially Mexican food—will continue to show solid growth in all segments of the industry. Chile peppers and food products will continue their penetration of eastern and midwestern markets, and new packaging techniques will increase the shelf life for fresh green chiles in produce departments, leading to the availability of New Mexican varieties of chile all over the country. Exotic chiles, particularly the hotter varieties such as habaneros and ajís, will increase in popularity.

An increased number of locally produced salsas and hot sauces will be introduced, despite the fact that there are more than 300 different brands already. More sales will be seen by pepper-oriented products prevalent in cuisines other than just Mexican and Southwestern; some examples are hot Asian oils, serrano sauces, Caribbean sauces and marinades, and East Indian condiments.

Fiery food and New Southwest restaurants will increase in number and will develop their own gourmet product lines, as evidenced by the fact that the East Coast Grill in Cambridge, Massachusetts, has long produced a habanero chile and mustard sauce called Inner Beauty.

Throughout this book, I have shown how chiles have conquered nations; therefore, we advise chile lovers to take pity on those skeptics who say the pungent pods are just a fad. Simply serve them some of the recipes contained in this book, and, while they are sweating, tell them that if chiles are a fad, they have been so for about 10,000 years.

FEATURED CHILE PEPPER: *CAPSICUM ANNUUM* 'NUMEX CENTENNIAL'

Ornamentals are a unique class of chile peppers. They are not really a "pod type" but a distinct group of capsicums. Ornamental peppers as a potted plant are very popular in Europe and are gaining in popularity in the United States. Advantages of ornamental chile peppers as potted plants include easy seed propagation, relatively short cropping time, heat and drought tolerance, and excellent keeping

quality. Although they are edible, ornamentals are not particularly flavorful and are grown primarily for their unusual pod shapes, colorful fruits, or their dense and sometimes variegated foliage. Ornamental chile peppers have all the colors of the rainbow, often displaying pods in four or five colors on the same plant at the same time. The earliest ornamentals were known as "Christmas peppers" and were given at Christmastime as a gift because the green and red fruits were the colors of Christmas. Ornamentals also work well in landscaping as border plants.

'NuMex Centennial' was the first ornamental chile pepper released by New Mexico State University, and it honored NMSU's centennial in 1988. The plant grows from 18 to 24 inches tall, and it has purple flowers and green and purple foliage. It matures in 70 to 80 days after the bedding plants are placed in the ground, and this cultivar is also a good container plant. The pods measure 0.5 to 0.75 inches long by 0.375 to 0.5 inches wide; grow erect; have thin flesh; and start purple, then ripen to yellow, orange, and finally red. They are edible but are not particularly flavorful. The yield per plant is often more than 50 pods, and they are spectacular in landscaping because the plants usually show all their colors at the same time.

recipes

These recipes were invented by yours truly, Dave DeWitt.

TOURNEDOS CON SALSA CHIPOTLE

yield 4 servings   *heat scale* medium

This recipe, of Mexican origin from the state of Jalisco, is the fiery version of the famous tournedos béarnaise. I have provided a chipotle salsa recipe, although any other commercial chipotle sauce can be substituted. The chipotle chiles are found dried in packages or canned in adobo sauce.

THE SAUCE

1	onion, finely chopped
2	cloves garlic
2	tablespoons olive oil
6	dried chipotle chiles, soaked in water until soft, finely chopped
1	large tomato, peeled, seeded, finely chopped
½	tablespoon oregano
½	teaspoon sugar
	Salt and pepper to taste

Sauté the onion and garlic in the oil until soft, then add all other ingredients and cook over low heat until done, about a half hour. Remove from heat and puree in a blender until smooth. Return to the pan and keep warm until ready for serving.

Grill or sauté the tournedos to taste, usually rare or medium rare. Place each tournedo on a slice of fried bread, and spread the chipotle sauce over each. Serve warm.

THE TOURNEDOS

4	tournedos, cut from the best part of the fillet mignon
4	slices French bread, fried in butter until golden brown

EGGS BENEDICT ARNOLD WITH HOT HOLLANDAZE SAUCE

yield 2 servings *heat scale* medium

Yes, I have taken on yet another classic dish and spiced it up. This classic breakfast dish is made pungent by the addition of both green chiles and the spicy sauce.

HOT HOLLANDAZE SAUCE

½	teaspoon cayenne powder	1	tablespoon lemon juice
3	egg yolks, slightly beaten	⅔	cup butter, softened
			Salt and pepper

EGGS BENEDICT ARNOLD

½   cup green chile strips

2   English muffins, halved and toasted

4   eggs, poached

4   slices ham or Canadian bacon

½   cup green chile strips

½   cup grated cheddar cheese

Place the cayenne powder in a double boiler over a pan of simmering water. Add the egg yolks to the bowl with the lemon juice and whisk until light and creamy. Whisk in half the butter a little at a time until a thick emulsion is formed and the whisk leaves a trail. Reduce the heat and gradually whisk in the remaining butter. Beat well until sauce is glossy. Season with the salt and pepper to taste.

To assemble, place one slice of ham on each muffin half, and place chile strips on the ham. Top with the poached egg, then the hollandaze sauce, and finally the grated cheese.

STEAK Á LA DAVE, PART DEUX

yield 4 servings   *heat scale* medium

I've been working on this recipe for many years and I'm not done yet. Hot sauces add a new dimension to a dish that was originally treated with chunks of green chile. Serve with a spinach salad.

4   teaspoons lemon juice

1   tablespoon your favorite
    commercial hot sauce

2   large, 2-inch-thick steaks, sirloin or
    fillets preferred

2   teaspoons freshly ground black
    pepper

2 t easpoons fresh garlic, minced

1   cup cheddar cheese, grated

Combine the lemon juice and the hot sauce in a small bowl, and then sprinkle the mixture over each side of the steak. Then sprinkle the garlic and black pepper over each side of each steak, and pound them gently into the meat. Let the steaks sit at room temperature for at least an hour.

Grill the steaks over a fire of mesquite wood or use a gas grill on high. About 4 or 5 minutes before they are done, spread the cheese over each steak. Serve just when the cheese has melted.

HERB- AND CHILE-INFUSED ROASTED LEG OF LAMB WITH THREE-CHILE PAN SAUCE

yield 6 to 8 servings   *heat scale* medium

In New Mexico, sometimes we are fortunate and can find churro lamb, which is grown in the northern part of the state. It is the most flavorful lamb I have ever tasted, and I use it with fresh herbs and chiles from the garden. Okay, okay, Pan Sauce is a fancy name for a gravy, but what is a gravy but a meat-infused sauce? And this one happens to be flavored with my favorite combination of chile powders. Serve it over the carved meat and pan-roasted potatoes, rice pilaf, or other starchy accompaniment.

THE LAMB		THE PAN SAUCE	
¼	cup fresh rosemary leaves		Pan juices from the lamb
¼	cup fresh oregano	2	cups rich, organic, low-sodium beef broth
3	fresh red serrano or jalapeño chiles, seeds and stems removed, minced	½	cup white wine
4	cloves garlic, minced	½	teaspoon Worcestershire sauce
1	three- or four-pound leg of lamb	2	teaspoons finely ground ancho chile
4	large potatoes, cut into 2-inch cubes	½	teaspoon ground habanero chile
3	tablespoons olive oil	1	teaspoon ground New Mexican red chile
			Flour as need
			Salt and ground black pepper to taste

Preheat the oven to 325 degrees F.

In a mortar, crush together the rosemary, oregano, chiles, and garlic to make a coarse paste.

Cut slits in the leg of lamb about 1 inch deep and 2 inches apart. With a spoon and fingers, work the paste into the slits.

Combine the potatoes and olive oil in a bowl, and mix well until the potatoes are coated. Transfer to a roasting pan.

Place the lamb in another roasting pan and cook for 20 minutes per pound for medium-rare lamb. Every half hour, turn the potatoes. The potatoes should be well browned by the time the lamb is done. Remove the lamb and potatoes, and keep warm while making the Pan Sauce.

Skim off all but 2 tablespoons of fat from the pan juices, and scrape up all the browned bits from the bottom of the roasting pan. Transfer this to a saucepan, gradually adding the flour only until a thick and medium-brown roux is formed, whisking over medium heat.

Add the broth, wine, Worcestershire sauce, and ground chiles; whisk well, and bring to a boil. Add salt and pepper to taste. Reduce the heat and cook over medium heat until sauce reaches desired consistency.

Serve the sauce over the sliced lamb and potatoes.

CURED AND PECAN-SMOKED KING SALMON WITH TWO CLASSIC SAUCES

serves 10 or more   *heat scale* pungent

Thanks to Mark Preston for the cure recipe, which he researched in out-of-print manuals for curing seafood and meats. The key to preparing salmon this way is to make certain that your smoke is rather cool, about 100 degrees F. If it is warmer, decrease the smoking time. Incidentally, this recipe was most recently tested by using salmon caught in Monterey Bay by David Humphrey. Note that this recipe requires a lot of preparation time for appetizers, but most of that time is spent waiting rather than working. It's not traditional, but feel free to add hot-chile powder to the sauce recipes to heat them up.

ENGLISH HORSERADISH SAUCE   *yield* ¾ cup

1 teaspoon dry hot mustard	½ teaspoon lemon juice
¼ teaspoon sugar	½ cup plus 1 tablespoon sour cream
¼ teaspoon salt	2 tablespoons cold heavy cream
Freshly ground black pepper	2 tablespoons grated horseradish
1 tablespoon white-wine vinegar	

To make the English Horseradish Sauce, in a small bowl combine the mustard, sugar, salt, a sprinkling of black pepper, the vinegar, and the lemon juice to make a smooth paste.

Whip the cream in a cold bowl until peaks form. Add the whipped cream and horseradish to the mustard paste, stirring the mixture to blend it. Refrigerate before serving.

CLASSIC BRITISH MUSTARD SAUCE *yield* about 1 ¼ cups

1	tablespoon unsalted butter
1	tablespoon flour
1 ¼	cups rich beef stock
1	tablespoon grated horseradish
1	tablespoon hot English mustard, coarse or smooth (or more to taste)
½	teaspoon salt
	Freshly ground black pepper

To make the Classic British Mustard Sauce, melt the butter in a small saucepan over low heat, add the flour, and stir to make a roux. Cook the roux for 2 to 3 minutes, stirring constantly. Remove from the heat and stir in the beef stock. Add the horseradish sauce, mustard, salt, and pepper to taste.

Return the pan to the stove and heat to boiling, stirring constantly, and cook for 2 to 3 minutes until slightly thickened. Serve immediately.

THE SALMON AND THE CURE

2	large salmon fillets, about 2 to 5 pounds each, or 5 small but thicker fillets
2 ½	cups kosher salt
¾	cup brown sugar
1	tablespoon freshly ground black pepper
1	teaspoon powdered oregano
1	teaspoon crushed dillweed (not seeds)

To make the salmon, combine the ingredients for the cure in a bowl and mix well. Place a sheet of plastic wrap on an aluminum baking sheet. Spread about an ⅛-inch-thick layer of the cure blend onto the plastic, and place the salmon fillets on the cure mixture. Top the fillets with 1/8 inch of cure. Cover the fillets with plastic wrap and cure in the refrigerator for at least 2 hours; a 4-hour cure is preferable.

Remove the fillets from the wrap and rinse the cure off each fillet. Allow the fillets to air-dry for about 2 hours.

Prepare a fire in the smoker's fire box with pecan wood, or other fruit or nut hardwood of choice, such as apple, apricot, peach, or walnut. When the fire stabilizes and the smoke is no longer hot, place the fillets skin-side down on racks or on the aluminum baking sheet. Smoke the fillets for 4 to 5 hours, depending on their thickness. Regularly check the fire and fillets to make sure that the fish is smoking, not cooking.

Serve with crackers and the two sauces as an appetizer. Refrigerate any leftovers, which will keep for weeks.

Alt, Jim
  1993. Personal correspondence.
Anderson, E. N.
  1988. *The Food of China*. Yale University Press, New Haven.
Andrews, Jean
  1984. *Peppers: The Domesticated Capsicums*. University of Texas Press, Austin.
Anonymous
  1956. Some Like Them Hot (Hot Pepper–Eating Contest). *Newsweek* 48(Oct. 22):41.
  2018a. *Transcendental Capsaicinophilic Society*. http://www.chetbacon.com/tcs/tcs.html.
  2018b. *Charm Xiazi*. Booklet celebrating China's Spice Town—Xiazi. Distributed at the Third China (Zunyi) International Chilli Expo, August 18.
  2019a. Annual Consumption Volume of Chili Peppers per Capita in South Korea from 2011 to 2017 (in Kilograms). *Statista*. Statistics, electronic document, https://www .statista.com/statistics/692749/south-korea-chili-pepper-consumption-per-capita/.
  2019b. 2019 Chilli Events. *Clifton Chilli Club*. https://www.cliftonchilliclub.com/chilli -festival-events-finder.
Arnstein, Tom
  2018. Exploring the Chilies of China. *The Beijinger* March–April. https://www.the beijinger.com/sites/default/files/2018.03-04_thebeijinger.pdf.
Athenaeus
  1909 [ca. AD 200]. *Deipnosophistai*, or *The Gastronomers*. Reprinted as *The Deipnosophists; or, Banquet of the Learned*. Translated by C. D. Yonge. George Bell and Sons, London.
Ayto, John
  1990. *The Glutton's Glossary: A Dictionary of Food and Drink Terms*. Routledge, London and New York.
Bannister, Justin
  2016. NMSU Researchers Investigate How Super-Hot Peppers Pack Their Powerful Punch. New Mexico State University News Center. 1 February. https://newscenter .nmsu.edu.
Baudin, Louis
  2003. *Daily Life of the Incas*. Dover Publications, Mineola, New York.
Benghiat, Norma
  1985. *Traditional Jamaican Cookery*. Penguin UK, London.
Billing, Jennifer, and Paul W. Sherman
  1998. Antimicrobial Functions of Spices: Why Some Like It Hot. *The Quarterly Review of Biology* 73(1)[March]:3–49.

Bowen, T. J.

1857. *Central Africa*. Southern Baptists Publication Society, Charleston, South Carolina.

Brennan, Jennifer

1986. Tantalizing Thai Curries. *Food and Wine*. May:77.

Bryden, Lynn

1977. Snacks and Stews from Ghana. In *The Anthropologists' Cookbook*, edited by Jessica Kuper. Universe Books, New York.

Burton, Sir Richard Francis

1860. *The Lake Regions of Central Africa: A Picture of Exploration*, Vol. 2. Longman, Green, Longman, and Roberts, London.

1863. *Wanderings in West Africa from Liverpool to Ferdinand Po*, Vol. 2. Tinsley Brothers, London.

Cameron, Verney Lovett

2016. *Across Africa*, Vol. 1. BoD [Books on Demand], May 25.

Chopra, R. N., R. L. Badhwar, and S. P. Ghosh

1984. *Poisonous Plants of India*. Scientific Publishers, Jodhpur, India.

Christie, Robert H.

1975. *Twenty-Two Authentic Banquets from India*. Reprinted. Dover, New York. Originally published 1911, J. & J. Gray, London.

Cobo, Father Bernabé

1979. *History of the Inca Empire*. Translated by Roland Hamilton from the 1653 work. University of Texas Press, Austin.

Coetzee, Renata

1977. *The South African Culinary Tradition*. C. Struik Publishers, Cape Town.

Columbus, Christopher

2004. *The Four Voyages of Christopher Columbus*. Penguin UK, London.

Conneau, Captain Theophilus

1976. *A Slaver's Log Book of 20 Years' Residence in Africa* (unedited version). Howard S. Mott, Sheffield, Massachusetts.

Coyle, L. Patrick

1985. *Cook's Books*. Facts on File, New York.

de Acosta, José

2002. *Natural and Moral History of the Indies*. Edited by Jane Mangan. Translated by Frances López-Morillas. Duke University Press, Durham, North Carolina.

de la Vega, Garcilaso (El Inca)

1966. *Royal Commentaries of the Incas*. Translated by Harold V. Livermore from the 1609 work. University of Texas Press, Austin.

del Castillo, Bernal Diaz

2003. *The Conquest of New Spain*. Penguin UK, London.

De Orta, Garcia

    2017. *Colloquies on the Simples & Drugs of India*. Creative Media Partners.

de Sahagún, Bernardino

    1963 [1590]. *The General History of the Things of New Spain*. Monograph No. 14. Translated by A. J. O. Anderson and C. E. Dibble. School of American Research, Santa Fe.

de Schlippe, Pierre

    1956. *Shifting Cultivation in Africa: The Zande System of Agriculture*. Humanities Press, London.

DeWitt, Dave

    1992. Singapore Fling. *FieryFoodsCentral.com*, republished November 30, 2008.

    1999. *The Chile Pepper Encyclopedia*. William Morrow, New York.

    2000. Tasting the Heat in Oz. *FieryFoodsCentral.com*, republished July 2, 2008.

    2005a. From Seed to Salsa: Episode 2 of Heat Up Your Life. Produced but unpublished video script, author's personal collection.

    2005b. Hot Plates: Episode 3 of Heat Up Your Life. Produced but unpublished video script, author's personal collection.

    2008a. Pepper Profile: Ancho/Poblano. *FieryFoodsCentral.com*, June 1.

    2008b. Pepper Profile: Jalapeño. *FieryFoodsCentral.com*, June 1.

    2008c. A Peri-Peri Good Time: Spiced Up South Africa. *FieryFoodsCentral.com*, June 26.

    2008d. The Japanese Scovie Awards. *FieryFoodsCentral.com*, June 30.

    2008e. Out of the Ash: The Prehistoric Chile Cuisine of Cerén. *FieryFoodsCentral.com*, July 2.

    2008f. Bonney Barbados: A Travel Retrospective, 1996. *FieryFoodsCentral.com*, July 2.

    2008g. Chile Peppers in Legend and Lore. *FieryFoodsCentral.com*, July 2.

    2008h. Why Chiles Conquered America. *FieryFoodsCentral.com*, July 2.

    2008i. Piment d'Espelette: The AOC-Protected Chile Pepper. *FieryFoodsCentral.com*, July 3.

    2008j. The Former Colonies Strike Back: Part 1, England. *FieryFoodsCentral.com*, July 3.

    2008k. The Former Colonies Strike Back: Part 3, Amsterdam. *FieryFoodsCentral.com*, July 3.

    2008l. Yo soy un chiltepínero! FieryFoodsCentral.com, November 29.

    2008m. Down de Islands: A Trinidad and Tobago Travel Retrospective, 1992. *FieryFoodsCentral.com*, December 6.

    2010. *The Founding Foodies: How Washington, Jefferson, and Franklin Revolutionized American Cuisine*. Sourcebooks, Naperville, IL.

    2011. *The Southwest Table: Traditional Foods from Texas, New Mexico, and Arizona*. Lyon's Press, New York.

2013. Personal correspondence with Harald Zoschke.

2014a. *Precious Cargo: How Foods from the Americas Changed the World*. Counterpoint Press, Berkeley.

2014b. *Dishing Up New Mexico*. Storey Publishing, North Adams, Massachusetts.

2016. Development of Superhot Chile Peppers in Trinidad and Tobago. *FieryFoodsCentral.com*, February 19.

2017. Watch Your Back, Hatch—Pueblo Chiles Are Making a Move. *FieryFoodsCentral. com*, February 5.

DeWitt, Dave, and Arthur J. Pais

1994. *A World of Curries*. Little, Brown, Boston.

DeWitt, Dave, and Chuck Evans

1996. *The Hot Sauce Bible*. The Crossing Press, Freedom, California.

DeWitt, Dave, and Mary Jane Wilan

1993. *Callaloo, Calypso & Carnival: The Cuisines of Trinidad & Tobago*. The Crossing Press, Freedom, California.

DeWitt, Dave, Mary Jane Wilan, and Melissa T. Stock

1994. *Hot & Spicy Chili*. Prima Publishing, Rocklin, California.

1995a. *Hot & Spicy Latin Dishes*. Prima Publishing, Rocklin, California.

1995b. *Hot & Spicy Southeast Asian Dishes*. Prima Publishing, Rocklin, California.

1996a. *Hot & Spicy Caribbean*. Prima Publishing, Rocklin, California.

1996b. *Hot & Spicy Mexican*. Prima Publishing, Rocklin, California.

1998. *The Flavors of Africa*. Prima Publishing, Rocklin, California.

DeWitt, Dave, and Nancy Gerlach

1990. *The Whole Chile Pepper Book*. Little, Brown, Boston.

1995. *The Habanero Cookbook*. Ten Speed Press, Berkeley.

1996. *The Hot Sauce Bible*. The Crossing Press, Freedom, California.

2000. *The Whole Chile Pepper Book*. Little, Brown, Boston.

2008. In Search of Hot Stuff in Costa Rica. *FieryFoodsCentral.com*, December 4.

2014. *Precious Cargo: How Foods from the Americas Changed the World*. Counterpoint Press, Berkeley.

DeWitt, Dave, and Paul W. Bosland

2009. *The Complete Chile Pepper Book*. Timber Press, Portland, Oregon.

Dobie, James Frank

1936. *The Flavor of Texas*. Dealey and Lowe, Dallas.

Doland, Gwyneth

2008. Jalape-oh-no! *FieryFoodsCentral.com*, July 2.

Drotleff, Laura

2018. How Bonnie Plants and ScottsMiracle-Gro Are Investing in Consumer Success. *GreenhouseGrower.com*, July 9.

Ducote, Jay D.

    2019. Cajun vs. Creole Food—What Is the Difference? *LouisianaTravel.com*.

Eshbaugh, W. Hardy

    1970a. A Biosystematic and Evolutionary Study of *Capsicum baccatum* (Solanaceae). *Brittonia* 22:31–33.

    1970b. Genetic and Biochemical Systematic Studies of Chili Peppers. *Bulletin of the Torrey Botanical Club* 102:396–403.

Eshbaugh, W. Hardy, and P. G. Smith

    1983. The Origin and Evolution of Domesticated *Capsicum* Species. *Journal of Ethnobiology* 3:49–54.

Fisher, M. F. K.

    1968. *With Bold Knife and Fork*. G. P. Putnam's, New York.

Food and Agriculture Organization of the United Nations (FAO)

    2013. faostat3.fao.org (chile pepper production statistics from FAO).

Fritz, Lorenzo

    1997. Personal communication with the author.

Fuentes y Guzmán, D. Francisco Antonio de

    1882. *History of Guatemala*, Num. 6. Colegiata, Madrid.

Gerber, Hilda

    1957. *Traditional Cookery of the Cape Malays: Food Customs and 200 Old Cape Recipes*. A. A. Balkema, Rotterdam.

Gonzalez Estrada, Tomas

    2008. The Habaneros of Yucatán. Edited by Dave DeWitt. *FieryFoodsCentral.com*, June 1.

Hachten, Harva

    1970a. *Best of Regional African Cooking*. Hippocrene Books, New York.

    1970b. *Kitchen Safari: A Gourmet's Tour of Africa*. Atheneum, New York.

Halász, Zoltán

    1963. *Hungarian Paprika through the Ages*. Corvina Press, Budapest.

Hall, Captain Basil

    1931. *Travels in India, Ceylon, and Borneo*. George Handy, London.

Harris, Jessica

    1992. *Tasting Brazil: Regional Recipes and Reminiscences*. Macmillan, New York.

Hatch, Peter J.

    2012. *"A Rich Spot of Earth": Thomas Jefferson's Revolutionary Garden at Monticello*, pp. 145–148. Yale University Press, New Haven.

Heiser, Charles B.

    1976. Peppers: Capsicum (Solanaceae). In *Evolution of Crop Plants*, edited by N. W. Simmonds, pp. 265–268. Longman, London.

Heiser, Charles B., and Barbara Pickersgill

    1968. Names for the Cultivated Capsicum Species (Solanaceae). *Taxon* 18: 277–283.

    1975. Names for the Bird Peppers (*Capsicum*—Solanaceae). *Baileya* 19:151–156.

Helms, Mary W.

    1976. *Ancient Panama*. University of Texas Press, Austin.

Higman, B. W.

    2008. *Jamaican Food: History, Biology, Culture*. University of the West Indies Press, Kingston, Jamaica.

Hillman, Howard

    1979. *The Book of World Cuisines*. Penguin, New York.

Hudgins, Sharon

    2008. Surprisingly Spicy Spain. *FieryFoodsCentral.com*, July 2.

Jaffrey, Madhur

    1975. *An Invitation to Indian Cooking*. Vintage, New York.

Jenne, Jeremiah

    2018. Tracing Heated Roots: How the Beloved Chili Arrived in China. *The Beijinger*, April 17. https://www.thebeijinger.com/blog/2018/04/17/tracing-heated-roots-how-beloved-chili-arrived-china.

Johns, Yohanni

    1971. *Dishes from Indonesia*. Chilton, Philadelphia.

Kaufman, William, and Saraswathi Lakshmanan

    1964. *The Art of India's Cookery*. Doubleday, Garden City, New York.

Kelly, Isabel

    2014. *Folk Practices in North Mexico: Birth Customs, Folk Medicine, and Spiritualism in the Laguna Zone*. University of Texas Press, Austin.

Kendall, Ann

    1973. *Everyday Life of the Incas*. Dorsett Press, New York.

Kennedy, Diana

    1972. *The Cuisines of Mexico*. Harper & Row, New York.

Kifer, Cassie

    2019. 10 Cajun Dishes to Try in Louisiana. *EverinTransit.com*.

Kloss, Jethro

    1989. *Back to Eden: A Human Interest Story of Health and Restoration to Be Found in Herb, Root, and Bark*. Lotus Press, Twin Lakes, Wisconsin.

Laas, William

    1967. *Cuisines of the Eastern World*. Golden Press, New York.

Lamson, Janie

    2019. Centennial. *ChilePlants.com*.

Lang, George

    1993. *Cuisine of Hungary*. Penguin Press, New York.

Lawrence, Blaise

    2008. The Portuguese Piri-Piri Expedition. *FieryFoodsCentral.com*, July 3.

Lee, Karen

    1984. *Chinese Cooking Secrets*. Doubleday, New York.

Leipoldt, Christian Louis

    1976. *Leipoldt's Cape Cookery*. W. J. Flesch, Cape Town.

    2003. Culinary Treasures. In *Leipoldt's Food and Wine*, edited by T. S. Emslie and
        P. L. Murray. Stonewall Books, Cape Town.

Lentz, David L., Marilyn P. Beaudry-Corbet, Maria Luisa Reyna de Aguilar,

and Lawrence Kaplan

    1996. Foodstuffs, Forests, Fields, and Shelter: A Paleoethnobotanical Analysis
        of Vessel Contents from the Cerén Site, El Salvador. *Latin American Antiquity* 7(3)
        [September 1996]:247–262.

Ligon, Richard

    2011 [1647]. *A True and Exact History of the Island of Barbados*. Edited by Karen
        Kupperman. Hackett, Indianapolis.

Lissy, Marin

    2017. Gardening Boom: 1 in 3 American Households Grow Food. *FarmerFoodShare.org*,
        June 15.

MacCormack, Carol

    2012. Queens of Sherbro. In *Gender and Power in Sierra Leone: Women Chiefs of the Last
        Two Centuries*, by L. Day. Palgrave Macmillan, London.

Marks, Copeland

    1979. Indonesian Cookery. *Gourmet* 39(November):50.

Meakin, Budgett

    1902. *The Moors: A Comprehensive Description*. S. Sonnenschein, London.

Mesfin, Daniel J.

    1990. *Exotic Ethiopian Cooking*. Ethiopian Cookbook Enterprises, Falls Church,
        Virginia.

Murray, Paul

    2007. The C. Louis Leipoldt Trail. *Litnet*. https://www.litnet.co.za/the-c-louis-leipoldt
        -trail/.

Nabhan, Gary

    1978. Chiltepines! *El Palacio* (Museum of New Mexico) 84(2):30–34.

    1985. For the Birds: The Red-Hot Mother of Chiles. In *Gathering the Desert*, pp. 123–133.
        University of Arizona Press, Tucson.

    1998. Personal communication with the author.

Naj, Amal

  1992. *Peppers: A Story of Hot Pursuits*. Vintage Books, New York.

Oon, Violet

1986. *Singapore: 101 Meals*. Singapore Tourist Promotion Board, Singapore.

Perry, Linda

  2007. Starch Fossils and the Domestication and Dispersal of Chili Peppers (*Capsicum* spp. L.) in the Americas. *Science* 315(5814)[16 February 2007]:986–988. https://10.1126/science.1136914.

Pfefferkorn, Ignaz

  1949 [1794]. *Sonora: A Description of the Province*. Translated by Theodore Treutlein. University of New Mexico Press, Albuquerque.

Pickersgill, Barbara

  1969a. The Archaeological Record of Chili Peppers (*Capsicum* spp.) and the Sequence of Plant Domestication in Peru." *American Antiquity* 34:54–61.

  1969b. The Domestication of Chili Peppers. In *The Domestication and Exploitation of Plants and Animals*, edited by Peter J. Ucko and G. W. Dimbleby, p. 443. Gerald Duckworth, London.

  1984. Migration of Chili Peppers, *Capsicum* spp., in the Americas. In *Pre-Columbian Plant Migration*, edited by Doris Stone, pp. 106–122. Peabody Museum of Archaeology and Ethnology, Harvard University, Cambridge.

Powis, Terry G., et al.

  2013. Prehispanic Use of Chili Peppers in Chiapas, Mexico. *PLOS ONE* 8(11):e79013. https://doi.org/10.1371/journal.pone.0079013.

Purseglove, John William

  1981. *Spices*, Vol. 2. Longman, London.

Rajah, Carol Selva

1987. *Makan-Lah!: The True Taste of Malaysia*. Toppan, Jurong Town, Singapore.

Rau, Santha Rama

  1969. *The Cooking of India*. Time-Life Books, New York.

Robertshaw, Peter, and Jill Rubalcaba

  2004. *The Early Human World*. Oxford University Press, New York.

Roeder, Beatrice A.

  1984. *Chicano Folk Medicine from Los Angeles, California*. University of California Press, Berkeley.

Rozin, Elisabeth

  1994. *The Primal Cheeseburger*. Penguin Books, New York.

Sahni, Julie

  1980. *Classic Indian Cookery*. William Morrow, New York.

Saparamadu, Anura

    Personal correspondence with the author, n.d.

Schell, H. A.

    1909. *Bazar Cook Book*. First Congregational Church Ladies Aid Society, Tucson, AZ.

Sheets, Payson D.

    2003. Tropical Time Capsule. In *Secrets of the Maya*, edited by the editors of *Archaeology Magazine*, pp. 48–52. Hatherleigh Press, New York.

Sherman, Paul W., and Geoffrey A. Hash.

    2001. Why Vegetable Recipes Are Not Very Spicy. *Evolution and Human Behavior* 22(3):147–163.

Singh, Dharam Jit

    1956. *Classic Cooking from India*. Houghton Mifflin, Boston.

Spaeth, Anthony

    1988. In Guntur, India, Even at 107 Degrees, It's Always Chili, Chili, and More Chili. *Wall Street Journal*, June 30. New York.

Stobart, Tom

    1980. *The Cook's Encyclopedia*. Harper & Row, New York.

Tindall, Robynne

    2018. Beyond Sichuan: Exploring the Spicy Traditions of Four Chinese Provinces. *The Beijinger* March–April. https://www.thebeijinger.com/sites/default/files /2018.03-04_thebeijinger.pdf.

United States International Trade Commission

    2008. Monitoring of U.S. Imports of Peppers, Investigation No. 332–51. Publication 4049, November.

Valcárcel, L. E.

    1925. *Del ayllu al imperio*. Lima.

Van der Post, Laurens

    1970. *African Cooking*. Time-Life Books, New York.

    1982. *First Catch Your Eland*. F. A. Thorpe, Leicestershire, UK.

Vogt, Evon Z. (editor)

    1969. *Ethnology*. Handbook of Middle American Indians Vol. 7. University of Texas Press, Austin.

Von Hagen, Victor W.

    1957. *Realm of the Incas*. Mentor Books, New York.

West, Richard

    1977. From Mexico with Love. *Texas Monthly*, June.

Whitlock, Ralph

    1976. *Everyday Life of the Maya*. Dorset Press, New York.

Wilson, Ellen Gibson

    1971. *A West African Cookbook*. M. Evans, Philadelphia.

Wiseman, James

    2003. The Art of Gardening. In *Secrets of the Maya*, edited by the editors of *Archaeology Magazine*. Hatherleigh Press, New York.

Wolfert, Paula

    2013. *Couscous and Other Good Food from Morocco*. Harper Collins, New York.

Xiaobing, Wang

    2018. Speech at the Opening Ceremony. *Opening Ceremony Information*. The Third China (Zunyi) International Chilli Expo, August 18.

Zoschke, Harald

    2008. Calabria, Part 8: Spicy Calabrian Recipes. *FieryFoodsCentral.com*, July 2.

Latin America, arrival of Spanish, 67

Lee, Karen (author and chef), popularity of chiles, 241–42

Leipoldt, C. Louis (South African poet), food history, 174–75, 182–84

Lentz, Dr. David (botanist), on Cerén chiles, 14

Ligon, Richard (author on history of Barbados), 47

Liten, Joe (pepper importer), 54

Louisiana (US), Creole and Cajun cuisines, 101–5

Lutz, Arlene (chef), Costa Rica cooking show, 77–79

MacCormack, Carol (anthropologist), on palaver sauce, 172

MacNeish, R. S. (archaeologist), on history of chile seeds, 2

maize (corn), evidence of domestication, 15

malagueta peppers, 179

Malaya, legacy of chile cuisine, 138–39

Malaysia, 228. See also Singapore
—influence of Indonesian cuisines, 234–37
—satays, 234–35, 258–59

marinades, recipes 86, 258–59, 263

Markuson, Chris, on 'Pueblo' chiles, 115

masala (Indian spice mixture), 206–7

Mayas and chile peppers, legacy of, 7–13
—ceremonial uses of chiles, 10
—cochinita pibil (recipe), 94
—food habits of Mayan civilization, 9–11
—how chile meals are prepared, 7–8
—indigenous people and, 56–57
—Jocón, 72–73
—spicy beverages, 9–10

Matheson, Lloyd (chemist), on inhaling toxic fumes, 268–69

McClean, Pat (L. G. Miller Import and Export), 48

McIlhenny, Edmund (first patent on Tabasco Sauce), 99–101

McIlhenny, Paul (Tabasco Sauce maker), 100–103

medical benefits of chiles, 287–93
—anti-bacterial properties of, 315–17
—cancer cure?, 287
—cures stomachaches, 288

—fiber and starch for diet, 292
—folk remedies, 288–89
—low-sodium diet, 292–93
—lowers cholesterol, 291–92
—New World uses discovered, 19
—panacea effect, 287–88
—Vitamins A and C, 289–90
—weight management (low calories), 290–91

Meakin, Budgett (traveler to North Africa), couscous recipe, 177

Mendocino Codex, famous codices with chile mentions, 20

Mesfin, Daniel J. (author), on Ethiopian cuisine, 180

Mexico and Mexican cuisine, 25–33, 73–76
—chile peppers in diet, 6–7, 73
—chile seeds discovered in excavation, 2
—early pungency chart, 12
—history of Mexican cookery, 73–76
—legacy of the Mayas, 7–13
—legend and lore around chile peppers, 299, 303–4
—recipes, 25–33
—spicy travel adventures, 84–87
—why most popular cuisine in US, 322–23

Miller, Mark (author and chef), 54, 112–13

Millward, Robynne (editor and publisher), 250–52

Minshall, Peter (Trinidadian cuisine), 44

Mohenjo-Dara (Indus Valley), ancient spices grown, 197

mole sauces, 7–8, 74–75, 86
—competitions, 74
—Mexican chiles used, 74–75
—Mole Poblano (classic recipe), 75–76

Monaco, Enzo (Italian Pepper Academy), 154

Monte, Albán, early Mexico, 7

Monteiro, Angola Joachim (early trader), on wild chiles, 169

Morera, Jorge (chile expert), 81

Morocco (Kasbah), Chicken Jajine meal, 177

'Mosco' chile (Colorado), 114

Mozambique and piri-piri, 172–73, 179

Mumbai (India), culinary tour, 215–17

Muro, Angel (cookbook author), on paprika, 131–33

—original ratings for chile peppers, 280–81
—Scoville Organoleptic Test, 277–78, 280–81
seeds, sizes and collecting, 16–17, 69–70
Serrano peppers (Mexico), 74
Sheets, Dr. Payson (anthropologist Cerén), 13–14
Sichuan style, 243
Singapore, travel adventure, 233–39
—culinary heritage, 234–36
—"dry" and "wet" markets, 236–37
Singh, Chattar (Indian chef), 214
Singh, Dharam Jit (author Indian cookbooks), 199
slavery (West Africa), influence on food culture,
     39–40, 41
—curries of Cape of Good Hope, 181–182
—sugarcane and slave labor, 71
—technique of jerking, 55
sodium content, chiles as low salt spice, 292–93
sofrito (hot sauce), 39
Sonora (Mexico) and chiltepín harvest, 22–24
'Sonoran style' (Arizona Mexican cuisine), 117–19
Sopmi, Selat Elbis (owner London curry
     restaurant), 199
"Sosaties" (curried kebabs), 184
South Africa (travel adventure)
—curries (called "ambrosia"), 181–82
—hot sauces, 173–75
—mixture of styles (Dutch, English and
     Malay), 181
—national landmarks, 185–88
South America chile peppers, 1–3, 68
—reputation for medical remedies, 288
Southey, Trevor (Zimbabwe-born artist), on
     curries, 182
Southwestern (US) chile cuisine, 105–8
—Arizona chile history, 116–19
—Colorado 'Pueblo' chiles, 113–16
—New Mexico and cultivation of chiles,
     110–13
—Southwest defined, 105–6
—Tex-Mex, advent of, 108–10
Spain and influence of Spanish paprika, 131–34
Spanish Conquest
—influence on Mexico's chile cuisine, 85
—Latin America, foods introduced, 67
spices
—anti-microbial functions of, 315–17
—countries using most spice seasonings, 317

—most traded (black pepper and chile
     peppers), 316–17
—why humans use, 315–17
Spiegel, Robert (Fiery Foods), 311
squash (recipes), 25–26, 32, 63
Sri Lanka, and curries, 211
sriracha chiles (Thai), 230
Stein, Sylvester (editor), on chiles, 182
Suchilquitongo bowl (used for grinding), 7
superhot peppers, 277
—Congo peppers, 42–43
—folk beliefs surrounding, 38
—genetic mutations to develop new varieties,
     37–38
—hot sauces made from, 39–40
—oleoresin capsicum mash using, 276–77
Széchy, Margit (aristocrat), paprika seeds and,
     143
Szent-Györgyi, Albert (discoverer of ascorbi
     acid), 289

Tabasco Sauce, 98–105, 308
—effect on stomach lining, 286–87
—history behind family recipe, 99–101
—travel adventure to see how made, 100–103
Taj Lake Palace Hotel (Udaipur), 215–17
Taj Mahal (New Delhi, India), 215
Taj Mahal Palace Hotel (Mumbai), 212, 215–17
tajines (stew cooked in earthenware pot), 176–77
tamales, 12
Tello Obelisk (Peru), 6
ten Cate, Peter (restaurant owner), 158
Tex-Mex cuisine, 108–10
—beans and, 109–10
—most commonly used chile peppers, 109
—role restaurants played in development, 109
Texas (US), and chile cuisine, 108–10
—chile con carne cookoff, 306–7
—chile con carne (red chili), 106–8
—first Mexican restaurant opens, 108–9
—love of jalapeños, 109
—Texan chilipiquin, 190
Thailand and chile cuisine, 228–32
—Bangkok as hottest chile city, 229
—curry dishes, most popular, 230–32
—popularity of Thai restaurants, 229
—Thai cuisine and nam prik, 230